Ethics: *The Classic Readings*

PHILOSOPHY: *The Classic Readings*

This series of collections offers classic readings by philosophers ranging from ancient times to the first part of the twentieth century, and contains seminal writings from both Western and non-Western traditions of philosophy. Combined with valuable editorial guidance, including a substantial Introduction to each volume as well as to individual pieces, they are intended to serve as core texts for historically orientated philosophy courses.

Already published:

Aesthetics: *The Classic Readings*

Forthcoming:

Epistemology: *The Classic Readings*
Philosophy of Religion: *The Classic Readings*
Metaphysics: *The Classic Readings*
Political Philosophy: *The Classic Readings*

Ethics:

The Classic Readings

Edited by David E. Cooper

University of Durham

Advisory Editors
Robert L. Arrington
James Rachels

BLACKWELL
Publishers

First published 1998

2 4 6 8 10 9 7 5 3 1

Blackwell Publishers Ltd
108 Cowley Road
Oxford OX4 1JF
UK

Blackwell Publishers Inc.
350 Main Street
Malden, Massachusetts 02148
USA

British Library Cataloguing in Publication Data
A CIP catalogue record for this book is available from the British Library.

Library of Congress Cataloging-in-Publication Data
Ethics: the classic readings / edited by David E. Cooper
        p.   cm. — (Philosophy: the classic readings)
    Includes index.
    ISBN 0–631–20632–9 (alk. paper). — ISBN 0–631–20633–7 (pbk. : alk. paper)
    1. Ethics.   I. Cooper, David Edward.   II. Series.
BJ1012.E8957   1997
170—DC21   97–8622
                                                              CIP

Typeset in 10½ on 12 pt Galliard
by Ace Filmsetting Ltd, Frome, Somerset
Printed and bound in Great Britain by MPG Books Ltd, Bodmin, Cornwall

This book is printed on acid-free paper.

Contents

Series Preface   vi

Acknowledgements   vii

Introduction   1

1 Plato, *Gorgias*, 482–4, 488–500   11

2 Aristotle, *Nicomachean Ethics*, Book I   29

3 Epicurus, 'Letter to Menoeceus' and 'Leading Doctrines'   47

4 Mencius, 'Human Nature is Good'   59
   Hsun Tzu, 'Man's Nature is Evil'

5 *The Book of Chuang Tzu*, chapters 9, 13–14   77

6 *The Bhagavad Gita*, chapters 1–5   93

7 Sāntideva, *The Bodhicaryāvatāra*, chapter 8 (verses 89–140)   110
   Tsongkapa and Pabongka Rinpoche, 'The Second Path'

8 St Thomas Aquinas, *Summa Theologica*, I–II, Questions   125
   55, 58, 61–3

9 Joseph Butler, Sermon 'Upon the Love of Our Neighbour'   136

10 David Hume, *A Treatise of Human Nature*, Book III, Part I   149
   (Sections 1–2)

11 Immanuel Kant, *Fundamental Principles of the Metaphysic*   166
   of Morals, Preface and Section 1

12 Søren Kierkegaard, *Fear and Trembling*, Problema I   181

13 John Stuart Mill, *Utilitarianism*, chapter 2   194

14 Friedrich Nietzsche, *On the Genealogy of Morals*, First Essay,   212
   Sections 2–14, 16

15 G. E. Moore, *Principia Ethica*, chapter 1, sections 1–2, 5–15   230

16 W. D. Ross, *The Right and the Good*, chapter 2   246

17 Charles L. Stevenson, 'The Emotive Meaning of Ethical Terms'   262

Index   281

Series Preface

Philosophers in the English-language world are becoming increasingly aware of the importance of the history of their subject. *Philosophy: The Classic Readings* is a series which provides students and teachers with the central historical texts in the main branches of philosophy. The texts selected range from ancient times to the first part of the twentieth century. In response to a growing and laudable interest in the contributions of non-Western philosophers, the volumes in the series will contain seminal writings from the Indian, Chinese and other traditions as well as the classics of Western philosophical literature.

Each volume in the series begins with a substantial introduction to the relevant area of philosophy and its history, and to the bearing of this history on contemporary discussion. Each selected text is prefaced by a discussion of its importance within the development of that area.

Taken individually, each volume will serve as a core text for courses which adopt a historical orientation towards the relevant branch of philosophy. Taken together, the volumes in the series will constitute the largest treasury of classic philosophical writings available.

The books in the series are edited and introduced by David E. Cooper, Professor of Philosophy at the University of Durham, England, and author of many books, including *World Philosophies: An Historical Introduction*, also published by Blackwell.

Acknowledgements

The source of each reading is given underneath the relevant chapter title. The editor and publishers gratefully acknowledge all copyright holders for permission to reproduce copyright material. The publishers apologise for any errors or omissions in the copyright information, and would be grateful to be notified of any corrections that should be incorporated in the next edition or reprint of this book.

Introduction

A liaison group of British business people and university teachers was recently reported to have rejected the suggestion that 'business ethics' should form part of their agenda. Ethics, it was decided, was something too 'esoteric' to occupy such a practically minded group of people. Lurking behind this decision, I suspect, was the feeling that ethics is a 'personal', perhaps religious, matter, and one to skirt around, therefore, when the business in hand is hard-headed public policy. If so, the group's understanding of ethics and morality corresponds to that of many politicians for whom, it seems, only a few select issues – abortion, say, or fox-hunting – count as moral or ethical ones and hence as issues on which there is a 'free vote', so that personal sensibilities need not collide with party line.

Doubtless there is an interesting story to be told of how this narrow understanding of ethics, as a bolt-on extra to the practical business of life, came about. The story would surely have to mention the powerful twentieth-century sense, endorsed by many philosophers, that morality, unlike science, belongs in the realm of 'subjective' opinion and conviction, not of fact and reason. Be that as it may, this current understanding is much narrower than that of professional philosophers who describe themselves as moral philosophers and as 'doing' ethics. Nor do we find a reliable clue as to the nature of ethics or moral philosophy by consulting the original Greek and Latin words from which 'ethics' and 'moral' derive. The Greek *ethos* meant 'character', so that when Aristotle (chapter 2) wrote of *ethikai aretai*, his subject was 'excellences of character' and not, as often rendered, 'moral virtues'. The Latin *mos* (pl. *mores*) meant 'custom' or 'tradition'. Again, there is an interesting story to be told of how these terms came to alter meaning over the centuries and of the differ-ences between ancient and modern thinking thereby indicated. For the moment, I simply note that the ancient terms give no precise idea of the preoccupations of later moral philosophy. Questions about character and customs certainly figure among, but hardly exhaust, those preoccupations.

It would be nice, at this stage, to provide a short, sharp definition of 'ethics' as understood by modern philosophers, but any such definition would beg questions and ruffle feathers. For example, to define it as the study of practical, as opposed to 'speculative', reason will offend those who deny that reason plays *any* significant role in moral life. To define it, as many philosophers did earlier in this century,[1] as the examination of evaluative language will hardly satisfy those who think that ethics can be something larger and more exciting than that. More helpful than such definitions, therefore, will be a rough demarcation of the main areas of ethics into which the many questions addressed by moral philosophers fall.

Before attempting this, however, an obvious ambiguity should be noted. When I speak of Aristotle's ethics, I am probably referring to his theory of the good, virtue, justice and so on. But when I speak of my neighbour's ethics, or lack of them, I am probably referring to his character, behaviour and principles (or lack of them). So we need to distinguish between ethics as a branch of philosophical study and the ethics of people, groups or whole societies which form an important part of the subject-matter of that study. A philosopher – Rousseau, for instance – may be famous for his ethics in the first sense and infamous for his lack of ethics in the second.

What activities and concerns, then, does philosophical ethics embrace? It has become standard to distinguish between (a) applied ethics and (b) meta-ethics.[2] But if justice is to be done to the main concerns of some moral philosophers, including several represented in this book, we need to add a third area which I shall call (c) fundamental ethics.

(a) *Applied ethics.* Moral philosophers come to the public's attention when they appear on TV or radio programmes discussing some currently 'hot' issue – gay marriage, say, or the use of a dead man's sperm. And it is indeed true that, over the last twenty-five years, philosophers have once again addressed such 'applied' or 'practical' problems with the aim, if not of 'solving' them, then at any rate of clarifying them and sorting the wheat from the chaff among the arguments that surround the problems. I say 'once again' for, while philosophers in earlier centuries often addressed the

---

[1] See, for example, A. J. Ayer, *Language, Truth and Logic*, London: Gollancz, 1936, chapter 6.
[2] See the useful survey article on ethics by John Skorupski, in N. Bunnin and E. Tsui-James (eds), *The Blackwell Companion to Philosophy*, Oxford: Blackwell, 1996, pp. 198ff.

practical issues of their day, it was for a time an orthodoxy of twentieth-century English-language philosophers that they had little or nothing professionally to contribute to practical moral debate. If a professor of ethics made an interesting proposal about the limits of justifiable euthanasia, all well and good: but that proposal, unlike his analysis of the meaning of 'justifiable', was not itself a piece of philosophizing, but of 'moralizing'. Such an eccentrically self-limiting conception of ethics is now largely a thing of the (recent) past. There is, today, general recognition that someone who approaches practical moral issues with the skills and knowledge associated with philosophical enquiry is engaged in a legitimate branch of ethics.

(b) *Meta-ethics.* Perhaps in order to disclaim any intent to 'moralize', many philosophers have described the enterprise in which they are professionally engaged as meta-ethics. They are engaged, that is, with questions *about* morality, not *of* morality. These questions range from ones about the ordinary meanings of terms like 'good', to ones about the logical relations between moral concepts (between rights and duties, say), to perennial ones about the relativity or otherwise of moral judgements. Several of the texts in this reader – those of Plato (chapter 1), Aristotle (chapter 2) and Butler (chapter 9), for example – include meta-ethical discussions of this kind. Special mention should perhaps be made of the selections from Hume (chapter 10) and Moore (chapter 15), for the questions they raise about the relationship between moral judgements and empirical judgements of fact have been at the centre of twentieth-century philosophical debate in such forms as 'Can an "ought" be derived from an "is"?' and 'Does "good" refer to a property in the way "yellow" does?' (For contrasting approaches to such questions, see Ross and Stevenson, chapters 16 and 17.)

(c) *Fundamental ethics.* Meta-ethical questions are often characterized as ones which have no direct bearing on the 'practical' issues of applied ethics. But if that is what they are then it is surely wrong to suppose that moral philosophy consists, without remainder, of those two areas. Take the case of John Stuart Mill (chapter 13). In his *Utilitarianism*, he defends a general view of how human beings should act, arguing for an overarching principle ('the greatest happiness' principle) to which their actions should conform. In doing so, Mill engages in meta-ethical discussion – about the relation between the concepts of good and right, say – and from his view he draws implications for various practical issues, such as the sale of drugs. But it is in neither the meta-ethical analyses nor the practical lessons drawn that Mill's importance resides. This lies, rather, in his attempt to provide a rational foundation for morality. Parallel remarks can be made about Kant's text (chapter 11), taken from the tellingly titled *Fundamental Principles [or Groundwork] of the Metaphysic of Morals*. Kant's ambition is neither conceptual analysis of moral terms nor resolution of particular practical issues – though he offers a bit of both – but the grander one of establishing the fundamental principle of right behaviour.

It is this kind of endeavour I mean by 'fundamental ethics', and it is the endeavour that many of the writers represented in this reader are embarked upon – Aristotle, Epicurus (chapter 3), Mencius (chapter 4), Aquinas (chapter 8), the anonymous authors of *The Bhagavad Gita* (chapter 6), as well as Mill and Kant. And perhaps one should also include among the practitioners of fundamental ethics certain 'rogue' or 'limiting' cases – authors like Nietzsche (chapter 14) who *reject* the whole enterprise of 'grounding' morality, of identifying any rational foundation for it, but who, in doing so, must perforce engage with the works and arguments of those who do pursue that enterprise.

Although the division into applied, meta-, and fundamental ethics is convenient, it should not be regarded as hard and sharp. As noted in the case of Mill, a philosopher may move smoothly between defending a fundamental principle of morality, analysing our moral concepts and proposing solutions to particular moral problems, but without any obvious sense of switching from one kind of enquiry to another. More important, there is often a degree of arbitrariness in judging that one enquiry has given way to another. There is no determinate point, for example, at which questions about life and death become sufficiently concrete and 'practical' to deserve treatment in the *Journal of Applied Philosophy* rather than in some more 'theoretical' publication. More important still, it can sometimes be a matter of genuine contention how or whether a boundary can be drawn. Is it, for example, possible to isolate the meta-ethical issue of moral relativity from ones about the proper attitudes to adopt towards other cultures? Some people think so, but not, certainly, those who insist that tolerance and respect for the values of other societies are implied by the alleged relativity of values.[3]

One difficulty in demarcating the province of ethics – and hence in editing a book of readings in ethics – is that this province lies close to, and may intersect with, others. Readers of the first volume in this series, *Aesthetics: The Classic Readings*, will have noticed that several of the texts are concerned with art and morality, and might have been happily included in the present volume. The same will be true of future volumes on political

---

[3] For a useful discussion of this issue, see Bernard Williams, *Morality*, Cambridge: Cambridge University Press, 1976, pp. 34ff.

philosophy and the philosophy of religion. People interested in art, politics or religion – or anthropology, economics, medicine, even archaeology and artificial intelligence – are bound to encounter moral questions germane to their subjects. Indeed, there are few, if any, areas of human conduct and enquiry which do not, at some point, throw up or impinge upon ethical issues. This is why applied ethics will never run short of material.

There is a second way, moreover, in which moral philosophy adjoins or intersects with other areas of enquiry. Even when a moral question has been isolated from political, religious and other considerations, it is not only the philosopher who will have something to say about it. So, typically, will the psychologist, the sociologist and other scientists, social or natural. It is difficult, for example, to imagine dissociating questions of how human beings ought to act from ones about human nature (see, e.g., the debate between Mencius and Hsun Tzu, chapter 4). After all, there is little purpose in exhorting us to love our neighbour as we love ourselves if that is a psychological impossibility. Again, in recent years – but see as well the text of Nietzsche's – some philosophers and scientists have argued that evolutionary and genetic theory has direct relevance to questions about the grounding of morality.

One reason I mention the affinities and intersections between ethics and other areas of enquiry is that this helps to explain certain inclusions and omissions. I have had to exercise judgement in deciding whether such-and-such a text is primarily a text of *moral* philosophy (*versus*, say, aesthetics), and whether a certain text is primarily one of moral *philosophy* (*versus*, say, the sociology of morals). That the volume is just one in a series has the advantage, of course, that some texts which would certainly deserve inclusion may, with equal or greater justice, be placed in other volumes. To take two important examples: I have not included any discussions of either the 'contractarian' or 'natural law' traditions in ethics, vital as these have been and still are. The explanation is that these traditions have secured an even more vital place in that discipline known as political philosophy. Thus Thomas Hobbes's view that morality rests upon, and should be shaped by, a 'social contract' into which people enter, is not represented here, but will be in *Political Philosophy: The Classic Readings*. Equally, my selection from St Thomas Aquinas does not include, as that later reader will, his discussion of morality as natural law, as God's rational dictates for the regulation of human conduct.

Mention of Aquinas prompts a third example. Apart from his discussion of the virtues, the only text I have included where religious – or, at any rate, theistic – considerations directly impinge upon ethical issues is a section from Kierkegaard's *Fear and Trembling* (chapter 12). In both cases, I judge, the influence of the discussions on our understanding of morality (and its limits) has been more considerable than upon theological debate. Texts which address the notorious and theological 'problem of evil' – of how evil can occur in a divinely created world – are reserved, on the other hand, for the volume on the philosophy of religion. It is true, no doubt, that *The Bhagavad Gita* and the two Buddhist texts (chapter 7) belong as much to the history of religious thought as to that of ethics: but as far as I can see, the main considerations which are advanced in the passages I have chosen are ones to which a non-religious person could also subscribe.

As for the problem of deciding when a text is sufficiently a work of philosophy, as distinct from psychology, say, the present climate is, fortunately, a relaxed one in which such distinctions are not rigidly regarded. In an earlier climate – that of my own undergraduate days, for example – there were philosophers who would have pigeon-holed Nietzsche's *On the Genealogy of Morals* as a work, not of philosophy, but of anthropology, psychology or what-not: but it is surely clear that, whatever the contributions from such disciplines Nietzsche exploits, the use that he makes of them in his critique of modern morality makes his book an important episode in the history of moral philosophy. Only a peculiarly stunted conception of the subject could warrant relegation of such a work to whatever nether regions were supposed to lurk beneath the realm of philosophy proper.

Other considerations, naturally, have also influenced my selection of texts. I will mention only the desirability of representing a wide variety of approaches to meta-ethical and fundamental ethical issues. (I have not included any texts which fall paradigmatically under the heading of 'applied ethics', the subject perhaps of a further volume.) Moral philosophy has, over the centuries, displayed a number of characteristic tensions – that between 'teleological' and 'deontological' approaches, for example, or between appeals to reason and to 'passion' as the proper guide to moral understanding. It is important that both sides to such disputes should be represented. If certain authors are unexpectedly missing, the explanation is often that, in my judgement, the kinds of position they occupy are better represented by other authors. For example, I include nothing by the 'father of utilitarianism', Jeremy Bentham: but only because a more measured and plausible version of that approach is to be found in the writings of his godson, J. S. Mill. Or, to take another of the great ethical traditions, Confucianism, sections from Confucius' follower, Mencius, provide a fuller understanding of its leading themes than would a pot-pourri of the Master's own aphoristic remarks.

I cannot, in this Introduction, provide a potted history of the subject to which the following texts belong. A mere chronology of the 'highlights' of two and a half thousand years of moral thought would be tedious, while a history in the more interesting sense of an attempt, inevitably contentious, to chart developments, continuities and 'revolutions' would deserve more pages than I have at my disposal.[4] Nevertheless, I shall indicate, towards the end, some significant differences between older and more recent perspectives. And I shall do so in the course of identifying some main categories into which the issues of moral theory fall and some of the axes along which competing positions on these issues lie. Identifying these will provide a fuller picture of the concerns of moral philosophy and help to locate the texts I have selected.

All these texts can, at a pinch, be seen to fall into one or more of three categories of concern: concerns with, as I shall label them, moral *grounds*, moral *knowledge*, and moral *scope*.

(a) *Moral grounds.* By concerns with moral grounds, I have in mind such questions as 'Why, if at all, should a person be moral?', 'What, if any, are the reasons or grounds for acting virtuously or for doing what is deemed one's duty?'. The broadest division among answers to these questions is between those which postulate some end or purpose which moral conduct allegedly promotes and those which do not: between, for example, Epicurus and the utilitarians on the one hand, who argue that the justification of morality is its promotion of pleasure or happiness, and, on the other hand, Kant who denies that the justification of, say, promise-keeping is to be given in terms of contributing to some end. This is, roughly, the famous division between 'teleological' ethics (from the Greek word for end) and 'deontological' ethics (from the Greek word for what is binding). Venerable as it is, this division needs to be handled gingerly. For example, Aristotle is usually classed as a teleologist, but the 'end' he speaks of virtue as achieving – *eudaimonia* ('happiness' or 'flourishing') – is not some end-product in which, conveniently, honesty and justice happen to result. It would be truer to say that *eudaimonia* consists *in* virtuous action.

Cutting across this division is another axis, on which are ranged different positions as to the kinds of ground on which a certain end can be shown to be desirable or, for deontologists, on which certain principles can be shown to be binding. The grounds appealed to have been extremely varied. For many philosophers – Aristotle, Epicurus and Mencius, for instance – the

---

[4] For histories in this more adventurous sense, see Alasdair MacIntyre, *A Short History of Ethics*, New York: Macmillan, 1966, and Robert L. Arrington, *An Historical Introduction to Ethics*, Oxford: Blackwell, 1997.

appeal has been to human nature: the good life is the one which best accords with man's true nature, though what that nature is has, needless to
say, been contested. For others – Hsun Tzu and Kant, for example – human nature is too vile, inconstant or fragile to provide the foundation for
morality, which must therefore be sought either in something that transcends our natural existence or in cultural conventions designed to con-
strain our natural proclivities. The distinctions here are not always sharp
and some philosophers appeal to a number of grounds. Aquinas, for example, is happy to base some of the virtues on our nature as rational beings,
while holding that other, 'theological' virtues can be discerned only by
someone with an understanding of God's purpose. And in *The Bhagavad
Gita*, the traditional duties of caste to which appeal is made turn out to be
part of the divine plan for humankind.

Thinkers who invoke convention and tradition may do so in order to
explain and justify moral practices: but they may, instead, do so in a de-
bunking, 'nihilist' spirit. Moral practices, it gets said, are 'mere' conventions, and hence without any genuine justificatory basis. Such is the view of
Plato's opponents in the *Gorgias* (chapter 1). It's worth noting, though,
that the denial of any grounds for moral principles need not be made in
this nihilistic spirit: for the point may not be to debunk morality but to
urge that moral beliefs do not require, nor perhaps permit, a grounding in
anything. Such, for instance, is W. D. Ross's view (chapter 16): that certain
actions are prima facie right is a matter of *sui generis* intuitive knowledge.
Here we are passing to the second of the categories of concern.

(b) *Moral knowledge.*   Two philosophers could agree that the moral life
is to be justified by appealing to, say, human nature, but disagree as to how
the relevant knowledge of human nature is to be secured. For one – Mill,
perhaps – it may be through ordinary empirical investigation of human
motivation; for the other – Aristotle, say – such knowledge may require
metaphysical reflection on the distinguishing end or *telos* of human existence. Again, several thinkers might agree that morality requires some transcendental grounding, but differ as to how the relevant transcendental
knowledge is arrived at. For one – Aquinas, say – faith and revelation may
be essential for discerning at least some of the virtues we ought to cultivate. For another – Chuang Tzu (chapter 5), perhaps – a more 'mystical'
insight into the 'way' of the universe is necessary if we are to recognize the
contours of the good life. For another – Kant, for example – it may be
through pure reason alone that the overarching principle of all moral duties is to be identified. Then again, there are philosophers for whom it is a
mistake to assimilate moral knowledge to any of the kinds just mentioned
– empirical, rational, 'mystical' or whatever. Thus, for Moore and Ross, as

for their 'intuitionist' predecessors in the eighteenth century, moral knowledge is *sui generis*, and any attempt to derive it from other forms of knowledge is to be guilty of a fallacy.

Finally, one must mention those philosophers for whom the very notion of moral knowledge is to be abandoned. These will include, of course, the debunkers of morality, such as Nietzsche, for whom there are no 'moral facts' to be known, only the various moral 'perspectives' which reflect the ways in which people of different kinds seek to increase their power. But they will include, as well, those philosophers for whom the idea of moral knowledge betrays a misunderstanding of the status of moral judgements. Thus, for 'emotivists' like C. L. Stevenson (chapter 17), such judgements are not, despite their grammatical form, statements which can be true or false, but merely ways of expressing and influencing feelings. The question, therefore, of how we can know whether such a judgement is true simply evaporates.

(c) *Moral scope.* There is a third category of issues which can divide moral philosophers, even when they are agreed on the general justifying grounds of moral principles and on the manner in which knowledge of these principles is secured. I shall call them issues of *scope*. It is, in fact, differences over these issues which loom largest when ancient and modern approaches to morality are contrasted. I remarked earlier on the absence in ancient writings of terms that are happily translated by 'moral' or 'ethical': and a main reason for this is the absence from the ancient approaches of certain doctrines about the scope of moral principles which have become part of received, though not unchallenged, modern wisdom. For all the important differences between them, the two most influential movements in modern ethics – utilitarianism and Kantianism – both incorporate two important tenets concerning the scope of moral principles. Both of these could be expressed by saying that the scope of these principles is *universal*.

The first of these tenets is that moral principles, unlike rules of etiquette or the laws of the land, apply to human beings in general, irrespective of, for example, nationality. If it is morally wrong for me to treat you in a certain manner – to break a promise made to you, for example – then it is morally wrong for anyone to treat anyone else in that manner, assuming that the circumstances are relevantly similar. The second tenet is that moral principles have authority in all walks of life so that where, say, the demands of morality conflict with aesthetic considerations, the former 'trump' the latter. Put differently, moral requirements are not just one kind of requirement, which may be suspended or set aside in favour of others, but those which have sovereign authority in people's lives. That moral principles have universal applicability and overriding authority are doctrines so pervasive in modern thought that, in the writings of some recent philosophers, they are built into the very definition of 'morality'.[5]

In an ancient writer like Aristotle, conversely, the scope of the *ethikai aretai* (misleadingly translated as 'moral virtues') are, in a double sense, only 'local'. To begin with, these are not 'virtues' incumbent on people in general: rather, they are the 'excellences' only of certain people living in certain communities. Nor is it required that these 'virtues' be exercised towards people in general, but only towards fellow-members of one's community. For Aristotle and most other ancient writers, there is no assumption that there are or should be principles of behaviour that are binding on human beings *as such* and demanding treatment of human beings *as such*. Nor, second, is it assumed that virtues and principles which we would nowadays describe as moral have sovereign authority in people's lives. Thus Aristotle, in the final book of his *Ethics*, argues for the superior value of the contemplative life, for those who are capable of it, over the ethical life. In that respect, at least, his position is akin to that of the Indian traditions. Moral rectitude, in those traditions, may be an important prerequisite for the 'liberation' from our mundane condition which people should aim at, but it is only one means among several and, for the virtuoso sage, may be a dispensable one.[6]

I do not want to exaggerate the ancient *versus* modern divide over issues of scope. There are ancient thinkers, especially among Buddhists, who argue for the universal applicability of moral precepts (see chapter 7), just as there are nineteenth- and twentieth-century thinkers who contradict the prevailing modern wisdom. Nietzsche mocks the very idea of universally applicable principles, while Kierkegaard argues, it seems, for the 'suspension', under certain circumstances, of the demands of ethics, implying thereby that there can be a 'higher' call than that of morality. And certainly several moral philosophers over the last quarter of a century have expressed their disquiet over the 'universalistic' predilections of modern ethics and their sympathy for older traditions in which the scope of moral principles and their place within the good life as a whole are open questions.

There are alternative ways, no doubt, of carving up the issues and concerns of moral philosophy over the millennia to the one I have just suggested. Whichever way it is done, the texts in this reader represent some of the most profound stances on those issues and the most influential expressions of those concerns to be found in the history of thought.

---

[5] See especially R. M. Hare, *Freedom and Reason*, Oxford: Oxford University Press, 1963.
[6] Not untypical is the position of Hinduism's most famous philosopher, Śaṃkara, who held that attention to one's duties is only a 'preliminary' or 'auxiliary' to the acquisition of liberating knowledge – a knowledge which some might attain even without such attention. *A Śaṃkara Source-Book*, vol. 5, London: Shanti-Sadan, 1989, pp. 107ff.

Plato, *Gorgias*, 482–4, 488–500

From Plato, *Gorgias*, trans. W. Hamilton. Harmondsworth: Penguin, 1960, pp. 77–9, 84–105 [notes and some passages omitted]; copyright © Walter Hamilton 1960.

The *Gorgias* of the great Athenian philosopher, Plato (*c.* 427–347 BCE), is one of his early dialogues, free as yet of his mature metaphysical doctrines, notably the theory of the Forms. Dark intimations of the fate of Socrates, the main character in the dialogue, and unusually bitter animosity towards Socrates' opponents suggest that it may have been written by Plato not long after his teacher's trial and death in 399. As such, the *Gorgias* is one of the very first sustained discussions of morality to have come down to us from the Greeks – and one of the most influential, for it announces themes that have continued to occupy philosophers ever since, such as the relation between goodness and pleasure. Above all, in the person of Callicles, the dialogue introduces a stark prototype of a 'might is right' amoralism which, ever since, has had its advocates in Western thought, right down to the apologists of *Realpolitik* and Fascism.

Callicles, like many of Socrates' adversaries, was a Sophist, one of those teachers of the skills – notably in oratory – deemed essential to success in Athenian public life. Like today's PR-men, advertising executives and 'spin doctors', the Sophists had a not disadvantageous reputation for nonchalance towards accepted morality. For the go-ahead Athenian orator or litigant, it might be useful to wear 'the appearance of goodness', but of no particular benefit to worry about its substance. And by the more philosophically-minded Sophists, like Protagoras and Thrasymachus, the very prospect of rational, objective moral norms is rejected. '[T]he just and the unjust . . . are in truth to each state such as it thinks they are . . . in these matters no citizen or state is wiser than another,' said Protagoras, the 'father' of moral relativism; while, for Thrasymachus – anticipating Marx's views – justice is simply 'the interest of the stronger' and morality only a system of rules furthering that interest.[1]

---

[1] For Protagoras, see Plato's *Theaetetus*, 172; for Thrasymachus, Plato's *Republic*, Book I.

Callicles' position, while equally dismissive of conventional morality itself or of people's usual understanding of it, is rather different. That morality varies from society to society is not the relevant point; nor is it that conventional morality is a tool exploited by the strong. Rather, the point is the more Nietzschean one (see chapter 14) that conventional morality is a crutch used by inferior, weaker people, and something to despise in comparison with the 'natural' morality of the unbridled strong man. (Callicles thereby stands behind another long tradition in Western thought, the opposition – in Rousseau, for instance – between 'natural' and 'social' man).[2] Callicles introduces this point at the stage where our extract from the *Gorgias* begins, after he has impatiently listened to the reasons Socrates has given for denying both that oratory is a beneficial art and that it confers on a man the power to get what he wants. Socrates, he exclaims, cannot be in earnest in holding that 'it is better to suffer wrong than to do wrong' and that the wrongdoer is 'more miserable than the man who is wronged' (479). For Callicles, Socrates' previous interlocutors, Gorgias and Polus, have conceded too much to familiar concepts of good and justice. What is needed is a blunt equation of 'better' and 'stronger', a radical rejection of familiar moral understanding.

This very bluntness and radicalism, however, lays him open to Socrates' objections. What, after all, can Callicles mean by terms like 'better' if he has broken completely with ordinary conceptions? Callicles is soon forced to qualify his initial equation and to shift towards a notion of good in terms of a lusty pursuit of pleasure, a move that is brought to a halt by Socrates' forcing of the concession that pleasures, too, can be appraised as good and bad. Not all of Socrates' arguments are good ones, notably the one which relies on the example of thirst and its quenching to show that pleasure and pain, unlike good and evil, can be found combined (494ff). But much of the argumentation is exemplary for subsequent attempts (G.E. Moore's, for instance, see chapter 15) to stop the radical moral revisionist or amoralist in his tracks. By appealing to how terms in the moral lexicon are actually employed, Socrates endeavours to show that the radical debars himself from saying what he wants to: for by loosing terms like 'good' and 'just' from their moorings, the radical is precluded from using them to approve the courses of action, or ways of life, which he urges. Readers will need to look at some of the other texts in this volume to decide whether that endeavour was necessarily a decisive one.

▶ ▶ ▶ CALLICLES: . . . Generally speaking, nature and convention are inconsistent with one another; so if from a feeling of shame a man does not dare
483   to say what he thinks he necessarily involves himself in an inconsistency.

---

[2] See Alasdair MacIntyre, *A Short History of Ethics*, New York: Macmillan, 1966, pp. 17ff.

You have discovered this subtle truth and make a dishonest use of it in argument; if a man speaks the language of convention, you meet him with a question framed in the language of nature; if he uses words in their natural sense you take them in their conventional meaning. That is what has happened in this discussion of doing wrong and suffering wrong. Polus meant what is conventionally baser, and you took up his conventional use of the word as if he had intended its natural meaning. In the natural sense anything that is a greater evil is also baser – in this case suffering wrong; but conventionally doing wrong is the baser of the two. The experience of suffering wrong does not happen to anyone who calls himself a man; it happens to a slave who had better die than live, seeing that when he is wronged and insulted he cannot defend himself or anyone else for whom he cares. Conventions, on the other hand, are made, in my opinion, by the weaklings who form the majority of mankind. They establish them and apportion praise and blame with an eye to themselves and their own interests, and in an endeavour to frighten those who are stronger and capable of getting the upper hand they say that ambition is base and wrong, and that wrong-doing consists in trying to gain an advantage over others; being inferior themselves, they are content, no doubt, if they can stand on an equal footing with their betters.

That is why by convention an attempt to gain an advantage over the majority is said to be wrong and base, and men call it criminal; nature, on the other hand, herself demonstrates that it is right that the better man should prevail over the worse and the stronger over the weaker. The truth of this can be seen in a variety of examples, drawn both from the animal world and from the complex communities and races of human beings; right consists in the superior ruling over the inferior and having the upper hand. By what right, for example, did Xerxes invade Greece and his father Scythia, to take two of the countless instances that present themselves? My conviction is that these actions are in accordance with nature; indeed, I would go so far as to say that they are in accordance with natural law, though not perhaps with the conventional law enacted by us. Our way is to take the best and strongest among us from an early age and endeavour to mould their character as men tame lions; we subject them to a course of charms and spells and try to enslave them by 484 repetition of the dogma that men ought to be equal and that equality is fine and right. But if there arises a man sufficiently endowed by nature, he will shake off and break through and escape from all these trammels; he will tread underfoot our texts and spells and incantations and unnatural laws, and by an act of revolt reveal himself our master instead of our slave, in the full blaze of the light of natural justice. Pindar seems to me to express the same thought as mine in the poem in which he speaks of 'Law, the king of all, men and gods alike', and goes on to say that this law 'carries things off with a high hand, making might to be right. Witness the deeds of Heracles when without paying a price . . .' or words to that effect. I do not know the poem by heart, but his meaning is that Heracles drove off the oxen of Geryon without paying for them or receiving them as a gift, because this was natural justice, and that oxen and all the other possessions of those who are weaker and inferior belong to the man who is better and superior.

That is the truth of the matter, and you will realize it if you abandon philosophy and turn to more important pursuits. . . .

488   SOCRATES: . . . Go back to the beginning and tell me again what you and Pindar mean by natural right. Am I mistaken in thinking that according to you right consists in the stronger seizing the property of the weaker and the better ruling the worse and the more gifted having an advantage over the less?

CALLICLES: No; that is what I said and what I still maintain.

SOCRATES: But do you mean that 'better' and 'stronger' are the same? I couldn't quite make out your meaning on this point. Do you mean by 'stronger' those who have greater physical strength, and must the weaker obey the stronger, as you seemed to imply when you spoke of big states attacking small in accordance with natural right, because they are stronger and physically more powerful, as if 'more powerful' and 'stronger' and 'better' were synonymous terms? Is it possible to be better, but at the same time less powerful and weaker, and stronger, but also more vicious? Or are 'better' and 'stronger' to be defined as the same? This is the point on which I want a clear statement; are 'stronger' and 'better' and 'more powerful' synonymous or not?

CALLICLES: I tell you quite explicitly that they are synonymous.

SOCRATES: Now are not the mass of men naturally stronger than the individual man? And these are the people, as you said a while ago, who impose their conventional laws upon the individual.

CALLICLES: Of course.

SOCRATES: Then the laws imposed by the majority are laws imposed by the stronger.

CALLICLES: Certainly.

SOCRATES: And therefore by the better? The stronger are also the better by your account, I think.

CALLICLES: Yes.

SOCRATES: Then since they are stronger the laws which they establish are by nature good?

CALLICLES: I agree.

SOCRATES: But is it not the conventional belief of the majority, as you said yourself just now, that equality is right and that it is a baser thing to do wrong than to suffer wrong? Answer yes or no, and take care that you in your turn are not betrayed by a feeling of shame. Do the majority believe or do they not that equality, not inequality, is right, and that it is baser to do wrong than to suffer wrong? Don't grudge me an answer to this question, Callicles. If you agree with me, let me hear the point established on your authority, the authority of a man well able to distinguish truth from falsehood.   489

CALLICLES: Very well, that is the belief of the masses.

SOCRATES: Then the belief that it is baser to do wrong than to suffer wrong and that equality is right appears to be founded in nature as well as in convention. It looks as if what you said earlier were not true, and you were wrong when you accused me of knowing that convention and nature were inconsistent, and of making a dishonest use of this knowledge in argument, by taking in a conventional sense words intended by the speaker in a natural sense, and vice versa.

CALLICLES: There is no end to the rubbish this fellow talks. Tell me, Socrates, aren't you ashamed at your age of laying these verbal traps and counting it a god-send if a man makes a slip of the tongue? Do you really suppose that by 'stronger' I mean anything but 'better'? Haven't I already told you that they are the same? Do you take me to mean that, if you sweep together a heap of slaves and riff-raff useful only for their brawn, and they say this or that, what they say is to have the force of law?

SOCRATES: Ah! my clever friend, is that the line you take?

CALLICLES: Certainly it is.

SOCRATES: Well, my good sir, I guessed some time ago that that or something like it was what you understood by 'stronger' and my repeating the question arises from my eagerness to grasp your precise meaning. Clearly you don't believe that two men are better than one or your slaves better than you, simply because they are physically more powerful. Tell me again from the start what you mean by 'better' if you don't mean 'more powerful'. And I must ask you, honoured sir, to be a little milder in your style of teaching; otherwise I shall run away from your school.

CALLICLES: You are pleased to be sarcastic, Socrates.

SOCRATES: No, Callicles, I am not; I swear it by Zethus, whose person you borrowed just now to utter a number of sarcasms at my expense. Come now, tell me whom you mean by 'better' men.

CALLICLES: I mean those who are more gifted.

SOCRATES: Then don't you see that you too are uttering mere words without meaning? Tell me, pray, do you mean by 'better' and 'stronger' those who are more intelligent, or something else?

CALLICLES: That is exactly what I do mean, most emphatically.

490   SOCRATES: Then on your theory it must often happen that one wise man is stronger than ten thousand fools, and that he ought to rule over them as subjects and have the lion's share of everything. That is what you seem to mean – there is no verbal trap here, I assure you – if one man is stronger than ten thousand.

CALLICLES: That is exactly what I do mean. My belief is that natural right consists in the better and wiser man ruling over his inferiors and having the lion's share.

SOCRATES: Stop there one moment. What would you say in the following situation? Suppose a number of us were collected in the same spot, as we are now, with plenty of food and drink between us, a heterogeneous crowd of strong and weak together, but containing one man wiser than the rest of us about such matters by virtue of his medical knowledge. And suppose that this man, as is quite likely, were physically more powerful than some but less powerful than other members of the crowd. Should we say that for the present purpose the doctor, being wiser than we, is also better and stronger?

CALLICLES: Certainly.

SOCRATES: Is he then to have more of the food than we because he is better, or is his authority over us to be shown by his being in control of the distribution? If he is not to suffer for it, he will not appropriate the largest ration for his personal consumption; he will have more than some and less than others, and if he happens to be the greatest invalid of the party the best man will get the smallest share. Isn't that how it will be, Callicles?

CALLICLES: You talk of food and drink and doctors and nonsense of that sort. That is not what I am referring to.

SOCRATES: Then do you maintain that the wiser man is also the better? Yes or no.

CALLICLES: Yes.

SOCRATES: And that the better man ought to have the larger share?

CALLICLES: Yes, but not of food and drink.

SOCRATES: Very well; perhaps you mean of clothes, and the best weaver ought to have the biggest coat, and go about the town in more and finer clothes than other people.

CALLICLES: Clothes, forsooth!

SOCRATES: As for shoes, obviously the man who is best and wisest about them will have the advantage there; the shoemaker will walk about in the largest shoes and have the greatest number of them.

CALLICLES: Shoes indeed! Bosh!

SOCRATES: If you don't mean that sort of thing, perhaps you mean, for example, that a farmer, who is intelligent and a fine fellow where land is concerned, should have a larger share of seed than other people, and use the greatest possible quantity of seed on his own farm.

CALLICLES: Still the same stale old language, Socrates.

SOCRATES: Yes, Callicles, and on the same subjects.

CALLICLES: You simply never stop talking of cobblers and fullers and cooks and doctors; as if our argument were concerned with them! 491

SOCRATES: Then kindly tell me in what sphere a man must show his greater strength and intelligence in order to establish a right to an advantage over others. Or are you going to refuse to entertain any of my suggestions, and at the same time make none of your own?

CALLICLES: I have told you already what I mean, Socrates. First of all, when I speak of 'stronger' I don't mean cobblers or cooks; I mean people with the intelligence to know how political matters should be handled, and not only intelligence but courage; people who have the ability to carry out their ideas, and who will not shrink from doing so through faintness of heart.

SOCRATES: Do you notice, my dear Callicles, how you and I find fault with one another for quite different reasons? You blame me for constantly using the same language, while I, on the contrary, find it a defect in you that you never keep to the same line about the same subject. At one moment you defined the better and stronger as the more powerful; next as the more intelligent; and now you come out with yet another idea; you say that the better and stronger are a braver sort of people. Tell us my good friend, and be done with it, what you mean by the better and stronger and how they differ from other people.

CALLICLES: I have told you that I mean people who are intelligent in political matters and have the courage of their convictions. They are the people who ought to rule states, and right consists in them as rulers having an advantage over the rest, who are their subjects.

SOCRATES: Tell me, will they be rulers of themselves?

CALLICLES: What do you mean?

SOCRATES: I mean each man being master of himself. Or is there no need for self-mastery as long as one is master of others?

CALLICLES: What do you mean by self-mastery?

SOCRATES: Nothing in the least recondite. I use the word simply in the popular sense, of being moderate and in control of oneself and master of one's own passions and appetites.

CALLICLES: What a funny fellow you are, Socrates. The people that you call moderate are the half-witted.

SOCRATES: How so? Anybody can see that I don't mean them.

CALLICLES: Oh! but you do, Socrates. For how can a man be happy that is in subjection to anyone whatever? I tell you frankly that natural good and right consist in this, that the man who is going to live as a man ought should encourage his appetites to be as strong as possible instead of repressing them, and be able by means of his courage and intelligence to satisfy them in all their intensity by providing them with whatever they happen to desire.

For the majority, I know, this is an impossible ideal; that is why, in an endeavour to conceal their own weakness, they blame the minority whom they are ashamed of not being able to imitate, and maintain that excess is a disgraceful thing. As I said before, they try to make slaves of men of better natural gifts, and because through their own lack of manliness they are unable to satisfy their passions they praise moderation and right-eousness. To those who are either of princely birth to begin with or able by their own qualities to win office or absolute rule or power what could in truth be more disgraceful or injurious than moderation, which in-volves their voluntary subjection to the conventions and standards and criticism of the majority, when they might enjoy every advantage with-out interference from anybody? How can they fail to be wretched when they are prevented by your fine righteousness and moderation from favouring their friends at the expense of their enemies, even when they are rulers in their own city?

The truth, Socrates, which you profess to be in search of, is in fact this; luxury and excess and licence, provided that they can obtain sufficient backing, are virtue and happiness; all the rest is mere flummery, un-natural conventions of society, worthless cant.

SOCRATES: Your frank statement of your position, Callicles, certainly does not lack spirit. You set out plainly in the light of day opinions which other people entertain but are loth to express. Don't weaken at all, I beseech you, so that we may come to a clear conclusion how life should be lived. And tell me this. You maintain, do you not, that if a man is to be what he ought he should not repress his appetites but let them grow as strong as possible and satisfy them by any means in his power, and that such behaviour is virtue?

CALLICLES: Yes, I do.

SOCRATES: Then the view that those who have no wants are happy is wrong?

CALLICLES: Of course; at that rate stones and corpses would be supremely happy.

SOCRATES: Nevertheless even the life which you describe has its alarming side. I should not wonder if Euripides may not be right when he says:

> Who knows if life be death or death be life? (*Polyidus*)

and if perhaps it may not be we who are in fact dead. This is a view that   493
I have heard maintained before now by one of the pundits, who declares that we in our present condition are dead. Our body is the tomb in which we are buried, and the part of the soul in which our appetites reside is liable by reason of its gullibility to be carried in the most contrary directions. This same part, because of its instability and readiness to be influenced, a witty man, Sicilian perhaps or Italian, has by a play upon words allegorically called a pitcher.[1] In the same vein he labels fools 'uninitiated' (or 'leaky'), and that part of their soul which contains the appetites, which is intemperate and as it were the reverse of watertight, he represents as a pitcher with holes in it, because it cannot be filled up. Thus in direct opposition to you, Callicles, he maintains that of all the inhabitants of Hades – meaning by Hades the invisible world – the uninitiated are the most wretched, being engaged in pouring water into a leaky pitcher out of an equally leaky sieve. The sieve, according to my informant, he uses as an image of the soul, and his motive for comparing the souls of fools to sieves is that they are leaky and unable to retain their contents on account of their fickle and forgetful nature.

This comparison is, no doubt, more or less grotesque, but it demonstrates the point which I want to prove to you, in order to persuade you, if I can, to change your mind, and, instead of a life of intemperate craving which can never be satisfied, to choose a temperate life which is content with whatever comes to hand and asks no more.

Does what I say influence you at all towards a conviction that the temperate are happier than the intemperate, or will any number of such allegories fail to convert you?

CALLICLES: The latter is nearer the truth, Socrates.

SOCRATES: Well, let me produce another simile from the same school as the first. Suppose that the two lives, the temperate and the intemperate, are typified by two men, each of whom has a number of casks. The casks of the first are sound and full, one of wine, one of honey, one of milk, and so on, but the supply of each of these commodities is scanty and he can procure them only with very great difficulty. This man, when once he has filled his casks, will not need to increase his store and give himself any further concern about it; as far as this matter goes his mind will be at rest. Now take the second man. He, like the first, can obtain a supply, though only with difficulty; but his vessels are leaky and rotten, so that if he is to avoid the extremity of privation he must be perpetually filling them, day and night. If such is the condition of the two lives respectively, can you say that the life of the intemperate man is happier than the life of the temperate? Am I making any progress towards making you admit that the temperate life is better than the intemperate, or not?

494

CALLICLES: No, Socrates, you are not. The man who has filled his casks no longer has any pleasure left. It is just as I said a moment ago; once his casks are filled his existence is the existence of a stone, exempt alike from enjoyment and pain. But the pleasure of life consists precisely in this, that there should be as much running in as possible.

SOCRATES: But if much is to run in much must necessarily run out, and there must be large holes for it to escape by.

CALLICLES: Certainly.

SOCRATES: Then the existence which you are describing, so far from being that of a stone or a corpse, is the existence of a greedy and dirty bird. Tell me now; are you speaking of such things as being hungry and eating when one is hungry?

CALLICLES: Yes.

SOCRATES: And of being thirsty and drinking when one is thirsty?

CALLICLES: Certainly, and of having all the other appetites and being able to satisfy them with enjoyment. That is the happy life.

SOCRATES: Excellent, my good sir. Only you must stick to your point and not give way out of shame. No more must I, for that matter, it seems. Tell me first of all; can a man who itches and wants to scratch and whose opportunities of scratching are unbounded be said to lead a happy life continually scratching?

CALLICLES: How fantastic you are, Socrates, and how thoroughly vulgar.

SOCRATES: That, Callicles, is why I shocked Polus and Gorgias and made them feel shame. But you are a brave man, and will never give way to such emotions. Just answer me.

CALLICLES: Then I say that even the man who scratches lives a pleasant life.

SOCRATES: And if pleasant then happy?

CALLICLES: Of course.

SOCRATES: But suppose that the itch were not confined to his head. Must I go on with my questions? Consider what answer you will make, Callicles, if you are asked all the questions which are corollaries of this. To bring the matter to a head, take the life of a catamite; is not that dreadful and shameful and wretched? Or will you dare to say that such people are happy provided that they have an abundant supply of what they want?

CALLICLES: Aren't you ashamed to introduce such subjects into the discussion, Socrates?

SOCRATES: Who is responsible for their introduction, my fine sir? I or the person who maintains without qualification that those who feel enjoyment of whatever kind are happy, and who does not distinguish between good and bad pleasures? Tell me once more; do you declare that pleasure is identical with good, or are there some pleasures which are not good? 495

CALLICLES: To say that they are different would involve me in an inconsistency. I declare that they are identical.

SOCRATES: If you say what you do not think, Callicles, you are destroying the force of your first speech, and I can no longer accept you as a satisfactory ally in my attempt to discover the truth.

CALLICLES: But you are doing just the same, Socrates.

SOCRATES: If I am, I am wrong, and so are you. Can it be, my good friend, that good is not identical with enjoyment of whatever kind? Otherwise, many shameful consequences will ensue besides those at which I have just hinted.

CALLICLES: That is what *you* think, Socrates.

SOCRATES: Do you really persist, Callicles, in what you affirm?

CALLICLES: Yes, I do.

SOCRATES: Shall we then continue the argument on the assumption that you are serious?

CALLICLES: By all means.

SOCRATES: Very well then; if that is your decision, solve this problem. You recognize the existence of something called knowledge, I presume?

CALLICLES: Yes.

SOCRATES: You were speaking just now, were you not, of courage existing together with knowledge?

CALLICLES: I was.

SOCRATES: Meaning, I suppose, that courage and knowledge are two different things.

CALLICLES: Undoubtedly.

SOCRATES: Now then; would you call pleasure and knowledge the same or different?

CALLICLES: Different, of course, my wiseacre.

SOCRATES: And courage different from pleasure?

CALLICLES: Naturally.

SOCRATES: We must make a note of this. 'Callicles of Acharnae declared that pleasure and good are the same, but knowledge and courage are different from one another and different from good.'

CALLICLES: 'But Socrates of Alopece does not agree with him', or does he?

SOCRATES: He does not. Nor, I think, will Callicles, when he has examined himself properly. Tell me; do you not think that the fortunate are in the opposite state to the unfortunate?

CALLICLES: Yes.

SOCRATES: Then, if these states are opposite, is not the same true of them as of health and sickness? A man, I presume, is never both well and sick at the same time, and never ceases to be well and sick at the same time.

CALLICLES: What do you mean?

SOCRATES: Take any part of the body you like by itself; suppose a man has a malady of the eyes, what is called ophthalmia.

CALLICLES: Very well.

SOCRATES: He does not, I presume, enjoy health in his eyes at the same time?

CALLICLES: By no manner of means.

SOCRATES: Now, when he loses his ophthalmia, does he at that moment lose health in his eyes, so that he ends by losing both together?

CALLICLES: Certainly not.

SOCRATES: Such a conclusion would be illogical as well as surprising, wouldn't it?

CALLICLES: It would indeed.

SOCRATES: The truth is, I imagine, that he acquires and loses each condition by turns.

CALLICLES: I agree.

SOCRATES: Is the same true of strength and weakness?

CALLICLES: Yes.

SOCRATES: And of quickness and slowness?

CALLICLES: Of course.

SOCRATES: Now take good and happiness and their opposites, evil and misery; are both of these acquired by turns and lost by turns?

CALLICLES: Unquestionably.

SOCRATES: Then, if we find any pair of things that a man loses together and possesses together, those things will not be good and evil. Are we agreed about this? Think well before you answer.

CALLICLES: I agree most emphatically.

SOCRATES: Go back now to what we agreed before. Did you say that hunger was pleasant or painful? I mean just hunger by itself.

CALLICLES: I should call that painful; but to eat when one is hungry is pleasant.

SOCRATES: I understand. Still, hunger in itself is painful, is it not?

CALLICLES: Yes.

SOCRATES: And thirst also?

CALLICLES: Certainly.

SOCRATES: Shall I go on with further questions, or do you agree that every state of want and desire is painful?

CALLICLES: You need not labour the point. I agree.

SOCRATES: Very well. But drinking when one is thirsty you would call pleasant, wouldn't you?

CALLICLES: Yes.

SOCRATES: When you say 'drinking when one is thirsty', 'thirsty' is equivalent to 'in pain', is it not?

CALLICLES: Yes.

SOCRATES: And drinking is the satisfaction of the want and a pleasure?

CALLICLES: Yes.

SOCRATES: So it is in connection with drinking that you speak of enjoyment?

CALLICLES: Certainly.

SOCRATES: When one is thirsty?

CALLICLES: Yes.

SOCRATES: And therefore in pain?

CALLICLES: Yes.

SOCRATES: Do you see what follows? When you speak of drinking, when one is thirsty, you imply the experience of pleasure and pain together. Can you say that these sensations don't occur together at the same time and in the same part of something which you may equally well, I think, call body or soul? Is this true or not?

CALLICLES: Quite true.

SOCRATES: Yet you say that it is impossible to be fortunate and unfortunate at the same time.

CALLICLES: I do.

SOCRATES: But you have agreed that it is possible to feel enjoyment when 497 one is in pain.

CALLICLES: So it appears.

SOCRATES: Then enjoyment is not the same as good fortune nor pain as bad fortune, and pleasure is a different thing from good.

CALLICLES: I don't understand your quibbles, Socrates.

SOCRATES: Oh yes, you do, Callicles; only it suits you to feign ignorance. Just carry the argument a little further.

CALLICLES: What is the point of continuing this nonsense?

SOCRATES: To show you how clever you are, my self-appointed instructor.

Is it not true that at the moment when each of us ceases to feel thirst he ceases also to feel the pleasure of drinking?

CALLICLES: I don't know what you mean.

SOCRATES: . . . tell me whether thirst and pleasure don't come to an end together for us all.

CALLICLES: Yes, they do.

SOCRATES: And the same with hunger and the other appetites? Does not the pleasure of satisfying them cease at the same moment as the desire?

CALLICLES: True.

SOCRATES: Then pains and pleasures come to an end together?

CALLICLES: Yes.

SOCRATES: But, as you agreed, good and evil do not come to an end together. Or do you wish to retract that admission?

CALLICLES: By no means. What then?

SOCRATES: The conclusion is, my friend, that good is not identical with pleasure nor evil with pain. The one pair of contraries comes to an end together and the other does not, because they are different. How then can pleasure possibly be the same as good or pain as evil? Look at the matter in another way if you like; the conclusion will still, I think, be at variance with yours. When you call people good, you imply, do you not, the presence of good in them, in the same way as you call those in whom beauty is present beautiful?

CALLICLES: Yes.

SOCRATES: Well, do you call fools and cowards good? You didn't a while ago; you reserved the term for the brave and intelligent. They are the people you call good, aren't they?

CALLICLES: Certainly.

SOCRATES: Well, have you ever seen a foolish child enjoying itself?

CALLICLES: Yes.

498   SOCRATES: And for that matter a foolish man enjoying himself?

CALLICLES: I suppose so. But what is the point of this?

SOCRATES: Never mind; just answer.

CALLICLES: Yes, then.

SOCRATES: Have you seen an intelligent man feeling pain or pleasure?

CALLICLES: Yes.

SOCRATES: Well, which class feels greater pain or pleasure, the fools or the wise men?

CALLICLES: I don't know that there is much in it.

SOCRATES: That is enough for my purpose. Now, have you seen a coward in war?

CALLICLES: Of course.

SOCRATES: And when the enemy retreated, which did you think felt greater joy, the cowards or the brave men?

CALLICLES: Greater joy? Both, as far as I could see. Anyhow, the difference was trifling.

SOCRATES: No matter for that. At any rate cowards feel joy as well as the brave?

CALLICLES: Undoubtedly.

SOCRATES: And fools too, it seems.

CALLICLES: Yes.

SOCRATES: But when the enemy advances, is pain confined to cowards or do the brave feel it too?

CALLICLES: Both feel it.

SOCRATES: Equally?

CALLICLES: Perhaps cowards feel it more.

SOCRATES: And don't they feel greater joy when the enemy retreats?

CALLICLES: Perhaps.

SOCRATES: Then by your account pain and joy are felt in practically the same degree by fools and wise men, cowards and heroes, but if anything more keenly by cowards than by brave men?

CALLICLES: Yes.

SOCRATES: Yet the wise and brave are good, and cowards and fools bad?

CALLICLES: Yes.

SOCRATES: Then good and bad feel joy and pain in about the same degree?

CALLICLES: Yes.

SOCRATES: In that case are we to conclude that there is very little to choose in goodness and badness between the good and the bad, or even that the bad are somewhat better than the good?

CALLICLES: I simply do not know what you mean.

SOCRATES: Don't you remember that you are maintaining that the good owe their goodness to the presence in them of good, and the bad their badness to the presence of evil, and that good is identical with pleasure and evil with pain?

CALLICLES: Yes.

SOCRATES: Doesn't the sensation of joy involve the presence of pleasure or good in those who experience it?

CALLICLES: Of course.

SOCRATES: Then since good is present in them, those who feel joy are good?

CALLICLES: Yes.

SOCRATES: Again, is not pain or evil present in those who suffer pain?

CALLICLES: It is.

SOCRATES: And you say that the bad owe their badness to the presence of evil in them. Or do you retract that?

CALLICLES: No, I affirm it.

SOCRATES: Then whoever feels joy is good and whoever feels pain is bad?

CALLICLES: Certainly.

SOCRATES: And people are more or less or equally good or bad according as their experience of joy is more or less or equally intense?

CALLICLES: Yes.

SOCRATES: You say, I think, that joy and pain are felt in almost equal degree by wise men and fools, cowards and heroes, or possibly somewhat more keenly by cowards?

CALLICLES: Yes.

SOCRATES: Now give me your help in drawing the conclusion that emerges
499   from what we have agreed. It is good to repeat and contemplate fine things two or three times, they say. We affirm that a wise and brave man is good, don't we?

CALLICLES: Yes.

SOCRATES: And a fool and a coward bad?

CALLICLES: Certainly.

SOCRATES: But a man who feels joy is good?

CALLICLES: Yes.

SOCRATES: And a man who feels pain bad?

CALLICLES: Inevitably.

SOCRATES: And the good and bad feel pain and joy alike, but the bad perhaps more keenly?

CALLICLES: Yes.

SOCRATES: Then the bad man is as good and as bad as the good, or perhaps rather better. Isn't this the conclusion that follows from our premises, if one begins by equating pleasure and good? Is there any escape from it, Callicles?

CALLICLES: I've been listening to you and expressing agreement for a long time, Socrates, with the thought in my mind all along that if one gives in to you on any point even in jest, you seize on the admission triumphantly with all the eagerness of a child. As if you didn't know that like everybody else I distinguish between better and worse pleasures.[2]

SOCRATES: Come, come, Callicles, what a cheat you are. You are treating me like a child, changing your ground from moment to moment, in order to mislead me. When we began I never supposed that you would wilfully mislead me, because I thought that you were my friend. But now it appears that I was mistaken in you, and I suppose that I must make the best of it, as the saying goes, and do what I can with what you choose to give me. What you are now saying, apparently, is that some pleasures are good and some bad. Is that right?

CALLICLES: Yes.

SOCRATES: Are good pleasures those which bring benefit and bad pleasures those which bring harm?

CALLICLES: Of course.

SOCRATES: And the beneficial are those which produce some good result, and the harmful those which produce the reverse?

CALLICLES: Yes.

SOCRATES: Do you mean the sort of pleasures we were speaking of before, the physical pleasures of eating and drinking, for example? Are we to regard those which produce bodily health or strength or some other desirable physical quality as good and those which have the opposite effect as bad?

CALLICLES: Certainly.

SOCRATES: And does the same apply to pains? Are some good and some bad?

CALLICLES: Naturally.

SOCRATES: Then we must prefer to embrace the good of both kinds, pains as well as pleasures?

CALLICLES: By all means.

SOCRATES: And reject the bad?

CALLICLES: Obviously.

SOCRATES: If you remember, Polus and I agreed that all actions should be performed as a means to the good. Do you also agree with this, that good is the object of all actions, and that all that we do should be a means to the good, and not vice versa? Are you prepared to add your vote to our two?

CALLICLES: Yes, I am.

500

SOCRATES: Then it follows that we should embrace pleasure among other things as a means to good, and not good as a means to pleasure. . . .

Notes

1 The word-play cannot be brought out in English, relying as it does on the similarity between the Greek words meaning 'pitcher' and 'readily influenced' respectively. The Sicilian and Italian are probably Empedocles and Pythagoras, and

it is the latter's doctrine of the soul entombed in the body which was referred to a few lines earlier.

2 Callicles is typically incapable of appreciating that the distinction he now concedes has fatal implications, soon exposed by Socrates, for his earlier equation of pleasure and goodness.

Aristotle, *Nicomachean Ethics*, Book I

From J. L. Ackrill (ed.), *Aristotle's Ethics*, trans. W. D. Ross (with amendments by J. L. Ackrill). London: Faber & Faber, 1973, pp. 41–60; reprinted by permission of Oxford University Press.

The *Nicomachean Ethics*, the second of three works which Plato's student Aristotle (384–322 BCE) devoted to ethics, is the most influential of all writings in Western moral philosophy. Indeed, it is the work which virtually defined this branch of philosophy, and Aristotle's discussions of its main topics – man's ' function', justice, the 'mean', responsibility and the will, the nature of practical reason, and more – have shaped nearly all later treatments. Moreover, one would have to go back to the Islamic and medieval Christian scholars, for whom Aristotle was 'The Philosopher', to find a time when his ethics was as live a subject of interest as it is today. A main reason is that, for many contemporary philosophers, Aristotle's conception of the moral life as the rational exercise of virtues within socio-political life is the only sensible alternative to the 'universalism' of Enlightenment thought and the stark 'individualism' of Kierkegaard and other critics of Enlightenment. To, that is, dreams of the betterment of mankind or of securing 'the universal rights of man', on the one hand, and to ideals of an 'inner' personal authenticity, on the other.[1]

In Book I, Aristotle sets out the conception of ethics that provides the framework for his ensuing discussions. His is not, he explains, a disinterested enquiry into the nature and vocabulary of ethics, but the practical endeavour to show people, in broad terms, how they might best achieve the good at which all of them aim – a flourishing life or 'happiness' (*eudaimonia*). (In this he differs from the Socrates of Plato's early dialogues, who typically restricts himself to exposing his opponents' confusions.) Since this is the life of humans, it must be one which accords with the distinctively human 'function', namely 'activity of the soul implying a rational principle'. Since this activity must be 'excellently' or 'virtuously' conducted, the human good turns out to be 'activity of the soul in accordance with virtue' (1098a). And since it is no less part of the distinctive

---

[1] See, especially, Alasdair MacIntyre, *After Virtue: A Study in Moral Theory*, London: Duckworth, 1982.

human essence to be a 'political animal', the requisite virtues – justice, magnan-
imity, friendship, and others – are those needed for effective conduct in the
public life of one's community.

For all its influence, Aristotle's ethics has attracted many critics. Do human
beings as such have a 'function' and single 'end'? Are all of Aristotle's virtues
really moral ones? Does he not exaggerate the centrality of politics? Did he
not, unforgivably, exclude women and slaves from the compass of ethical life?
Some, at least, of such objections can be defused by careful attention, avoiding anachronism, to Aristotle's key terms.[2] Man's *ergon* is not his 'function' in
the sense of a pre-set objective, but the dimension of his existence which best
explains characteristically human behaviour. *Eudaimonia* is not a psychological
state of 'happiness' which virtuous activities produce, not an 'end' to which
they are 'means', but the flourishing, fully realized life of which they are constituents. The *ethikai aretai* are not necessarily 'moral virtues' on today's connotation, but the 'excellences of character' conducive to flourishing within the
polis. And that is what 'political' life is – responsible, public activity within
one's *polis* or community, not the electioneering, wheeler-dealing, and the
like which 'political' today conjures up. Women and slaves are excluded from
ethical life, not because they are immoral or just don't count, but because,
Aristotle believed for antiquated reasons, they do not have the qualifications
for rational participation in the affairs of the *polis*.

Readers of the *Ethics* should be warned of a surprise in store in the final
Book X. Despite an early reference in Book I (1103a) to the 'intellectual' virtues, the work will have given the impression that the best life is the ethical
one. Yet, in Book X, we are told that philosophical contemplation, the para-
mount exercise of the intellectual virtues, is 'the highest form of activity' (1177a).
Any attempt to reconcile this claim with the general thrust of the work, it has
been said, is bound to be 'broken-backed'.[3] Perhaps Aristotle is indeed inconsistent here, but then he was not the first or last of those – including the
author(s) of *The Bhagavad Gita* (see chapter 6 below) – who have struggled,
successfully or otherwise, to reconcile the ideal of contemplative truth with
the importance of ethical conduct.

▶▶▶▶ Every art and every inquiry, and similarly every action and pursuit, is thought   1
to aim at some good; and for this reason the good has rightly been de-
1094a   clared to be that at which all things aim. But a certain difference is found
among ends; some are activities, others are products apart from the activi-

[2] For a clear account of these terms, see Jonathan Barnes, *Aristotle*, Oxford: Oxford University Press, 1986, pp. 77f.
[3] J. L. Ackrill, 'Aristotle on Eudaimonia', in A. Rorty (ed.), *Essays on Aristotle's Ethics*,
Berkeley: University of California Press, 1980, p. 33.

ties that produce them. Where there are ends apart from the actions, it is   5
the nature of the products to be better than the activities. Now, as there are
many actions, arts and sciences, their ends also are many; the end of the
medical art is health, that of shipbuilding a vessel, that of strategy victory,
that of economics wealth. But where such arts fall under a single capacity –   10
as bridle-making and the other arts concerned with the equipment of horses
fall under the art of riding, and this and every military action under strategy, in the same way other arts fall under yet others – in all of these the
ends of the master arts are to be preferred to all the subordinate ends; for it
is for the sake of the former that the latter are pursued. It makes no differ-   15
ence whether the activities themselves are the ends of the actions, or something else apart from the activities, as in the case of the sciences just
mentioned.

2   If, then, there is some end of the things we do, which we desire for its own
sake (everything else being desired for the sake of this), and if we do not
choose everything for the sake of something else (for at that rate the pro-   20
cess would go on to infinity, so that our desire would be empty and vain),
clearly this must be the good and the chief good. Will not the knowledge
of it, then, have a great influence on life? Shall we not, like archers who
have a mark to aim at, be more likely to hit upon what is right? If so, we   25
must try, in outline at least, to determine what it is, and of which of the
sciences or capacities it is the object. It would seem to belong to the most
authoritative art and that which is most truly the master art. And politics
appears to be of this nature; for it is this that ordains which of the sciences
should be studied in a state, and which each class of citizens should learn   1094b
and up to what point they should learn them; and we see even the most
highly esteemed of capacities to fall under this, e.g. strategy, economics,
rhetoric; now, since politics uses the rest of the sciences, and since, again, it
legislates as to what we are to do and what we are to abstain from, the end   5
of this science must include those of the others, so that this end must be
the good for man. For even if the end is the same for a single man and for
a state, that of the state seems at all events something greater and more
complete whether to attain or to preserve; though it is worth while to
attain the end merely for one man, it is finer and more godlike to attain it
for a nation or for city-states. These, then, are the ends at which our in-   10
quiry aims, since it is political science, in one sense of that term.

3   Our discussion will be adequate if it has as much clearness as the subject-
matter admits of, for precision is not to be sought for alike in all discussions, any more than in all the products of the crafts. Now fine and just

actions, which political science investigates, exhibit much variety and
fluctuation of opinion, so that they may be thought to exist only by convention, and not by nature. And goods also exhibit a similar fluctuation
because they bring harm to many people; for before now men have been
undone by reason of their wealth, and others by reason of their courage.
We must be content, then, in speaking of such subjects and with such
premises to indicate the truth roughly and in outline, and in speaking about
things which are only for the most part true and with premises of the same
kind to reach conclusions that are no better. In the same spirit, therefore,
should each type of statement be *received*; for it is the mark of an educated
man to look for precision in each class of things just so far as the nature of
the subject admits; it is evidently equally foolish to accept probable reasoning from a mathematician and to demand from a rhetorician demonstrative
proofs.

Now each man judges well the things he knows, and of these he is a
good judge. And so the man who has been educated in a subject is a good
judge of that subject, and the man who has received an all-round education is a good judge in general. Hence a young man is not a proper hearer
of lectures on political science; for he is inexperienced in the actions that
occur in life, but its discussions start from these and are about these; and,
further, since he tends to follow his passions, his study will be vain and
unprofitable, because the end aimed at is not knowledge but action. And it
makes no difference whether he is young in years or youthful in character;
the defect does not depend on time, but on his living, and pursuing each
successive object, as passion directs. For to such persons, as to the incontinent, knowledge brings no profit; but to those who desire and act in
accordance with a rational principle knowledge about such matters will be
of great benefit.

These remarks about the student, the sort of treatment to be expected,
and the purpose of the inquiry, may be taken as our preface.

Let us resume our inquiry and state, in view of the fact that all knowledge
and every pursuit aims at some good, what it is that we say political science
aims at and what is the highest of all goods achievable by action. Verbally
there is very general agreement; for both the general run of men and
people of superior refinement say that it is happiness, and identify living
well and doing well with being happy; but with regard to what happiness is
they differ, and the many do not give the same account as the wise. For the
former think it is some plain and obvious thing, like pleasure, wealth or
honour; they differ, however, from one another – and often even the same
man identifies it with different things, with health when he is ill, with wealth

when he is poor; but, conscious of their ignorance, they admire those who proclaim some great thing that is above their comprehension. Now some thought that apart from these many goods there is another which is good in itself and causes the goodness of all these as well. To examine all the opinions that have been held were perhaps somewhat fruitless; enough to examine those that are most prevalent or that seem to be arguable.

Let us not fail to notice, however, that there is a difference between 30 arguments from and those to the first principles. For Plato, too, was right in raising this question and asking, as he used to do, 'are we on the way from or to the first principles?' There is a difference, as there is in a race-course between the course from the judges to the turning-point and the way back. For, while we must begin with what is known, things are objects 1095b of knowledge in two senses – some to us, some without qualification. Presumably, then, *we* must begin with things known to *us*. Hence any one who is to listen intelligently to lectures about what is noble and just and, 5 generally, about the subjects of political science must have been brought up in good habits. For the fact is a starting-point, and if this is sufficiently plain to him, he will not need the reason as well; and the man who has been well brought up has or can easily get starting-points. And as for him who neither has nor can get them, let him hear the words of Hesiod:

> Far best is he who knows all things himself; 10
> Good, he that hearkens when men counsel right;
> But he who neither knows, nor lays to heart
> Another's wisdom, is a useless wight.

5 Let us, however, resume our discussion from the point at which we digressed. To judge from the lives that men lead, most men, and men of the most vulgar type, seem (not without some ground) to identify the good, 15 or happiness, with pleasure; which is the reason why they love the life of enjoyment. For there are, we may say, three prominent types of life – that just mentioned, the political, and thirdly the contemplative life. Now the mass of mankind are evidently quite slavish in their tastes, preferring a life 20 suitable to beasts, but they get some ground for their view from the fact that many of those in high places share the tastes of Sardanapallus. A consideration of the prominent types of life shows that people of superior refinement and of active disposition identify happiness with honour; for this is, roughly speaking, the end of the political life. But it seems too superficial to be what we are looking for, since it is thought to depend on those who bestow honour rather than on him who receives it, but the good we 25 divine to be something proper to a man and not easily taken from him.

Further, men seem to pursue honour in order that they may be assured of their goodness; at least it is by men of practical wisdom that they seek to be honoured, and among those who know them, and on the ground of their

30   virtue; clearly, then, according to them, at any rate, virtue is better. And perhaps one might even suppose this to be, rather than honour, the end of the political life. But even this appears somewhat incomplete; for possession of virtue seems actually compatible with being asleep, or with lifelong

1096a   inactivity, and, further, with the greatest sufferings and misfortunes; but a man who was living so no one would call happy, unless he were maintaining a thesis at all costs. But enough of this; for the subject has been sufficiently treated even in the current discussions. Third comes the contemplative life, which we shall consider later.

5   The life of money-making is one undertaken under compulsion, and wealth is evidently not the good we are seeking; for it is merely useful and for the sake of something else. And so one might rather take the aforenamed objects to be ends; for they are loved for themselves. But it is evident that not even these are ends; yet many arguments have been thrown away in

10   support of them. Let us leave this subject, then.

We had perhaps better consider the universal good and discuss thoroughly   6
what is meant by it, although such an inquiry is made an uphill one by the fact that the Forms have been introduced by friends of our own.[1] Yet it would perhaps be thought to be better, indeed to be our duty, for the sake

15   of maintaining the truth even to destroy what touches us closely, especially as we are philosophers or lovers of wisdom; for, while both are dear, piety requires us to honour truth above our friends.

The men who introduced this doctrine did not posit Ideas of classes within which they recognized priority and posteriority (which is the reason why they did not maintain the existence of an Idea embracing all numbers); but the term 'good' is used both in the category of substance and in

20   that of quality and in that of relation, and that which is *per se*, i.e. substance, is prior in nature to the relative (for the latter is like an offshoot and accident of being); so that there could not be a common Idea set over all these goods. Further, since 'good' has as many senses as 'being' (for it is

25   predicated both in the category of substance, as of God and of reason, and in quality, i.e. of the virtues, and in quantity, i.e. of that which is moderate, and in relation, i.e. of the useful, and in time, i.e. of the right opportunity, and in place, i.e. of the right locality and the like), clearly it cannot be something universally present in all cases and single; for then it could not have been predicated in all the categories but in one only. Further, since of

30   the things answering to one Idea there is one science, there would have

been one science of all the goods; but as it is there are many sciences even of the things that fall under one category, e.g. of opportunity, for opportunity in war is studied by strategics and in disease by medicine, and the moderate in food is studied by medicine and in exercise by the science of gymnastics. And one might ask the question, what in the world they *mean* by 'a thing itself', if (as is the case) in 'man himself' and in a particular man the account of man is one and the same. For in so far as they are man, they will in no respect differ; and if this is so, neither will 'good itself' and particular goods, in so far as they are good. But again it will not be good any the more for being eternal, since that which lasts long is no whiter than that which perishes in a day. The Pythagoreans seem to give a more plausible account of the good, when they place the one in the column of goods; and it is they that Speusippus seems to have followed.

But let us discuss these matters elsewhere; an objection to what we have said, however, may be discerned in the fact that the Platonists have not been speaking about *all* goods, and that the goods that are pursued and loved for themselves are called good by reference to a single Form, while those which tend to produce or to preserve these somehow or to prevent their contraries are called so by reason of these, and in a different way. Clearly, then, goods must be spoken of in two ways, and some must be good in themselves, the others by reason of these. Let us separate, then, things good in themselves from things useful, and consider whether the former are called good by reference to a single Idea. What sort of goods would one call good in themselves? Is it those that are pursued even when isolated from others, such as intelligence, sight, and certain pleasures and honours? Certainly, if we pursue these also for the sake of something else, yet one would place them among things good in themselves. Or is nothing other than the Idea of good good in itself? In that case the Form will be empty. But if the things we have named are also things good in themselves, the account of the good will have to appear as something identical in them all, as that of whiteness is identical in snow and in white lead. But of honour, wisdom and pleasure, just in respect of their goodness, the accounts are distinct and diverse. The good, therefore, is not something common answering to one Idea.

But what then do we mean by the good? It is surely not like the things that only chance to have the same name. Are goods one, then, by being derived from one good or by all contributing to one good, or are they rather one by analogy? Certainly as sight is in the body, so is reason in the soul, and so on in other cases. But perhaps these subjects had better be dismissed for the present; for perfect precision about them would be more appropriate to another branch of philosophy. And similarly with regard to

35
1096b

5

10

15

20

25

30

the Idea; even if there is some one good which is universally predicable of goods or is capable of separate and independent existence, clearly it could
35   not be achieved or attained by man; but we are now seeking something attainable. Perhaps, however, some one might think it worth while to rec-
1097a   ognize this with a view to the goods that *are* attainable and achievable; for having this as a sort of pattern we shall know better the goods that are good for us, and if we know them shall attain them. This argument has
5   some plausibility, but seems to clash with the procedure of the sciences; for all of these, though they aim at some good and seek to supply the deficiency of it, leave on one side the knowledge of *the* good. Yet that all the exponents of the arts should be ignorant of, and should not even seek, so great an aid is not probable. It is hard, too, to see how a weaver or a
10   carpenter will be benefited in regard to his own craft by knowing this 'good itself', or how the man who has viewed the Idea itself will be a better doctor or general thereby. For a doctor seems not even to study health in this way, but the health of man, or perhaps rather the health of a particular man; it is individuals that he is healing. But enough of these topics.

15   Let us again return to the good we are seeking, and ask what it can be. It   7
seems different in different actions and arts; it is different in medicine, in strategy, and in the other arts likewise. What then is the good of each?
20   Surely that for whose sake everything else is done. In medicine this is health, in strategy victory, in architecture a house, in any other sphere something else, and in every action and pursuit the end; for it is for the sake of this that all men do whatever else they do. Therefore, if there is an end for all that we do, this will be the good achievable by action, and if there are more than one, these will be the goods achievable by action.

So the argument has by a different course reached the same point; but
25   we must try to state this even more clearly. Since there are evidently more than one end, and we choose some of these (e.g. wealth, flutes, and in general instruments) for the sake of something else, clearly not all ends are final ends; but the chief good is evidently something final. Therefore, if there is only one final end, this will be what we are seeking, and if there are
30   more than one, the most final of these will be what we are seeking. Now we call that which is in itself worthy of pursuit more final than that which is worthy of pursuit for the sake of something else, and that which is never desirable for the sake of something else more final than the things that are desirable both in themselves and for the sake of that other thing, and therefore we call final without qualification that which is always desirable in itself and never for the sake of something else.

Now such a thing happiness, above all else, is held to be; for this we

choose always for itself and never for the sake of something else, but hon-   **1097b**
our, pleasure, reason and every virtue we choose indeed for themselves (for
if nothing resulted from them we should still choose each of them), but we
choose them also for the sake of happiness, judging that through them we   5
shall be happy. Happiness, on the other hand, no one chooses for the sake
of these, nor, in general, for anything other than itself.

From the point of view of self-sufficiency the same result seems to follow; for the final good is thought to be self-sufficient. Now by self-sufficient we do not mean that which is sufficient for a man by himself, for one
who lives a solitary life, but also for parents, children, wife, and in general   10
for his friends and fellow citizens, since man is born for citizenship. But
some limit must be set to this; for if we extend our requirement to ancestors and descendants and friends' friends we are in for an infinite series. Let
us examine this question, however, on another occasion; the self-sufficient
we now define as that which when isolated makes life desirable and lacking   15
in nothing; and such we think happiness to be; and further we think it most
desirable of all things, without being counted as one good thing among
others – if it were so counted it would clearly be made more desirable by
the addition of even the least of goods; for that which is added becomes an
excess of goods, and of goods the greater is always more desirable. Happi-   20
ness, then, is something final and self-sufficient, and is the end of action.

Presumably, however, to say that happiness is the chief good seems a
platitude, and a clearer account of what it is is still desired. This might
perhaps be given, if we could first ascertain the function of man. For just as   25
for a flute-player, a sculptor, or any artist, and, in general, for all things that
have a function or activity, the good and the 'well' is thought to reside in
the function, so would it seem to be for man, if he has a function. Have the
carpenter, then, and the tanner certain functions or activities, and has man   30
none? Is he born without a function? Or as eye, hand, foot, and in general
each of the parts evidently has a function, may one lay it down that man
similarly has a function apart from all these? What then can this be? Life
seems to be common even to plants, but we are seeking what is peculiar to
man. Let us exclude, therefore, the life of nutrition and growth. Next there   **1098a**
would be a life of perception, but *it* also seems to be common even to the
horse, the ox and every animal. There remains, then, an active life of the
element that has a rational principle; of this, one part has such a principle in
the sense of being obedient to one, the other in the sense of possessing one
and exercising thought. And, as 'life of the rational element' also has two   5
meanings, we must state that life in the sense of activity is what we mean;
for this seems to be the more proper sense of the term. Now if the function
of man is an activity of soul which follows or implies a rational principle,

and if we say 'a so-and-so' and 'a good so-and-so' have a function which is the same in kind, e.g. a lyre-player and a good lyre-player, and so without 10   qualification in all cases, eminence in respect of goodness being added to the name of the function (for the function of a lyre-player is to play the lyre, and that of a good lyre-player is to do so well): if this is the case, [and we state the function of man to be a certain kind of life, and this to be an activity or actions of the soul implying a rational principle, and the function 15   of a good man to be the good and noble performance of these, and if any action is well performed when it is performed in accordance with the appropriate excellence: if this is the case,] human good turns out to be activity of the soul in accordance with virtue, and if there are more than one virtue, in accordance with the best and most complete.

But we must add 'in a complete life'. For one swallow does not make a summer, nor does one day; and so too one day, or a short time, does not make a man blessed and happy.

20   Let this serve as an outline of the good; for we must presumably first sketch it roughly, and then later fill in the details. But it would seem that any one is capable of carrying on and articulating what has once been well outlined, and that time is a good discoverer or partner in such a work; to 25   which facts the advances of the arts are due; for any one can add what is lacking. And we must also remember what has been said before, and not look for precision in all things alike, but in each class of things such precision as accords with the subject-matter, and so much as is appropriate to 30   the inquiry. For a carpenter and a geometer investigate the right angle in different ways; the former does so in so far as the right angle is useful for his work, while the latter inquires what it is or what sort of thing it is; for he is a spectator of the truth. We must act in the same way, then, in all other matters as well, that our main task may not be subordinated to minor questions. Nor must we demand the cause in all matters alike; it is enough in 1098b   some cases that the *fact* be well established, as in the case of the first principles; the fact is a primary thing or first principle. Now of first principles we see some by induction, some by perception, some by a certain habituation, and others too in other ways. But each set of principles we must try 5   to investigate in the natural way, and we must take pains to determine them correctly, since they have a great influence on what follows. For the beginning is thought to be more than half of the whole, and many of the questions we ask are cleared up by it.

We must consider it, however, in the light not only of our conclusion and   8 10   our premises, but also of what is commonly said about it; for with a true view all the data harmonize, but with a false one the facts soon clash. Now

goods have been divided into three classes, and some are described as external, others as relating to soul or to body; we call those that relate to soul most properly and truly goods, and psychical actions and activities we class   15
as relating to soul. Therefore our account must be sound, at least according to this view, which is an old one and agreed on by philosophers. It is correct also in that we identify the end with certain actions and activities; for thus it falls among goods of the soul and not among external goods. Another belief which harmonizes with our account is that the happy man   20
lives well and does well; for we have practically defined happiness as a sort of good life and good action. The characteristics that are looked for in happiness seem also, all of them, to belong to what we have defined happiness as being. For some identify happiness with virtue, some with practical wisdom, others with a kind of philosophic wisdom, others with these, or   25
one of these, accompanied by pleasure or not without pleasure; while others include also external prosperity. Now some of these views have been held by many men and men of old, others by a few eminent persons; and it is not probable that either of these should be entirely mistaken, but rather that they should be right in at least some one respect or even in most respects.

With those who identify happiness with virtue or some one virtue our   30
account is in harmony; for to virtue belongs virtuous activity. But it makes, perhaps, no small difference whether we place the chief good in possession or in use, in state of mind or in activity. For the state of mind may exist without producing any good result, as in a man who is asleep or in some   1099a
other way quite inactive, but the activity cannot; for one who has the activity will of necessity be acting, and acting well. And as in the Olympic Games it is not the most beautiful and the strongest that are crowned but those who compete (for it is some of these that are victorious), so those who act   5
win, and rightly win, the noble and good things in life.

Their life is also in itself pleasant. For pleasure is a state of *soul*, and to each man that which he is said to be a lover of is pleasant; e.g. not only is a horse pleasant to the lover of horses, and a spectacle to the lover of sights,   10
but also in the same way just acts are pleasant to the lover of justice and in general virtuous acts to the lover of virtue. Now for most men their pleasures are in conflict with one another because these are not by nature pleasant, but the lovers of what is noble find pleasant the things that are by nature pleasant; and virtuous actions are such, so that these are pleasant for such men as well as in their own nature. Their life, therefore, has no further   15
need of pleasure as a sort of adventitious charm, but has its pleasure in itself. For, besides what we have said, the man who does not rejoice in noble actions is not even good; since no one would call a man just who did

not enjoy acting justly, nor any man liberal who did not enjoy liberal
20   actions; and similarly in all other cases. If this is so, virtuous actions must
be in themselves pleasant. But they are also *good* and *noble*, and have each
of these attributes in the highest degree, since the good man judges well
about these attributes; his judgement is such as we have described. Happi-
25   ness then is the best, noblest and most pleasant thing in the world, and
these attributes are not severed as in the inscription at Delos –

> Most noble is that which is justest, and best is health;
> But pleasantest is it to win what we love.

For all these properties belong to the best activities; and these, or one – the
30   best – of these, we identify with happiness.
   Yet evidently, as we said, it needs the external goods as well; for it is
1099b   impossible, or not easy, to do noble acts without the proper equipment. In
many actions we use friends and riches and political power as instruments;
and there are some things the lack of which takes the lustre from happiness, as good birth, goodly children, beauty; for the man who is very ugly
5   in appearance or ill-born or solitary and childless is not very likely to be
happy, and perhaps a man would be still less likely if he had thoroughly bad
children or friends or had lost good children or friends by death. As we
said, then, happiness seems to need this sort of prosperity in addition; for
which reason some identify happiness with good fortune, though others
identify it with virtue.

For this reason also the question is asked, whether happiness is to be   9
10   acquired by learning or by habituation or some other sort of training, or
comes in virtue of some divine providence or again by chance. Now if there
is *any* gift of the gods to men, it is reasonable that happiness should be
god-given, and most surely god-given of all human things inasmuch as it is
the best. But this question would perhaps be more appropriate to another
15   inquiry; happiness seems, however, even if it is not god-sent but comes as
a result of virtue and some process of learning or training, to be among the
most godlike things; for that which is the prize and end of virtue seems to
be the best thing in the world, and something godlike and blessed.
   It will also on this view be very generally shared; for all who are not
20   maimed as regards their potentiality for virtue may win it by a certain kind
of study and care. But if it is better to be happy thus than by chance, it is
reasonable that the facts should be so, since everything that depends on
the action of nature is by nature as good as it can be, and similarly everything that depends on art or any rational cause, and especially if it depends

on the best of all causes. To entrust to chance what is greatest and most noble would be a very defective arrangement.

The answer to the question we are asking is plain also from the definition of happiness; for it has been said to be a virtuous activity of soul, of a certain kind. Of the remaining goods, some must necessarily pre-exist as conditions of happiness, and others are naturally co-operative and useful as instruments. And this will be found to agree with what we said at the outset; for we stated the end of political science to be the best end, and political science spends most of its pains on making the citizens to be of a certain character, viz. good and capable of noble acts.

It is natural, then, that we call neither ox nor horse nor any other of the animals happy; for none of them is capable of sharing in such activity.[2] For this reason also a boy is not happy; for he is not yet capable of such acts, owing to his age; and boys who are called happy are being congratulated by reason of the hopes we have for them. For there is required, as we said, not only complete virtue but also a complete life, since many changes occur in life, and all manner of chances, and the most prosperous may fall into great misfortunes in old age, as is told of Priam in the Trojan Cycle; and one who has experienced such chances and has ended wretchedly no one calls happy.

10 Must no one at all, then, be called happy while he lives; must we, as Solon says, see the end? Even if we are to lay down this doctrine, is it also the case that a man *is* happy when he is *dead*? Or is not this quite absurd, especially for us who say that happiness is an activity? But if we do not call the dead man happy, and if Solon does not mean this, but that one can then safely *call* a man blessed as being at last beyond evils and misfortunes, this also affords matter for discussion; for both evil and good are thought to exist for a dead man, as much as for one who is alive but not aware of them; e.g. honours and dishonours and the good or bad fortunes of children and in general of descendants. And this also presents a problem; for though a man has lived happily up to old age and has had a death worthy of his life, many reverses may befall his descendants – some of them may be good and attain the life they deserve, while with others the opposite may be the case; and clearly too the degrees of relationship between them and their ancestors may vary indefinitely. It would be odd, then, if the dead man were to share in these changes and become at one time happy, at another wretched; while it would also be odd if the fortunes of the descendants did not for *some* time have *some* effect on the happiness of their ancestors.

But we must return to our first difficulty; for perhaps by a consideration of it our present problem might be solved. Now if we must see the end and

only then call a man happy, not as being happy but as having been
so before, surely this is a paradox, that when he is happy the attribute
that belongs to him is not to be truly predicated of him because we do not
wish to call living men happy, on account of the changes that may
befall them, and because we have assumed happiness to be something
permanent and by no means easily changed, while a single man may
suffer many turns of fortune's wheel. For clearly if we were to follow his
fortunes, we should often call the same man happy and again wretched,
making the happy man out to be a 'chameleon and insecurely based'. Or is
this following his fortunes quite wrong? Success or failure in life does not
depend on these, but human life, as we said, needs these as well, while
virtuous activities or their opposites are what determine happiness or the
reverse.

The question we have now discussed confirms our definition. For no
function of man has so much permanence as virtuous activities (these are
thought to be more durable even than knowledge of the sciences), and of
these themselves the most valuable are more durable because those who
are happy spend their life most readily and most continuously in these; for
this seems to be the reason why we do not forget them. The attribute in
question, then, will belong to the happy man, and he will be happy throughout his life; for always, or by preference to everything else, he will be engaged in virtuous action and contemplation, and he will bear the chances
of life most nobly and altogether decorously, if he is 'truly good' and 'four-
square beyond reproach'.

Now many events happen by chance, and events differing in importance;
small pieces of good fortune or of its opposite clearly do not weight down
the scales of life one way or the other, but a multitude of great events if
they turn out well will make life happier (for not only are they themselves
such as to add beauty to life, but the way a man deals with them may be
noble and good), while if they turn out ill they crush and maim happiness;
for they both bring pain with them and hinder many activities. Yet even in
these nobility shines through, when a man bears with resignation many
great misfortunes, not through insensibility to pain but through nobility
and greatness of soul.

If activities are, as we said, what determine the character of life, no happy
man can become miserable; for he will never do the acts that are hateful
and mean. For the man who is truly good and wise, we think, bears all the
chances of life becomingly and always makes the best of circumstances, as a
good general makes the best military use of the army at his command and
a good shoemaker makes the best shoes out of the hides that are given him;
and so with all other craftsmen. And if this is the case, the happy man can

never become miserable – though he will not reach *blessedness*, if he meet with fortunes like those of Priam.

Nor, again, is he many-coloured and changeable; for neither will he be 10 moved from his happy state easily or by any ordinary misadventures, but only by many great ones, nor, if he has had many great misadventures, will he recover his happiness in a short time, but if at all, only in a long and complete one in which he has attained many splendid successes.

Why then should we not say that he is happy who is active in accordance 15 with complete virtue and is sufficiently equipped with external goods, not for some chance period but throughout a complete life? Or must we add 'and who is destined to live thus and die as befits his life'? Certainly the future is obscure to us, while happiness, we claim, is an end and something in every way final. If so, we shall call happy those among living men in whom these conditions are, and are to be, fulfilled – but happy *men*. So 20 much for these questions.

11   That the fortunes of descendants and of all a man's friends should not affect his happiness at all seems a very unfriendly doctrine, and one op- posed to the opinions men hold; but since the events that happen are nu- merous and admit of all sorts of difference, and some come more near to 25 us and others less so, it seems a long – nay, an infinite – task to discuss each in detail; a general outline will perhaps suffice. If, then, as some of a man's own misadventures have a certain weight and influence on life while others are, as it were, lighter, so too there are differences among the misadventures 30 of our friends taken as a whole, and it makes a difference whether the various sufferings befall the living or the dead (much more even than whether lawless and terrible deeds are presupposed in a tragedy or done on the stage), this difference also must be taken into account; or rather, perhaps, the fact that doubt is felt whether the dead share in any good or evil. For it 35 seems, from these considerations, that even if anything whether good or 1101b evil penetrates to them, it must be something weak and negligible, either in itself or for them, or if not, at least it must be such in degree and kind as not to make happy those who are not happy nor to take away their blessed- ness from those who are. The good or bad fortunes of friends, then, seem 5 to have some effects on the dead, but effects of such a kind and degree as neither to make the happy unhappy nor to produce any other change of the kind.

12   These questions having been definitely answered, let us consider whether 10 happiness is among the things that are praised or rather among the things that are prized; for clearly it is not to be placed among *potentialities*. Every-

thing that is praised seems to be praised because it is of a certain kind and is related somehow to something else; for we praise the just or brave man
15   and in general both the good man and virtue itself because of the actions and functions involved, and we praise the strong man, the good runner, and so on, because he is of a certain kind and is related in a certain way to something good and important. This is clear also from the praises of the gods; for it seems absurd that the gods should be referred to our standard,
20   but this *is* done because praise involves a reference, as we said, to something else. But if praise is for things such as we have described, clearly what applies to the best things is not praise, but something greater and better, as is indeed obvious; for what we do to the gods and the most godlike of men
25   is to call them blessed and happy. And so too with good *things*; no one praises happiness as he does justice, but rather calls it blessed, as being something more divine and better.

Eudoxus also seems to have been right in his method of advocating the supremacy of pleasure; he thought that the fact that, though a good, it is not praised indicated it to be better than the things that are praised, and
30   that this is what God and the good are; for by reference to these all other things are judged. *Praise* is appropriate to virtue, for as a result of virtue men tend to do noble deeds; but *encomia* [or panegyrics – Ed.] are bestowed on acts, whether of the body or of the soul. But perhaps nicety in
35   these matters is more proper to those who have made a study of encomia;
1102a   to us it is clear from what has been said that happiness is among the things that are prized and perfect. It seems to be so also from the fact that it is a first principle; for it is for the sake of this that we all do everything else, and the first principle and cause of goods is, we claim, something prized and divine.

5   Since happiness is an activity of soul in accordance with perfect virtue, we   13
must consider the nature of virtue; for perhaps we shall thus see better the nature of happiness. The true student of politics, too, is thought to have studied virtue above all things; for he wishes to make his fellow citizens
10   good and obedient to the laws. As an example of this we have the lawgivers of the Cretans and the Spartans, and any others of the kind that there may have been. And if this inquiry belongs to political science, clearly the pursuit of it will be in accordance with our original plan. But, clearly the virtue
15   we must study is human virtue; for the good we were seeking was human good and the happiness human happiness. By human virtue we mean not that of the body but that of the soul; and happiness also we call an activity of soul. But if this is so, clearly the student of politics must know somehow the facts about soul, as the man who is to heal the eyes must know about

the whole body also; and all the more since politics is more prized and better than medicine; but even among doctors the best educated spend much labour on acquiring knowledge of the body. The student of politics, then, must study the soul, and must study it with these objects in view, and do so just to the extent which is sufficient for the questions we are discussing; for further precision is perhaps something more laborious than our purposes require.

Some things are said about it, adequately enough, even in the discussions outside our school, and we must use these; e.g. that one element in the soul is irrational and one has a rational principle. Whether these are separated as the parts of the body or of anything divisible are, or are distinct by definition but by nature inseparable, like convex and concave in the circumference of a circle, does not affect the present question.

Of the irrational element one division seems to be widely distributed, and vegetative in its nature, I mean that which causes nutrition and growth; for it is this kind of power of the soul that one must assign to all nurslings and to embryos, and this same power to full-grown creatures; this is more reasonable than to assign some different power to them. Now the excellence of this seems to be common to all species and not specifically human; for this part or faculty seems to function most in sleep, while goodness and badness are least manifest in sleep (whence comes the saying that the happy are no better off than the wretched for half their lives; and this happens naturally enough, since sleep is an inactivity of the soul in that respect in which it is called good or bad), unless perhaps to a small extent some of the movements actually penetrate to the soul, and in this respect the dreams of good men are better than those of ordinary people. Enough of this subject, however; let us leave the nutritive faculty alone, since it has by its nature no share in human excellence.

There seems to be also another irrational element in the soul – one which in a sense, however, shares in a rational principle. For we praise the rational principle of the continent man and of the incontinent, and the part of their soul that has such a principle, since it urges them aright and towards the best objects; but there is naturally found in them also another element beside the rational principle, which fights against and resists that principle. For exactly as paralysed limbs when we intend to move them to the right turn on the contrary to the left, so is it with the soul; the impulses of incontinent people move in contrary directions. But while in the body we see that which moves astray, in the soul we do not. No doubt, however, we must none the less suppose that in the soul too there is something beside the rational principle, resisting and opposing it. In what sense it is distinct from the other elements does not concern us. Now even this seems to have

20

25

30

1102b

5

10

15

20

25

a share in a rational principle, as we said; at any rate in the continent man it obeys the rational principle – and presumably in the temperate and brave man it is still more obedient; for in him it speaks, on all matters, with the same voice as the rational principle.

Therefore the irrational element also appears to be twofold. For the veg-
30   etative element in no way shares in a rational principle, but the appetitive and in general the desiring element in a sense shares in it, in so far as it listens to and obeys it; this is the sense in which we speak of 'taking account' of one's father or one's friends, not that in which we speak of 'accounting' for a mathematical property. That the irrational element is in some sense persuaded by a rational principle is indicated also by the giving
1103a   of advice and by all reproof and exhortation. And if this element also must be said to have a rational principle, that which has a rational principle (as well as that which has not) will be twofold, one subdivision having it in the strict sense and in itself, and the other having a tendency to obey as one does one's father.

Virtue too is distinguished into kinds in accordance with this difference;
5   for we say that some of the virtues are intellectual and others moral, philosophic wisdom and understanding and practical wisdom being intellectual, liberality and temperance moral. For in speaking about a man's character we do not say that he is wise or has understanding but that he is good-tempered or temperate; yet we praise the wise man also with respect to his
10   state of mind [or disposition – Ed.]; and of states of mind we call those which merit praise virtues.

Notes

1 In this difficult chapter, Aristotle is preparing to distinguish his own view that there is a single end, *eudaimonia*, at which all our activities finally aim from the Platonists' – our 'friends' – idea that there is a single Form of the Good by reference to which justice, happiness and so on are deemed good. Readers not acquainted with the debate between Plato and Aristotle over the Forms are advised to proceed to chapter 7.
2 This denial that children can enjoy *eudaimonia* is, of course, an excellent reason for questioning the translation of that term by 'happiness'.

Epicurus, 'Letter to Menoeceus' and 'Leading Doctrines'

From The Philosophy of Epicurus, trans. G. K. Strodach. Evanston, Ill.: Northwestern University Press, n.d., pp. 178–85, 196–203.

It comes as a surprise to modern readers to learn that, during the centuries of the 'Hellenistic Age' following Aristotle's death, it was not he and Plato who had the greatest influence upon the thought and practice of Greeks and Romans, but some slightly later schools of philosophy, notably the Stoics and Epicureans. The man who gave his name to the latter was born in Samos in 341 and died in 271 BCE near Athens, where he had founded his famous 'Garden', a kind of *ashram* of which he was the *guru*. Today's connotations of 'epicurean' and 'epicure' might suggest that the Garden was a place of sybaritic indulgence. In fact it was a community of people living, if not Spartan, then simple and austere lives. For Epicurus himself, 'barley bread and water' could 'yield the peak of pleasure', and 'a little pot of cheese' was a true luxury.

This indicates that care is needed with the usual labelling of Epicurus as a 'hedonist', for while he indeed declares that 'pleasure is the goal of living', he has something different in mind from the 'epicure'. Still, the claim that pleasure is the goal of life, and that the virtues are simply means – albeit necessary ones – to that goal, is sufficient to put Epicurus importantly at odds with Plato, Aristotle and his rivals, the Stoics. For Plato, we saw in chapter 1, pleasure cannot be identified with happiness and the good, and for all these other thinkers virtue is not a means to the good, but constitutive of it. (Aristotle's exercise of the virtues is *part of eudaimonia*.) In contemporary parlance, Epicurus was a 'consequentialist': something is morally good because of something – pleasure or whatever – it results in. Unjust acts, for example, are not bad in themselves, but because of the unpleasant fear of punishment they bring in their wake (*Leading Doctrines* 34).

Epicurus' ethics emerges from his view of nature. Human beings are purely material creatures (souls being composed of special physical 'atoms') and like everything else are 'naturally' in a state of equilibrium. This means, in the words of Epicurus' most famous disciple, Lucretius, that 'nature is clamouring for . . . a body free from pain, a mind released from worry and fear'.[1] And this gives the clue to the Master's understanding of pleasure. Even in the case of activities which yield positive or 'kinetic' pleasures, like drinking fine wine, the pleasure which counts is the 'static' one of being free from desire and its discomforts.[2] More generally, the pleasure which is the goal of life is 'freedom from pain and . . . fear' (*ataraxia*) (*Letter*, p. 51 below). Wine, women and song do very badly by this test: for not only do they cause a man subsequent remorse and suffering, they belong to a way of life ill-designed to achieve peace of mind.

Epicurus, then, is an early representative of that tradition – familiar among Indian thinkers, but popular too among French Enlightenment writers – which condemns the indulgent life, not out of puritanism, but for reasons of self-interest. He is no utilitarian, however: a person is equipped by nature only to aim at his or her own pleasure, and there can be no compelling reason to think that this requires promotion of the general happiness. Indeed, Epicurus – here at odds once more with Aristotle – is scornful of political, public life, which he describes as a 'prison house' we 'must get out of' (*Vatican Sayings* 58). Friendship, though, is a different matter, for it is only through the succour which close friends afford one another that peace of mind and freedom from anxiety are achievable.

Unfortunately, thinks Epicurus, few people appreciate that these achievements constitute the goal of pleasure. And a main reason for this failure, he famously argues, is due to the fear of death, something which prompts everything from a 'make hay while the sun shines' abandon to excessive asceticism performed in order to escape eternal punishment. Whether or not his argument for saying that death should 'mean nothing to us' (*Letter*, p. 49 below) is 'about as absurd as any I have seen',[3] readers must judge. But they should perhaps ask themselves whether such a reaction does not depend on commitments and attitudes which are indeed central to a certain way of life – our usual way – but which, if Epicurus is right, we should surely try to put aside or overcome.

▶ ▶ ▶ **Letter to Menoeceus**

No one should postpone the study of philosophy when he is young, nor should he weary of it when he becomes mature, because the search for

---

[1] *On the Nature of the Universe*, trans. R. Latham, Harmondsworth: Penguin, 1986, p. 60.
[2] See A. A. Long's excellent *Hellenistic Philosophy: Stoics, Epicureans, Sceptics*, London: Duckworth, 1986, pp. 64ff.
[3] Steven Luper, *Invulnerability: On Securing Happiness*, Chicago: Open Court, 1996, p. 109.

mental health is never untimely or out of season. To say that the time to study philosophy has not yet arrived or that it is past is like saying that the time for happiness is not yet at hand or is no longer present. Thus both the young and the mature should pursue philosophy, the latter in order to be rejuvenated as they age by the blessings that accrue from pleasurable past experience, and the youthful in order to become mature immediately through having no fear of the future. Hence we should make a practice of the things that make for happiness, for assuredly when we have this we have everything, and we do everything we can to get it when we don't have it.

The Preconditions of Happiness

(I) You should do and practise all the things I constantly recommended to you, with the knowledge that they are the fundamentals of the good life.

   (a) First of all, you should think of deity as imperishable and blessed being (as delineated in the universal conception of it common to all men), and you should not attribute to it anything foreign to its immortality or inconsistent with its blessedness. On the contrary, you should hold every doctrine that is capable of safeguarding its blessedness in common with its imperishability. The gods do indeed exist, since our knowledge of them is a matter of clear and distinct perception; but they are not like what the masses suppose them to be, because most people do not maintain the pure conception of the gods. The irreligious man is not the person who destroys the gods of the masses but the person who imposes the ideas of the masses on the gods. The opinions held by most people about the gods are not true conceptions of them but fallacious notions, according to which awful penalties are meted out to the evil and the greatest of blessings to the good. The masses, by assimilating the gods in every respect to their own moral qualities, accept deities similar to themselves and regard anything not of this sort as alien.

   (b) Second, you should accustom yourself to believing that death means nothing to us, since every good and every evil lies in sensation; but death is the privation of sensation. Hence a correct comprehension of the fact that death means nothing to us makes the mortal aspect of life pleasurable, not by conferring on us a boundless period of time but by removing the yearning for deathlessness. There is nothing fearful in living for the person who has really laid hold of the fact that there is nothing fearful in not living. So it is silly for a person to say that he dreads death – not because it will be painful when it arrives but because it pains him now as a future certainty;

for that which makes no trouble for us when it arrives is a meaningless pain when we await it. This, the most horrifying of evils, means nothing to us, then, because so long as we are existent death is not present and whenever it is present we are nonexistent. Thus it is of no concern either to the living or to those who have completed their lives. For the former it is nonexistent, and the latter are themselves nonexistent.

Most people, however, recoil from death as though it were the greatest of evils; at other times they welcome it as the end-all of life's ills. The sophisticated person, on the other hand, neither begs off from living nor dreads not living. Life is not a stumbling block to him, nor does he regard not being alive as any sort of evil. As in the case of food he prefers the most savoury dish to merely the larger portion, so in the case of time he garners to himself the most agreeable moments rather than the longest span.

Anyone who urges the youth to lead a good life but counsels the older man to end his life in good style is silly, not merely because of the welcome character of life but because of the fact that living well and dying well are one and the same discipline. Much worse off, however, is the person who says it were well not to have been born 'but once born to pass Hades' portals as swiftly as may be'. Now if he says such a thing from inner persuasion why does he not withdraw from life? Everything is in readiness for him once he has firmly resolved on this course. But if he speaks facetiously he is a trifler standing in the midst of men who do not welcome him.

It should be borne in mind, then, that the time to come is neither ours nor altogether not ours. In this way we shall neither expect the future outright as something destined to be nor despair of it as something absolutely not destined to be.

The Good Life

(II)   It should be recognized that within the category of desire certain desires are natural, certain others unnecessary and trivial; that in the case of the natural desires certain ones are necessary, certain others merely natural; and that in the case of necessary desires certain ones are necessary for happiness, others to promote freedom from bodily discomfort, others for the maintenance of life itself. A steady view of these matters shows us how to refer all moral choice and aversion to bodily health and imperturbability of mind, these being the twin goals of happy living. It is on this account that we do everything we do – to achieve freedom from pain and freedom from fear. When once we come by this, the tumult in the soul is calmed and the human being does not have to go about looking for something that is lacking or to search for something additional with which to supplement the welfare of soul and body. Accordingly we have need of pleasure only when we feel pain because of the absence of pleasure, but whenever we do not feel pain we no longer stand in need of pleasure. And so we speak of pleasure as the starting point and the goal of the happy life because we realize that it is our primary native good, because every act of choice and aversion originates with it, and because we come back to it when we judge every good by using the pleasure feeling as our criterion.

Because of the very fact that pleasure is our primary and congenital good we do not select every pleasure; there are times when we forgo certain pleasures, particularly when they are followed by too much unpleasantness. Furthermore, we regard certain states of pain as preferable to pleasures, particularly when greater satisfaction results from our having submitted to discomforts for a long period of time. Thus every pleasure is a good by reason of its having a nature akin to our own, but not every pleasure is desirable. In like manner every state of pain is an evil, but not all pains are uniformly to be rejected. At any rate, it is our duty to judge all such cases by measuring pleasures against pains, with a view to their respective assets and liabilities, inasmuch as we do experience the good as being bad at times and, contrariwise, the bad as being good.

In addition, we consider limitation of the appetites a major good, and we recommend this practice not for the purpose of enjoying just a few things and no more but rather for the purpose of enjoying those few in case we do not have much. We are firmly convinced that those who need expensive fare least are the ones who relish it most keenly and that a natural way of life is easily procured, while trivialities are hard to come by. Plain foods afford pleasure equivalent to that of a sumptuous diet, provided that the pains of penury are wholly eliminated. Barley bread and water yield the peak of pleasure whenever a person who needs them sets them in front of himself. Hence becoming habituated to a simple rather than a lavish way of life provides us with the full complement of health; it makes a person ready for the necessary business of life; it puts us in a position of advantage when we happen upon sumptuous fare at intervals and prepares us to be fearless in facing fortune.

Thus when I say that pleasure is the goal of living I do not mean the pleasures of libertines or the pleasures inherent in positive enjoyment, as is supposed by certain persons who are ignorant of our doctrine or who are not in agreement with it or who interpret it perversely. I mean, on the contrary, the pleasure that consists in freedom from bodily pain and mental agitation. The pleasant life is not the product of one drinking party after another or of sexual intercourse with women and boys or of the sea food and other delicacies afforded by a luxurious table. On the contrary, it is the result of sober thinking – namely, investigation of the reasons for every act of choice and aversion and elimination of those false ideas about the gods and death which are the chief source of mental disturbances.

The starting point of this whole scheme and the most important of its values is good judgement, which consequently is more highly esteemed even than philosophy.[1] All the other virtues stem from sound judgement, which shows us that it is impossible to live the pleasant Epicurean life without also living sensibly, nobly and justly and, vice versa, that it is impossible to live sensibly, nobly and justly without living pleasantly. The traditional virtues grow up together with the pleasant life; they are indivisible. Can you think of anyone more moral than the person who has devout beliefs about the gods, who is consistently without fears about death, and who has pondered man's natural end? Or who realizes that the goal of the good life is easily gained and achieved and that the term of evil is brief, both in extent of time and duration of pain? Or the man who laughs at the 'decrees of Fate', a deity whom some people have set up as sovereign of all? * * * * [A lacuna in the MSS here – Ed.]

The good Epicurean believes that certain events occur deterministically, that others are chance events, and that still others are in our own hands. He sees also that necessity cannot be held morally responsible and that chance is an unpredictable thing, but that what is in our own hands, since it has no master, is naturally associated with blameworthiness and the opposite. (Actually it would be better to subscribe to the popular mythology than to become a slave by accepting the determinism of the natural philosophers, because popular religion underwrites the hope of supplicating the gods by offerings but determinism contains an element of necessity, which is inexorable.) As for chance, the Epicurean does not assume that it is a deity (as in popular belief)[2] because a god does nothing irregular; nor does he regard it as an unpredictable cause of all events. It is his belief that good and evil are not the chance contributions of a deity, donated to mankind for the happy life, but rather that the initial circumstances for great good and evil are sometimes provided by chance. He thinks it preferable to have bad luck rationally than good luck irrationally. In other words, in human action it is better for a rational choice to be unsuccessful than for an irrational choice to succeed through the agency of chance.

Think about these and related matters day and night, by yourself and in company with someone like yourself. If you do, you will never experience anxiety, waking or sleeping, but you will live like a god among men. For a human being who lives in the midst of immortal blessings is in no way like mortal man!

Leading Doctrines

1–5: Five Fundamental Teachings Bearing on the Good Life

(1)   The blessed and indestructible being of the divine has no concerns of its own, nor does it make trouble for others. It is not affected by feelings of anger or benevolence, because these are found where there is lack of strength.

(2)   Death means nothing to us, because that which has been broken down into atoms has no sensation and that which has no sensation is no concern of ours.

(3)   The quantitative limit of pleasure is the elimination of all feelings of pain. Wherever the pleasurable state exists, there is neither bodily pain nor mental pain nor both together, so long as the state continues.

(4)   Bodily pain does not last continuously. The peak is present for a very brief period, and pains that barely exceed the state of bodily pleasure do not continue for many days. On the other hand, protracted illnesses show a balance of bodily pleasure over pain.

(5)   It is impossible to live the pleasant life without also living sensibly, nobly and justly, and conversely it is impossible to live sensibly, nobly and justly without living pleasantly. A person who does not have a pleasant life is not living sensibly, nobly and justly, and conversely the person who does not have these virtues cannot live pleasantly.

6–7: Personal Security and the Good Life

(6)   Any means by which it is possible to procure freedom from fearing other men is a natural good.

(7)   Some men have desired to gain reputation and to be well regarded, thinking in this way to gain protection from other people. If the lives of such men are secure, they have acquired a natural blessing; but if they are not, they do not possess what they originally reached for by natural instinct.

8–9: How to Choose Pleasures

(8)   No pleasure is bad in itself. But the things that make for pleasure in certain cases entail disturbances many times greater than the pleasures themselves.

(9)   If all pleasures could be compressed in time and intensity, and were characteristic of the whole man or his more important aspects, the various pleasures would not differ from each other.

10–13: The Good Life is Dependent on Science*

(10)   If the things that produce the debauchee's pleasures dissolved the mind's fears regarding the heavenly bodies, death and pain and also told us how to limit our desires, we would never have any reason to find fault with such people, because they would be glutting themselves with every sort of pleasure and never suffer physical or mental pain, which is the real evil.

(11)   We would have no need for natural science unless we were worried by apprehensiveness regarding the heavenly bodies, by anxiety about the meaning of death, and also by our failure to understand the limitations of pain and desire.

(12)   It is impossible to get rid of our anxieties about essentials if we do not understand the nature of the universe and are apprehensive about some of the theological accounts. Hence it is impossible to enjoy our pleasures unadulterated without natural science.

(13)   There is no advantage in gaining security with regard to other people if phenomena occurring above and beneath the earth – in a word, everything in the infinite universe – are objects of anxiety.

14: Withdrawal into Obscurity is the Best Form of Security

(14)   The simplest means of procuring protection from other men (which is gained to a certain extent by deterrent force) is the security of quiet solitude and withdrawal from the mass of people.

15: Wealth, Natural and Unnatural

(15)   Nature's wealth is restricted and easily won, while that of empty convention runs on to infinity.

* I.e. knowledge.

16: Luck Versus Reason in the Good Life

(16)   Bad luck strikes the sophisticated man in a few cases, but reason has directed the big, essential things, and for the duration of life it is and will be the guide.

17: Justice and Mental Health

(17)   The just man is the least disturbed by passion, the unjust man the most highly disturbed.

18–21: The Limits of True Pleasure

(18)   Bodily pleasure is not enlarged once the pains brought on by need have been done away with; it is only diversified. And the limit of mental pleasure is established by rational reflection on pleasures themselves and those kindred emotions that once instilled extreme fear in human minds.

(19)   Infinite time contains no greater pleasure than does finite time, if one determines the limits of pleasure rationally.

(20)   The body takes the limits of pleasure to be infinite, and infinite time would provide such pleasure. But the mind has provided us with the complete life by a rational examination of the body's goal and limitations and by dispelling our fears about a life after death; and so we no longer need unlimited time. On the other hand, it does not avoid pleasure, nor, when conditions occasion our departure from life, does it come to the end in a manner that would suggest that it had fallen short in any way of the best possible existence.

(21)   One who understands the limits of the good life knows that what eliminates the pains brought on by need and what makes the whole of life perfect is easily obtained, so that there is no need for enterprises that entail the struggle for success.

22–25: Empirical Considerations

(22)   It is necessary to take into account both the actual goal of life and the whole body of clear and distinct percepts to which we refer our judgements. If we fail to do this, everything will be in disorder and confusion.

(23)   If you reject all sensations, you will not have any point of reference by which to judge even the ones you claim are false.

(24)   If you summarily rule out any single sensation and do not make a distinction between the element of belief that is superimposed on a percept that awaits verification and what is actually present in sensation or in the feelings or some percept of the mind itself, you will cast doubt on all other sensations by your unfounded interpretation and consequently abandon all the criteria of truth. On the other hand, in cases of interpreted data, if you accept as true those that need verification as well as those that do not, you will still be in error, since the whole question at issue in every judgement of what is true or not true will be left intact.

(25)   If at any time you fail to refer each of your acts to nature's standard, and turn off instead in some other direction when making a choice to avoid or pursue, your actions will not be consistent with your creed.

26, 29, 30: Classification of Human Desires

(29)   Some desires are (1) natural and necessary, others (2) natural but not necessary, still others (3) neither natural nor necessary but generated by senseless whims.

(26)   All desires that do not lead to physical pain if not satisfied are unnecessary, and involve cravings that are easily resolved when they appear to entail harm or when the object of desire is hard to get.

(30)   If interest is intense in the case of those natural desires that do not lead to physical pain when they are not satisfied, then such desires are generated by idle fancy, and it is not because of their own nature that they are not dissipated but because of the person's own senseless whims.

27–28: Friendship

(27)   Of all the things that wisdom provides for the happiness of the whole man, by far the most important is the acquisition of friendship.

(28)   It is the same judgement that has made us feel confident that nothing fearful is of long duration or everlasting, and that has seen personal security during our limited span of life most nearly perfected by friendship.

31–38: Justice and Injustice

(31)   The justice that seeks nature's goal is a utilitarian pledge of men not to harm each other or be harmed.[3]

(32)   Nothing is either just or unjust in the eyes of those animals that have been unable to make agreements not to harm each other or be harmed. The same is true of those peoples who are unable or unwilling to make covenants not to harm or be harmed.

(33)   Justice was never an entity in itself. It is a kind of agreement not to harm or be harmed, made when men associate with each other at any time and in communities of any size whatsoever.

(34)   Injustice is not an evil in itself. Its evil lies in the anxious fear that you will not elude those who have authority to punish such misdeeds.

(35)   It is impossible for a person who underhandedly breaks the agreement not to harm or be harmed to feel sure that he will escape punishment, even though he manages to do so time after time; for up to the very end of his life he cannot be sure that he will actually escape.

(36)   In its general meaning, justice is the same for all because of its utility in the relations of men to each other, but in its specific application to countries and various other circumstances it does not follow that the same thing is just for all.

(37)   In the case of actions that are legally regarded as just, those that are of tested utility in meeting the needs of human society have the hallmark of justice, whether they turn out to be equally just in all cases or not. On the other hand, if somebody lays down a law and it does not prove to be of advantage in human relations, then such a law no longer has the true character of justice. And even if the element of utility should undergo a change after harmonizing for a time with the conception of justice, the law was still just during that period, in the judgement of those who are not confused by meaningless words but who look at the actualities.

(38)   In cases where the surrounding conditions are not new and where laws regarded as just have been shown to be inconsistent with the conception of justice in their actual workings, such laws are unjust. Again, in cases where the circumstances are new and where the same laws, once deemed to be just, are no longer serviceable, the laws in this case were just as long as they were useful to the community of citizens, but later when they were no longer useful they became unjust.

39–40: The Sectarian Spirit and Life

(39)   The person who is the most successful in controlling the disturbing elements that come from the outside world has assimilated to himself what he could, and what he could not assimilate he has at least not alienated. Where he could not do even this, he has dissociated himself or eliminated all that it was expedient to treat in this way.

(40)   All who have the capacity to gain security, especially from those who live around them, live a most agreeable life together, since they have the firm assurance of friendship; and after enjoying their comradeship to the full they do not bewail the early demise of a departed friend as if it were a pitiable thing.

Notes

1 The targets here are Plato and Aristotle, who elevated the 'intellectual virtues' of contemplative philosophy over prudence or 'practical wisdom'.
2 The reference here is to the Greek cults of gods or goddesses of 'Fate' and 'Fortune'.
3 Notice, however, that Epicurus' position is not that of later 'social contract' theorists, who think we ought to act justly *because* we have pledged to do so. For Epicurus, my own peace of mind is the reason for acting justly.

(A) Mencius, 'Human Nature is Good'
(B) Hsun Tzu, 'Man's Nature is Evil'

(A) *From The Works of Mencius*, trans. James Legge. London: Trübner, 1861, pp. 270–97. (B) *From Basic Writings of Mo Tzu, Hsun Tzu and Han Fei Tzu*, trans. Burton Watson. New York: Columbia University Press, 1967, pp. 157–71 [some passages omitted and some Chinese names given standard spellings]. Copyright © 1967 by Columbia University Press; reprinted with permission of the publisher.

Historically, moral philosophy has been intimately related to moral psychology and the study of human nature. Even when the propounders of ethical systems have not tried to justify them by appeal to human nature, they have been keen to show that their proposals are not vitiated by any innate recalcitrance of human beings. In the absence of an account of human nature, moreover, it is hard to envisage the shape that moral and political education should take. It was unsurprising, therefore, to find the Greek thinkers represented in the opening chapters of this volume devoting attention to people's nature and motivation. No less attention was paid further east, in China, where philosophical interest was almost exclusively 'centred in human needs, in the improvement of government, [and] in morals'.[1]

The most abiding ethical system of China – and indeed of anywhere else – was Confucianism. The primary emphases of Confucian ethics were altruistic benevolence (*jen*) and 'righteousness' (*yi*), the latter largely understood as the correct performance of 'rites' (*li*), pre-eminently those of 'filial piety' towards relatives and ancestors. The defence of this system offered by Confucius (6th–5th century BCE) himself was primarily by way of appeal to ancient tradition, but he hints as well that benevolence and righteousness are in accordance with both human nature and 'the way of Heaven'. Unfortunately, these were two topics, so a disciple tells us, on which it was impossible to persuade the Master to elaborate.[2] Elaboration had to await Confucius' best-known followers, Mencius (Mengzi, Master Meng, c.372–289 BCE) and Hsun Tzu (Xunzi,

[1] A. C. Graham, 'The place of reason in the Chinese philosophical tradition', in R. Dawson (ed.), *The Legacy of China*, Oxford: Clarendon Press, 1964, p. 54.
[2] Confucius, *The Analects*, Harmondsworth: Penguin, 1979, V, 13.

Master Hsun, c.298–238 BCE). Their articulations of the Confucian tradition could hardly have been more different, however – on the surface at least. The two selections which follow are from Book 6, Part 1, of Mencius' works and from the critical rejoinder to this in §23 of Hsun Tzu's writings.

Mencius develops Confucius' hint that morality accords with human nature, asserting that 'human nature is good'. Just as water will flow downwards and grains ripen unless obstacles are placed in the way, so human beings will behave rightly unless circumstances are adverse. Various evidence is cited in favour of this claim – the fact that people prefer to die than to do something utterly shameful, for example, or the 'gut' sympathy people feel when seeing a child drown or an animal suffer. These are not things we learn to do or to feel, and the difference between the 'sage' and the ordinary person is that the former has not lost something – his natural 'heart-mind' (hsin) – which, in the case of the latter, has atrophied as a result of adverse circumstances and lack of diligence. Morality, for Mencius, belongs to human nature in the further sense that it, and the 'heart-mind' which predisposes towards it, distinguish human beings from all other creatures.

Since the view that the 'good heart' is innate was held by most Confucians,[3] Hsun Tzu is maverick in arguing, against Mencius, that 'man's nature is evil', though few Confucians were more zealous than he in defence of the performance of 'rites'.[4] In Hsun Tzu's view, what is natural to human beings is desire and desire inevitably leads to conflict: since this is an evil, so is the nature which results in it. Even if the young child possesses innate benevolence, it is no less natural for this to disappear and it is absurd, Hsun Tzu holds, to suppose that something as obviously acquired and requiring training as moral behaviour is natural in the way sight is to the eye. Far from the 'sage' being a person who has not lost some innate endowment, he is someone who has fought much harder than the rest of us to acquire the virtues. Performance of 'rites' is not something that flows from our inner being, but must be instilled in us in order to prevent social conflict.

The distance between the two philosophers may be rather less than it appears. Mencius does not deny that most human beings behave badly most of the time, no more than Hsun Tzu denies that they have a capacity to act out of altruistic motives. (He is not a philosophical egoist.) Again, it is clear that at various points they mean different things by 'natural'. Mencius' claim that a capacity for morality is what distinguishes human from animal nature is not contradicted by Hsun Tzu's insistence that the exercise of this capacity is the

---

[3] See Xinzhong Yao, *Confucianism and Christianity: A Comparative Study of Jen and Agape*, Brighton: Sussex Academic Press, 1996, pp. 132ff.
[4] In the first volume of this series, *Aesthetics: The Classic Readings*, chapter 3, we encountered Hsun Tzu's robust defence (in §20 of his works) of musical and artistic 'rites' against Mo Tzu's attack.

result of training, environment and the disciplining of natural desires. Arguably, the most interesting difference between the two men is that, for Mencius, the precepts of Confucian 'righteousness' are ones which the uncorrupted 'sage' will intuitively assent to, while for Hsun Tzu, their only warrant is their success, over the centuries, in effectively controlling social conflict and in lending order (the primary imperative of 'Heaven') to the affairs of men.[5]

Although Mencius' position was to become Confucian orthodoxy, the debate between him and Hsun Tzu was to be replayed many times within Chinese philosophy, right down to recent arguments over the malleability of human nature that Marxism seems to presuppose. Similar debates, of course, were to be conducted by philosophers in the West – by, for example, the advocates of 'moral sentiment' and their critics (see Butler's discussion, chapter 9 below).

(A) Mencius, 'Human Nature is Good'

Chapter 1

(1)   The philosopher Kao Tzu said, 'Man's nature is like the *ch'i* willow, and righteousness is like a cup or a bowl. The fashioning benevolence and righteousness out of man's nature is like the making cups and bowls from the *ch'i* willow.'

(2)   Mencius replied, 'Can you, leaving untouched the nature of the willow, make with it cups and bowls? You must do violence and injury to the willow, before you can make cups and bowls with it. If you must do violence and injury to the willow in order to make cups and bowls with it, on your principles you must in the same way do violence and injury to humanity in order to fashion from it benevolence and righteousness! Your words, alas! would certainly lead all men on to reckon benevolence and righteousness to be calamities.'

Chapter 2

(1)   The philosopher Kao said, 'Man's nature is like water whirling round in a corner. Open a passage for it to the east, and it will flow to the east; open a passage for it to the west, and it will flow to the west. Man's nature is indifferent to good and evil, just as the water is indifferent to the east and west.'

[5] See Chad Hansen, *A Daoist Theory of Chinese Thought*, New York: Oxford University Press, 1992, c.p. 195, and c.p. 312.

(2)   Mencius replied, 'Water indeed will flow indifferently to the east or west, but will it flow indifferently up or down? The tendency of man's nature to good is like the tendency of water to flow downwards. There are none but have this tendency to good, just as all water flows downwards.

(3)   'Now by striking water and causing it to leap up, you may make it go over your forehead, and, by damming and leading it, you may force it up a hill – but are such movements according to the nature of water? It is the force applied which causes them. When men are made to do what is not good, their nature is dealt with in this way.'

Chapter 3

(1)   The philosopher Kao said, 'Life is what is to be understood by nature.'

(2)   Mencius asked him, 'Do you say that by nature you mean life, just as you say that white is white?' 'Yes, I do,' was the reply. Mencius added, 'Is the whiteness of a white feather like that of white snow, and the whiteness of white snow like that of a white gem?' Kao again said 'Yes.'

(3)   'Very well,' pursued Mencius. 'Is the nature of a dog like the nature of an ox, and the nature of an ox like the nature of a man?'

Chapter 4

(1)   The philosopher Kao said, 'To enjoy food and delight in colours is nature. Benevolence is internal and not external; righteousness is external and not internal.'

(2)   Mencius asked him, 'What is the ground of your saying that benevolence is internal and righteousness external?' He replied, 'There is a man older than I, and I give honour to his age. It is not that there is first in me a principle of such reverence to age. It is just as when there is a white man, and I consider him white – according as he is so externally to me. On this account, I pronounce of righteousness that it is external.'

(3)   Mencius said, 'There is no difference between our pronouncing of a white horse to be white and our pronouncing a white man to be white. But is there no difference between the regard with which we acknowledge the age of an old horse and that with which we acknowledge the age of an old man? And what is it which is called righteousness? – the fact of a man's being old? or the fact of our giving honour to his age?'

(4)   Kao said, 'There is my younger brother – I love him. But the younger brother of a man of Ch'in I do not love: that is, the feeling is determined by myself, and therefore I say that benevolence is internal. On the other hand, I give honour to an old man of Ch'u and I also give honour to an old man of my own people: that is, the feeling is determined by the age, and therefore I say that righteousness is external.'

(5)   Mencius answered him, 'Our enjoyment of meat roasted by a man of Ch'in does not differ from our enjoyment of meat roasted by ourselves. Thus, what you insist on takes place also in the case of such things, and will you say likewise that our enjoyment of a roast is external?'

Chapter 5

(1)   The disciple Meng Chi-Tzu asked Kung-tu Tzu [another disciple of Mencius – Ed.] saying, 'On what ground is it said that righteousness is internal?'

(2)   Kung-tu Tzu replied, 'We therein act out our feeling of respect, and therefore it is said to be internal.'

(3)   The other objected, 'Suppose the case of a villager older than your elder brother by one year, to which of them would you show the greater respect?' 'To my brother,' was the reply. 'But for which of them would you first pour out wine at a feast?' 'For the villager.' Meng Chi-Tzu argued, 'Now your feeling of reverence rests on the one, and now the honour due to age is rendered to the other – this is certainly determined by what is without, and does not proceed from within.'

(4)   Kung-tu Tzu was unable to reply, and told the conversation to Mencius. Mencius said, 'You should ask him, "Which do you respect most, your uncle, or your younger brother?" He will answer, "My uncle." Ask him again, "If your younger brother be personating a dead ancestor, to which do you show the greater respect, to him or to your uncle?" He will say, "To my younger brother." You can go on, "But where is the respect due, as you said, to your uncle?" He will reply to this, "I show the respect to my younger brother, because of the position which he occupies," and you can likewise say, "So my respect to the villager is because of the position which he occupies. Ordinarily, my respect is rendered to my elder brother; for a brief season, on occasion, it is rendered to the village."'

(5)   Meng chi-Tzu heard this and observed, 'When respect is due to my uncle, I respect him, and when respect is due to my younger brother, I respect him; the thing is certainly determined by what is without, and does not proceed from within.' Kung-tu Tzu replied, 'In winter we drink things

hot, in summer we drink things cold; and so, on your principle, eating and drinking also depend on what is external!'

Chapter 6

(1)   The disciple Kung-tu Tzu said, 'The philosopher Kao says "Man's nature is neither good nor bad."

(2)   'Some say, "Man's nature may be made to practise good, and it may be made to practise evil, and accordingly, under [Kings] Wen and Wu the people loved what was good, while under [Kings] Yu and Li they loved what was cruel." . . .

(4)   'And now you say, "The nature is good." Then are all those wrong?'

(5)   Mencius said, 'From the feelings proper to it, it is constituted for the practice of what is good. This is what I mean in saying that the nature is good.

(6)   'If men do what is not good, the blame cannot be imputed to their natural powers.

(7)   'The feeling of commiseration belongs to all men; so does that of shame and dislike; and that of reverence and respect; and that of approving and disapproving. The feeling of commiseration implies the principle of benevolence; that of shame and dislike, the principle of righteousness; that of reverence and respect, the principle of propriety; and that of approving and disapproving, the principle of knowledge. Benevolence, righteousness, propriety and knowledge are not infused into us from without. We are certainly furnished with them. And a different view is simply from want of reflection. Hence it is said "Seek and you will find them. Neglect and you will lose them." Men differ from one another in regard to them; some as much again as others, some five times as much, and some to an incalculable amount – it is because they cannot carry out fully their natural powers.

(8)   'It is said in the *Book of Poetry* [or *Book of Odes* – Ed.],

> Heaven in producing mankind,
> Gave them their various faculties and relations with *their specific* laws.
> These are the invariable rules of nature for all to hold,
> And *all* love this admirable virtue.

Confucius said, "The maker of this ode knew indeed the principle of our nature!" We may thus see that every faculty and relation must have its law, and since there are invariable rules for all to hold, they consequently love this admirable virtue.'

Chapter 7

(1)   Mencius said, 'In good years the children of the people are most of them good, while in bad years the most of them abandon themselves to evil. It is not owing to their natural powers conferred by Heaven that they are thus different. The abandonment is owing to the circumstances through which they allow their minds to be ensnared and drowned in evil.

(2)   'There now is barley. Let it be sown and covered up; the ground being the same, and the time of sowing likewise the same, it grows rapidly up, and when the full time is come, it is all found to be ripe. Although there may be inequalities of produce, that is owing to the difference of the soil, as rich or poor, to the unequal nourishment afforded by the rains and dews, and to the different ways in which man has performed his business in reference to it.

(3)   'Thus all things which are the same in kind are like to one another; why should we doubt in regard to man, as if he were a solitary exception to this? The sage and we are the same in kind.

(4)   'In accordance with this the scholar Lung said, "If a man make hempen sandals without knowing the size of people's feet, yet I know that he will not make them like baskets." Sandals are all like one another, because all men's feet are like one another.

(5)   'So with the mouth and flavours; all mouths have the same relishes. Yi-ya [a famous chef – Ed.] only apprehended before me what my mouth relishes. Suppose that his mouth in its relish for flavours differed from that of other men, as is the case with dogs or horses which are not the same in kind with us, why should all men be found following Yi-ya in their relishes? In the matter of tastes the whole empire models itself after Yi-ya; that is, the mouths of all men are like one another.

(6)   'And so also it is with the ear. In the matter of sounds, the whole empire models itself after the music-master K'uang; that is, the ears of all men are like one another.

(7)   'And so also it is with the eye. In the case of Tzu-tu, there is no man but would recognize that he was beautiful. Any one who would not recognize the beauty of Tzu-tu must have no eyes.

(8)   'Therefore I say, men's mouths agree in having the same relishes; their ears agree in enjoying the same sounds; their eyes agree in recognizing the same beauty – shall their minds alone be without that which they similarly approve? What is it then of which they similarly approve? It is, I say, the principles of our nature, and the determinations of righteousness. The sages only apprehended before me that of which my mind approves

along with other men. Therefore the principles of our nature and the determinations of righteousness are agreeable to my mind, just as the flesh of grass and grain-fed animals is agreeable to my mouth.'

Chapter 8

(1)   Mencius said, 'The trees of the New mountain were once beautiful. Being situated, however, in the borders of a large State, they were hewn down with axes and billhooks; and could they retain their beauty? Still through the activity of the vegetative life day and night, and the nourishing influence of the rain and dew, they were not without buds and sprouts springing forth, but then came the cattle and goats and browsed upon them. To these things is owing the bare and stripped appearance of the mountain, which when people see, they think it was never finely wooded. But is this the nature of the mountain?

(2)   'And so also of what properly belongs to man – shall it be said that the mind of any man was without benevolence and righteousness? The way in which a man loses his proper goodness of mind is like the way in which the trees are denuded by axes and billhooks. Hewn down day after day, can it – the mind – retain its beauty? But there is a development of its life day and night, and in the calm air of the morning, just between night and day, the mind feels in a degree those desires and aversions which are proper to humanity, but the feeling is not strong, and it is fettered and destroyed by what takes place during the day. This fettering taking place again and again, the restorative influence of the night is not sufficient to preserve the proper goodness of the mind; and when this proves insufficient for that purpose, the nature becomes not much different from that of the irrational animals, which when people see, they think that it never had those powers which I assert. But does this condition represent the feelings proper to humanity?

(3)   'Therefore, if it receive its proper nourishment, there is nothing which will not grow. If it lose its proper nourishment, there is nothing which will not decay away.

(4)   'Confucius said, "Hold it fast, and it remains with you. Let it go, and you lose it. Its outgoing and incoming cannot be defined as to time or place." It is the mind of which this is said!'

Chapter 9

(1)   Mencius said, 'It is not to be wondered at that the king is not wise!

(2)   'Suppose the case of the most easily growing thing in the world – if you let it have one day's genial heat, and then expose it for ten days to cold, it will not be able to grow. It is but seldom that I have an audience of the king, and when I retire, there come all those who act upon him like the cold. Though I succeed in bringing out some buds of goodness, of what avail is it!

(3)   'Now chess-playing is but a small art,[2] but without his whole mind being given, and his will bent to it, a man cannot succeed at it. Yi Ch'iu is the best chess-player in all the kingdom. Suppose that he is teaching two men to play. The one gives to the subject his whole mind and bends to it all his will, doing nothing but listening to Yi Ch'iu. The other, although he seems to be listening to him, has his whole mind running on a swan which he thinks is approaching, and wishes to bend his bow, adjust the string to the arrow, and shoot it. Although he is learning along with the other, he does not come up to him. Why? Because his intelligence is not equal? Not so.'

Chapter 10

(1)   Mencius said, 'I like fish and I also like bear's palm. If I cannot have the two together, I will let the fish go, and take the bear's palm. So, I like life, and I also like righteousness. If I cannot keep the two together, I will let life go and choose righteousness.

(2)   'I like life indeed, but there is that which I like more than life, and therefore, I will not seek to possess it by any improper ways. I dislike death indeed, but there is that which I dislike more than death, and therefore there are occasions when I will not avoid danger.

(3)   'If among the things which man likes there were nothing which he liked more than life, why should he not use every means by which he could preserve it? If among the things which man dislikes there were nothing which he disliked more than death, why should he not do every thing by which he could avoid danger?

(4)   'There are cases when men by a certain course might preserve life, and they do not employ it; when by certain things they might avoid danger, and they will not do them.

(5)   'Therefore, men have that which they like more than life, and that which they dislike more than death. They are not men of distinguished talents and virtue only who have this mental nature. All men have it; what belongs to such men is simply that they do not lose it.' . . .

Chapter 11

(1)   Mencius said, 'Benevolence is man's mind, and righteousness is man's path.

(2)   'How lamentable is it to neglect the path and not pursue it, to lose this mind and not know to seek it again!

(3)   'When men's fowls and dogs are lost, they know to seek for them again, but they lose their mind, and do not know to seek for it.

(4)   'The great end of learning is nothing else but to seek for the lost mind.' . . .

Chapter 15

(1)   The disciple Kung-tu Tzu said, 'All are equally men, but some are great men, and some are little men – how is this?' Mencius replied, 'Those who follow that part of themselves which is great are great men; those who follow that part which is little are little men.'

(2)   Kung-tu Tzu pursued, 'All are equally men, but some follow that part of themselves which is great, and some follow that part which is little – how is this?' Mencius answered, 'The senses of hearing and seeing do not think, and are obscured by external things. When one thing comes into contact with another, as a matter of course it leads it away. To the mind belongs the office of thinking. By thinking, it gets the right view of things; by neglecting to think, it fails to do this. These – the senses and the mind – are what Heaven has given to us. Let a man first stand fast in the supremacy of the nobler part of his constitution, and the inferior part will not be able to take it from him. It is simply this which makes the great man.'

Chapter 16

(1)   Mencius said, 'There is a nobility of Heaven, and there is a nobility of man. Benevolence, righteousness, self-consecration and fidelity, with unwearied joy in these virtues – these constitute the nobility of Heaven. . . .

(2)   'The men of antiquity cultivated their nobility of Heaven, and the nobility of man came to them in its train.

(3)   'The men of the present day cultivate their nobility of Heaven in order to seek for the nobility of man, and when they have obtained that, they throw away the other – their delusion is extreme. The issue is simply this that they must lose that nobility of man as well.'

Chapter 17

(1)   Mencius said, 'To desire to be honoured is the common mind of men. And all men have in themselves that which is truly honourable. Only they do not think of it.

(2)   'The honour which men confer is not good honour. Those whom Chaou the Great ennobles he can make mean again.

(3)   'It is said in the *Book of Poetry* [or *Book of Odes* – Ed.],

> He has filled us with his wine,
> He has satiated us with his goodness.

"Satiated us with his goodness", that is, satiated us with benevolence and righteousness, and he who is so, consequently, does not wish for the fat meat and fine millet of men. A good reputation and far-reaching praise fall to him, and he does not desire the elegant embroidered garments of men.'

Chapter 18

(1)   Mencius said, 'Benevolence subdues its opposite just as water subdues fire. Those, however, who nowadays practise benevolence do it as if with one cup of water they could save a whole waggon-load of fuel which was on fire, and when the flames were not extinguished, were to say that water cannot subdue fire. This conduct, moreover, greatly encourages those who are not benevolent.

(2)   'The final issue will simply be this – the loss of that small amount of benevolence.'

Chapter 19

Mencius said, 'Of all seeds the best are the five kinds of grain, yet if they be not ripe, they are not equal to the *t'e* or the *pae*. So, the value of benevolence depends entirely on its being brought to maturity.'

Chapter 20

(1)   Mencius said, 'Yi, in teaching men to shoot, made it a rule to draw the bow to the full, and his pupils also did the same.

(2)   'A master workman, in teaching others, uses the compass and square, and his pupils do the same.'

Notes

1 More recent translators suggest 'the appetitite for sex' rather than 'delight in colours'.
2 Mencius' reference here is probably to the game of *go* rather than chess.

▶ ▶ ▶ (B) Hsun Tzu, 'Man's Nature is Evil'

Man's nature is evil; goodness is the result of conscious activity. The nature of man is such that he is born with a fondness for profit. If he indulges this fondness, it will lead him into wrangling and strife, and all sense of courtesy and humility will disappear. He is born with feelings of envy and hate, and if he indulges these, they will lead him into violence and crime, and all sense of loyalty and good faith will disappear. Man is born with the desires of the eyes and ears, with a fondness for beautiful sights and sounds. If he indulges these, they will lead him into licence and wantonness, and all ritual principles and correct forms will be lost. Hence, any man who follows his nature and indulges his emotions will inevitably become involved in wrangling and strife, will violate the forms and rules of society, and will end as a criminal. Therefore, man must first be transformed by the instructions of a teacher and guided by ritual principles, and only then will he be able to observe the dictates of courtesy and humility, obey the forms and rules of society, and achieve order. It is obvious from this, then, that man's nature is evil, and that his goodness is the result of conscious activity.

A warped piece of wood must wait until it has been laid against the straightening board, steamed and forced into shape before it can become straight; a piece of blunt metal must wait until it has been whetted on a grindstone before it can become sharp. Similarly, since man's nature is evil, it must wait for the instructions of a teacher before it can become upright, and for the guidance of ritual principles before it can become orderly. If men have no teachers to instruct them, they will be inclined towards evil and not upright; and if they have no ritual principles to guide them, they will be perverse and violent and lack order. In ancient times the sage kings realized that man's nature is evil, and that therefore he inclines toward evil and violence and is not upright or orderly. Accordingly they created ritual principles and laid down certain regulations in order to reform man's emotional nature and make it upright, in order to train and transform it and guide it in the proper channels. In this way they caused all men to become orderly and to conform to the Way. Hence, today any man who takes to heart the instructions of his teacher, applies himself to his studies, and abides by ritual principles may become a gentleman, but anyone who gives free rein to his emotional nature, is content to indulge his passions, and disregards ritual principles becomes a petty man. It is obvious from this, therefore, that man's nature is evil, and that his goodness is the result of conscious activity.

Mencius states that man is capable of learning because his nature is good, but I say that this is wrong. It indicates that he has not really understood man's nature nor distinguished properly between the basic nature and conscious activity. The nature is that which is given by Heaven; you cannot learn it, you cannot acquire it by effort. Ritual principles, on the other hand, are created by sages; you can learn to apply them, you can work to bring them to completion. That part of man which cannot be learned or acquired by effort is called the nature; that part of him which can be acquired by learning and brought to completion by effort is called conscious activity. This is the difference between nature and conscious activity.

It is a part of man's nature that his eyes can see and his ears can hear. But the faculty of clear sight can never exist separately from the eye, nor can the faculty of keen hearing exist separately from the ear. It is obvious, then, that you cannot acquire clear sight and keen hearing by study. Mencius states that man's nature is good, and that all evil arises because he loses his original nature. Such a view, I believe, is erroneous. It is the way with man's nature that as soon as he is born he begins to depart from his original naïveté and simplicity, and therefore he must inevitably lose what Mencius regards as his original nature. It is obvious from this, then, that the nature of man is evil.

Those who maintain that the nature is good praise and approve whatever has not departed from the original simplicity and naïveté of the child. That is, they consider that beauty belongs to the original simplicity and naïveté and goodness to the original mind in the same way that clear sight is inseparable from the eye and keen hearing from the ear. Hence, they maintain that [the nature possesses goodness] in the same way that the eye possesses clear vision or the ear keenness of hearing. Now it is the nature of man that when he is hungry he will desire satisfaction, when he is cold he will desire warmth, and when he is weary he will desire rest. This is his emotional nature. And yet a man, although he is hungry, will not dare to be the first to eat if he is in the presence of his elders, because he knows that he should yield to them, and although he is weary, he will not dare to demand rest because he knows that he should relieve others of the burden of labour. For a son to yield to his father or a younger brother to yield to his elder brother, for a son to relieve his father of work or a younger brother to relieve his elder brother – acts such as these are all contrary to man's nature and run counter to his emotions. And yet they represent the way of filial piety and the proper forms enjoined by ritual principles. Hence, if men follow their emotional nature, there will be no courtesy or humility; courtesy and humility in fact run counter to man's emotional nature. From this it is obvious, then, that man's nature is evil, and that his goodness is the result of conscious activity.

Someone may ask: if man's nature is evil, then where do ritual principles come from? I would reply: all ritual principles are produced by the conscious activity of the sages; essentially they are not products of man's nature. A potter moulds clay and makes a vessel, but the vessel is the product of the conscious activity of the potter, not essentially a product of his human nature. A carpenter carves a piece of wood and makes a utensil, but the utensil is the product of the conscious activity of the carpenter, not essentially a product of his human nature. The sage gathers together his thoughts and ideas, experiments with various forms of conscious activity, and so produces ritual principles and sets forth laws and regulations. Hence, these ritual principles and laws are the products of the conscious activity of the sage, not essentially products of his human nature.

Phenomena such as the eye's fondness for beautiful forms, the ear's fondness for beautiful sounds, the mouth's fondness for delicious flavours, the mind's fondness for profit, or the body's fondness for pleasure and ease – these are all products of the emotional nature of man. They are instinctive and spontaneous; man does not have to do anything to produce them. But that which does not come into being instinctively but must wait for some activity to bring it into being is called the product of conscious activity. These are the products of the nature and of conscious activity respectively, and the proof that they are not the same. Therefore, the sage transforms his nature and initiates conscious activity; from this conscious activity he produces ritual principles, and when they have been produced he sets up rules and regulations. Hence, ritual principles and rules are produced by the sage. In respect to human nature the sage is the same as all other men and does not surpass them; it is only in his conscious activity that he differs from and surpasses other men.

It is man's emotional nature to love profit and desire gain. Suppose now that a man has some wealth to be divided. If he indulges his emotional nature, loving profit and desiring gain, then he will quarrel and wrangle even with his own brothers over the division. But if he has been transformed by the proper forms of ritual principle, then he will be capable of yielding even to a complete stranger. Hence, to indulge the emotional nature leads to the quarrelling of brothers, but to be transformed by ritual principles makes a man capable of yielding to strangers.

Every man who desires to do good does so precisely because his nature is evil. A man whose accomplishments are meagre longs for greatness; an ugly man longs for beauty; a man in cramped quarters longs for spaciousness; a poor man longs for wealth; a humble man longs for eminence. Whatever a man lacks in himself he will seek outside. But if a man is already rich, he will not long for wealth, and if he is already eminent, he will not long for greater power. What a man already possesses in himself he will not bother to look for outside. From this we can see that men desire to do good precisely because their nature is evil. Ritual principles are certainly not a part of man's original nature. Therefore, he forces himself to study and to seek to possess them. An understanding of ritual principles is not a part of man's original nature, and therefore he ponders and plans and thereby seeks to understand them. Hence, man in the state in which he is born neither possesses nor understands ritual principles. If he does not possess ritual principles, his behaviour will be chaotic, and if he does not understand them, he will be wild and irresponsible. In fact, therefore, man in the state in which he is born possesses this tendency towards chaos and irresponsibility. From this it is obvious, then, that man's nature is evil, and that his goodness is the result of conscious activity.

Mencius states that man's nature is good, but I say that this view is wrong. All men in the world, past and present, agree in defining goodness as that which is upright, reasonable and orderly, and evil as that which is prejudiced, irresponsible and chaotic. This is the distinction between good and evil. Now suppose that man's nature was in fact intrinsically upright, reasonable and orderly – then what need would there be for sage kings and ritual principles? The existence of sage kings and ritual principles could certainly add nothing to the situation. But because man's nature is in fact evil, this is not so. Therefore, in ancient times the sages, realizing that man's nature is evil, that it is prejudiced and not upright, irresponsible and lacking in order, for this reason established the authority of the ruler to control it, elucidated ritual principles to transform it, set up laws and standards to correct it, and meted out strict punishments to restrain it. As a result, all the world achieved order and conformed to goodness. Such is the orderly government of the sage kings and the transforming power of ritual principles. Now let someone try doing away with the authority of the ruler, ignoring the transforming power of ritual principles, rejecting the order that comes from laws and standards, and dispensing with the restrictive power of punishments, and then watch and see how the people of the world treat each other. He will find that the powerful impose upon the weak and rob them, the many terrorize the few and extort from them, and in no time the whole world will be given up to chaos and mutual destruction. It is obvious from this, then, that man's nature is evil, and that his goodness is the result of conscious activity.

Those who are good at discussing antiquity must demonstrate the validity of what they say in terms of modern times; those who are good at discussing Heaven must show proofs from the human world. In discussions of all kinds, men value what is in accord with the facts and what can be proved to be valid. Hence if a man sits on his mat propounding some theory, he should be able to stand right up and put it into practice, and show that it can be extended over a wide area with equal validity. Now Mencius states that man's nature is good, but this is neither in accord with the facts, nor can it be proved to be valid. One may sit down and propound such a theory, but he cannot stand up and put it into practice, nor can he extend it over a wide area with any success at all. How, then, could it be anything but erroneous?

If the nature of man were good, we could dispense with sage kings and forget about ritual principles. But if it is evil, then we must go along with the sage kings and honour ritual principles. The straightening board is made because of the warped wood; the plumb line is employed because things are crooked; rulers are set up and ritual principles elucidated because the nature of man is evil. From this it is obvious, then, that man's nature is evil, and that his goodness is the result of conscious activity. A straight piece of wood does not have to wait for the straightening board to become straight; it is straight by nature. But a warped piece of wood must wait until it has been laid against the straightening board, steamed and forced into shape before it can become straight, because by nature it is warped. Similarly, since man's nature is evil, he must wait for the ordering power of the sage kings and the transforming power of ritual principles; only then can he achieve order and conform to goodness. From this it is obvious, then, that man's nature is evil, and that his goodness is the result of conscious activity.

Someone may ask whether ritual principles and concerted conscious activity are not themselves a part of man's nature, so that for that reason the sage is capable of producing them. But I would answer that this is not so. A potter may mould clay and produce an earthen pot, but surely moulding pots out of clay is not a part of the potter's human nature. A carpenter may carve wood and produce a utensil, but surely carving utensils out of wood is not a part of the carpenter's human nature. The sage stands in the same relation to ritual principles as the potter to the things he moulds and produces. How, then, could ritual principles and concerted conscious activity be a part of man's basic human nature? . . .

The man in the street can become a Yu. What does this mean? What made the sage emperor Yu a Yu, I would reply, was the fact that he practised benevolence and righteousness and abided by the proper rules and standards. If this is so, then benevolence, righteousness and proper standards must be based upon principles which can be known and practised. Any man in the street has the essential faculties needed to understand benevolence, righteousness and proper standards, and the potential ability to put them into practice. Therefore it is clear that he can become a Yu.

Would you maintain that benevolence, righteousness and proper standards are not based upon any principles that can be known and practised? If so, then even a Yu could not have understood or practised them. Or would you maintain that the man in the street does not have the essential faculties needed to understand them or the potential ability to put them into practice? If so, then you are saying that the man in the street in his family life cannot understand the duties required of a father or a son and in public life cannot comprehend the correct relationship between ruler and subject. But in fact this is not true. Any man in the street *can* understand the duties required of a father or a son and *can* comprehend the correct relationship between ruler and subject. Therefore, it is obvious that the essential faculties needed to understand such ethical principles and the potential ability to put them into practice must be a part of his make-up. Now if he takes these faculties and abilities and applies them to the principles of benevolence and righteousness, which we have already shown to be knowable and practicable, then it is obvious that he can become a Yu. If the man in the street applies himself to training and study, concentrates his mind and will, and considers and examines things carefully, continuing his efforts over a long period of time and accumulating good acts without stop, then he can achieve a godlike understanding and form a triad with Heaven and earth. The sage is a man who has arrived where he has through the accumulation of good acts.

You have said, someone may object, that the sage has arrived where he has through the accumulation of good acts. Why is it, then, that everyone is not able to accumulate good acts in the same way? I would reply: everyone is capable of doing so, but not everyone can be made to do so. The petty man is capable of becoming a gentleman, yet he is not willing to do so; the gentleman is capable of becoming a petty man but he is not willing to do so. The petty man and the gentleman are perfectly capable of changing places; the fact that they do not actually do so is what I mean when I say that they are capable of doing so but they cannot be made to do so. Hence, it is correct to say that the man in the street is *capable* of becoming a Yu but it is not necessarily correct to say that he will in fact find it possible to do so. But although he does not find it possible to do so does not prove that he is incapable of doing so.

A person with two feet is theoretically capable of walking to every corner of the earth, although in fact no one has ever found it possible to do so. Similarly, the artisan, the carpenter, the farmer and the merchant are theoretically capable of exchanging professions, although in actual practice they find it impossible to do so. From this we can see that, although someone may be theoretically capable of becoming something, he may not in practice find it possible to do so. But although he does not find it possible to do so, this does not prove that he is not capable of doing so. To find it practically possible or impossible to do something and to be capable or incapable of doing something are two entirely different things. It is perfectly clear, then, that a man is theoretically capable of becoming something else. . . .

From The Book of Chuang Tzu, trans. M. Palmer. Harmondsworth: Penguin, 1996, pp. 72–4, 106–14, 118, 122–7 [some passages omitted].

After the *Tao Te Ching*, *The Book of Chuang Tzu* is the most famous text of classical Taoism. Unlike the 'author' of the *Tao Te Ching*, Lao Tzu ('Old Master'), Chuang Tzu (or Zhuangzi, Master Chuang) seems to have been an actual historical figure, an official in the Lacquer Garden at Meng who lived from around 369 to 286 BCE. Which parts of his Book he himself penned, however, is unclear, and the chapters from which I have drawn are probably later accretions – so that when I refer to 'Chuang Tzu' from now on, it may not be the man from Meng himself whose views are presented.

Taoism is traditionally thought of as the great rival to Confucian ethics. But this can be misleading. One should recall that the division of Chinese philosophy into various 'schools' and '-isms' was made several centuries after Confucius, Mencius, Chuang Tzu and other leading thinkers flourished, and that in Taoist texts – though not in the chapters I have chosen – Confucius is often portrayed in a favourable light. Moreover, in later centuries, Confucianism and Taoism were often perceived 'not as rival systems', but as 'complementary doctrines, an ethical and political system for the conduct of public and family life, and a mystical philosophy for the spiritual nourishment of the individual' respectively.[1] Still, the fact that the 'systems' had to operate in distinct walks of life suggests that there are important differences between them, and in the following pages of *The Book of Chuang Tzu* Confucian ethics, while not ridiculed, are subjected to serious criticisms.

Chuang Tzu is often represented as a vitriolic critic of 'artifice' and 'conventions', including the 'rites' on which Confucians placed such a premium. But there is a sense in which, for Chuang Tzu, convention and artifice are unavoidable. He was a relativist for whom all beliefs and distinctions, including ethical ones, are the product of people's 'perspectives' and the languages they have

[1] Burton Watson, Introduction to his translation of *The Complete Works of Chuang Tzu*, New York: Columbia University Press, 1968, p. 10. The idea that Taoism is 'mystical' has been robustly challenged by Chad Hansen. See n.5. to chapter 4.

forged (see chapters 2 and 17 especially). His real complaint is against those who fail to appreciate this, who 'reify' our perspectival distinctions and treat them – as Confucians do their principles of benevolence and righteousness – as if they were naturally woven into the order of things. To this complaint are added the conviction, shared by the *Tao Te Ching*,[2] that people's obsession with moral principles is already a sign that their lives and society are awry, and the insistence that, while some reliance on 'convention' is unavoidable, any dogged clinging to artifice is destructive of authentic human existence (rather as horse-training is to authentic equine existence (chapter 9)).

For Chuang Tzu, the 'true man', by refusing to cling to conventional principles and distinctions, thereby 'follows the Way (*tao*)'. It is notoriously difficult to know what is meant by *tao*, which is anyway said to be 'almost indescribable', to have 'no name' (chapter 22). Suffice it to say that, as the 'source' and 'sustainer' of everything in Heaven and Earth, it is not dependent upon anything and has nothing against which to act or contend. In these respects, it can be described as 'free', and the 'true man' will emulate this freedom. In particular, his life will be one of 'actionless action' (*wu wei*): by acting without specific purpose, relatively unconstrained by particular conventions, and refusing to contend against circumstance and other men, he emulates the 'freedom' of the *tao* itself. Only such a person is capable of appreciating the role, limited though it is, which principles of benevolence and righteousness may play. The Taoist hero is not the busy Confucian official endeavouring to beef up the moral fibre of the body politic, but the retiring, contemplative sage who disdains the latest fashionable 'perspective', or the artisan (like the wheelwright in chapter 13) who responds smoothly and naturally to the demands of his materials, without the mediation of precepts and formulas. Each in his own way 'lets things be' and, in doing so, 'follows the Way'. (Chuang Tzu is said to have turned down offers of government office and, spurning Confucian principles, cheerfully practised his drumming after his wife's death.)

Taoism, unsurprisingly, did not enjoy the state sponsorship which Confucian ethics did for nearly two millennia. But Chinese painting and fiction testify to the enduring appeal of Taoism, one which in recent years has spread to the West, not least because of the feeling that, in Taoist calls to 'follow Nature', there is inspiration for an 'environmental ethic'.[3] Not that the West has itself lacked a tradition of ethical thought which, in its essentials, corresponds to that of Taoism. From Democritus to Heidegger, there have always been those who have located the proper life for human beings, not in adherence to what they see as the artifice of a moral system, but in obedience to something mysterious and indescribable.

[2] Harmondsworth: Penguin, 1985. See especially chapter 38, according to which benevolence, rectitude and rites emerged only 'when the Way was lost'.
[3] But see my 'Is Daoism green?', *Asian Philosophy*, 5, 1994.

Chapter 9: Horses' Hooves

Horses have hooves so that their feet can grip on frost and snow and hair so that they can withstand the wind and cold. They eat grass and drink water, they buck and gallop, for this is the innate nature of horses. Even if they had great towers and magnificent halls, they would not be interested in them. However, when [the horse-trainer] Po Lo came on the scene, he said, 'I know how to train horses.' He branded them, cut their hair and their hooves, put halters on their heads, bridled them, hobbled them and shut them up in stables. Out of ten horses at least two or three die. Then he makes them hungry and thirsty, gallops them, races them, parades them, runs them together. He keeps before them the fear of the bit and ropes, behind them the fear of the whip and crop. Now more than half the horses are dead.

The potter said, 'I know how to use clay, how to mould it into rounds like the compass and into squares as though I had used a T-square.' The carpenter said, 'I know how to use wood: to make it bend, I use the template; to make it straight, I use the plumb line.' However, is it really the innate nature of clay and wood to be moulded by compass and T-square, template and plumb line? It is true, nevertheless, that generation after generation has said, 'Po Lo is good at controlling horses, and indeed the potter and carpenter are good with clay and wood.' And the same nonsense is spouted by those who rule the world.

I think that someone who truly knows how to rule the world would not be like this. The people have a true nature, they weave their cloth, they farm to produce food. This is their basic Virtue.[1] They are all one in this, not separated, and it is from Heaven.[2] Thus, in an age of perfect Virtue the people walk slowly and solemnly. They see straight and true. In times such as these the mountains have neither paths nor tunnels, on the lakes there are neither boats nor bridges; all life lives with its own kind, living close together. The birds and beasts multiply in their flocks and herds, the grass and trees grow tall. It is true that at such a time the birds and beasts can be led around without ropes, and birds' nests can be seen with ease.

In this time of perfect Virtue, people live side by side with the birds and beasts, sharing the world in common with all life. No one knows of distinctions such as nobles and the peasantry! Totally without wisdom but with virtue which does not disappear; totally without desire they are known as truly simple. If people are truly simple, they can follow their true nature. Then the perfect sage comes,[3] going on about benevolence, straining for self-righteousness, and suddenly everyone begins to have doubts. They start to fuss over the music, cutting and trimming the rituals, and thus the whole world is disturbed. If the pure essence had not been so cut about, how could they have otherwise ended up with sacrificial bowls? If the raw jade was not broken apart, how could the symbols of power be made? If the Tao and Te – Way and Virtue – had not been ignored, how could benevolence and righteousness have been preferred? If innate nature had not been left behind, how could rituals and music have been invented? If the five colours had not been confused, how could patterns and designs have occurred? If the five notes had not been confused, how could they have been supplanted by the six tones? The abuse of the true elements to make artefacts was the crime of the craftsman. The abuse of the Tao and Te – Way and Virtue – to make benevolence and righteousness, this was the error of the sage.

Horses, when they live wild, eat grass and drink water; when they are content, they entwine their necks and rub each other. When angry, they turn their backs on each other and kick out. This is what horses know. But if harnessed together and lined up under constraints, they know to look sideways and to arch their necks, to career around and try to spit out the bit and rid themselves of the reins. The knowledge thus gained by the horse, and its wicked behaviour, is in fact the fault of Po Lo.

At the time of [Emperor] Ho Hsu, people stayed where they were, not knowing anything else; they walked but did not know where they were going; filled themselves with food and were happy slapping their bellies to show their contentment. This was what the people had. Then came the sage. He brought the cringing and grovelling of the rituals and music and infected all under Heaven with his offer of benevolence and righteousness, which he said would comfort the hearts of all.

As a result the people desired and longed for knowledge, and warred against each other to gain the advantage. Nothing could stop them. All this was the fault of the sage.

Chapter 13: Heaven's Tao

It is Heaven's Tao to journey and to gather no moss,
thus all the forms of life are brought to perfection.
It is the Emperor's Tao to journey and to gather no moss,
which is why the whole world comes to his feet.
It is the sages' Tao to journey and to gather no moss,
thus all that lies within the oceans venerates them.

To understand Heaven clearly,
to comprehend the sages,
to journey through the entire cosmos
following the Virtue of the Emperors and the kings
but also to be spontaneous themselves;
this is the nature of those who comprehend,
seeming not to know
but being centred in stillness.

The sages are quiescent, not because of any value in being quiescent, they simply are still. Not even the multitude of beings can disturb them, so they are calm. Water, when it is still, reflects back even your eyebrows and beard. It is perfectly level and from this the carpenter takes his level. If water stilled offers such clarity, imagine what pure spirit offers! The sage's heart is stilled! Heaven and Earth are reflected in it, the mirror of all life. Empty, still, calm, plain, quiet, silent, non-active, this is the centredness of Heaven and Earth and of the Tao and of Virtue. The Emperor, king and sages rest there. Resting, they are empty; empty, they can be full; fullness is fulfilment. From the empty comes stillness; in stillness they can travel; in travelling they achieve. In stillness they take actionless action. Through actionless action they expect results from those with responsibilities. Through actionless action they are happy, very happy; being so happy they are not afflicted by cares and worries, for these have no place, and their years of life are prolonged. Empty, still, calm, plain, quiet, silent, actionless action is the foundation of all life. If you are clear on this and facing south, it means you are a noble like [Emperor] Yao; if you are clear on this and facing north, you will become a minister like Shun.

Looking up to them, you observe the Virtue of Emperors, kings and the Sons of Heaven. Looking down on them, you observe the Tao of the dark sages and the uncrowned king. If you retire as they did, amongst the hermits of the rivers and oceans, mountains and forests, you will be considered like them as true scholars. Coming forward and offering help to this generation brings great fame and merit and the whole world becomes one. The sage is still; the king travels. Actionless action brings honour. The beauty radiated, since it arises from simplicity, outshines the rest of the world. Clarity is the Virtue of Heaven and Earth: this is the great Origin, the great Beginning. To have it is to be in harmony with Heaven, to bring equality with everything below Heaven and to be in harmony with all people. To be in harmony with all people is called human happiness; to be in harmony with Heaven, this is called Heavenly happiness.

Chuang Tzu said,

'My Master Teacher! My Master Teacher!
He judges all life but does not feel he is being judgemental;
he is generous to multitudes of generations
but does not think this benevolent;
he is older than the oldest
but he does not think himself old;
he overarches Heaven and sustains Earth,
shaping and creating endless bodies
but he does not think himself skilful.
This is what is known as Heavenly happiness.

'There is a saying: "If you know the happiness of Heaven, then you know that life is from Heaven and death is the transformation of things. In their stillness they are yin and in their journeying they are yang."[4] To know Heavenly happiness means that you do not upset Heaven, nor go against others. You are not reliant on material things, you are not rebuked by the ghosts. There is a saying: "He moves with Heaven and rests with Earth, his heart is one, he is the king of the whole world; the ghosts do not worry him and his soul is not wearied, his heart is one with all living beings." This means his emptiness and stillness enter all beings in Heaven and Earth, travelling alongside all beings. This is known as the Heavenly happiness. Heavenly happiness is the heart of the sage; this is how he cares for all under Heaven.'

The Virtue of Emperors and kings considers Heaven and Earth as its parents, the Tao and Virtue as its master and actionless action as its core. Through actionless action they can make the whole world do as they will and yet not be wearied. Through action they cannot even begin to fulfil what the world requires. This is why the ancient ones valued actionless action. When both the leaders and those below them are in actionless action, then both the leaders and the underlings have the same Virtue. If those below and those above share the same Virtue, then none of them is in the position of a minister. If those below act and those above act also, then those above and those below share the same Tao. If those above and those below share the same Tao, then there is no one to be the lord. However, those above tend to care for the world by actionless action, while those below care for the world by action. This has always been the case. Thus the ancient kings of the world, who knew everything about Heaven and Earth, had no designs; even though they understood the whole of life, they did not speak out; though their skills were greater than any in the lands bounded by oceans, they did nothing.

Heaven produces nothing,
yet all life is transformed;
Earth does not support,
yet all life is sustained;
the Emperor and the king take actionless action,
yet the whole world is served.
There is a saying that there is
nothing as spiritual as Heaven,
nothing as rich as Earth,
nothing as great as Emperors and kings.

It is also said that the Virtue of Emperors and kings finds its match in that of Heaven and Earth. Thus can one ascend with Heaven and Earth, gallop with all life and harness all people to the Tao.

The beginning lies with those above, the outworking with those below; the important lies with the ruler, the details with the minister.

The three armies and five types of weapons* are the irrelevant aspects of Virtue.

Handing down rewards and punishments, advantage and loss and the inflicting of the five types of sentence,† these are the irrelevant aspects of teaching.

Rituals and laws, weights and measures and all the attention to self and name are the irrelevant aspects of governing.

The sound of bells and drums, the attention to feathers and hangings, these are the irrelevant aspects of music.

The attributes of official mourning are the irrelevant aspects of grief.

These five unimportant aspects await the movement of the spirit and the liveliness of the heart's skills before they can be of service.

The ancient ones were aware of all these aspects but did not give them any importance.

The ruler precedes and the minister follows;
the father precedes and the son follows;
the elder brother precedes and the younger brother follows;
the senior one precedes and the junior follows;
the man precedes and the woman follows;
the husband precedes and the wife follows.

---

* The three armies are the standard subdivisions of a feudal state, and the five weapons are the spear, halberd, axe, shield and bow.
† The five sentences are branding or tattooing, cutting off the nose, cutting off the feet, castration and execution.

This progression of the greater followed by the lesser mirrors that of Heaven and Earth. The sages take their example from this. Heaven is elevated, Earth lowly, and this reflects their spiritual illumination. Spring and summer precede and autumn and winter follow: this is the pattern of the four seasons. In the growth of all life, their roots and buds have their appointed place and distinct shape, and from this comes maturation and then decay, the constant stream of transformation and change. If Heaven and Earth, the most perfect in spirit, have their hierarchy of precedence and sequence, then how much more should this be so with the people!

> In the ancestor shrine it is kinship which brings honour;
> in the court it is nobility;
> in the local areas it is age;
> in the governing of things it is wisdom.

This is the pattern of the great Tao. To speak about the Tao but not about its pattern of sequence goes against the Tao itself. If we speak about the Tao that has no Tao, then there is no Tao to guide!

Thus it was that the ancient ones clearly grasped the great Tao, seeking first the meaning of Heaven and then the meaning of its Tao and Virtue.

> When they clearly understood the Tao and Virtue,
> they then understood benevolence and righteousness.
> When they clearly grasped benevolence and righteousness,
> they could see how to perform their duties.
> When they grasped how to perform their duties,
> they came to understand form and fame.
> When they comprehended form and fame,
> they were able to make appointments.
> When they had made appointments,
> they went on to examining people and their efforts.
> When they had examined people's efforts,
> they moved to judgements of good or bad.
> When they had made judgements of good and bad,
> they went on to punishments and rewards.

Following this, the foolish and the wise knew what they should do and the elevated and the lowly went to their appropriate places. The good and the worthy as well as those below them found in their own selves that all had assignments adapted to their skills, appropriate to their rank. Thus did they serve those above them and encourage those below; external matters were governed and their own selves developed. Knowledge and plotting were never used and they relied upon Heaven.

This is known as the great peace and perfect government.

The Book says, 'There is form and there is title.' Form and title were known to the ancient ones, but they gave it no importance. In the olden days, when they talked of the great Tao, they spoke of the five steps which brought them to 'form and fame', or they went to nine steps and debated 'rewards and punishments'. If they had just gone straight to discussing 'form and fame' they would have shown up their ignorance of the origin; or if they had plunged straight into 'rewards and punishments' they would have shown their ignorance of the correct beginning. Those who turn the Tao upside down before talking of it, who in fact oppose the Tao before speaking of it, will be governed by other people, for they could not rule others! Those who plunge straight in, gabbling on about 'form and fame' or 'rewards and punishments', may have some understanding of the means of governing but do not understand the Tao of governing. They may be of use to the world, but they cannot use the world. They are typical pompous scholars, just stuck in their little corner. Rituals, laws, weights and measures, all the pointscoring of correct forms and titles: the ancient ones had all this, but they were the tools of those below to serve those above. Those above did not use this to rule those below.

In days gone by Shun spoke to Yao, saying, 'Being Heaven's king, how do you use your heart?'

'I do not abuse those who are defenceless,' said Yao, 'nor do I ignore the poor. I mourn for those who die, caring for the orphaned child and for the widow. This is how I use my heart.'

'Righteous as far as righteousness goes, but not that great,' commented Shun.

'What ought I to do, then?' said Yao.

'When Heaven's Virtue is found, the hills rejoice, the sun and moon shine and the four seasons are in line. The regular pattern of each day and night follows properly and the rain clouds are moved accordingly.'

Yao said, 'So all I've really been doing is getting worked up and bothered! You seek compliance with Heaven, whereas I have sought compliance with humanity.'

Since earliest times Heaven and Earth have been known as great. The Yellow Emperor, Yao and Shun have all praised them. The ancient kings who ruled all under Heaven, did they need to act? Heaven and Earth were sufficient for them.

Confucius travelled west to place his books in the archives of Chou. Tzu Lu offered advice, saying, 'I have heard that the official in charge of the Royal Archives is Lao Tzu. But he has resigned and lives at home. Sir, if you want to place your books there, go and see him and ask his assistance.'

'Splendid,' said Confucius. So off he went to see Lao Tzu,[5] but Lao Tzu refused to help. So Confucius took out his Twelve Classics, and started to preach.

When he was halfway through, Lao Tzu said, 'This is too much. Put it briefly.'

Confucius said, 'In essence, it is benevolence and righteousness.'

'May I ask,' said Lao Tzu, 'are benevolence and righteousness of the very essence of humanity?'

'Certainly,' said Confucius. 'If the nobleman is without benevolence, he has no purpose; if without righteousness, he has no life. Benevolence and righteousness, these are truly of the innate nature of humanity. How else could it be?'

'May I ask, what are benevolence and righteousness?'

'To be at one, centred in one's heart, in love with all, without selfishness, this is what benevolence and righteousness are,' replied Confucius.

'Really! Your words reveal misunderstanding,' said Lao Tzu. ' "Love of all", that's both vague and an exaggeration! "Without selfishness", isn't that rather selfish? Sir, if you want people to remain simple, shouldn't you look to the ways of Heaven and Earth?

'Heaven and Earth have their boundaries which are constant;
the sun and moon hold their courses in their brightness;
the stars and planets proceed in the boundaries of their order;
the birds and creatures find their confines within their herds and flocks.
Think of the trees which stand within their own boundaries in order.

'So Sir, walk with Virtue and travel with the Tao, and you will reach the perfect end. Why bother with all this benevolence and righteousness, prancing along as if you were beating a drum and looking for a lost child? Sir, you will just confuse people's true nature!'

Shih Cheng Chi came to see Lao Tzu and asked him, 'I have heard tell that you, Sir, are a sage, so I came to see you, regardless of the length of the journey. Over the hundred nights of the journey my feet became blistered, but I did not stop nor rest. Now I find, Sir, that you are not a sage. Even though you were wealthy enough for even the rat holes of your house to be full of left-over rice, you nevertheless kicked your poor little sister out of the house. What an unkind action! When your food is placed before you, even if you cannot eat it all, you hoard it, whether it is raw or cooked.'

Lao Tzu showed no emotion and made no reply. The next day Shih Cheng Chi came to see him again and said, 'Yesterday I was rude to you, Sir. Today I have no heart for it. Why is this?'

Lao Tzu said, 'I think I have freed myself from knowledge, from the spiritual and from being a sage. If you had called me an ox yesterday, Sir, then I would have said I was an ox. If you had called me a horse, I would have said I was a horse. If people name a reality, but someone won't have it, then he just makes life more problematic. I am always like this, I don't just put it on for certain occasions.'

Shih Cheng Chi shrank back so as not to be even near Lao Tzu's shadow, then he came forward once more in a humble way and asked how he could cultivate himself. Lao Tzu said, 'Your face is unpleasant; your eyes glare; your forehead is broad; your mouth hangs open; your style is pompous; you are like a tethered horse waiting to bolt, ready to go like an arrow from a crossbow; you examine everything in too much detail; you are cunning in your use of knowledge, yet you lounge around. All this makes me distrust you. Out on the frontier someone like you would be called a bandit.'

The Master said,

'The Tao does not hesitate before that which is vast,
nor does it abandon the small.
Thus it is that all life is enlivened by it.
So immense, so immense there is nothing which is not held by it;
so deep, so unfathomable beyond any reckoning.
The form of its Virtue is in benevolence and righteousness,
though this is a minor aspect of its spirit.
Who but the perfect man could comprehend all this?
The perfect man has charge of this age,
a somewhat daunting task!
However, this does not fool him or trap him.
He holds the reins of power over the whole world
but it is of little consequence to him.
His discernment unearths all falsehood
but he gives no thought to personal gain.
He gets to the heart of issues and knows how to protect the foundation of
    truth.
Thus Heaven and Earth are outside him,
he ignores all life and his spirit is never wearied.
He travels with the Tao,
is in agreement with Virtue,
bids farewell to benevolence and righteousness
and ignores ritual and music,
because the perfect man has set his heart upon what is right.'

This generation believes that the value of the Tao is to be found in books. But books are nothing more than words, and words have value but only in terms of their meaning. Meaning is constantly seeking to express what cannot be said in words and thus passed on. This generation values words and puts them into books, yet what it values is perhaps mistaken, because what it values is not really all that valuable. So we look at things and see things, but it is only an outward form and colour, and what can be heard is just the name and sound. How sad that this generation imagines that the form, colour, name and sound are enough to capture the essence of something! The form, colour, name and sound are in no way sufficient to capture or convey the truth, which is why it is said that the knowledgeable do not speak and those who speak are not knowledgeable. But how can this generation understand this?

Duke Huan was sitting up in his hall reading a book. The wheelwright Pien was down below in the courtyard making a wheel. He put down his chisel and hammer, went up to the hall and asked Duke Huan, 'May I ask you, Sir, what words you are reading?'

Duke Huan replied, 'The words of the sages.'

'Are these sages still living?'

'They are long dead,' said Duke Huan.

'Then, Sir, what you are reading is nothing but rubbish left over from these ancient men!'

'How dare you, a wheelwright, comment on what I read! If you can explain this, fine, if not you shall die!' thundered Duke Huan.

The wheelwright Pien replied, 'Your Lordship's servant looks at it from the perspective of his own work. When I work on a wheel, if I hit too softly, pleasant as this is, it doesn't make for a good wheel. If I hit furiously, I get tired and the thing doesn't work! So, not too soft, not too vigorous, I grasp it in my hand and hold it in my heart. I cannot express this by word of mouth, I just know it. I cannot teach this to my son, nor can my son learn it from me. So for seventy years I have gone along this path and here I am still making wheels. The ancient ones, when they died, took their words with them. Which is why I can state that what Your Lordship is reading is nothing more than rubbish left over from these ancient ones!'

Chapter 14: Does Heaven Move?

. . . Tang, the Prime Minister of Shang, asked Chuang Tzu about benevolence. Chuang Tzu said, 'Tigers and wolves are benevolent.'

'What do you mean?'

'The father cares for his children,' said Chuang Tzu. 'Is this not benevolence?'

'But it is perfect benevolence that I am interested in.'

'Perfect benevolence has nothing to do with affection,' said Chuang Tzu.

But the Prime Minister replied, 'I have heard that where there is no affection, there is no love; where there is no love, there is no filial piety. Do you mean to say that perfect benevolence is without filial piety?'

'Certainly not. Perfect benevolence is of the highest order, and words such as "filial piety" cannot describe it. What you want to say is not that filial piety is surpassed, but that nothing even comes close to it. When a traveller goes south and then turns to face north when he has reached Ying, he cannot see Ming mountain. Why is this? Because it is far away. There is the saying: filial piety arising from respect is easy, filial piety arising from love is hard. If filial piety from love is easy, then to forget your parents is hard. It is easy to forget your parents, but it is hard to make my parents forget me. It is easy to make my parents forget me, but it is hard to make me forget the whole world. It is easy to forget the whole world, but it is hard for the whole world to forget me.

'Virtue ignores Yao and Shun and dwells in actionless action. Its benefits embrace every generation, though no one in the world understands this. Despite your protestations, how can you talk of benevolence and filial piety? Filial piety, mutual respect, benevolence, righteousness, loyalty, integrity, resoluteness and purity, all of these can be of service to Virtue. But they are not worthy in themselves. So it is said,

> ' "Perfect nobility disregards the honours of state;
> Perfect richness ignores the wealth of the country;
> Perfect fulfilment ignores fame and glory.
> Alone of all, the Tao never alters." ' . . .

. . . Confucius had pottered along for fifty-one years and had never heard anyone speak of the Tao until he went south to Pei and went to see Lao Tzu.

Lao Tzu said, 'So you've come then, Sir? I have heard of you, that you are the wise man of the north. Have you, Sir, followed the Tao?'

'I have not yet followed it,' replied Confucius.

'Well, Sir, where have you looked?'

'I looked for it in what can be measured and regulated, but even after five years I still haven't been able to find it.'

'So, Sir, what did you do then?' asked Lao Tzu.

'I looked for it in yin and yang, but ten, twelve years went by and I still couldn't find it.'

'Obviously!' said Lao Tzu. 'If the Tao could be served up, everyone would serve it up to their lords. If the Tao could be offered, there is no one who would not offer it to their parents. If the Tao could be spoken of, there is no one who would not speak of it to their brothers and sisters. If the Tao could be passed on, there is no one who would not pass it on to their heirs. However, it obviously cannot be so and the reason is as follows.

'If there is no true centre within to receive it,
it cannot remain;
if there is no true direction outside to guide it,
it cannot be received.
If the true centre is not brought out
it cannot receive on the outside.
The sage cannot draw it forth.
If what comes in from the outside is not welcomed by the true centre,
then the sage cannot let it go.
Fame is something sought by all,
but don't go for too much of it.
Benevolence and righteousness are as the houses of the former kings,
useful for one night's shelter,
but don't stay there too long.
To stay long causes considerable adverse comment.

'The perfect man of old walked the Tao of benevolence, a path which he took on loan; he used righteousness as a place to lodge for a night. So it was that he ambled through the void and uncontrolled places; found food in the open fields and enjoyed the gardens which were not his. To be in such freedom, you must take actionless action. The open fields make living easy. He gives nothing and requires nothing. The ancient ones knew this as the wandering of the Truth Gatherer.

'Someone who believes wealth is the most important thing cannot give up their income; someone who seeks pre-eminence cannot give up the hunt for fame; those who love power cannot hand it over to others.

'Those who cling to things like these are usually fearful. Letting them go just once causes such agony that they will not consider even once doing so, although it would show them the folly of their ways. These are people bearing the punishment of Heaven. Hatred and kindness, taking and giving, correction and instruction, life and death, these eight things are tools of reform. However, only the one who abides by the great change and who does not stand in its way can use them. So it is said, to correct is to reform. If the heart cannot accept this, then the gate of Heaven is not opened.'

Confucius went to see Lao Tzu and talked with him about benevolence and righteousness. Lao Tzu said, 'If you get grit in your eye from winnowing chaff, then Heaven and Earth and the four directions get mixed up. A mosquito or gadfly which stings you can keep you awake all night. And benevolence and righteousness, when forced upon us, disturb your heart and produce great distress. You, Sir, if you want to stop everything below Heaven losing its original simplicity, you must travel with the wind and stand firm in Virtue. Why do you exert yourself so much, banging a big drum and hunting for a lost child? The snow goose doesn't need a daily bath to stay white, nor does the crow need to be stained every day to stay black. Black and white comes from natural simplicity, not from argument. Fame and fortune, though sought after, do not make people greater than they actually are. When the waters dry up and the fish are stranded on the dry land, they huddle together and try to keep each other moist by spitting and wetting each other. But wouldn't it be even better if they could just forget each other, safe in their lakes and rivers?'

After seeing Lao Tzu, Confucius went home and for three days he said nothing.

. . . Confucius said to Lao Tzu, 'I have mastered the *Poems*, the *Histories*, the *Rites*, the *Music*, the *I Ching* and the *Spring and Autumn* – all of the Six Classics. I know them inside out. However, I have discussed them with seventy-two rulers, telling them of the Tao of the first kinds and the illumination of the path trodden by Chou and Shao, but not one king has been interested. They've done nothing! It is so difficult to preach to such people! How can I make the Tao clear to them?'

Lao Tzu said, 'It is very lucky, Sir, that you did not discover a ruler who would try to govern this generation in such a way! The Six Classics are the tired footpaths of the first kings, not the actual feet that trod those paths! Now, Sir, what you are going on about is just these worn footpaths. But footpaths are created by the feet that first walked them. They are not the feet themselves! The white herons only have to look into each other's eyes without blinking for impregnation to happen. A male insect buzzes above and the female replies from below and impregnation takes place, borne upon the air. The creature called Lei contains both male and female and so impregnates itself. Innate nature does not change; fate is unalterable; time cannot be stopped and the Tao cannot be halted. Hold fast to the Tao and there is nothing it cannot do; lose it and there is nothing that can be done.'

Confucius did not go out for three months, then he went to see Lao Tzu and said, 'I've grasped it! The raven hatches its young; the fish spew forth their eggs; the slim-waisted wasp transforms, and when a younger brother comes along the elder brother weeps. For too long I have not been able to work in harmony with these changes. So, given that I did not play my part in harmony with others, how could I expect to change people?'

Lao Tzu replied, 'Well done. So now you've grasped it.'

Notes

1 'Virtue' (*te*) sometimes refers, as here, to something like people's nature or dispositions. Elsewhere it has more of the ethical connotation that we associate with the word.

2 'Heaven' (*tsien*) seems to have no 'supernatural' meaning for Chuang Tzu. Often it seems to mean no more than 'Nature'.

3 Here, but not always, 'the perfect sage' is used ironically, to refer to the sage as portrayed by Confucians.

4 *Yin* and *Yang* in ancient Chinese cosmology are the two opposed, yet mutually dependent, principles – 'dark', 'feminine' and 'hidden' *versus* 'bright', 'masculine' and 'open' – whose interaction produces balance in the universe.

5 The references to Lao Tzu should not be taken as evidence that the author(s) regard him as an actual person. Many of the figures in whose mouths words are put are clearly fictitious.

The Bhagavad Gita, chapters 1–5   6

From The Bhagavad Gita, trans. W. J. Johnson. Oxford: Oxford University Press, 1994, pp. 4–24 [first part of chapter 1 and last part of chapter 5 omitted; asterisked notes are the translator's]; reprinted by permission of Oxford University Press.

For hundreds of millions of people over the centuries, *The Bhagavad Gita* ('The Song of the Lord') has been the most important text ever composed. Its canonical status for many Hindus, especially the devotees of Vishnu, is primarily due to the later chapters' articulation – for the first time in Indian literature – of a theistic, devotional religion. But the *Gita* begins with and is structured by a concrete moral dilemma and the account of moral action within which that dilemma is resolved has, despite its ambiguities, been inspirational for countless later writers, not least Mahatma Gandhi, for whom it was an 'infallible guide', a 'dictionary of daily reference'.[1]

The *Gita*, probably composed around the third century BCE, is a short philosophical interlude within the massive epic *The Mahabharata*, which tells of the rivalry between two branches of a royal clan which eventually leads to war. Just before the decisive battle, the leading hero of one branch, Arjuna, is assailed by doubt. Although it is his duty as a member of the *kshatriya* (nobleman warrior) caste to fight and although justice is on the side of his branch of the family, ought he really to kill his kinsmen in what is bound to be a devastating war from which he can expect no peace or happiness? The *Gita* records the attempt of Arjuna's charioteer – who, it turns out, is Krishna, the embodiment or avatar of the god Vishnu – to dispel the hero's doubts and urge him to fight. (I take it as obvious that, while Arjuna's predicament may be sharpened by his caste allegiance, the kind of dilemma he faces is one that people outside of any caste system might face – a modern-day soldier, for example, embroiled in a civil war.)

Krishna's strategy of argument, wisely enough, is not simply to remind Arjuna of a code of duties and the dishonour that disobedience will bring – for of course it is precisely the validity of this code which Arjuna is questioning. The

---

[1] *The Sayings of Mahatma Gandhi*, Singapore: Brash, 1984, p. 78.

strategy, rather, is to impart a philosophical understanding of the cosmos, and of the individual's place within it, which will enable the reluctant hero to see that fighting is his proper course. Krishna's emphasis on understanding and knowledge – on seeing, for example, that only *bodies* can be killed, not the selves or souls of their owners (2.18) – soon prompts Arjuna to wonder, however, why *action*, including the performance of soldierly duties, should matter at all. In wondering this, he gives voice to the central problem in traditional Hindu or Brahminical thought. According to that scheme of thought, the true human goal is that of freedom or release (*moksha*) from the round of rebirth, with the apparent implication that morality is, as the philosopher Śaṃkara was to say, a mere 'preliminary' – useful but inessential training, perhaps, for the acquisition of that knowledge of *Brahman* (the underlying principle of reality) which enables release.[2] It is remarks like this which prompted Western commentators like Albert Schweitzer to deny that Indian thought was genuinely ethical.[3]

In replying to Arjuna's question, Krishna offers a retort to this downgrading of ethics and rejects the idea that it is through renunciation and navel-gazing contemplation that freedom and release are to be obtained. Human beings, he insists, cannot avoid acting (3.5): even the contemplative yogi must beg and eat. The real issue, therefore, is to ascertain which actions are without those karmic consequences which bind a person to the cycle of rebirth. For Krishna, these are actions performed without 'attachment' – without desires, interests and future consequences in mind (3.7ff. (Readers will note a parallel with the Taoist ideal of 'actionless action', see chapter 5 above.) Arjuna is encouraged to adopt this detached stance towards his action by reflecting that, strictly speaking, it is never the *self* which acts, for the self is something separate from the physical processes of the world which owe to the operation of underlying material constituents. Provided Arjuna does his duty purely for its own sake, and hence without attachment, he will obtain release. There is, therefore, no conflict between the two 'disciplines' (*yogas*) of action and knowledge: for proper action is what is conducted with true understanding of one's self and reality at large. Through a true 'vision of cosmic reality', Arjuna is 'in a position to act from the motive of duty alone'.[4]

There are anticipations, here, of Immanuel Kant, although it needs to be stressed that the duty Arjuna is exhorted to perform is that of his 'station in life', not one which, as for Kant, is binding on all rational beings as such (see chapter 11 below). Certainly the ethical position urged in the *Gita* has been

---

[2] A. J. Alston, *A Śaṃkara Source-Book*, vol. 5, London: Shanti Sadan, 1989, p. 107.
[3] See S. Radhakrishnan, *Eastern Religions and Western Thought*, Oxford: Clarendon Press, 1939, chapter 3.
[4] M. M. Agrawal, 'Arjuna's moral predicament', in B. K. Motilal (ed.), *Moral Dilemmas in the Mahabharata*, M. Banarsidass: Delhi, 1989, p. 140.

subjected to the same criticism as Kant's: that of preaching an unacceptable 'coldness' in our affective relations to one another. (In gaudier editions of the *Gita*, pictures of Arjuna and Krishna, serene and smiling as they scythe their way through the enemy, can indeed be chilling.)[5] Nobody, however, can gainsay the seriousness of the *Gita*'s attempt to seek for a resolution of moral dilemmas and an articulation of a moral stance within the framework of a metaphysical system.

Several Indian names occur in the chapters selected. Sanjaya, the narrator, is court bard to Dhritarashtra, King of Arjuna's enemies. Most of the other names, such as Govinda and Bharata, are alternative names or titles of either Krishna or Arjuna. Some other names are explained in the notes.

Chapter 1

◀ ◀ ◀

[. . .]

26   There Arjuna saw, standing their ground, fathers, grandfathers, teachers, maternal uncles, brothers, sons, grandsons, friends,

27   Fathers-in-law, and companions in both armies. And looking at all these kinsmen so arrayed, Arjuna, the son of Kunti,

28   Was overcome by deep compassion; and in despair he said: 'Krishna, when I see these my own people eager to fight, on the brink,

29   'My limbs grow heavy, and my mouth is parched, my body trembles and my hair bristles,

30   'My bow, Gandiva, falls from my hand, my skin's on fire, I can no longer stand – my mind is reeling,

31   'I see evil omens, Krishna: nothing good can come from slaughtering one's own family in battle – I foresee it!

32   'I have no desire for victory, Krishna, or kingship, or pleasures. What should we do with kingship, Govinda? What are pleasures to us? What is life?

33   'The men for whose sake we desire kingship, enjoyment and pleasures are precisely those drawn up for this battle, having abandoned their lives and riches.

34   'Teachers, fathers, sons, as well as grandfathers, maternal uncles, fathers-in-law, grandsons, brothers-in-law, and kinsmen –

35   'I have no desire to kill them, Madhusudana, though they are killers themselves – no, not for the lordship of the three worlds,* let alone the earth!

---

[5] See Arthur Danto, *Mysticism and Morality*, Harmondsworth: Penguin, 1976, p. 99.
* Heaven, earth, and the atmosphere or sometimes the lower regions.

36   'Where is the joy for us, Janardana, in destroying Dhritarashtra's people? Having killed these murderers, evil would attach itself to us.

37   'It follows, therefore, that we are not required to kill the sons of Dhritarashtra – they are our own kinsmen, and having killed our own people, how could we be happy, Madhava?

38   'And even if, because their minds are overwhelmed by greed, *they* cannot see the evil incurred by destroying one's own family, and the degradation involved in the betrayal of a friend,

39   'How can *we* be so ignorant as not to recoil from this wrong? The evil incurred by destroying one's own family is plain to see, Janardana.

40   'With the destruction of family the eternal family laws are lost; when the law is destroyed, lawlessness overpowers the entire family.

41   'Krishna, because of overpowering lawlessness, the women of the family are corrupted; when women are corrupted, Varshneya, there is inter-mingling of the four estates.[1]

42   'And intermingling leads to hell for the family-destroyers *and* the family, for their ancestors, robbed of their rice-ball and water offerings, fall back.

43   'Through these evils of the family-destroyers, which cause inter-mingling of the four estates, caste laws and the eternal family laws are obliterated.

44   'For men whose family laws have been obliterated we have heard that a place in hell is certain, Janardana.

45   'Oh, ignominy! We are about to perpetrate a great evil – out of sheer greed for kingdoms and pleasures, we are prepared to kill our own people.

46   'It would be better for me if Dhritarashtra's armed men were to kill me in battle, unresisting and unarmed.'

47   Having spoken this on the field of conflict, Arjuna sank down into the chariot, letting slip his bow and arrow, his mind distracted with grief.

Chapter 2

Sanjaya said:

1   Then, Krishna, the destroyer of the demon Madhu, spoke these words to the dejected Arjuna, who, eyes blurred and brimming with tears, was so overcome by pity:

The Lord said:

2   Arjuna, where do you get this weakness from at a moment of crisis? A

noble should not experience this. It does not lead to heaven, it leads to disgrace.

3 No impotence, Partha, it does not become you. Abandon this base, inner weakness. Get up, Incinerator of the Foe!

Arjuna said:

4 Destroyer of Madhu, destroyer of the enemy, how can I shoot arrows at Bhishma and Drona in battle when they should be honoured?

5 Better to eat begged food among common people than to kill such worthy teachers. For having killed my teachers, who desire legitimate worldly ends, I should be consuming food smeared with blood.

6 And we do not know which is better for us – that we should overcome Dhritarashtra's men, standing there before us, or that they should overcome us. For if we were to kill them, we should have no desire to go on living.

7 My inner being is disabled by that vice of dejection. My mind is bewildered as to what is right. I ask you, which would be better? Tell me for certain. I am your student, I have come to you for help. Instruct me!

8 Though I were to obtain a prosperous, unrivalled kingdom on earth, and even mastery over the gods, I cannot imagine what could dispel my grief, which withers the senses.

Sanjaya said:

9 And having spoken thus to Krishna, to Govinda, having said 'I will not fight!' Arjuna, the Incinerator of the Foe, fell silent.

10 O Dhritarashtra, between the two armies, Krishna, with the shadow of a smile, spoke these words to that dejected man:

The Lord said:

11 You utter wise *words*, yet you have been mourning those who should not be mourned; the truly wise do not grieve for the living or the dead.

12 There never was a time when I was not, or you, or these rulers of men. Nor will there ever be a time when we shall cease to be, all of us hereafter.

13 Just as within this body the embodied self passes through childhood, youth and old age, so it passes to another body. The wise man is not bewildered by this.

14 But contacts with matter, Son of Kunti, give rise to cold and heat, pleasure and pain. They come and go, Bharata; they are impermanent and you should endure them.

15 For these things, Bull among men, do not perturb that wise man for whom pleasure and pain are the same; he is ready for immortality.

16   For the non-existent there is no coming into existence, for the existent there is no lapsing into non-existence; the division between them is observed by those who see the underlying nature of things.

17   But know that that on which all this is stretched is indestructible. No one can destroy this imperishable one.

18   It is just these *bodies* of the indestructible, immeasurable, and eternal embodied self that are characterized as coming to an end – therefore fight, Bharata!

19   Anyone who believes this a killer, and anyone who thinks this killed, they do not understand: it does not kill, it is not killed

20   It is not born, it never dies; being, it will never again cease to be. It is unborn, invariable, eternal, primeval. It is not killed when the body is killed.

21   Partha, how can that man who knows it to be indestructible, invariable, unborn and imperishable bring about the death of anyone? Whom does he kill?

22   Just as a man casting off worn-out clothes takes up others that are new, so the embodied self, casting off its worn-out bodies, goes to other, new ones.

23   Blades do not pierce it, fire does not burn it, waters do not wet it, and the wind does not parch it.

24   It cannot be pierced, it cannot be burned, it cannot be wetted, it cannot be parched. It is invariable, everywhere, fixed, immovable, eternal.

25   It is said to be imperceptible, unthinkable and immutable; knowing it to be so, you should not therefore grieve.

26   And even if you believe that it is regularly born and regularly dead, you should not grieve for it, Great Arm.

27   Death is inevitable for those who are born; for those who are dead birth is just as certain. Therefore you must not grieve for what is ineluctable.

28   Bharata, beings have imperceptible beginnings; the interim is clear; their ends are again indistinct. What is there to lament in this?

29   Quite exceptionally does anyone see it, and quite exceptionally does anyone speak of it; it is quite exceptional for anyone to hear of it, but even when they have heard of it, no one in fact knows it.

30   Bharata, this embodied self in the body of everyone is eternally unkillable. Therefore you must not grieve for any beings at all.

31   Recognizing your inherent duty, you must not shrink from it. For there is nothing better for a warrior than a duty-bound war.

32 It is a door to heaven, opened fortuitously. Fortunate are the warriors, Partha, who are presented with such a war.

33 But if, careless of your inherent duty and renown, you will not undertake this duty-bound conflict, you shall transgress.

34 Moreover, people will recount your limitless disgrace – and disgrace is worse than death for the man who has once been honoured.

35 The great warriors will suppose that you withdrew from the battle out of fear. And you will fade from their high regard into insignificance.

36 Then your enemies will say many things that would be better unsaid, slighting your strength – and what could be more painful than that?

37 You will either be killed and attain heaven, or conquer and enjoy the earth. So rise, Son of Kunti, determined to fight.

38 Making yourself indifferent to pleasure and pain, gain and loss, victory and defeat, commit yourself to battle. And in that way you shall not transgress.

39 You have received this intelligence according to Sankhya theory,[2] now hear it as it applies to practice. Disciplined with such intelligence, Partha, you shall throw off the bondage of action.

40 In this there is no wasted effort, no reverse; just a little of this truth saves from great danger.

41 Son of the Kurus, in this the resolute intelligence is one, the intellects of the irresolute are without limit and many-branched.

42 Partha, that florid speech the uninspired utter, addicted to the words of the Veda,* claiming that there is nothing else.

43 Their nature desire, their aim heaven – that speech which produces rebirth as the fruit of action, and which is dense with specific ritual acts aimed at the attainment of enjoyment and power,

44 Robs those addicted to enjoyment and power of their minds. For them no resolute intelligence is established in concentration.

45 The Vedas' sphere of activity is the three constituents of material nature. Arjuna, be free from the three constituents, free from duality, forever grounded in purity, beyond getting and keeping, possessed of the self.

46 For the brahmin who knows, there is no more purpose in all the Vedas than in a water-tank surrounded by a flood.

47 You are qualified simply with regard to action, never with regard to its results. You must be neither motivated by the results of action nor attached to inaction.

48 Grounded in yogic discipline, and having abandoned attachment,

* The revealed texts of Brahminical religion and mainstream Hinduism.

undertake actions, Dhananjaya, evenly disposed as to their success or failure. Yoga is defined as evenness of mind.

49   For action in itself is inferior by far to the discipline of intelligence, Dhananjaya. You must seek refuge in intelligence. Those motivated by results are wretched.

50   The man disciplined in intelligence renounces in this world the results of both good and evil actions. Therefore commit yourself to yogic discipline; yogic discipline is skill in actions.

51   For, having abandoned the result produced from action, those who understand, who are disciplined in intelligence, are freed from the bondage of rebirth and achieve a state without disease.

52   When your intelligence emerges from the thicket of delusion, then you will become disenchanted with what is to be heard and has been heard in the Veda.

53   When, turned away from the Veda, your intelligence stands motionless, immovable in concentration, then you will attain yogic discipline.

Arjuna said:

54   O Keshava, how do you describe that man whose mentality is stable, whose concentration is fixed? What should the man whose thought is settled say? How should he sit? How should he walk?

The Lord said:

55   Partha, when he abandons every desire lodged in the mind, by himself content within the self, then he is called a man of stable mentality.

56   He is called a holy man, settled in thought, whose mind is not disturbed in the midst of sorrows, who has lost the desire for pleasures, whose passion, fear and anger have disappeared.

57   His mentality is stabilized who feels no desire for anything, for getting this or that good or evil, and who neither rejoices in nor loathes anything.

58   When this man, like a tortoise retracting its limbs, entirely withdraws his senses from the objects of sense, his mentality is stabilized.

59   For the embodied being who does not feed on them the objects of sense disappear, except flavour; flavour fades too for the one who has seen the highest.

60   Son of Kunti, even for the man of discernment who strives, the harassing senses forcibly seize the mind.

61   Restraining all the senses, one should sit, yogically disciplined, focused on me; for if one's senses are under control one's mentality is grounded.

62   When a man meditates on the objects of sense he becomes attached

to them; from attachment desire is born, from desire anger.

63 Out of anger confusion arises, through confusion memory wanders, from loss of memory the intelligence is destroyed; from the destruction of intelligence a man is lost.

64 But engaging the objects of sense with his senses separated from desire and loathing, and subject to the will of the self, a man who is self-controlled attains calmness.

65 In calm all his miseries are ended, for the intelligence of the man whose mind is calm is immediately stabilized.

66 The undisciplined man has no intelligence, and no capacity to produce anything, and one who has no capacity is without serenity. And how can there be happiness for the man who lacks serenity?

67 For a mind conforming to the wandering senses carries away one's insight, as the wind a ship on the water.

68 Therefore, Great Arm, whoever has entirely withheld the senses from the objects of sense has stabilized his insight.

69 When it is night for all creatures, the man who restrains himself is awake; when creatures are awake, it is night for the perceptive seer.

70 Just as waters enter the sea, which is forever being filled although its depths are unmoving, so the man whom all desires enter in the same way attains peace – but not the desirer of desires.

71 The man who, having abandoned all desires, lives free from longing, unpossessive and unegoistical, approaches peace.

72 This, Partha, is the Brahman state; having attained it, one is not deluded; fixed in it, even at the moment of death one reaches the nirvana of Brahman.[3]

Chapter 3

Arjuna said:

1 Krishna, if it is your belief that the way of intelligence is superior to action, then why do you enjoin me, Keshava, to this terrible undertaking?

2 With such equivocal words you seem to confuse my intelligence. Describe clearly an unambiguous way through which I may attain what is best.

The Lord said:

3 Blameless one, I have taught of old that in this world two ways are open: the discipline of knowledge for Sankhya theorists, and the discipline of action for yogins.

4   A man does not attain freedom from the results of action by abstaining from actions, and he does not approach perfection simply by renunciation.

5   For no one ever, even for a moment, exists without acting; everyone, regardless of their will, is made to perform actions by the constituents which originate from material nature.

6   The man who, having restrained his action organs, then sits with his mind preoccupied with sense objects, is called a self-deluding hypocrite.

7   But the man who, controlling his senses with his mind, undertakes through his action organs the discipline of action without attachment, distinguishes himself, Arjuna.

8   You should perform enjoined action, for action is better than non-action; even the minimum of bodily subsistence would be impossible without action.

9   The entire world is bound by actions; the only exception is action undertaken for sacrificial purposes. Therefore, Son of Kunti, free from attachment, you should perform that kind of action.

10   When he created creatures in the beginning, along with the sacrifice, Prajapati* said: 'May you be fruitful by this sacrifice, let this be the cow which produces all you desire.

11   'You should nourish the gods with this so that the gods may nourish you; nourishing each other, you shall achieve the highest good.

12   'For nourished by the sacrifice, the gods will give you the pleasures you desire. The man who enjoys these gifts without repaying them is no more than a thief.'

13   The virtuous who eat the remainder of the sacrifice are released from all faults; the wicked who cook for the sake of themselves consume impurity.

14   Beings exist through food, the origin of food is rain, rain comes from sacrifice, sacrifice derives from action.

15   Know that action originates from Brahman – Brahman whose source is the imperishable. Therefore all-pervading Brahman is eternally established in the sacrifice.

16   Whoever in this world does not turn the wheel thus set in motion, Partha, lives in vain, making a pleasure garden of his senses, intent upon evil.

17   But it is clear that, for the man who delights in the self, and is satisfied with the self, and fulfilled only in the self, there is nothing that has to be done.[4]

* The 'Lord of Creatures' . . . protector of life and procreation.

18 For him there is no significance whatsoever in what has been done or has not been done in this world, and he has no kind of dependence at all on any being.

19 Therefore, without attachment, always do whatever action has to be done; for it is through acting without attachment that a man attains the highest.

20 Indeed, it was by action alone that King Janaka and others attained perfection. Looking only to what maintains the world, you too must act.

21 Whatever the superior man does, so do the rest; whatever standard he sets, the world follows it.

22 Partha, as for me there is nothing whatever that has to be done in the three worlds; there is nothing unaccomplished to be accomplished. Yet I still engage in action.

23 For were I not to engage tirelessly in action, humans everywhere would follow in my wake, Partha.

24 If I did not engage in action, these worlds would fall into ruin; I should be the instrument of anarchy; I should destroy these creatures.

25 Just as the ignorant act out of attachment to action, Bharata, so the wise should also act, but without attachment, intent upon maintaining the world.

26 The wise man should not disturb the minds of those ignorant people who are attached to action; acting in a disciplined manner himself, he should encourage involvement in all actions.

27 In every case, actions are performed by the constituents of material nature; although the man who is deluded by egotism thinks to himself, '*I* am the actor.'

28 But he who knows the principle underlying the division of constituents and actions, understanding that it is constituents that are acting on constituents, is not attached, Great Arm.

29 The person whose knowledge is comprehensive should not agitate those dullards whose knowledge is not so great – those who are deluded by the constituents of material nature and attached to the actions of the constituents.

30 Giving up all actions to me, with your mind on what relates to the self, desireless and not possessive, fight! Your fever is past.

31 Faithful, uncontentious men, who constantly practise this doctrine of mine, are also released from the results of action.

32 But you should know that those who object to this, who do not follow my doctrine, and who are blind to all knowledge, are mindless and lost.

33 Even the one who knows acts in accordance with his own material nature. Creatures conform to material nature – what good will repression do?

34 In the case of a sense, desire and aversion adhere to the object of that sense; you should not fall into the power of those two, for they will block your path.

35 It is better to practise your own inherent duty deficiently than another's duty well. It is better to die conforming to your own duty; the duty of others invites danger.

Arjuna said:

36 So what is it that impels a man to do evil, Varshneya, even unwillingly, as though compelled to it by force?

The Lord said:

37 It is desire, it is anger, produced from the constituent of passion, all-consuming, all-injuring; know that that is the enemy here.

38 As a fire is covered by smoke and a mirror by dust; as an embryo is covered by a sac, this world is enveloped by that.

39 By this perpetual enemy of the wise, by this insatiable fire in the form of desire, knowledge is obscured, Son of Kunti.

40 It is said that the senses, the mind and the intelligence are its locality; having obscured a man's knowledge with these, it deludes the embodied self.

41 Therefore, having first restrained the senses, Bull of the Bharatas, strike down this evil thing, the destroyer of insight and knowledge.

42 They say that the senses are great; the mind is greater than the senses. Yet greater than the mind is the intelligence; but he [i.e. the true self – Ed.] is that which is still greater than the intelligence.

43 So, Great Arm, having learned what is higher than the intelligence, and having strengthened yourself through the self, kill that enemy in the shape of desire, so difficult to pin down.

Chapter 4

The Lord said:

1 I taught this eternal way to Vivasvat; Vivasvat showed it to Manu; Manu told it to Ikshvaku.*

* Vivasvat [is] a sun god and the father of the original ancestor of the human race, Manu. Ikshvaku is one of Manu's sons.

2   And it was this way, passed on from teacher to teacher in an unbroken line, that the royal seers knew. Over a long period of time here on earth that track was obliterated, Incinerator of the Foe.

3   It is this very same ancient way that I have shown you now, for you are devoted, and my friend, and this is the most secret teaching.

Arjuna said:

4   You were born recently, Vivasvat was born a long time ago, so what should I understand by the saying that you taught it in the beginning?

The Lord said:

5   I have passed through many births, and so have you, Arjuna. I know them all, you do not, Incinerator of the Foe.

6   Although I am unborn and have a self that is eternal, although I am lord of beings, by controlling my own material nature I come into being by means of my own incomprehensible power.

7   Whenever there is a falling away from the true law and an upsurge of unlawfulness, then, Bharata, I emit myself.

8   I come into being age after age, to protect the virtuous and to destroy evil-doers, to establish a firm basis for the true law.

9   Whoever knows my divine birth and action as they really are is not born again on leaving the body. He comes to me, Arjuna.

10 There are many, free of passion, fear and anger, at one with me, taking refuge in me, who, refined in the heat of knowledge, have come to my state of being.

11 I favour them according to the manner in which they approach me. Men, Partha, universally follow my path.

12 Desiring the attainment that comes from ritual acts, men here sacrifice to the gods; for in the human world the attainment born of sacrificial action comes quickly.

13 The four estates were created by me, divided according to constituents and actions. Although I alone am the one who did this, know that I am an eternal non-actor.

14 Actions do not taint me. I have no desire for the results of action. Whoever understands that I am like this is not bound by actions.

15 Men of old who desired release knew this and acted. Therefore you should act as they once acted.

16 What is action, what is non-action? Even inspired seers are confused about this. Such action I shall explain to you, and understanding it you shall be freed from evil.

17 You should know what constitutes action, wrong action, and non-action. The way of action runs deep.

18   He who sees action in non-action, non-action in action, is wise among men; performing all actions he is disciplined.

19   The wise call him a man of learning whose every activity is free from desire and specific intention; his actions are consumed in the fire of knowledge.

20   That man who depends upon nothing, who has given up attachment to the results of action, is perpetually satisfied, and even though engaged in action he does nothing whatsoever.

21   Acting for the body alone, without expectation, having abandoned possessions, restrained in thought and self, he incurs no defilement.

22   Content with what comes by chance, having gone beyond dualities, free from envy, the same in success and in failure, even when he has acted he is not bound.

23   For the man who is rid of attachment, who has attained release, whose thought is anchored in knowledge, action is sacrificial and melts entirely away.

24   The offering is Brahman, the oblation is Brahman, poured by Brahman into the fire that is Brahman. Brahman is to be attained by that man who concentrates intensely on the action that is Brahman.[5]

25   Some skilled performers concentrate on sacrifice to one of the deities; some offer sacrifice through the sacrifice itself into the fire of Brahman;

26   Others offer the senses (such as hearing) into the fires of restraint; others again offer the objects of the senses (such as sound) into the fires of the senses;

27   Some offer all actions of sense and breath into the fire of the discipline of self-restraint, kindled by knowledge.

28   Similarly there are others, sacrificers with material substance, with bodily mortification, with spiritual exercise, with Vedic study and knowledge – ascetics with uncompromising vows.

29   And again, those whose object is breath-control offer the inhaled into the exhaled breath, and the exhaled into the inhaled, restricting their passage.

30   Others, who have put limits on their consumption of food, offer their inhalation into their inhalation. All these, who know what sacrifice is, have their imperfections obliterated by sacrifice.

31   Those who eat the immortality-conferring remnants of the sacrifice go to primeval Brahman. Best of Gurus, this world, let alone the other, is not for non-sacrificers.

32   Thus many kinds of sacrifice are stretched out in the mouth of

Brahman. Remember that they are all born of action; knowing that, you will be liberated.

33 Incinerator of the Foe, the sacrifice of knowledge is better than the sacrifice of material substance. There is no action whatsoever, Partha, which is not concluded in knowledge.

34 Know this: through your submission, through the questions you ask, through your service, those who have knowledge, who see things as they are, will teach you knowledge.

35 And having it, you will never be bewildered in such a way again, Pandava. Through it you shall see all creatures in yourself, and then in me.

36 Even if you are the very worst of all transgressors, with the boat of knowledge you shall plot a safe course through all crookedness.

37 As a lighted fire reduces kindling to ash, in the same way, Arjuna, the fire of knowledge incinerates all actions.

38 Nothing on earth has the purificatory power of knowledge; eventually, the man who has perfected his disciplined practice discovers it in himself.

39 Restraining his senses, the man of faith who is devoted to knowledge attains it. And having attained knowledge, he rapidly achieves supreme peace.

40 The faithless and ignorant man, whose nature it is to doubt, perishes. Not this world, nor the one beyond, nor happiness exists for the doubter.

41 But the self-possessed man, Dhananjaya, who has renounced action through discipline, and cut through doubt with knowledge, is not bound by actions.

42 Therefore, having severed with the blade of knowledge this doubt of yours, which stems from ignorance and is fixed in the heart, act with discipline, Bharata – arise!

Chapter 5

Arjuna said:

1 Krishna, you approve the renunciation of actions, and then again the practice of yogic discipline. Tell me unambiguously, which is the better of these two? The Lord said:

2 Both renunciation and the practice of yogic action lead to ultimate bliss, but, of the two, the practice of yogic action is superior to the renunciation of action.

3 Great Arm, the man who neither desires nor hates is considered a perpetual renouncer; free from duality, he is easily liberated.

4 Fools hold that the way of Sankhya and the practice of yogic action are different, but not those who know. Through either one of them, carried out properly, one attains the reward of both.

5 The state achieved by Sankhyas is also achieved by yogic actors; whoever sees the ways of Sankhya and yogic action as one truly sees.

6 But renunciation, Great Arm, is hard to attain without yogic practice; the sage disciplined in yogic practice swiftly reaches Brahman.

7 Even when he is acting, the man who is disciplined in yogic practice, whose self is pure, whose self and senses are controlled, whose self is the self of all beings, is not defiled.

8–9 The disciplined man, who knows the underlying principle of reality, thinks: 'I really don't do anything at all,' certain that whether seeing, hearing, touching, smelling, eating, walking, sleeping, breathing, talking, excreting, grasping, opening or shutting the eyes, it is merely the senses acting on the objects of sense.

10 The man who acts, having rendered his actions to Brahman and abandoned attachment, is untainted by evil, in the same way that a lotus leaf is unstained by water.

11 Having abandoned attachment, yogins undertake action with the body, mind and intelligence, even with the senses alone, for the sake of self-purification.

12 The disciplined man, having abandoned the result of action, attains complete peace; the undisciplined man, whose action is impelled by desire, and who is attached to the result, is bound.

13 Having renounced all actions with the mind, the embodied self sits easily, ruler in its nine-gated city,* neither acting nor causing action.

14 The lord of the body does not create agency or actions for the world, or the connection of action and result; rather it is inherent nature that accomplishes this. . . .

Notes

1 I.e. the four castes of Indian society: priests (*brahmins*), warrior-nobles, merchants and labourers.

2 The two main tenets of the Sankhya school of philosophy to which the *Gita* appeals are (a) the separation of the true self or soul from the natural world, and

* I.e. the body.

(b) the explanation of the natural world in terms of three material constituents (*gunas*).

3 The *Gita* is an eclectic work. Sankhyan and Yogic thought figures large, and in this verse we find a reference to the Buddhist notion of *nirvana* and the Vedantic concept of *Brahman*.

4 The reference here is clearly to the 'pure' or 'true' self, to be distinguished from the empirical ego, the psychological subject of desires, motives etc.

5 *Brahman* came to be the name of absolute or underlying reality in Hindu thought; but earlier the word had referred, first, to prayers and invocations used in sacrificial rituals and then to the power supposedly invoked in such rituals.

7

(A) Śāntideva, *The Bodhicaryāvatāra*, chapter 8 (verses 89–140)
(B) Tsongkapa and Pabongka Rinpoche, 'The Second Path'

(A) *From* Śāntideva, *The Bodhicaryāvatāra*, trans. K. Crosby and A. Skilton. Oxford: Oxford University Press, 1996, pp. 96–100; reprinted permission of Oxford University Press. (B) *From* Tsongkapa, *The Principal Teachings of Buddhism*, with a commentary by Pabongka Rinpoche, trans. L. Tharchin and M. Roach. New Jersey: Mahayana Sutra and Tantra Press, 1988, pp. 93–104 [some passages omitted]; reprinted by permission of the publisher.

In recent years, Buddhism has won many converts in the West. It appears to offer a perspective which is at once religious and free from the theistic notion, unacceptable to many modern minds, of a personal creator-God. But its attraction owes, as well, to a moral doctrine of universal compassion that knows no boundaries of nation, class, sex or even species. The exhortation 'whatever living beings there be: feeble or strong . . . seen or unseen . . . far or near . . . may all beings be happy!¹ seems more congenial to the modern sensibility than the *Gita's* call (see chapter 6 above) to performance of duties, military ones included, for their own sake.

The importance of compassion and 'loving-kindness' seems to be implied by the first of the 'four noble truths' announced by Gotama, the Buddha, in the sixth or fifth century BCE – that life is 'suffering', 'sorrow', 'dis-ease', 'unsatisfactoriness' (just some of the suggested translations of the Pali word *dukkha*). But other Buddhist doctrines make it problematic as to why and how moral concern should have a central role. The other noble truths suggest that it is essentially through understanding and wisdom that 'suffering' is to be overcome – through, above all, recognizing that the desires or 'cravings' which are responsible for 'suffering' are due to a mistaken 'clinging' to a non-existent 'self'. Morality, it can seem, is at most a useful preparation for that

---

¹ *The Sutta-Nipata*, London: Curzon Press, 1985, 16: 4–5.

'renunciation' of self-centred desire which is a prerequisite for entry into the enlightened condition of *nirvana* ('extinction'). Moreover, one is bound to ask, if this 'extinction', this release from the round of rebirth, is the proper goal, why should one care too much about improving conditions for creatures still caught up in this process? Anyway, if a person is 'not-self', but perhaps merely a bundle of passing mental states without any centre of identity, to whom exactly are compassion and loving-kindness directed?

It is unsurprising, therefore, that some commentators, such as Max Weber and Albert Schweitzer, have regarded Buddhism as a 'cold', amoral religion – and certainly in the Theravada tradition of Buddhism, the emphasis has tended to be upon renunciation and asceticism rather than moral action.[2] But in the Mahayana ('Great Vehicle') tradition which arose in opposition to the earlier one, a central tenet is that of universal compassion, understood as a loving commitment to help all creatures escape from 'suffering'. The pledge of the *bodhisattva* ('the being of enlightenment'), who postpones his or her attainment of *nirvana*, is 'However numerous are the sentient beings that exist, I vow to save them all!'.[3]

While there are many moral 'manuals' in the Buddhist literature, edifying precepts enjoining temperance, charity, friendship and so on, there is a dearth of sustained discussion attempting to reconcile the importance of morality with the doctrines mentioned above. In my two selections – both from the Mahayana tradition – one discerns, however, arguments for universal compassion compatible with, or even grounded in, those doctrines. In his commentary on the poem *Three Principal Paths* by the most famous Buddhist philosopher of Tibet, Tsongkapa (1357–1419), the monk and university teacher Pabongka Rinpoche (1878–1941) mentions two methods of 'training one's mind' for aiming at 'saving' all creatures – the 'seven-part, cause-and-effect instruction' and 'exchanging self and others'. It is the former which he adumbrates, the latter being the main theme in my selection from the eighth-century CE Indian monk Śāntideva's 'Guide to the Buddhist Path to Awakening', 'one of the great spiritual poems of mankind'[4] and a text especially influential in Tibetan Buddhism. Although both authors speak of 'methods' for inducing a compassionate attitude, we might instead think of these as arguments for why one *ought* to adopt such an attitude.

---

[2] In the authoritative Theravada treatise, Buddhaghosa's *The Path of Purification*, Kandy: Buddhist Publication Society, 1991, 'virtue' is only the first stage, before 'concentration' and 'understanding', on this path. But see Steven Collins, *Selfless Persons*, Cambridge: Cambridge University Press, p.194f, on not exaggerating the difference between the two traditions.

[3] Quoted in Heinrich Dumoulin, *Understanding Buddhism*, New York: Weatherhill, 1994, p. 76.

[4] Paul Williams, *Mayahana Buddhism: The Doctrinal Foundations*, London: Routledge, 1989, p. 198.

The two 'methods' or arguments are, I think, fairly self-explanatory: both aim to cultivate a 'selfless' or 'neutral' attitude towards ourselves and others. In the Tibetan text, the argument is based on our relationships with other people in past and future lives. This raises the question of the relevance of such arguments to those non-Buddhists who are unable to accept the doctrine of rebirth. I invite readers to try amending the arguments, to treat them as grounded in reflections not on how we *actually* were and will be related to other people in past and future lives, but on how we *might* have been related to them in this one. Instead, for example, of reflecting, like Tsongkapa, that this woman, whom I may be treating badly, *was* my mother in a previous life, reflect on the facts that she *might* have been my mother in this one and that she probably is the mother of someone who *might* have been my best friend.

A residual worry may be that, for all the talk of selfless compassion, the motive for it remains a selfish one – ensuring *nirvana* for oneself. But, as a great commentator pointed out, 'if a Buddhist undergoes the discipline that leads to *nirvana* . . . it is in order to diminish by one the number of living and suffering beings'.[5] In other words, someone with a selfless or neutral attitude will regard his own future lives as just one more series of 'bundles of suffering', no more, but no less, deserving of compassion than any other. Moreover, as Śāntideva reminds us (e.g. verse 98), the doctrine of 'not-self' entails that these future lives are not in any substantial sense 'mine', but only loosely continuous with 'my' present one, so that aiming to forestall them (by achieving *nirvana*) is no more egocentric than it is altruistic.[6]

▷ ▷ ▷ (A) Śāntideva, *The Bodhicaryāvatāra*, Chapter 8

[. . .]

89 By developing the virtues of solitude . . ., distracted thoughts being calmed, one should now develop the Awakening Mind.[1]

90 At first one should meditate intently on the equality of oneself and others as follows: 'All equally experience suffering and happiness. I should look after them as I do myself.'

91 Just as the body, with its many parts from division into hands and other limbs, should be protected as a single entity, so too should this entire world which is divided, but undivided in its nature to suffer

[5] Louis de la Vallée Poussin, quoted in Collins, *Selfless Persons*, p. 193.
[6] For an interesting attempt by a modern Western philosopher to explore the implications of something like the Buddhist 'not-self' doctrine, see Derek Parfit, *Reasons and Persons*, Oxford: Clarendon Press, 1984.

and be happy.

92　Even though suffering in me does not cause distress in the bodies of others, I should nevertheless find their suffering intolerable because of the affection I have for myself,

93　In the same way that, though I cannot experience another's suffering in myself, his suffering is hard for him to bear because of his affection for himself.

94　I should dispel the suffering of others because it is suffering like my own suffering. I should help others too because of their nature as beings, which is like my own being.

95　When happiness is liked by me and others equally, what is so special about me that I strive after happiness only for myself?

96　When fear and suffering are disliked by me and others equally, what is so special about me that I protect myself and not the other?

97　If I give them no protection because their suffering does not afflict me, why do I protect my body against future suffering when it does not afflict me?

98　The notion 'it is the same me even then' is a false construction, since it is one person who dies, quite another who is born.

99　If you think that it is for the person who has the pain to guard against it, a pain in the foot is not of the hand, so why is the one protected by the other?

100　If you argue that, even though this conduct is inappropriate, it proceeds from the sense of self-identity, [our response is that] one should avoid what is inappropriate in respect of self and others as far as one can.

101　The continuum of consciousnesses, like a queue, and the combination of constituents, like an army, are not real. The person who experiences suffering does not exist. To whom will that suffering belong?

102　Without exception, no sufferings belong to anyone. They must be warded off simply because they are suffering. Why is any limitation put on this?[2]

103　If one asks why suffering should be prevented, no one disputes that! If it must be prevented, then all of it must be. If not, then this goes for oneself as for everyone.

104　You may argue: compassion causes us so much suffering, why force it to arise? Yet when one sees how much the world suffers, how can this suffering from compassion be considered great?

105　If the suffering of one ends the suffering of many, then one who has compassion for others and himself must cause that suffering to arise.

106 That is why [the monk] Supuṣpacandra, though undergoing torture at the hands of the king, did nothing to prevent his own suffering out of sacrifice for many sufferers.

107 Those who have developed the continuum of their mind in this way, to whom the suffering of others is as important as the things they themselves hold dear, plunge down into the Avīci hell as geese into a cluster of lotus blossoms.³

108 Those who become oceans of sympathetic joy when living beings are released, surely it is they who achieve fulfilment. What would be the point in a liberation without sweetness?

109 In fact, though acting for the good of others, there is neither intoxication nor dismay, nor desire for the resulting reward, with a thirst solely for the well-being of others.

110 Therefore, just as I protect myself to the last against criticism, let me develop in this way an attitude of protectiveness and of generosity towards others as well.

111 Through habituation there is the understanding of 'I' regarding the drops of sperm and blood of two other people, even though there is in fact no such thing.⁴

112 Why can I not also accept another's body as my self in the same way, since the otherness of my own body has been settled and is not hard to accept?

113 One should acknowledge oneself as having faults and others as oceans of virtues. Then one should meditate on renouncing one's own self-identity and accepting other people.

114 In the same way that the hands and other limbs are loved because they form part of the body, why are embodied creatures not likewise loved because they form part of the universe?

115 In the same way that, with practice, the idea of a self arose towards this, one's own body, though it is without a self, with practice will not the same idea of a self develop towards others too?

116 Though acting like this for the good of others, there is neither intoxication nor dismay. Even after giving oneself as food, there arises no hope for reward.

117 Therefore, in the same way that one desires to protect oneself from affliction, grief and the like, so an attitude of protectiveness and of compassion should be practised towards the world.

118 That is why the Protector, Avalokita, empowered even his own name to drive away even such fear as the shyness people have in front of an audience.⁵

119 One should not turn away from difficulty, because by the power of

practice the very thing one once feared to hear becomes something without which one has no delight.

120 Whoever longs to rescue quickly both himself and others should practise the supreme mystery: exchange of self and other.

121 If even slight danger causes fear because of overfondness for oneself, who would not detest that self like a fear-inspiring enemy?

122 One who, wishing to fend off hunger, thirst and weakness, kills birds, fish and animals, or lurks in wait on the highway,

123 One who, motivated by possessions and honour, would even kill his parents, or would take the property of the Three Jewels, who would thereby become fuel in the Avīci hell,

124 What wise person would want such a self, protect it, worship it, and not see it as an enemy? Who would treat it with regard?

125 'If I give, what shall I enjoy?' Such concern for one's own welfare is fiendish. 'If I enjoy, what shall I give?' Such concern for the welfare of others is divine.

126 By oppressing another for one's own sake, one is roasted in hells, but by oppressing oneself for the sake of another, one meets with success in everything.

127 A bad rebirth, inferiority and stupidity result from the mere desire for self-advancement. By transferring that same desire to others, one achieves a good rebirth, honour and intelligence.

128 By commanding another to one's own end one attains positions of servitude, whereas by commanding oneself to the benefit of others one attains positions of power.

129 All those who suffer in the world do so because of their desire for their own happiness. All those happy in the world are so because of their desire for the happiness of others.

130 Why say more? Observe this distinction: between the fool who longs for his own advantage and the sage who acts for the advantage of others.

131 For one who fails to exchange his own happiness for the suffering of others, Buddhahood is certainly impossible – how could there even be happiness in cyclic existence?

132 Never mind the next life! Even right here and now the objective of a servant who does not work or of a master who does not pay the wages cannot be achieved.

133 Having forsaken the promotion of one another's happiness, the fountain of happiness now and in the future, by causing mutual distress, the deluded seize upon gruesome suffering.

134 The calamities which happen in the world, the sufferings and fears,

many as they are, they all result from clinging on to the notion of self, so what good is this clinging of mine?

135 If one does not let go of self one cannot let go of suffering, as one who does not let go of fire cannot let go of burning.

136 Therefore, in order to allay my own suffering and to allay the suffering of others, I devote myself to others and accept them as myself.

137 Hey Mind, make the resolve, 'I am bound to others'! From now on you must have no other concern than the welfare of all beings.

138 It is not right to look to one's own good with others' eyes and other senses. It is not right to set in motion one's own good with others' hands and other limbs.

139 So having become devoted to others, remove from this body everything you see in it, and use that to benefit others.

140 Creating a sense of self in respect of inferiors and others, and a sense of other in oneself, imagine envy and pride with a mind free from false notions!

Notes

1 I.e. 'the Mind resolved on Awakening' or enlightenment, as Śāntideva explains in chapter 1, verses 15–16.

2 This is Śāntideva's reply to the familiar charge that Buddhism is 'impersonal'. That states of suffering are not those of any self is morally irrelevant, for what matters is, simply, that they are states of *suffering*, and hence ones which should inspire compassion.

3 The meaning here is that the 'awakened' person is willing to suffer for the sake of others. The Avīci hell is the most gruesome of the hells portrayed in some Mahayana texts.

4 'According to ancient Indian physiology, the sperm of the father and the blood of the mother give rise to the individual who, in Buddhist terms, then mistakenly perceives the product as his self' [Tr.].

5 Avalokita (or Avalokitesvara) is the Buddha of compassion, whose name means something like 'The Lord who looks down [to see the suffering of the world]' [Tr.].

(B) Tsongkapa and Pabongka Rinpoche, 'The Second Path: The Wish to Achieve Enlightenment for Every Living Being'

11: Why You Need the Wish for Enlightenment

We have now reached the second of the four parts in the actual body of the text [i.e. the poem *Three Principal Paths* – Ed.]. This is an explanation of the wish to achieve enlightenment for the sake of every living being. This explanation itself will include three sections: why you need the wish for enlightenment, how to go about developing this wish, and how to know when you've finally developed it. The next verse of the root text tells us why we need this great wish:

(6)

> Renunciation though can never bring
> The total bliss of matchless Buddhahood
> Unless it's bound by the purest wish; and so,
> The wise seek the high wish for enlightenment.

You may be able to gain some fierce feelings of renunciation . . ., any good deeds you do under their influence though can only bring you an ordinary nirvana – they alone can never serve to bring you to omniscient enlightenment. We can see this from the fact that even practitioners of lower paths – people we call 'listeners' and 'self-made victors' – can possess true renunciation.

For full enlightenment then a person needs to develop within his mind all three of the principal paths – and more specifically, he must have gained the second path: the wish to achieve enlightenment for every living being. You may possess extra-sensory powers, you may be able to perform miracles, you may have any number of fantastic qualities – but unless you have this precious jewel in your heart, you will never enter that select group of people who practise the greater way. Without this highest wish, none of your qualities will ever bring you total bliss – none of them, none of them at all, will bring you Buddhahood: the ability to free each and every living being from all the troubles of cyclic life, and from those of a lower escape from cyclic life.

Those great practitioners of the lower paths – 'enemy destroyers' of the 'listener' or 'self-made' type – possess fine qualities like a huge mountain made of pure gold; even such qualities as the ability to perceive emptiness directly. But these paths never bring them to Buddhahood. Why? Because they lack the wish to achieve enlightenment for every living being.

If you do gain this great wish, you become a person who truly deserves to have the entire world – with all its different kinds of beings up to humans and gods – bow down at your feet, just as holy books like *The Bodhisattva's Life*, and *Entering the Middle Way*, and *The Rare Stack* describe it.[1] You find yourself in a different class of being, and then you completely outshine listeners and self-made victors – practitioners of the lower paths. Every virtuous act you do, even down to throwing a scrap of food to some wild bird, becomes a practice of the greater way; becomes a cause for your future Buddhahood; becomes the way of life of a bodhisattva.

If a person possesses this holy wish to achieve enlightenment for the sake of every living being, then all the countless Buddhas in all the ten directions of space look upon him as their son. And all the great bodhisattvas look upon him as their brother.

But that's not all; the whole question of whether you have reached the greater way, and the whole question of whether you will be able to achieve Buddhahood in this one short life, depend on whether you have truly gained this wish. . . .

12: How to Develop the Wish for Enlightenment

The second section in our explanation of the wish to achieve enlightenment for every living being describes how to develop this wish. As the next two verses say,

(7,8)

They're swept along on four fierce river currents,
Chained up tight in past deeds, hard to undo,
Stuffed in a steel cage of grasping 'self',
Smothered in the pitch-black ignorance.

In a limitless round they're born, and in their births
Are tortured by three sufferings without a break;
Think how your mothers feel, think of what's happening
To them: try to develop this highest wish.

We may begin with another pair of verses, from *The Bodhisattva's Life*:

Even just wishing you could stop
A headache another person has

Can bring you merit without measure
Because of the helpful intent you feel.

What need then to mention the wish
That you could stop the immeasurable pain
Of every being, and put every one
In a state of measureless happiness?

The *Sutra that Viradatta Requested* says as well,

Were the merit of the wish for enlightenment
To take on some kind of physical form
It would fill the reaches of space itself
And then spill over farther still.

The benefits of this wish to achieve enlightenment for all living beings are thus described, in these and other texts, as limitless. And so here are the mass of living beings, all of them our mothers, *swept along* the flow of *four river currents*, all *fierce suffering*. From one viewpoint, while they are acting as causes, these four are the torrent of desire, the torrent of views, the torrent of the ripe force of deeds, and the torrent of ignorance. Later, when they serve as results, they are the four torrents of birth, and aging, and illness, and death.

And these mother beings are not just hurtling along in these four great rivers; it's just as if their hands and feet too were bound fast – they are *chained up tight*, they are snared, *in* their own *past deeds, hard to undo*.

But that's not all; the bonds which hold them tight are no regular ties, like our twined ropes of yak-skin or hair. It's more like our mothers are clasped in fetters of iron, ever so hard to sever, ever so hard to unshackle – for while they are swept along they are *stuffed in a steel cage of grasping* to some non-existent '*self*'.

And there's more. If there were some daylight, these mother beings would have some glimmer of hope – they could at least cry out, and try to get some help. But it is night, and the darkest hour of the night, and in pitch-black dark they are swept downstream the mighty river: they are *smothered* completely *in pitch-black ignorance*.

In a limitless round, in an endless round, *they are born* into the ocean of life, *and in these births* they *are tortured by three* different kinds of *suffering*: the suffering of suffering, the suffering of change, and the all-pervading suffering. And their torture comes to them *without a break* – it is always there.

This is *what's happening to them*, to our mother beings, this is their situation: unbearable pain. There's nothing they can do like this to help themselves; the son though has a chance at hand to pull his mother free. He must find a way, and find it now, to grasp her hand and draw her out. And the way he must *try* is *to develop this* jewel *wish* for enlightenment: he must do so first by *thinking how* his *mothers feel*, tortured by pain; then by deciding to take personal responsibility, the duty of freeing them, upon himself; and so on, all in the proper stages.

To actually gain the wish for enlightenment he must first contemplate it. To contemplate it, he must first learn about it from another. 'Loving-kindness' is an almost obsessive desire that each and every living being find happiness. 'Compassion' is an almost obsessive desire that they be free of any pain. Think of how a mother feels when her one and only and most beloved son is in the throes of a serious illness. Wherever she goes, whatever she does, she is always thinking how wonderful it would be if she could find some way of freeing him quickly from his sickness. These thoughts come to her mind in a steady stream, without a break, and all of their own, automatically. They become an obsession with her. When we feel this way towards every living being, and only then, we can say we have gained what they call 'great compassion'.

Here in the teachings of the Buddha there are two methods given for training one's mind in this precious jewel, the wish for enlightenment. The first is known as the 'seven-part, cause-and-effect instruction'. The second we call 'exchanging self and others'. No matter which of the two you use to train your mind, you can definitely gain the wish for enlightenment. The way to train oneself in the wish, the way which is complete and which never errs, the way unmatched by any other here upon this earth, is the instruction of the Steps of the path to Buddhahood, the very essence of all the teachings of our gentle protector, the great Tsongkapa. Thus you should train your mind in the wish for enlightenment by using this very instruction.

Here we'll give just a brief summary of how one trains himself in the wish to achieve enlightenment for every living being. The start-off is to practise feelings of neutrality towards all beings; after that, one begins meditation on each of the steps from 'mother recognition' on up. The first three steps are to recognize all beings as one's mothers, to feel gratitude for their kindness, and to wish to repay that kindness. These three act as a cause for what we call 'beautiful' loving-kindness. This type of loving-kindness is itself the fourth step; it is both an effect brought about by the first three, and a cause for the fifth: great compassion. . . .

Once you develop great compassion, then you can develop the extraordinary form of personal responsibility, where you take upon yourself the load of working for others' benefit. And the wish to achieve enlightenment for every living being comes from this.

The meditation on neutrality goes like this. First you put your thoughts in an even state, free of feelings of like and dislike, by thinking about someone who is for you a neutral figure: neither your enemy nor your friend. Then you imagine that two people are sitting before you: one of your best-loved friends, and one of your ugliest enemies. Next you think very carefully about how the friend has, in many of your previous lives, taken birth as your enemy and hurt you. You think too about how the enemy has, in so many of your past lives, taken birth as your friend and helped you. This puts your mind in the even state, free of feelings of like and dislike.

You go on then to think about how all living beings are equal in that, from his own point of view, each one of them wants to be happy. They are equal too in not wanting pain. And they are equal in that every one has acted as both my enemy and my friend, many many times. So who am I supposed to like? And who am I supposed to dislike? You have to keep on practising this way until, one day, you gain neutral feelings towards all sentient beings, as vast in extent as space itself.

The next step is the meditation where you recognize that every living being is your mother. Gaining this recognition is much easier if you apply the line of reasoning mentioned in the *Commentary on Valid Perception* [by Dharmakirti, seventh century CE] for demonstrating the infinite regression of one's awareness. We'll present this reasoning here, in brief.

Your awareness of today is a mental continuation of the awareness you had yesterday. This year's awareness is a mental continuation of the awareness you had the year before. Just so, your awareness over this entire life is a mental continuation of the awareness you had in your former life. The awareness you had in your former life was, in turn, a mental continuation of the awareness you had in the life before that. You can continue back in a regression like this and absolutely never reach some point where you can say, 'Prior to this, I had no awareness.' This then proves the infinite regression of one's awareness.

My own circle of life then must also be beginningless, and the births I have taken as well can have no starting point. There exists no place where I have never taken birth. I have taken birth in every single place, countless times. There exists no creature whose body I have not worn. I have worn every kind of body, countless times. Just the lives I have taken as a dog are themselves beyond any number to count. And the same is true for every living being.

Therefore there exists no being who has never been my mother. Absolutely every single one of them has been my mother a countless number of times. Even the number of times that each has been my mother in just my births as a human is past all counting too.

Do this meditation over and over until you gain a deep-felt certainty that each and every living being has been your mother, over and over, countless times.

Developing a sense of gratitude is the next step, and you can start by taking your mother in this present life. She began her hardships for me while I was still in her womb, gladly taking it upon herself to avoid anything she felt might hurt me – even down to the food she ate – treating herself with care, as though she were sick. For nine months and ten days she carried me in her womb, looking at her own body as though it belonged to someone else, someone very ill, and hesitating even to take big steps.

As she gave me birth, my mother was torn with violent suffering, excruciating pain, and yet still felt an overwhelming joy, as though she had discovered some precious gem that would grant her any wish.

Right then I knew absolutely nothing more than to cry and wave my arms around somehow. I was totally helpless. Totally stupid. Incapacitated. Nothing more than some baby chick with a red-rubber beak still yet to harden. But she swayed me on her fingertips, and pressed me to her body's warmth, and greeted me with a smile of love.

With joyful eyes she gazed on me, and wiped the snot from my face with her lips, and cleaned my filthy shit with her hands. Sometimes she chewed my food for me, and fed me things like milky porridge straight from her mouth to mine. She did her best to protect me from any hurt. She did her best to get me any good.

In those days I had to look to her for everything; good or bad, happy or sad, all the hope I could have lay in one person: mother. But for her kindness, I wouldn't have lasted an hour; they could have set me out in the open right then and some birds or a dog would have come and made a meal of me – I'd have no hope of coming out alive. Every single day she protected me from harms that could have taken my life, no less than a hundred times. Such was her kindness.

And while I was growing up she gathered together whatever I needed, avoiding no bad deed, and no suffering, and caring nothing for what other people might say of her. All the money and things she had she handed over to me, hesitating to use anything for herself.

For those of us who are fortunate enough to be practising the monastic life, it was Mother who put forth all the necessary expenses, giving without reservation, to arrange our admission into the monastery. And from that time on she supported us here, from whatever resources she had. Thus the kindness she has shown us is truly without measure.

And this is not the only life in which my present mother has given this kindness to me. She has showered me with this kindness, great kindness, over and over, countless times, in my many lives before. And she is not the only one; every single living being has been my mother in my past lives, and during those lives cared for me no less than my present mother does – it is only my transitions from death to birth that prevent me from recognizing all these mothers now.

Look now . . . at the way any common animal – a dog or bird, even the tiny sparrow – shows shows affection for its young, and cares for it well. From watching this we can imagine what kindness we were given too.

The next step in gaining the wish for enlightenment is to develop a wish to repay this great kindness. So every living being is my mother, and has given me her loving care over and over endlessly, for time with no beginning. And we know from what was described above that they are being swept along by four great currents, out to sea – to the vast expanse of the ocean of cyclic life. They are tormented, without a break, by the three types of suffering, and all the other pains. Their situation is desperate.

And here am I, their child. Right now I have a chance to rescue them from this ocean of cyclic life. Suppose I simply sit and bide my time, and give no thought to them. This is the lowest a person could stoop – base and absolutely shameless.

Right now I could give them things that they would be happy to get – food, or clothes, or beds to sleep on, whatever. But these are only some temporary happiness within the circle of life. The very highest way of repaying their kindness would be to put them into the state of ultimate happiness. So let me decide within myself that every living being must come to have every happiness. And every one should be freed as well from every form of pain.

Right now it's absurd to say that these beings have any kind of pure happiness – they don't even have any of the impure kinds. Every single thing they think is happiness is, in its essence, nothing more than pain. They want wantables but don't want to know about doing the good deeds that bring happiness. They want no unwantables but don't want to know about giving up the bad deeds that bring pain. They act ass backwards: they do what they shouldn't and don't what they should. And so my dear aged mothers, these living beings, are made to suffer.

> How good it would be if they could all find every happiness, and every cause of happiness. I wish they could. I'll see that they do.

> How good it would be if they could all be free of every pain, and every cause of pain. I wish they could. I'll see that they do.

Let these two trains of thought run through your mind; meditate on them over and over again. Then you will come to feel the very strongest loving-kindness and compassion.

Some people might come up with the idea that 'Why should I take upon myself this great load, of every living being? There are plenty of Buddhas and bodhisattvas around to guide them on their way.' This kind of thought though is absolutely improper. It's base. It's shameless. It's as if your mother in this life was hungry, and parched, and you expected someone else's child to go and give her food and drink. But it's you for whom she has cared, and the responsibility of paying her back has fallen only to you.

It's the same with all these living beings, who for beginningless time have served as my mother so many times, and who in each of these times cared for me in every way with the kindness of this present mother. Returning their kindness is no business of anyone else at all, not for some Buddha or bodhisattva – it is my responsibility, and only mine.

So someone is going to do it – to make sure every sentient being has every happiness, and never a single pain. It is going to be myself; I'll rely on no one else. I by myself will see to it that every single being comes to have every single happiness. And I by myself will see to it that every single being gets free of every single pain. I will by myself put them into . . . the state of Buddhahood. Meditate strongly on these thoughts; they are the step we call the 'extraordinary form of personal responsibility'.

I may be able to develop this noble intention, but the fact is that I'm completely incapable of leading a single being to Buddhahood – much less every one of them. Who then has the capacity? This power is had by a fully enlightened Buddha – only by him, and by no one else at all. If I can reach the same state, I will by definition have brought both mine and others' benefit to its perfection. And then every single ray of light that emanates from me, whether it be an action of my body, or my speech, or my thoughts, will have the power to accomplish the ends of countless sentient beings.

And so, for the sake of every living being, I will do anything I can to achieve this one great goal – the state of a Buddha – with every speed. Think this way to yourself, and do anything you can to develop the genuine wish to reach enlightenment for every living being. . . .

Note

1 The first of the works mentioned here is Śāntideva's *The Bodhicaryāvatāra*, which is then quoted a few lines later.

St Thomas Aquinas, *Summa Theologica*, I–II, Questions 55, 58, 61–3

From Aquinas Ethicus: or, The Moral Teaching of St Thomas, vol. 1, trans. J. Rickaby. London: Burns & Oates, 1896, pp. 155, 167–74, 179–87, reprinted by permission of the publisher.

During the Middle Ages, in both the Islamic and Christian worlds, a battle was fought between 'the philosophers' and 'the theologians' over the respective authority of unaided reason and of revelation and faith. In Islam, it was Al-Ghazali and other theologians who were victorious, with the result that ever since philosophy has been at best a suspect enterprise in Muslim countries, Persia excepted. That a similar fate did not befall philosophy in Christendom was largely due to the genius of a Dominican friar, Thomas Aquinas (1225–74). Ironically, it was Aquinas's debt to the Aristotelianism of Muslim *falasifah* such as Averroës that enabled his own compromise between reason and faith, not least in the domain of ethics.

So much the 'official' philosopher of Roman Catholicism has Aquinas become that it surprises people to learn that several of his doctrines were officially condemned by the Church three years after his death – though in a rapid ecclesiastical volte-face, sainthood was to be bestowed fifty years later. Certainly Aquinas's ethical position ran strongly counter to prevailing orthodoxy. According to the view inherited from St Augustine, St Bernard and others, man is a 'fallen', sinful creature, quite incapable of true understanding and moral virtue without the help of God. Moral life is an uphill struggle of the soul against man's corrupt nature, 'imprisoned' as it is 'in th[e] body . . . sunk in its mire'.[1] Without knowledge of God, indeed, there could be no genuine moral understanding and virtue, for what is morality but the commandments of God?

Doubtless the label of 'Aristotle baptized' sometimes attached to Thomism is rather too cute, but St Thomas's discussion of virtue – in the first division of the second part of the gigantic *Summa Theologica*, from which the following 'Ques-

---

[1] St Bernard of Clairvaux, quoted in Etienne Gilson, *The Mystical Theology of Saint Bernard*, London: Sheed & Ward, 1940, p. 133.

tions' are selected – is a fine example of his judicious use of the Greek philosopher in combating the orthodox view and of his conviction that 'Grace does not destroy nature, but completes it' (*Sum. Th.*, I.1.8). Prior to that discussion, Aquinas presents an amended version of Aristotle's notion of *eudaimonia* as the final end of all our 'appetites' and hence the good. As a devout Christian, Aquinas substitutes for Aristotelian 'happiness' that 'final happiness' which comes with direct, visionary knowledge of God. The virtues are then understood as the 'habits' or dispositions which, reason shows us, equip us to realize beatitude. Since it is our 'nature' to seek this end, the virtues are not 'acquired', nor are they exercised in conflict with our other natural tendencies. The rational 'man should be attracted by the good', performing for example 'acts of kindness with pleasure [rather] than . . . with set teeth, as it were'.[2] Indeed, the 'continent' and 'persevering' person who does need to set his teeth is, for that reason, not fully virtuous (I–II.68.3). (Compare Kant's account of 'the good will' in chapter 11 below.)

Aquinas, of course, does not subscribe to the whole list of Aristotelian virtues, geared as they were to the *eudaimonia* of the Athenian citizen. More importantly, that God has revealed Himself and that it is beatitude rather than 'happiness' in the here and now which is our final end mean that there are some virtues which would have been foreign to even the most rational and reflective Greek. These are the 'theological virtues' of faith, hope and, above all, charity, this last to be understood, not as alms-giving, but as loving God 'with thy whole soul' and 'thy neighbour as thyself'.

But even in the case of these 'theological virtues', we can rationally grasp why they are required of us given our understanding of God. Moral principles are never simply the arbitrary commandments of God, as they were for St Thomas's fourteenth-century critic William of Ockham. God does, to be sure, command us to follow them, as Aquinas indicates in his famous definition of 'natural law' as 'participation in the eternal law by rational creatures' (I–II.91.2). But as that definition also makes clear, such principles are never arbitrary: for given our nature, conferred on us by God in His own image, there are only certain ways in which human beings can fulfil their, and God's, purpose. It is to Aquinas's formulation of this position that the tradition of rational Christian ethics owes its primary debt.

▶ ▶ ▶ **Question 55: Of Virtues in Their Essence**

Article 1: Is Human Virtue a Habit?

R. Virtue denotes some perfection of a power. The perfection of everything is estimated chiefly in regard to its end: now the end of power is

---

[2] F. C. Copleston, *Aquinas*, Harmondsworth: Penguin, 1982, p. 214.

action: hence a power is said to be perfect inasmuch as it is determined to its act. Now there are powers which are determined of themselves to their acts, as the active powers of physical nature. But the rational powers, which are proper to man, are not determined to one line of action, but are open indeterminately to many, and are determined to acts by habits. And therefore human virtues are habits [or dispositions – Ed.].

§3.   We are said to merit by a thing in two ways: in one way as by the merit itself, in the same way that we are said to run by running; and in this way we merit by acts. In another way we are said to merit by a thing as by a principle of merit, as we are said to run by motive power; and thus we are said to merit by virtues and habits.

Question 58: Of the Distinction of Moral Virtues from Intellectual

Article 1: Is All Virtue Moral?

R. We must consider what the (Latin) word *mos* means; for so we shall be able to know what *moral* virtue is. *Mos* has two meanings: sometimes it means *custom*; sometimes it means a sort of *natural* or *quasi-natural inclination* to do a thing. These two meanings are distinguished in Greek, ἔθος, ἦθος. *Moral* virtue is so called from *mos*, inasmuch as the word signifies a certain *natural* or *quasi-natural inclination* to do a thing. And to this meaning the other meaning of *custom* is allied: for custom in a manner turns into nature, and makes an inclination like to that which is natural. But it is manifest that the inclination to act is properly to be attributed to the appetitive faculty, the function whereof is to move the other powers to action. And therefore not every virtue is called *moral*, but that only which is in the appetitive faculty.

Article 2: Is Moral Virtue Distinct from Intellectual?

R. Reason is the first principle of all human acts: all other principles obey reason, though in different degrees. Some obey reason's every beck without any contradiction, as do the limbs of the body if they are in their normal state. Hence the Philosopher [i.e. Aristotle – Ed.] says that 'the soul rules the body with a despotic command,' as the master rules the slave, who has no right to contradict. Some authorities have laid it down that all the active principles in man stand in this way subordinate to reason. If that were true, it would suffice for well-doing to have the reason perfect. Hence as virtue is a habit whereby we are perfected towards well-doing, it would follow that virtue was in reason alone; and thus there would be no virtue but that which is intellectual. Such was the opinion of Socrates, who said that all virtues were modes of prudence. Hence he laid it down that man, while knowledge was present in him, could not sin, but that whoever sinned, sinned through ignorance. This argumentation, however, goes on a false supposition: for the appetitive part is obedient to reason, not to every beck, but with some contradiction. Hence the Philosopher says that 'reason commands appetite with a constitutional command', like to that authority which a parent has over his children, who have in some respects the right of contradiction. Hence Augustine says, 'sometimes understanding goes before, and tardy or none the affection that follows after': inasmuch as, owing to passions or habits in the appetitive faculty, the use of reason on some particular point is impeded. And to this extent it is in some sort true what Socrates said that 'in the presence of knowledge sin is not', provided that the knowledge here spoken of be taken to include the use of reason on the particular point that is matter of choice. Thus then for well-doing it is required that not only reason be well disposed by the habit of intellectual virtue, but also that the appetitive power be well disposed by the habit of moral virtue. As then appetite is distinct from reason, so is moral virtue distinct from intellectual. Hence as appetite is a principle of human action by being in a manner partaker of reason, so a moral habit has the character of a human virtue by being conformable to reason.

Article 3: Is the Division of Virtues into Moral and Intellectual an Exhaustive Division?

R. Human virtue is a habit perfecting man unto well-doing. Now the principle of human acts in man is only twofold, namely, intellect or reason, and appetite. Hence every human virtue must be perfective of one or other of these two principles. If it is perfective of the speculative or practical intellect towards a good human act, it will be intellectual virtue: if it is perfective of the appetitive part, it will be moral virtue.

§1.   Prudence in its essence is an intellectual virtue: but in its subject-matter it falls in with the moral virtues, being *a right method of conduct*; and in this respect it is counted among the moral virtues.

§2.   Continence and perseverance are not perfections of the sensitive appetite, as is evident from this, that in the continent and in the persevering man there are inordinate passions to excess, which would not be the case if the sensitive appetite were perfected by any habit conforming it to reason. But continence, or perseverance, is a perfection of the rational faculty, holding out against passion so as not to be carried away. Nevertheless it falls short of the character and rank of virtue; because that intellectual virtue which makes the reason stand well in moral matters supposes the appetitive faculty to be rightly bent upon the end, which is not the case with the continent and with the persevering man. For no operation proceeding from two powers can be perfect, unless each of the two powers be perfected by the due habit: as there does not follow a perfect action on the part of one acting through an instrument, if the instrument be not well disposed, however perfect be the principal agent. Hence, if the sensitive appetite, which the rational faculty moves, be not perfect, however perfect be the rational faculty itself, still the action ensuing will not be perfect: hence the principle of action will not be a virtue. And therefore continence from pleasures and perseverance in the midst of sorrows are not virtues, but something less than virtue, as the Philosopher says.[1]

§3. Faith, hope and charity are above human virtues; for they are the virtues of man as he is made partaker of divine grace.

Article 4: Can There Be Moral Virtue Without Intellectual?

R. Moral virtue may be without some intellectual virtues, as without wisdom, science and art, but it cannot be without intuition [or intellect – Ed.] and prudence. Moral virtue cannot be without prudence, because moral virtue is an *elective habit*, making a good election. Now to the goodness of an election two things are requisite: first, a due intention of the end – and that is secured by moral virtue, which inclines the appetitive powers to good in accordance with reason, which is the due end; secondly, it is required that the person make a right application of means to the end, and this cannot be except by the aid of reason, rightly counselling, judging and prescribing: all which offices belong to prudence and the virtues annexed thereto. Hence moral virtue cannot be without prudence, and consequently not without intuition either: for by the aid of intuition principles are apprehended, such principles as are naturally knowable, both in speculative and in practical matters. Hence as right reason in matters of speculation, proceeding on principles naturally known, presupposes the intuition of principles, so also does prudence, being right reason applied to conduct, presuppose the same intuition or insight.

§2. In a virtuous person it is not necessary for the use of reason to be vigorous on all points, but only in those things that are to be done according to virtue, and to this extent the use of reason is vigorous in all virtuous persons. Hence even they who seem to be simple, and to lack worldly wisdom, may be prudent persons for all that, according to the text: 'Be ye wise as serpents and simple as doves' [Matthew x.16].

§3.   A natural inclination to the good that is in virtue is a beginning of virtue, but it is not perfect virtue. For the more perfect such inclination is, the more dangerous may it prove, unless right reason be conjoined with it, to make a right election of proper means to a due end. Thus a blind horse runs amuck; and the higher its speed, the more it hurts itself.

Article 5: Can There Be Intellectual Virtue Without Moral?

R. Other intellectual virtues can be without moral virtue, but prudence cannot. The reason is because prudence is right reason applied to conduct, and that not only in general, but also in particular, as actions are particular. But right reason demands pre-established principles, and on them it proceeds. Now in particular matters reason must proceed not only on general but also on particular principles. As for general principles of conduct, man is kept right on these points by his natural insight into principles, whereby he knows that no evil is to be done, or again by some piece of practical knowledge. But this is not sufficient for reasoning aright in particular cases. For it happens sometimes that a general principle of this sort, ascertained by intuition or by science, is set aside in a particular case by some passion. Thus when desire gets the better of a man, that seems good which he desires, though it be against the general judgement of reason. And therefore as man is disposed by natural insight, or by a habit of science, to hold himself aright in respect of general principles, so, to keep right in respect of particular principles of conduct, which are ends of action, he must be perfected by certain habits that make it in a manner connatural to him to judge rightly of the end. And this is done by moral virtue: for the virtuous man judges rightly of the end that virtue should aim at, because 'as each one is, so does the end appear to him.' And therefore for prudence, or the application of right reason to conduct, it is requisite for man to have moral virtue.

Question 61: Of the Cardinal Virtues

Article 2: Are There Four Cardinal Virtues?

R. The formal principle of virtue is rational good; and that may be considered in two ways – in one way as consisting in the mere consideration of reason; and in that way there will be one principal virtue, which is called *prudence*: in another way according as a rational order is established in some matter, and that, either in the matter of actions, and so there is *justice*; or in the matter of passions, and so there must be two virtues. For rational order must be established in the matter of the passions with regard to their repugnance to reason. Now this repugnance may be in two ways: in one way by passion impelling to something contrary to reason; and for that, passion must be *tempered*, or repressed: hence *temperance* takes its name; in another way by passion holding back from that which reason dictates; and for that, man must put his foot down there where reason places him, not to budge from thence: and so *fortitude* gets its name. And in like manner according to subjects the same number is found. For we observe a fourfold subject of this virtue whereof we speak: to wit, the part *rational by essence*, which prudence perfects; and the part *rational by participation*, which is divided into three, namely, the *will*, the subject of justice; the *concupiscible* faculty, the subject of temperance; and the *irascible* faculty, the subject of fortitude.

Article 4: Do the Four Cardinal Virtues Differ One from Another?

R. The four virtues above-mentioned are differently understood by different authors. Some take them as meaning certain general conditions of the human mind which are found in all virtues, so that *prudence* is nothing else than a certain correctness of discernment in any acts or matters whatsoever, *justice* is a certain rectitude of mind whereby a man does what he ought to do in any matter; *temperance* is a disposition of mind, which sets bounds to all manner of passions or actions, that they may not exceed; while *fortitude* is a disposition of the soul whereby it is strengthened in what is according to reason against all manner of assaults of passion or toil of active labours. This fourfold distinction does not involve any difference of virtuous habits so far as justice, temperance and fortitude are concerned. For to every virtue by the fact of its being a *habit* there attaches a certain firmness, so that it may not be moved by any impulse to the contrary; and this has been said to be a point of *fortitude*. Also from the fact of its being a *virtue* it has a direction towards good, wherein is involved the notion of something right and due, which was said to be a point of *justice*. Again, by the fact of its being a *moral* virtue partaking in reason, it has that which makes it observe the bounds of reason in all things, and not go beyond, which was said to be a point of *temperance*. Only the having of discretion, which was attributed to *prudence*, seems to be distinguished from the other three points, inasmuch as this belongs to reason essentially so called, whereas the other three involve only a certain participation in reason by way of application thereof to passions or acts. Thus then on the foregoing reckoning, prudence would be a virtue distinct from the other three; but the other three would not be virtues distinct from one another. For it is manifest that one and the same virtue is at once a *habit*, and a *virtue*, and is *moral*.

Others better understand these four virtues as being determined to special matters, each of them to one matter, so that every virtue which produces that goodness which lies in the consideration of reason, is called *prudence*; and every virtue which produces that goodness which consists in what is due and right in action, is called *justice*; and every virtue which restrains and represses the passions, is called *temperance*; and every virtue which produces a firmness of soul against all manner of sufferings, is called *fortitude*. On this arrangement it is manifest that the aforesaid virtues are different habits, distinct according to the diversity of their objects.

Question 62: Of the Theological Virtues

Article 1: Are There Any Theological Virtues?

R. By virtue man is perfected unto the acts whereby he is set in the way to happiness. Now there is a twofold happiness of man: one proportionate to human nature, whereunto man can arrive by the principles of his own nature. Another happiness there is exceeding the nature of man, whereunto man can arrive only by a divine virtue involving a certain participation in the Deity, according as it is said that by Christ we are made 'partakers of the divine nature' [Peter i. 4]. And because this manner of happiness exceeds the capacities of human nature, the natural principles of human action, on which man proceeds to such well-doing as is in proportion with himself, suffice not to direct man unto the aforesaid happiness. Hence there must be superadded to man by the gift of God certain principles, whereby he may be put on the way to supernatural happiness, even as he is directed to his connatural end by natural principles, yet not without the divine aid. Such principles are called *theological virtues*: both because they have God for their object, inasmuch as by them we are directed aright to God; as also because it is only by divine revelation in Holy Scripture that such virtues are taught.

Article 2: Are Theological Virtues Distinct from Virtues Intellectual and Moral?

R. Habits are specifically distinct according to the formal difference of their objects. But the object of the theological virtues is God Himself, the last end of all things, as He transcends the knowledge of our reason: whereas the object of the intellectual and moral virtues is something that can be comprehended by human reason. Hence theological virtues are specifically distinct from virtues moral and intellectual.

§1.   The intellectual and moral virtues perfect the intellect and appetite of man according to the capacity of human nature, but the theological virtues supernaturally.

Article 3: Are Faith, Hope and Charity Fitly Assigned as the Theological Virtues?

R. The theological virtues set man in the way of supernatural happiness, as he is directed to his connatural end by a natural inclination. This latter direction is worked out in two ways: first, by way of the reason or intellect, as that power holds in its knowledge the general principles of rational procedure, theoretical and practical, known by the light of nature: secondly, by the rectitude of the will naturally tending to rational good. But both these agencies fall short of the order of supernatural good. Hence for both of them some supernatural addition was necessary to man, to direct him to a supernatural end. On the side of the intellect man receives the addition of certain supernatural principles, which are perceived by divine light; and these are the objects of belief, with which *faith* is conversant. Secondly, there is the will, which is directed to the supernatural end, both by way of an affective movement directed thereto as to a point possible to gain, and this movement belongs to *hope*; and by way of a certain spiritual union, whereby the will is in a manner transformed into that end, which union and transformation is wrought by *charity*. For the appetite of every being has a natural motion and tendency towards an end connatural to itself; and that movement arises from some sort of conformity of the thing to its end.

§2.   Faith and hope denote a certain imperfection: because faith is of the things that are seen not, and hope of the things that are possessed not. Hence to have faith in and hope of the things that are amenable to human power, is a falling short of the character of virtue. But to have faith in and hope of the things that are beyond the ability of human nature, transcends all virtue proportionate to man, according to the text: 'The weakness of God is stronger than men' [I Corinthians i. 25].

Question 63: Of the Cause of Virtues

Article 1: Is Virtue in Us by Nature?

R. As regards sciences and virtues some have laid it down that they are totally from within, meaning that all virtues and sciences naturally pre-exist in the soul, and that discipline and exercise do no more than remove the obstacles to virtue and science, which arise in the soul from the lumpishness of the body, as when iron is polished by filing; and this was the opinion of the Platonists. Others, on the contrary, have said that they are totally from without. Others again have said that in aptitude the sciences and virtues are in us by nature, but not in perfection. So says the Philosopher, and this is the more correct thing to say. In evidence whereof we must consider that a thing is said to be natural to man in two ways: in one way according to the nature of the species, in another way according to the nature of the individual. And because everything has its species according to its form, and is individualized according to its matter: and man's form is his rational soul, and his matter his body; therefore that which belongs to man by virtue of his rational soul is natural to him in point of his species; while that which is natural to him by his having a given complexion of body is natural to him according to his nature as an individual. Now in both these ways a rudimentary phase of virtue is natural to man. First, as regards his specific nature, in this way, that there are by nature in the reason of man certain naturally known principles, theoretical and practical, which are seminal principles of virtues intellectual and moral; and again inasmuch as there is in the will a natural craving after the good that is according to reason. Secondly, as regards his individual nature, inasmuch as by conformation of body some are better and some worse disposed to certain virtues: the explanation being this, that the sensitive powers are energies of corresponding parts of the body; and according to the disposition of those parts the said powers are helped or hindered in their operations; and consequently the rational powers also, which these sensitive powers serve, are helped or hindered in like manner. Thus one man has a natural aptitude for knowledge, another for fortitude, another for temperance. And in these ways the virtues, as well intellectual as moral, are in us by nature to the extent of a certain rudimentary aptitude, but not in their perfect completeness: the reason being that nature is limited to one fixed course of action, whereas the perfection of the said virtues does not lead to one fixed course of action, but is varied according to the diversity of matters wherein the virtues operate, and the diversity of circumstances. It appears then that virtues are in us by nature, in aptitude, and in a rudimentary phase, but not in their perfection – except the theological virtues, which are wholly from without.[2]

Article 2

§2. Virtue divinely infused, considered in its perfection, is incompatible with any mortal sin. But virtue humanly acquired is compatible with an act even of mortal sin, because the use of a habit in us is subject to our will. Nor is a habit of acquired virtue destroyed by one act of sin: for the direct contrary of a habit is not an act, but another habit. And therefore, though without grace a man cannot avoid mortal sin so as never to sin mortally, still there is nothing to hinder him from acquiring a habit of virtue, enough to keep him from evil acts for the most part, and especially from those that are very much opposed to reason. There are, however, some mortal sins that man can nowise avoid without grace, to wit, the sins that are directly contrary to the theological virtues which are in us by the gift of grace.

Notes

1 The point Aquinas and Aristotle (*Nicomachean Ethics*, Book 7) are making is that, while continence, self-discipline, perseverance and the like are to be admired, the truly virtuous person would not require them, since he or she would not be subject to the temptations that they are required to overcome. For such a person, acting virtuously has become, as we might say, 'second nature'.
2 It may seem odd to say that the theological virtues, being 'infused' in us by God, can in any sense be 'in us by nature'. But 'natural' here contrasts, not with 'supernatural', but with 'acquired'. A gift of Grace is not an acquisition of mine.

Joseph Butler, Sermon 'Upon the Love of Our Neighbour'

From Joseph Butler, *Fifteen Sermons: Preached at the Rolls Chapel*. London: Bell & Sons, 1964, 11th Sermon, pp. 165–83.

Beyond their wearing of the cloth, one might expect little in common between a thirteenth-century Dominican friar and an eighteenth-century Anglican Bishop of Durham. Yet both Aquinas and Bishop Butler (1692–1752) were combating prevalent doctrines of their contemporaries incompatible, as they saw it, with a rational approach to morality based on a proper appreciation of human nature. In Aquinas's case, the enemy was the doctrine of morality as the arbitrary edicts of God; in Butler's case, it was the egoistic hedonism embraced by many Enlightenment thinkers, especially those of a 'materialist' bent. As he explains in the Preface to his *Sermons*, 'perhaps the finest ethical work in English',[1] the targets of the 11th Sermon are Epicurus, Thomas Hobbes, the Duc de la Rochefoucauld and others who try to 'represent . . . the whole of life as nothing but one continued exercise of self-love' (§35). Such a doctrine means that either there is no such thing as moral conduct ('our virtues are only vices in disguise', as the Duc's cynical maxim has it), or moral conduct just *is* enlightened self-interest.

Not the least objection to this doctrine is its tendency to provoke barely more acceptable views at the other extreme: its inspiration, for example, of puritanical hostility to *any* exercise of self-love, or of the view that morality is benevolent devotion to what Francis Hutcheson, ahead of Bentham, called 'the greatest happiness of the greatest number' – a view Butler rejects on the grounds that conscience often requires actions which there is no reason to suppose will promote general happiness. For Butler, both egoism and these reactions to it share a false premise, namely that self-love and benevolence or 'disinterestedness' are in conflict. Hence the 11th Sermon has two aims: to discredit egoism as a general theory of human nature and motivation, and to

[1] T. L. S. Sprigge, 'Butler', in *The Oxford Companion to Philosophy*, Oxford: Oxford University Press, 1995, p. 112.

show that, in so far as we do act out of self-love, this need not be antithetical to benevolent, moral conduct.

Butler's sharp arguments have convinced many that egoism is either trivial or false, indeed incoherent. It is trivial if it boils down to saying that all my voluntary actions are *mine*, empirically false or worse if it means that some state of myself is always the goal of my actions, thereby ignoring the 'particular external things' – be it my reputation, my mother's health, or peace on earth – which I may be aiming at. Even if self-love and wanting some such 'external thing' coincided in the actions each would produce, it cannot follow that the latter reduces to the former. 'Everything is what it is, and not another thing' (Preface §39), to cite Butler's famous legacy to analytic philosophy. Indeed, unless I typically aimed at something other than my own pleasure, it is impossible to see how I could get any pleasure from succeeding (11th Sermon §9). Readers have always been puzzled, however, by the concluding lines of §19, where Butler himself seems to endorse hedonism, apparently suggesting that we cannot justify anything to ourselves unless 'we are convinced that it will be for our own happiness'. But a careful reading of his words suggests that his point is this: *even if* our sole goal were self-love, we could still morally justify some actions.[2] The lines belong, therefore, to the other purpose of the Sermon, to show that self-love and moral action need not conflict.

Whether Butler is as successful here as in his arguments against psychological egoism is doubtful. Presumably he is right to claim, as John Stuart Mill did over a century later, that a person's happiness is often dependent on that of others, since the latter is an ingredient in it. But there is surely eighteenth-century over-optimism in the assumption that all human beings are so constituted by nature that the well-being of others is an important factor in their own well-being. Perhaps this is recognized by Butler when, like Aquinas (though for different reasons), he introduces God to round off his account of morality. Ultimately, the suggestion seems to be in §22, Christian belief in the prospect of eternal salvation is required to 'lay us under . . . obligations to a good life' and to 'afford additional motives' for virtuous behaviour beyond those of benevolence and self-love.

And if there be any other commandment, it is briefly comprehended in this saying, namely, Thou shalt love thy neighbour as thyself.

(Romans xiii. 9)

(1)   It is commonly observed that there is a disposition in men to complain of the viciousness and corruption of the age in which they live, as

---

[2] See Austin Duncan-Jones, *Butler's Moral Philosophy*, Harmondsworth: Penguin, 1952, pp. 113ff.

greater than that of former ones; which is usually followed with this further observation, that mankind has been in that respect much the same in all times. Now, not to determine whether this last be not contradicted by the accounts of history; thus much can scarce be doubted, that vice and folly takes different turns, and some particular kinds of it are more open and avowed in some ages than in others: and, I suppose, it may be spoken of as very much the distinction of the present to profess a contracted spirit, and greater regards to self-interest, than appears to have been done formerly. Upon this account it seems worth while to inquire whether private interest is likely to be promoted in proportion to the degree in which self-love engrosses us, and prevails over all other principles; *or whether the contracted affection may not possibly be so prevalent as to disappoint itself, and even contradict its own end, private good.*

(2)   And since further, there is generally thought to be some peculiar kind of contrariety between self-love and the love of our neighbour, between the pursuit of public and of private good; insomuch that when you are recommending one of these, you are supposed to be speaking against the other; and from hence arises a secret prejudice against, and frequently open scorn of, all talk of public spirit, and real good-will to our fellow-creatures; it will be necessary to *inquire what respect benevolence hath to self-love, and the pursuit of private interest to the pursuit of public*: or whether there be anything of that peculiar inconsistence and contrariety between them, over and above what there is between self-love and other passions and particular affections, and their respective pursuits.

(3)   These inquiries, it is hoped, may be favourably attended to: for there shall be all possible concessions made to the favourite passion, which hath so much allowed to it, and whose cause is so universally pleaded: it shall be treated with the utmost tenderness and concern for its interests.

(4)   In order to [do] this, as well as to determine the forementioned questions, it will be necessary to *consider the nature, the object and end of that self-love, as distinguished from other principles or affections in the mind, and their respective objects.*

(5)   Every man hath a general desire of his own happiness; and likewise a variety of particular affections, passions and appetites to particular external objects. The former proceeds from, or is self-love; and seems inseparable from all sensible creatures, who can reflect upon themselves and their own interest or happiness, so as to have that interest an object to their minds: what is to be said of the latter is, that they proceed from, or together make up that particular nature, according to which man is made. The object the former pursues is somewhat internal, our own happiness, enjoyment, satisfaction; whether we have, or have not, a distinct particular

perception what it is, or wherein it consists: the objects of the latter are this or that particular external thing which the affections tend towards, and of which it hath always a particular idea or perception. The principle we call self-love never seeks anything external for the sake of the thing, but only as a means of happiness or good: particular affections rest in the external things themselves. One belongs to man as a reasonable creature reflecting upon his own interest or happiness. The other, though quite distinct from reason, are as much a part of human nature.

(6)   That all particular appetites and passions are towards *external things themselves*, distinct from the *pleasure arising from them*, is manifested from hence; that there could not be this pleasure, were it not for that prior suitableness between the object and the passion: there could be no enjoyment or delight from one thing more than another, from eating food more than from swallowing a stone, if there were not an affection or appetite to one thing more than another.

(7)   Every particular affection, even the love of our neighbour, is as really our own affection as self-love; and the pleasure arising from its gratification is as much my own pleasure as the pleasure self-love would have, from knowing I myself should be happy some time hence would be my own pleasure. And if, because every particular affection is a man's own, and the pleasure arising from its gratification his own pleasure, or pleasure to himself, such particular affection must be called self-love; according to this way of speaking, no creature whatever can possibly act but merely from self-love; and every action and every affection whatever is to be resolved up into this one principle. But, then, this is not the language of mankind: or if it were, we should want words to express the difference between the principle of an action, proceeding from cool consideration that it will be to my own advantage; and an action, suppose of revenge, or of friendship, by which a man runs upon certain ruin, to do evil or good to another. It is manifest the principles of these actions are totally different, and so want different words to be distinguished by: all that they agree in is that they both proceed from, and are done to gratify, an inclination in a man's self. But the principle or inclination in one case is self-love: in the other, hatred or love of another. There is then a distinction between the cool principle of self-love, or general desire of our own happiness, as one part of our nature and one principle of action; and the particular affections towards particular external objects, as another part of our nature and another principle of action. How much soever therefore is to be allowed to self-love, yet it cannot be allowed to be the whole of our inward constitution; because, you see, there are other parts or principles which come into it.

(8)   Further, private happiness or good is all which self-love can make us desire, or be concerned about: in having this consists its gratification; it is an affection to ourselves; a regard to our own interest, happiness and private good: and in the proportion a man hath this, he is interested, or a lover of himself. Let this be kept in mind; because there is commonly, as I shall presently have occasion to observe, another sense put upon these words. On the other hand, particular affections tend towards particular external things: these are their objects; having these is their end; in this consists their gratification, no matter whether it be, or be not, upon the whole, our interest or happiness. An action done from the former of these principles is called an interested action. An action proceeding from any of the latter has its denomination of passionate, ambitious, friendly, revengeful or any other, from the particular appetite or affection from which it proceeds. Thus self-love as one part of human nature, and the several particular principles as the other part, are themselves their objects and ends, stated and shewn.

(9)   From hence it will be easy to see how far, and in what ways, each of these can contribute and be subservient to the private good of the individual. Happiness does not consist in self-love. The desire of happiness is no more the thing itself, than the desire of riches is the possession or enjoyment of them. People may love themselves with the most entire and unbounded affection, and yet be extremely miserable. Neither can self-love any way help them out, but by setting them on work to get rid of the causes of their misery, to gain or make use of those objects which are by nature adapted to afford satisfaction. Happiness or satisfaction consists only in the enjoyment of those objects, which are by nature suited to our several particular appetites, passions and affections. So that if self-love wholly engrosses us, and leaves no room for any other principle, there can be absolutely no such thing at all as happiness, or enjoyment of any kind whatever; since happiness consists in the gratification of particular passions, which supposes the having of them. Self-love, then, does not constitute *this* or *that* to be our interest or good; but, our interest or good being constituted by nature and supposed, self-love only puts us upon obtaining and securing it. Therefore, if it be possible that self-love may prevail and exert itself in a degree or manner which is not subservient to this end; then it will not follow that our interest will be promoted in proportion to the degree in which that principle engrosses us, and prevails over others. Nay further, the private and contracted affection, when it is not subservient to this end, private good, may, for anything that appears, have a direct contrary tendency and effect. And if we will consider the matter, we shall see that it often really has. *Disengagement* is absolutely necessary to enjoyment: and a person may have so steady and fixed an eye upon his own interest, what-

ever he places it in, as may hinder him from *attending* to many gratifications within his reach, which others have their minds *free* and *open* to. Over-fondness for a child is not generally thought to be for its advantage; and, if there be any guess to be made from appearances, surely that character we call selfish is not the most promising for happiness. Such a temper may plainly be and exert itself in a degree and manner which may give unnecessary and useless solicitude and anxiety, in a degree and manner which may prevent obtaining the means and materials of enjoyment, as well as the making use of them. Immoderate self-love does very ill consult its own interest: and, how much soever a paradox it may appear, it is certainly true, that even from self-love we should endeavour to get over all inordinate regard to, and consideration of ourselves. Every one of our passions and affections hath its natural stint and bound, which may easily be exceeded; whereas our enjoyments can possibly be but in a determinate measure and degree. Therefore such excess of the affection, since it cannot procure any enjoyment, must in all cases be useless; but is generally attended with inconveniences, and often is downright pain and misery. This holds as much with regard to self-love as to all other affections. The natural degree of it, so far as it sets us on work to gain and make use of the materials of satisfaction, may be to our real advantage; but beyond or besides this, it is in several respects an inconvenience and disadvantage. Thus it appears that private interest is so far from being likely to be promoted in proportion to the degree in which self-love engrosses us, and prevails over all other principles, that *the contracted affection may be so prevalent as to disappoint itself, and even contradict its own end, private good.*

(10)   'But who, except the most sordidly covetous, ever thought there was any rivalship between the love of greatness, honour, power, or between sensual appetites, and self-love? No, there is a perfect harmony between them. It is by means of these particular appetites and affections that self-love is gratified in enjoyment, happiness and satisfaction. The competition and rivalship is between self-love and the love of our neighbour: that affection which leads us out of ourselves, makes us regardless of our own interest, and substitute that of another in its stead.' Whether then there be any peculiar competition and contrariety in this case shall now be considered.

(11)   Self-love and interestedness was stated to consist in or be an affection to ourselves, a regard to our own private good: it is therefore distinct from benevolence, which is an affection to the good of our fellow-creatures. But that benevolence is distinct from, that is, not the same thing with self-love, is no reason for its being looked upon with any peculiar suspicion; because every principle whatever, by means of which self-love is

gratified, is distinct from it; and all things which are distinct from each other are equally so. A man has an affection or aversion to another: that one of these tends to and is gratified by doing harm, does not in the least alter the respect which either one or the other of these inward feelings has to self-love. We use the word *property* so as to exclude any other persons having an interest in that of which we say a particular man has the property. And we often use the word *selfish* so as to exclude in the same manner all regards to the good of others. But the cases are not parallel: for though that exclusion is really part of the idea of property; yet such positive exclusion, or bringing this peculiar disregard to the good of others into the idea of self-love, is in reality adding to the idea or changing it from what it was before stated to consist in, namely, in an affection to ourselves. This being the whole idea of self-love, it can no otherwise exclude good-will or love of others, than merely by not including it, no otherwise than it excludes love of arts or of reputation, or of anything else. Neither on the other hand does benevolence, any more than love of arts or reputation, exclude self-love. Love of our neighbour then has just the same respect to, is no more distant from self-love, than hatred of our neighbour, or than love or hatred of anything else. Thus the principles from which men rush upon certain ruin for the destruction of an enemy, and for the preservation of a friend, have the same respect to the private affection, and are equally interested, or equally disinterested; and it is of no avail, whether they are said to be one or the other. Therefore to those who are shocked to hear virtue spoken of as disinterested, it may be allowed that it is indeed absurd to speak thus of it; unless hatred, several particular instances of vice, and all the common affections and aversions in mankind are acknowledged to be disinterested too. Is there any less inconsistence between the love of inanimate things, or of creatures merely sensitive, and self-love, than between self-love and the love of our neighbour? Is desire of and delight in the happiness of another any more a diminution of self-love, than desire of and delight in the esteem of another? They are both equally desire of and delight in somewhat external to ourselves: either both or neither are so. The object of self-love is expressed in the term self; and every appetite of sense, and every particular affection of the heart, are equally interested or disinterested, because the objects of them all are equally self or somewhat else. Whatever ridicule therefore the mention of a disinterested principle or action may be supposed to lie open to, must, upon the matter being thus stated, relate to ambition, and every appetite and particular affection, as much as to benevolence. And indeed all the ridicule, and all the grave perplexity, of which this subject hath had its full share, is merely from words. The most intelligible way of speaking of it seems to be this: that self-love, and the actions done in consequence of it (for these will presently appear to be the same as to this question) are interested; that particular affections towards external objects, and the actions done in consequence of those affections, are not so. But every one is at liberty to use words as he pleases. All that is here insisted upon is that ambition, revenge, benevolence, all particular passions whatever, and the actions they produce, are equally interested or disinterested.

(12)   Thus it appears that there is no peculiar contrariety between self-love and benevolence; no greater competition between these than between any other particular affections and self-love. This relates to the affections themselves. Let us now see whether there be any peculiar contrariety between the respective courses of life which these affections lead to; whether there be any greater competition between the pursuit of private and of public good, than between any other particular pursuits and that of private good.

(13)   There seems no other reason to suspect that there is any such peculiar contrariety, but only that the course of action which benevolence leads to, has a more direct tendency to promote the good of others, than that course of action which love of reputation, suppose, or any other particular affection leads to. But that any affection tends to the happiness of another, does not hinder its tending to one's own happiness too. That others enjoy the benefit of the air and the light of the sun, does not hinder but that these are as much one's own private advantage now, as they would be if we had the property of them exclusive of all others. So a pursuit which tends to promote the good of another, yet may have as great tendency to promote private interest as a pursuit which does not tend to the good of another at all, or which is mischievous to him. All particular affections whatever, resentment, benevolence, love of arts, equally lead to a course of action for their own gratification, i.e. the gratification of ourselves; and the gratification of each gives delight: so far then it is manifest they have all the same respect to private interest. Now take into consideration further, concerning these three pursuits, that the end of the first is the harm, of the second, the good of another, of the last, somewhat indifferent; and is there any necessity that these additional considerations should alter the respect which we before saw these three pursuits had to private interest, or render any one of them less conducive to it than any other? Thus one man's affection is to honour as his end; in order to obtain which he thinks no pains too great. Suppose another with such a singularity of mind as to have the same affection to public good as his end, which he endeavours with the same labour to obtain. In case of success, surely the man of benevolence hath as great enjoyment as the man of ambition; they both equally having

the end of their affections, in the same degree, tended to: but in case of disappointment, the benevolent man has clearly the advantage, since endeavouring to do good considered as a virtuous pursuit is gratified by its own consciousness, i.e. is in a degree its own reward.

(14)   And as to these two, or benevolence and any other particular passions whatever, considered in a further view as forming a general temper, which more or less disposes us for enjoyment of all the common blessings of life, distinct from their own gratification: is benevolence less the temper of tranquillity and freedom than ambition or covetousness? Does the benevolent man appear less easy with himself, from his love to his neighbour? Does he less relish his being? Is there any peculiar gloom seated on his face? Is his mind less open to entertainment, to any particular gratification? Nothing is more manifest than that being in good humour, which is benevolence whilst it lasts, is itself the temper of satisfaction and enjoyment.

(15)   Suppose then a man sitting down to consider how he might become most easy to himself, and attain the greatest pleasure he could, all that which is his real natural happiness. This can only consist in the enjoyment of those objects which are by nature adapted to our several faculties. These particular enjoyments make up the sum total of our happiness; and they are supposed to arise from riches, honours and the gratification of sensual appetites. Be it so; yet none profess themselves so completely happy in these enjoyments but that there is room left in the mind for others, if they were presented to them: nay these, as much as they engage us, are not thought so high but that human nature is capable even of greater. Now there have been persons in all ages, who have professed that they found satisfaction in the exercise of charity, in the love of their neighbour, in endeavouring to promote the happiness of all they had to do with, and in the pursuit of what is just and right and good, as the general bent of their mind, and end of their life; and that doing an action of baseness or cruelty would be as great violence to *their* self, as much breaking in upon their nature, as any external force. Persons of this character would add, if they might be heard, that they consider themselves as acting in the view of an infinite Being, who is in a much higher sense the object of reverence and of love, than all the world besides; and therefore they could have no more enjoyment from a wicked action done under his eye, than the persons to whom they are making their apology could, if all mankind were the spectators of it; and that the satisfaction of approving themselves to his unerring judgement, to whom they thus refer all their actions, is a more continued settled satisfaction than any this world can afford; as also that they have, no less than others, a mind free and open to all the common innocent gratifications of it, such as they are. And if we go no further, does there

appear any absurdity in this? Will any one take upon him to say that a man cannot find his account in this general course of life, as much as in the most unbounded ambition and the excesses of pleasure? Or that such a person has not consulted so well for himself, for the satisfaction and peace of his own mind, as the ambitious or dissolute man? And though the consideration, that God himself will in the end justify their taste and support their cause, is not formally to be insisted upon here, yet thus much comes in, that all enjoyments whatever are much more clear and unmixed from the assurance that they will end well. Is it certain then that there is nothing in these pretensions to happiness? Especially when there are not wanting persons who have supported themselves with satisfactions of this kind in sickness, poverty, disgrace, and in the very pangs of death; whereas it is manifest all other enjoyments fail in these circumstances. This surely looks suspicious of having somewhat in it. Self-love methinks should be alarmed. May she not possibly pass over greater pleasures than those she is so wholly taken up with?

(16) The short of the matter is no more than this. Happiness consists in the gratification of certain affections, appetites, passions, with objects which are by nature adapted to them. Self-love may indeed set us on work to gratify these; but happiness or enjoyment has no immediate connection with self-love, but arises from such gratification alone. Love of our neighbour is one of those affections. This, considered as a *virtuous principle* is gratified by a consciousness of *endeavouring* to promote the good of others; but considered as a natural affection, its gratification consists in the actual accomplishment of this endeavour. Now indulgence or gratification of this affection, whether in that consciousness or this accomplishment, has the same respect to interest as indulgence of any other affection; they equally proceed from or do not proceed from self-love, they equally include or equally exclude this principle. Thus it appears that *benevolence and the pursuit of public good hath at least as great respect to self-love and the pursuit of private good as any other particular passions, and their respective pursuits.*

(17) Neither is covetousness, whether as a temper or pursuit, any exception to this. For if by covetousness is meant the desire and pursuit of riches for their own sake, without any regard to or consideration of the uses of them, this hath as little to do with self-love as benevolence hath. But by this word is usually meant, not such madness and total distraction of mind, but immoderate affection to and pursuit of riches as possessions in order to some further end, namely, satisfaction, interest or good. This therefore is not a particular affection or particular pursuit, but it is the general principle of self-love, and the general pursuit of our own interest;

for which reason, the word selfish is by every one appropriated to this temper and pursuit. Now as it is ridiculous to assert that self-love and the love of our neighbour are the same, so neither is it asserted that following these different affections hath the same tendency and respect to our own interest. The comparison is not between self-love and the love of our neighbour, between pursuit of our own interest, and the interest of others; but between the several particular affections in human nature towards external objects, as one part of the comparison, and the one particular affection to the good of our neighbour, as the other part of it: and it has been shewn that all these have the same respect to self-love and private interest.

(18)   There is indeed frequently an inconsistence or interfering between self-love or private interest, and the several particular appetites, passions, affections, or the pursuits they lead to. But this competition or interfering is merely accidental; and happens much oftener between pride, revenge, sensual gratifications and private interest, than between private interest and benevolence. For nothing is more common than to see men give themselves up to a passion or an affection to their known prejudice and ruin, and in direct contradiction to manifest and real interest, and the loudest calls of self-love: whereas the seeming competitions and interfering between benevolence and private interest relate much more to the materials or means of enjoyment than to enjoyment itself. There is often an interfering in the former, when there is none in the latter. Thus as to riches: so much money as a man gives away, so much less will remain in his possession. Here is a real interfering. But though a man cannot possibly give without lessening his fortune, yet there are multitudes might give without lessening their own enjoyment, because they may have more than they can turn to any real use or advantage to themselves. Thus the more thought and time any one employs about the interests and good of others, he must necessarily have less to attend his own; but he may have so ready and large a supply of his own wants that such thought might be really useless to himself, though of great service and assistance to others.

(19)   The general mistake, that there is some greater inconsistence between endeavouring to promote the good of another and self-interest than between self-interest and pursuing anything else, seems, as hath already been hinted, to arise from our notions of property, and to be carried on by this property's being supposed to be itself our happiness or good. People are so very much taken up with this one subject, that they seem from it to have formed a general way of thinking, which they apply to other things that they have nothing to do with. Hence, in a confused and slight way, it might well be taken for granted, that another's having no interest in an affection (i.e. his good not being the object of it) renders, as one may

speak, the proprietor's interest in it greater; and that if another had an interest in it, this would render his less, or occasion that such affection could not be so friendly to self-love or conducive to private good, as an affection or pursuit which has not a regard to the good of another. This, I say, might be taken for granted, whilst it was not attended to, that the object of every particular affection is equally somewhat external to ourselves; and whether it be the good of another person, or whether it be any other external thing, makes no alteration with regard to its being one's own affection, and the gratification of it one's own private enjoyment. And so far as it is taken for granted that barely having the means and materials of enjoyment is what constitutes interest and happiness, that our interest or good consists in possessions themselves, in having the property of riches, houses, lands, gardens, not in the enjoyment of them; so far it will even more strongly be taken for granted, in the way already explained, that an affection's conducing to the good of another must even necessarily occasion it to conduce less to private good, if not to be positively detrimental to it. For, if property and happiness are one and the same thing, as by increasing the property of another you lessen your own property, so by promoting the happiness of another you must lessen your own happiness. But whatever occasioned the mistake, I hope it has been fully proved to be one, as it has been proved that there is no peculiar rivalship or competition between self-love and benevolence; that as there may be a competition between these two, so there may also between any particular affection whatever and self-love; that every particular affection, benevolence among the rest, is subservient to self-love by being the instrument of private enjoyment; and that in one respect benevolence contributes more to private interest, i.e. enjoyment or satisfaction, than any other of the particular common affections, as it is in a degree its own gratification.

(20)   And to all these things may be added, that religion, from whence arises our strongest obligation to benevolence, is so far from disowning the principle of self-love, that it often addresses itself to that very principle, and always to the mind in that state when reason presides; and there can no access be had to the understanding, but by convincing men, that the course of life we would persuade them to is not contrary to their interest. It may be allowed, without any prejudice to the cause of virtue and religion, that our ideas of happiness and misery are of all our ideas the nearest and most important to us; that they will, nay, if you please, that they ought to prevail over those of order, and beauty, and harmony, and proportion, if there should ever be, as it is impossible there ever should be, any inconsistence between them; though these last too, as expressing the fitness of actions, are real as truth itself. Let it be allowed, though virtue or moral rectitude

does indeed consist in affection to and pursuit of what is right and good, as such; yet, that when we sit down in a cool hour, we can neither justify to ourselves this or any other pursuit, till we are convinced that it will be for our happiness, or at least not contrary to it.

(21)   Common reason and humanity will have some influence upon mankind, whatever becomes of speculations; but, so far as the interests of virtue depend upon the theory of it being secured from open scorn, so far its very being in the world depends upon its appearing to have no contrariety to private interest and self-love. The foregoing observations therefore, it is hoped, may have gained a little ground in favour of the precept before us; the particular explanation of which shall be the subject of the next Discourse.

(22)   I will conclude at present, with observing the peculiar obligation which we are under to virtue and religion, as enforced in the verses following the text, in the epistle for the day, from our Saviour's coming into the world. *The night is far spent, the day is at hand; let us therefore cast off the works of darkness, and let us put on the armour of light, etc.* The meaning and force of which exhortation is that Christianity lays us under new obligations to a good life, as by it the will of God is more clearly revealed, and as it affords additional motives to the practice of it, over and above those which arise out of the nature of virtue and vice; I might add, as our Saviour has set us a perfect example of goodness in our own nature. Now love and charity is plainly the thing in which he hath placed his religion; in which therefore, as we have any pretence to the name of Christians, we must place ours. He hath at once enjoined it upon us by way of command with peculiar force; and by his example, as having undertaken the work of our salvation out of pure love and good-will to mankind. The endeavour to set home this example upon our minds is a very proper employment of this season, which is bringing on the festival of his birth: which as it may teach us many excellent lessons of humility, resignation and obedience to the will of God; so there is none it recommends with greater authority, force and advantage, than this of love and charity; since it was *for us men, and for our salvation,* that *he came down from heaven, and was incarnate, and was made man*; that he might teach us our duty, and more especially that he might enforce the practice of it, reform mankind, and finally bring us to that *eternal salvation* of which *he is the Author to all those that obey him.*

David Hume, *A Treatise of Human Nature*, Book III, Part I (Sections 1–2)

From David Hume, *A Treatise of Human Nature*, ed. L. A. Selby-Bigge. Oxford: Clarendon Press, 1960, pp. 455–76 [asterisked notes are Hume's own; some notes omitted]; reprinted by permission of Oxford University Press.

Butler, we saw, is not without today's champions, but the accolade of 'the greatest of all English moralists, were he not a Scotsman' usually goes to the Edinburgh philosopher David Hume (1711–76).[1] Certainly Hume's moral philosophy had an immense impact, immediately upon the *philosophes* of French Enlightenment and, in the twentieth century, upon analytic philosophers seeking precursors of their own theories of moral discourse.

Hume shared the concern of Butler, to whom he acknowledged a debt, to counter the fashionable egoism of his day. Beyond self-love, he insists, there is a common human 'sentiment' which is 'no other than a feeling for the happiness of mankind, and a resentment of their misery', the two ends which 'virtue and vice' respectively promote.[2] Even rules of justice, which may not immediately arouse this 'sentiment', are approved of because they contribute to a system of behaviour which does promote general happiness. But in the famous text I have selected from his *Treatise*, Hume's main target is at an opposite extreme from egoism. It might be called 'ethical rationalism'. Among both followers of Descartes and the English Neo-Platonists, it was held that moral truths were discoverable in the same manner as those of mathematics or science, either by unaided reason or by reason in conjunction with empirical enquiry into the objective order of the world. For example, it was held by the theologian William Wollaston, whom Hume demolishes in a long footnote (omitted), that all bad actions are a species of falsehood – the adulterer, for instance, representing another's wife as his own. Others imagined that moral

---

[1] Alasdair MacIntyre, *A Short History of Ethics*, London: Macmillan, 1966, p. 168.
[2] *An Inquiry Concerning the Principles of Morals*, Indianapolis: Bobbs-Merrill, 1957, p. 105.

principles were innately implanted in us just as, allegedly, were the truths of logic.

It is views such as these which Hume rejects in claiming that 'moral distinctions [are] not deriv'd from reason'. Care is needed, however, over his use of 'reason'. He is no irrationalist denying, say, the role of rational enquiry in ascertaining which rules of justice best contribute to a society's well-being. Nor, when he famously remarks that ' 'tis not contrary to reason to prefer the destruction of the whole world to the scratching of my finger' (*Treatise*, II.III.3), is he embracing moral nihilism. Reason, he explains, enables us to establish only 'relations of ideas' and 'matters of fact': its scope, in modern parlance, is the truths of logic and the truths ascertainable by empirical investigation. The point of the scratched finger example, then, is that no amount of logical and scientific enquiry – excluding as it does considerations of 'sentiment' or emotion – can by itself show why mass destruction is worse than a minor wound.

Hume advances several arguments against the rationalists, of which the most enduring is presaged in his earlier remark that 'reason is, and ought only to be the slave of the passions' (II.III.3). This is not a wild romantic manifesto, enjoining submission of the head to the heart, but the insistence that reason *per se* is incapable of moving people to action. Since our moral convictions *necessarily* move us to action, and to praise and blame, it follows that these convictions involve the 'passions' and cannot therefore merely be judgements of logic or empirical fact.

So one conclusion Hume draws is clear enough: 'since vice and virtue are not discoverable merely by reason, . . . it must be by means of . . . sentiment . . . that we are able to mark the difference' (III.I.2). But does he want to draw a stronger conclusion? Focusing on the notorious final paragraph of Section 1, many commentators attribute to Hume the view that no 'ought' can be derived from an 'is', that moral and evaluative judgements can never be inferred from statements of fact. This interpretation is then supported by citing lines where Hume seems to suggest that, in calling something 'good', I am simply expressing a favourable feeling towards it. Against this, other commentators hold that Hume is claiming only this: 'oughts' cannot be derived from factual statements which 'say nothing about human sentiments'.[3] Once we take into account the fact that a certain kind of action has a tendency to arouse general approval, Hume would have no objection, they argue, to concluding that the action is a good one. These latter commentators also draw attention to the passages, in Hume's aesthetic as well as his ethical writings, where he compares evaluative properties to 'secondary qualities', like colour. Nothing is coloured except in relation to our impressions, but it remains an empirical fact

---

[3] Geoffrey Hunter, 'A reply to Professor Flew', in W. D. Hudson (ed.), *The Is/Ought Question*, London: Macmillan, 1969, p. 71. The first six articles of this book are devoted to Hume.

that a thing has the colour it does. Why should it be any different with things' moral and aesthetic properties?[4]

It is fair to say that the jury is still out on the exact meaning of Hume's ambiguous remarks, as indeed it is on the issue of the relation between moral and empirical discourse which those remarks have done so much to place at the centre of modern philosophical ethics.

Section 1: Moral Distinctions not Deriv'd from Reason

There is an inconvenience which attends all abstruse reasoning, that it may silence, without convincing an antagonist, and requires the same intense study to make us sensible of its force, that was at first requisite for its invention. When we leave our closet, and engage in the common affairs of life, its conclusions seem to vanish, like the phantoms of the night on the appearance of the morning; and 'tis difficult for us to retain even that conviction, which we had attain'd with difficulty. This is still more conspicuous in a long chain of reasoning, where we must preserve to the end the evidence of the first propositions, and where we often lose sight of all the most receiv'd maxims, either of philosophy or common life. I am not, however, without hopes that the present system of philosophy will acquire new force as it advances; and that our reasonings concerning *morals* will corroborate whatever has been said concerning the *understanding* and the *passions*. Morality is a subject that interests us above all others: we fancy the peace of society to be at stake in every decision concerning it: and 'tis evident, that this concern must make our speculations appear more real and solid than where the subject is, in a great measure, indifferent to us. What affects us, we conclude can never be a chimera; and as our passion is engag'd on the one side or the other, we naturally think that the question lies within human comprehension; which, in other cases of this nature, we are apt to entertain some doubt of. Without this advantage I never should have ventur'd upon a third volume of such abstruse philosophy, in an age wherein the greatest part of men seem agreed to convert reading into an amusement, and to reject every thing that requires any considerable degree of attention to be comprehended.

---

[4] The viability of the comparison with secondary qualities has been an important topic in recent discussions of 'realism' *versus* 'anti-realism' in ethics. See, e.g., G. Sayre-McCord (ed.), *Essays on Moral Realism*, Ithaca, NY: Cornell University Press, 1988.

It has been observ'd that nothing is ever present to the mind but its perceptions; and that all the actions of seeing, hearing, judging, loving, hating and thinking fall under this denomination. The mind can never exert itself in any action, which we may not comprehend under the term of *perception*; and consequently that term is no less applicable to those judgments, by which we distinguish moral good and evil, than to every other operation of the mind. To approve of one character, to condemn another, are only so many different perceptions.

Now as perceptions resolve themselves into two kinds, viz. *impressions* and *ideas*, this distinction gives rise to a question, with which we shall open up our present enquiry concerning morals, *Whether 'tis by means of our* ideas *or* impressions *we distinguish betwixt vice and virtue, and pronounce an action blameable or praiseworthy?*[1] This will immediately cut off all loose discourses and declamations, and reduce us to something precise and exact on the present subject.

Those who affirm that virtue is nothing but a conformity to reason; that there are eternal fitnesses and unfitnesses of things, which are the same to every rational being that considers them; that the immutable measures of right and wrong impose an obligation, not only on human creatures, but also on the Deity himself: all these systems concur in the opinion, that morality, like truth, is discern'd merely by ideas, and by their juxtaposition and comparison. In order, therefore, to judge of these systems, we need only consider, whether it be possible, from reason alone, to distinguish betwixt moral good and evil, or whether there must concur some other principles to enable us to make that distinction.

If morality had naturally no influence on human passions and actions, 'twere in vain to take such pains to inculcate it; and nothing would be more fruitless than that multitude of rules and precepts, with which all moralists abound. Philosophy is commonly divided into *speculative* and *practical*; and as morality is always comprehended under the latter division, 'tis supposed to influence our passions and actions, and to go beyond the calm and indolent judgments of the understanding. And this is confirm'd by common experience, which informs us that men are often govern'd by their duties, and are deter'd from some actions by the opinion of injustice, and impell'd to others by that of obligation.

Since morals, therefore, have an influence on the actions and affections, it follows that they cannot be deriv'd from reason; and that because reason alone, as we have already prov'd, can never have any such influence. Morals excite passions, and produce or prevent actions. Reason of itself is utterly impotent in this particular. The rules of morality, therefore, are not conclusions of our reason.

No one, I believe, will deny the justness of this inference; nor is there any other means of evading it, than by denying that principle on which it is founded. As long as it is allow'd that reason has no influence on our passions and actions, 'tis in vain to pretend that morality is discover'd only by a deduction of reason. An active principle can never be founded on an inactive; and if reason be inactive in itself, it must remain so in all its shapes and appearances, whether it exerts itself in natural or moral subjects, whether it considers the powers of external bodies, or the actions of rational beings.

It would be tedious to repeat all the arguments, by which I have prov'd [Book II, Part III, Section 3], that reason is perfectly inert, and can never either prevent or produce any action or affection. 'Twill be easy to recollect what has been said upon that subject. I shall only recall on this occasion one of these arguments, which I shall endeavour to render still more conclusive, and more applicable to the present subject.

Reason is the discovery of truth or falshood. Truth or falshood consists in an agreement or disagreement either to the *real* relations of ideas, or to *real* existence and matter of fact. Whatever, therefore, is not susceptible of this agreement or disagreement, is incapable of being true or false, and can never be an object of our reason. Now 'tis evident our passions, volitions and actions are not susceptible of any such agreement or disagreement; being original facts and realities, compleat in themselves, and implying no reference to other passions, volitions and actions. 'Tis impossible, therefore, they can be pronounced either true or false, and be either contrary or conformable to reason.

This argument is of double advantage to our present purpose. For it proves *directly*, that actions do not derive their merit from a conformity to reason, nor their blame from a contrariety to it; and it proves the same truth more *indirectly*, by shewing us, that as reason can never immediately prevent or produce any action by contradicting or approving of it, it cannot be the source of moral good and evil, which are found to have that influence. Actions may be laudable or blameable; but they cannot be reasonable or unreasonable: laudable or blameable, therefore, are not the same with reasonable or unreasonable. The merit and demerit of actions frequently contradict, and sometimes control our natural propensities. But reason has no such influence. Moral distinctions, therefore, are not the offspring of reason. Reason is wholly inactive, and can never be the source of so active a principle as conscience, or a sense of morals.

But perhaps it may be said that tho' no will or action can be immediately contradictory to reason, yet we may find such a contradiction in some of the attendants of the action, that is, in its causes or effects. The action may cause a judgment, or may be *obliquely* caus'd by one, when the judgment concurs with a passion; and by an abusive way of speaking, which philosophy will scarce allow of, the same contrariety may, upon that account, be ascrib'd to the action. How far this truth or falshood may be the source of morals, 'twill now be proper to consider.

It has been observ'd that reason, in a strict and philosophical sense, can have an influence on our conduct only after two ways: either when it excites a passion by informing us of the existence of something which is a proper object of it; or when it discovers the connexion of causes and effects, so as to afford us means of exerting any passion. These are the only kinds of judgment, which can accompany our actions, or can be said to produce them in any manner; and it must be allow'd, that these judgments may often be false and erroneous. A person may be affected with passion by supposing a pain or pleasure to lie in an object, which has no tendency to produce either of these sensations, or which produces the contrary to what is imagin'd. A person may also take false measures for the attaining his end, and may retard, by his foolish conduct, instead of forwarding the execution of any project. These false judgments may be thought to affect the passions and actions, which are connected with them, and may be said to render them unreasonable, in a figurative and improper way of speaking. But tho' this be acknowledg'd, 'tis easy to observe, that these errors are so far from being the source of all immorality, that they are commonly very innocent, and draw no manner of guilt upon the person who is so unfortunate as to fall into them. They extend not beyond a mistake of *fact*, which moralists have not generally suppos'd criminal, as being perfectly involuntary. I am more to be lamented than blam'd, if I am mistaken with regard to the influence of objects in producing pain or pleasure, or if I know not the proper means of satisfying my desires. No one can ever regard such errors as a defect in my moral character. A fruit, for instance, that is really disagreeable appears to me at a distance, and thro' mistake I fancy it to be pleasant and delicious. Here is one error. I choose certain means of reaching this fruit, which are not proper for my end. Here is a second error; nor is there any third one which can ever possibly enter into our reasonings concerning actions. I ask, therefore, if a man, in this situation and guilty of these two errors, is to be regarded as vicious and criminal, however unavoidable they might have been? Or if it be possible to imagine that such errors are the sources of all immorality?

And here it may be proper to observe, that if moral distinctions be deriv'd from the truth or falshood of those judgments, they must take place wherever we form the judgments; nor will there be any difference, whether the question be concerning an apple or a kingdom, or whether the error be avoidable or unavoidable. For as the very essence of morality is suppos'd to consist in an agreement or disagreement to reason, the other circumstances are entirely arbitrary, and can never either bestow on any action the character of virtuous or vicious, or deprive it of that character. To which we may add, that this agreement or disagreement, not admitting of degrees, all virtues and vices would of course be equal.

Should it be pretended, that tho' a mistake of *fact* be not criminal, yet a mistake of *right* often is; and that this may be the source of immorality: I would answer, that 'tis impossible such a mistake can ever be the original source of immorality, since it supposes a real right and wrong; that is, a real distinction in morals, independent of these judgments. A mistake, therefore, of right may become a species of immorality; but 'tis only a secondary one, and is founded on some other, antecedent to it.

As to those judgments which are the *effects* of our actions, and which, when false, give occasion to pronounce the actions contrary to truth and reason; we may observe, that our actions never cause any judgment, either true or false, in ourselves, and that 'tis only on others they have such an influence. 'Tis certain that an action, on many occasions, may give rise to false conclusions in others; and that a person, who thro' a window sees any lewd behaviour of mine with my neighbour's wife, may be so simple as to imagine she is certainly my own. In this respect my action resembles somewhat a lye or falshood; only with this difference, which is material, that I perform not the action with any intention of giving rise to a false judgment in another, but merely to satisfy my lust and passion. It causes, however, a mistake and false judgment by accident; and the falshood of its effects may be ascribed, by some odd figurative way of speaking, to the action itself. But still I can see no pretext of reason for asserting that the tendency to cause such an error is the first spring or original source of all immorality.[2]

Thus upon the whole, 'tis impossible that the distinction betwixt moral good and evil can be made by reason; since that distinction has an influence upon our actions, of which reason alone is incapable. Reason and judgment may, indeed, be the mediate cause of an action, by prompting, or by directing a passion: but it is not pretended that a judgment of this kind, either in its truth or falshood, is attended with virtue or vice. And as to the judgments, which are caused by our judgments, they can still less bestow those moral qualities on the actions, which are their causes.

But to be more particular, and to shew that those eternal immutable fitnesses and unfitnesses of things cannot be defended by sound philosophy, we may weigh the following considerations.

If the thought and understanding were alone capable of fixing the boundaries of right and wrong, the character of virtuous and vicious either must lie in some relations of objects, or must be a matter of fact, which is discovered by our reasoning. This consequence is evident. As the operations of human understanding divide themselves into two kinds, the comparing of ideas, and the inferring of matter of fact; were virtue discover'd by the understanding; it must be an object of one of these operations, nor is there any third operation of the understanding which can discover it. There has been an opinion very industriously propagated by certain philosophers, that morality is susceptible of demonstration; and tho' no one has ever been able to advance a single step in those demonstrations; yet 'tis taken for granted, that this science may be brought to an equal certainty with geometry or algebra. Upon this supposition, vice and virtue must consist in some relations; since 'tis allow'd on all hands that no matter of fact is capable of being demonstrated. Let us, therefore, begin with examining this hypothesis, and endeavour, if possible, to fix those moral qualities, which have been so long the objects of our fruitless researches. Point out distinctly the relations, which constitute morality or obligation, that we may know wherein they consist, and after what manner we must judge of them.

If you assert that vice and virtue consist in relations susceptible of certainty and demonstration, you must confine yourself to those *four* relations, which alone admit of that degree of evidence; and in that case you run into absurdities, from which you will never be able to extricate yourself. For as you make the very essence of morality to lie in the relations, and as there is no one of these relations but what is applicable, not only to an irrational, but also to an inanimate object, it follows that even such objects must be susceptible of merit or demerit. *Resemblance, contrariety, degrees in quality*, and *proportions in quantity and number*, all these relations belong as properly to matter as to our actions, passions, and volitions. 'Tis unquestionable, therefore, that morality lies not in any of these relations, nor the sense of it in their discovery.*

---

* As a proof, how confus'd our way of thinking on this subject commonly is, we may observe, that those who assert that morality is demonstrable, do not say that morality lies in the relations, and that the relations are distinguishable by reason. They only say that reason can discover such an action, in such relations, to be virtuous, and such another vicious. It seems they thought it sufficient, if they could bring the word, relation, into the proposition, without troubling themselves whether it was to the purpose or not. But here, I think, is plain argument. Demonstrative reason discovers only relations. But that reason, according to this hypothesis, discovers also vice and virtue. These moral qualities, therefore, must be relations. When we blame any action, in any situation, the whole complicated object, of action and situation, must form certain relations, wherein the essence of vice consists. This hypothesis is not otherwise intelligible. For what does reason discover, when it pronounces any action vicious? Does it discover a relation or a matter of fact? These questions are decisive, and must not be eluded.

Should it be asserted that the sense of morality consists in the discovery of some relation, distinct from these, and that our enumeration was not compleat, when we comprehended all demonstrable relations under four general heads: to this I know not what to reply, till some one be so good as to point out to me this new relation. 'Tis impossible to refute a system which has never yet been explain'd. In such a manner of fighting in the dark, a man loses his blows in the air, and often places them where the enemy is not present.

I must, therefore, on this occasion, rest contented with requiring the two following conditions of any one that would undertake to clear up this system. *First*, as moral good and evil belong only to the actions of the mind, and are deriv'd from our situation with regard to external objects, the relations, from which these moral distinctions arise, must lie only betwixt internal actions and external objects, and must not be applicable either to internal actions, compared among themselves, or to external objects, when placed in opposition to other external objects. For as morality is supposed to attend certain relations, if these relations could belong to internal actions consider'd singly, it would follow, that we might be guilty of crimes in ourselves, and independent of our situation, with respect to the universe: and in like manner, if these moral relations could be apply'd to external objects, it would follow that even inanimate beings would be susceptible of moral beauty and deformity. Now it seems difficult to imagine that any relation can be discover'd betwixt our passions, volitions and actions, compared to external objects, which relation might not belong either to these passions and volitions, or to these external objects, compar'd among *themselves*.

But it will be still more difficult to fulfil the *second* condition, requisite to justify this system. According to the principles of those who maintain an abstract rational difference betwixt moral good and evil, and a natural fitness and unfitness of things, 'tis not only suppos'd, that these relations, being eternal and immutable, are the same, when consider'd by every rational creature, but their *effects* are also suppos'd to be necessarily the same; and 'tis concluded they have no less, or rather a greater, influence in directing the will of the deity, than in governing the rational and virtuous of our own species. These two particulars are evidently distinct. 'Tis one thing to know virtue, and another to conform the will to it. In order, therefore, to prove that the measures of right and wrong are eternal laws, *obligatory* on every rational mind, 'tis not sufficient to shew the relations upon which they are founded: we must also point out the connexion betwixt the relation and the will; and must prove that this connexion is so necessary, that in every well-disposed mind it must take place and have its influence; tho' the difference betwixt these minds be in other respects immense and infinite. Now besides what I have already prov'd, that even in human nature no relation can ever alone produce any action; besides this, I say, it has been shewn, in treating of the understanding, that there is no connexion of cause and effect, such as this is suppos'd to be, which is discoverable otherwise than by experience, and of which we can pretend to have any security by the simple consideration of the objects. All beings in the universe, consider'd in themselves, appear entirely loose and independent of each other. 'Tis only by experience we learn their influence and connexion; and this influence we ought never to extend beyond experience.

Thus it will be impossible to fulfil the *first* condition required to the system of eternal rational measures of right and wrong; because it is impossible to shew those relations, upon which such a distinction may be founded: and 'tis as impossible to fulfil the *second* condition; because we cannot prove *a priori*, that these relations, if they really existed and were perceiv'd, would be universally forcible and obligatory.

But to make these general reflexions more clear and convincing, we may illustrate them by some particular instances, wherein this character of moral good or evil is the most universally acknowledged. Of all crimes that human creatures are capable of committing, the most horrid and unnatural is ingratitude, especially when it is committed against parents, and appears in the more flagrant instances of wounds and death. This is acknowledg'd by all mankind, philosophers as well as the people; the question only arises among philosophers, whether the guilt or moral deformity of this action be discover'd by demonstrative reasoning, or be felt by an internal sense, and by means of some sentiment, which the reflecting on such an action naturally occasions. This question will soon be decided against the former opinion if we can shew the same relations in other objects, without the notion of any guilt or iniquity attending them. Reason or science is nothing but the comparing of ideas, and the discovery of their relations; and if the same relations have different characters, it must evidently follow that those characters are not discover'd merely by reason. To put the affair, therefore, to this trial, let us chuse any inanimate object, such as an oak or elm; and let us suppose that by the dropping of its seed it produces a sapling below it, which springing up by degrees, at last overtops and destroys the parent tree: I ask, if in this instance there be wanting any relation, which is discoverable in parricide or ingratitude? Is not the one tree the cause of the other's existence, and the latter the cause of the destruction of the former, in the same manner as when a child murders his parent? 'Tis not sufficient to reply, that a choice or will is wanting. For in the case of parricide, a will does not give rise to any *different* relations, but is only the cause from which the action is deriv'd; and consequently produces the *same* relations, that in the oak or elm arise from some other principles. 'Tis a will or choice that determines a man to kill his parent; and they are the laws of matter and motion that determine a sapling to destroy the oak, from which it sprung. Here then the same relations have different causes; but still the relations are the same: and as their discovery is not in both cases attended with a notion of immorality, it follows that that notion does not arise from such a discovery.

But to chuse an instance, still more resembling; I would fain ask anyone why incest in the human species is criminal, and why the very same action and the same relations in animals have not the smallest moral turpitude and deformity? If it be answer'd that this action is innocent in animals, because they have not reason sufficient to discover its turpitude; but that man, being endow'd with that faculty which *ought* to restrain him to his duty, the same action instantly becomes criminal to him; should this be said, I would reply that this is evidently arguing in a circle. For before reason can perceive this turpitude, the turpitude must exist; and consequently is independent of the decisions of our reason, and is their object more properly than their effect. According to this system, then, every animal that has sense, and appetite, and will; that is, every animal must be susceptible of all the same virtues and vices, for which we ascribe praise and blame to human creatures. All the difference is that our superior reason may serve to discover the vice or virtue, and by that means may augment the blame or praise: but still this discovery supposes a separate being in these moral distinctions, and a being which depends only on the will and appetite, and which, both in thought and reality, may be distinguish'd from the reason. Animals are susceptible of the same relations, with respect to each other, as the human species, and therefore would also be susceptible of the same morality, if the essence of morality consisted in these relations. Their want of a sufficient degree of reason may hinder them from perceiving the duties and obligations of morality, but can never hinder these duties from existing; since they must antecedently exist in order to their being perceiv'd. Reason must find them, and can never produce them. This argument deserves to be weigh'd as being, in my opinion, entirely decisive.

Nor does this reasoning only prove, that morality consists not in any relations, that are the objects of science; but if examin'd, will prove with equal certainty, that it consists not in any *matter of fact*, which can be discover'd by the understanding. This is the *second* part of our argument; and if it can be made evident, we may conclude that morality is not an object of reason. But can there be any difficulty in proving that vice and virtue are not matters of fact, whose existence we can infer by reason? Take any action allow'd to be vicious: wilful murder, for instance. Examine it in all lights, and see if you can find that matter of fact, or real existence, which you call *vice*. In whichever way you take it, you find only certain passions, motives, volitions and thoughts. There is no other matter of fact in the case. The vice entirely escapes you, as long as you consider the object. You never can find it till you turn your reflexion into your own breast, and find a sentiment of disapprobation, which arises in you, towards this action. Here is a matter of fact; but 'tis the object of feeling, not of reason. It lies in yourself, not in the object. So that when you pronounce any action or character to be vicious, you mean nothing but that from the constitution of your nature you have a feeling or sentiment of blame from the contemplation of it. Vice and virtue, therefore, may be compar'd to sounds, colours, heat and cold, which, according to modern philosophy, are not qualities in objects, but perceptions in the mind: and this discovery in morals, like that other in physics, is to be regarded as a considerable advancement of the speculative sciences; tho', like that too, it has little or no influence on practice. Nothing can be more real, or concern us more, than our own sentiments of pleasure and uneasiness; and if these be favourable to virtue and unfavourable to vice, no more can be requisite to the regulation of our conduct and behaviour.

I cannot forbear adding to these reasonings an observation which may, perhaps, be found of some importance. In every system of morality which I have hitherto met with, I have always remark'd that the author proceeds for some time in the ordinary way of reasoning, and establishes the being of a God, or makes observations concerning human affairs; when of a sudden I am surpriz'd to find that instead of the usual copulations of propositions, *is* and *is not*, I meet with no proposition that is not connected with an *ought* or an *ought not*. This change is imperceptible; but is, however, of the last consequence. For as this *ought*, or *ought not*, expresses some new relation or affirmation, 'tis necessary that it should be observ'd and explain'd; and at the same time that a reason should be given for what seems altogether inconceivable, how this new relation can be a deduction from others, which are entirely different from it. But as authors do not commonly use this precaution, I shall presume to recommend it to the readers; and am persuaded that this small attention would subvert all the vulgar systems of morality, and let us see that the distinction of vice and virtue is not founded merely on the relations of objects, nor is perceiv'd by reason.

Section 2: Moral Distinctions Deriv'd from a Moral Sense

Thus the course of the argument leads us to conclude that since vice and virtue are not discoverable merely by reason, or the comparison of ideas, it must be by means of some impression or sentiment they occasion, that we are able to mark the difference betwixt them. Our decisions concerning moral rectitude and depravity are evidently perceptions; and as all perceptions are either impressions or ideas, the exclusion of the one is a convincing argument for the other. Morality, therefore, is more properly felt than judg'd of; tho' this feeling or sentiment is commonly so soft and gentle that we are apt to confound it with an idea, according to our common custom of taking all things for the same, which have any near resemblance to each other.

The next question is, of what nature are these impressions, and after what manner do they operate upon us? Here we cannot remain long in suspense, but must pronounce the impression arising from virtue to be agreeable, and that proceeding from vice to be uneasy. Every moment's experience must convince us of this. There is no spectacle so fair and beautiful as a noble and generous action; nor any which gives us more abhorrence than one that is cruel and treacherous. No enjoyment equals the satisfaction we receive from the company of those we love and esteem; as the greatest of all punishments is to be oblig'd to pass our lives with those we hate or contemn. A very play or romance may afford us instances of this pleasure, which virtue conveys to us; and pain, which arises from vice.

Now since the distinguishing impressions, by which moral good or evil is known, are nothing but *particular* pains or pleasures; it follows, that in all enquiries concerning these moral distinctions, it will be sufficient to shew the principles, which make us feel a satisfaction or uneasiness from the survey of any character, in order to satisfy us why the character is laudable or blameable. An action, or sentiment, or character is virtuous or vicious; why? Because its view causes a pleasure or uneasiness of a particular kind. In giving a reason, therefore, for the pleasure or uneasiness, we sufficiently explain the vice or virtue. To have the sense of virtue is nothing but to *feel* a satisfaction of a particular kind from the contemplation of a character. The very *feeling* constitutes our praise or admiration. We go no farther; nor do we enquire into the cause of the satisfaction. We do not infer a character to be virtuous, because it pleases: but in feeling that it pleases after such a particular manner, we in effect feel that it is virtuous. The case is the same as in our judgments concerning all kinds of beauty, and tastes and sensations. Our approbation is imply'd in the immediate pleasure they convey to us.

I have objected to the system, which establishes eternal rational measures of right and wrong, that 'tis impossible to shew, in the actions of reasonable creatures, any relations which are not found in external objects; and therefore, if morality always attended these relations, 'twere possible for inanimate matter to become virtuous or vicious. Now it may, in like manner, be objected to the present system, that if virtue and vice be determin'd by pleasure and pain, these qualities must, in every case, arise from the sensations; and consequently any object, whether animate or inanimate, rational or irrational, might become morally good or evil, provided it can excite a satisfaction or uneasiness. But tho' this objection seems to be the very same, it has by no means the same force in the one case as in the other. For, *first*, 'tis evident that under the term *pleasure*, we comprehend sensations which are very different from each other, and which have only such a distant resemblance, as is requisite to make them be express'd by the same abstract term. A good composition of music and a bottle of good wine equally produce pleasure; and what is more, their goodness is determin'd merely by the pleasure. But shall we say upon that account that the wine is harmonious, or the music of a good flavour? In like manner an inanimate object, and the character or sentiments of any person may, both of them, give satisfaction; but as the satisfaction is different, this keeps our sentiments concerning them from being confounded, and makes us ascribe virtue to the one, and not to the other. Nor is every sentiment of pleasure or pain, which arises from characters and actions, of that *peculiar* kind which makes us praise or condemn. The good qualities of an enemy are hurtful to us, but may still command our esteem and respect. 'Tis only when a character is considered in general, without reference to our particular interest, that it causes such a feeling or sentiment, as denominates it morally good or evil. 'Tis true, those sentiments, from interest and morals, are apt to be confounded, and naturally run into one another. It seldom happens that we do not think an enemy vicious, and can distinguish betwixt his opposition to our interest and real villainy or baseness. But this hinders not, but that the sentiments are, in themselves, distinct; and a man of temper and judgment may preserve himself from these illusions. In like manner, tho' 'tis certain a musical voice is nothing but one that naturally gives a *particular* kind of pleasure; yet 'tis difficult for a man to be sensible, that the voice of an enemy is agreeable, or to allow it to be musical. But a person of a fine ear, who has the command of himself, can separate these feelings, and give praise to what deserves it.

Secondly, we may call to remembrance the preceding system of the passions, in order to remark a still more considerable difference among our pains and pleasures. Pride and humility, love and hatred are excited, when there is any thing presented to us that both bears a relation to the object of the passion, and produces a separate sensation related to the sensation of the passions. Now virtue and vice are attended with these circumstances. They must necessarily be plac'd either in ourselves or others, and excite either pleasure or uneasiness; and therefore must give rise to one of these four passions, which clearly distinguishes them from the pleasure and pain arising from inanimate objects, that often bear no relation to us: and this is, perhaps, the most considerable effect that virtue and vice have upon the human mind.

It may now be ask'd *in general*, concerning this pain or pleasure, that distinguishes moral good and evil, *From what principles is it derived, and whence does it arise in the human mind?* To this I reply, *first*, that 'tis absurd to imagine, that in every particular instance, these sentiments are produc'd by an *original* quality and *primary* constitution. For as the number of our duties is, in a manner, infinite, 'tis impossible that our original instincts should extend to each of them, and from our very first infancy impress on the human mind all that multitude of precepts, which are contain'd in the compleatest system of ethics. Such a method of proceeding is not conformable to the usual maxims, by which nature is conducted, where a few principles produce all that variety we observe in the universe, and every thing is carry'd on in the easiest and most simple manner. 'Tis necessary, therefore, to abridge these primary impulses, and find some more general principles, upon which all our notions of morals are founded.

But in the *second* place, should it be ask'd whether we ought to search for these principles in *nature*, or whether we must look for them in some other origin? I would reply, that our answer to this question depends upon the definition of the word, Nature, than which there is none more ambiguous and equivocal. If *nature* be oppos'd to miracles, not only the distinction betwixt vice and virtue is natural, but also every event which has ever happen'd in the world, *excepting those miracles on which our religion is founded*. In saying, then, that the sentiments of vice and virtue are natural in this sense, we make no very extraordinary discovery.

But *nature* may also be opposed to rare and unusual; and in this sense of the word, which is the common one, there may often arise disputes concerning what is natural or unnatural; and one may in general affirm that we are not possess'd of any very precise standard by which these disputes can be decided. Frequent and rare depend upon the number of examples we have observ'd; and as this number may gradually encrease or diminish, 'twill be impossible to fix any exact boundaries betwixt them. We may only affirm on this head, that if ever there was any thing, which could be call'd natural in this sense, the sentiments of morality certainly may; since there never was any nation of the world, nor any single person in any nation, who was utterly depriv'd of them, and who never, in any instance, shew'd the least approbation or dislike of manners. These sentiments are so rooted in our constitution and temper, that without entirely confounding the human mind by disease or madness, 'tis impossible to extirpate and destroy them.

But *nature* may also be opposed to artifice, as well as to what is rare and unusual; and in this sense it may be disputed, whether the notions of virtue be natural or not. We readily forget that the designs, and projects, and views of men are principles as necessary in their operation as heat and cold, moist and dry: but taking them to be free and entirely our own, 'tis usual for us to set them in opposition to the other principles of nature. Should it, therefore, be demanded whether the sense of virtue be natural or artificial, I am of opinion that 'tis impossible for me at present to give any precise answer to this question. Perhaps it will appear afterwards that our sense of some virtues is artificial, and that of others natural. The discussion of this question will be more proper, when we enter upon an exact detail of each particular vice and virtue [Book III, Parts II–III].

Meanwhile it may not be amiss to observe from these definitions of *natural* and *unnatural*, that nothing can be more unphilosophical than those systems which assert that virtue is the same with what is natural, and vice with what is unnatural. For in the first sense of the word, nature, as opposed to miracles, both vice and virtue are equally natural; and in the second sense, as oppos'd to what is unusual, perhaps virtue will be found to be the most unnatural. At least it must be own'd, that heroic virtue, being as unusual, is as little natural as the most brutal barbarity. As to the third sense of the word, 'tis certain, that both vice and virtue are equally artificial, and out of nature. For however it may be disputed, whether the notion of a merit or demerit in certain actions be natural or artificial, 'tis evident that the actions themselves are artificial, and are perform'd with a certain design and intention; otherwise they could never be rank'd under any of these denominations. 'Tis impossible, therefore, that the character of natural and unnatural can ever, in any sense, mark the boundaries of vice and virtue.

Thus we are still brought back to our first position, that virtue is distinguished by the pleasure, and vice by the pain, that any action, sentiment or character gives us by the mere view and contemplation. This decision is very commodious; because it reduces us to this simple question, *why any action or sentiment upon the general view or survey, gives a certain satisfaction or uneasiness*, in order to shew the origin of its moral rectitude or depravity, without looking for any incomprehensible relations and qualities, which never did exist in nature nor even in our imagination by any clear and distinct conception. I flatter myself I have executed a great part of my present design by a state of the question, which appears to me so free from ambiguity and obscurity.

Notes

1 Hume is referring here to his distinction made in Book I, Part I, between the 'impressions' which we experience through the senses or when our 'passions' are affected and the 'ideas' which are before the mind when we think and reflect. In the present context, his point is that moral distinctions cannot be drawn merely through reflection since they are functions of the different 'passions' actuated in us.
2 There follows the long footnote, which I have omitted, on Wollaston's construal of moral wrong as a species of falsehood. Hume argues that if what makes my adultery wrong is the false message it conveys that another's wife is my own, I could avoid the wrong by taking 'the precaution of shutting the windows, while I indulg'd myself'. Nobody then gets any message, true or false.

Immanuel Kant, *Fundamental Principles of the Metaphysic of Morals*, Preface and Section 1

From Immanuel Kant, *Fundamental Principles of the Metaphysic of Morals*, trans. T. K. Abbott. Buffalo, NY: Prometheus, 1987, pp. 9–13, 17–33 [some passages from Preface omitted; asterisked notes are Kant's own].

In moral philosophy, as in other branches of the subject, the man most responsible for setting the modern agenda was the German philosopher Immanuel Kant (1724–1804). Anyone now wanting to defend the *idées fixes* of the eighteenth-century Enlightenment – though their pedigree goes back to Aristotle or Epicurus – must do so against Kant's critique. There were at least three such dominant ideas, apparent in Hume's writings, for example. First, the 'teleological' or 'consequentialist' assumption that actions are right only if they tend to produce a certain result, such as, according to utilitarians, the general happiness. Second, the conviction that a result or goal is good if it is *natural*, in the sense of being one that people would, according to their human nature, aim at unless blinded by ignorance, indoctrination or whatever. Third, and relatedly, the view that a good person is one motivated by such natural dispositions – benevolence, sympathy, enlightened self-love or whatever.

In the remarkably rich few pages which follow, Kant challenges each of these claims. Driving his criticisms, one feels, is a nightmare scenario which he envisaged. What results our actions tend to produce, as well as our currently 'natural' make-up and aspirations, are contingent matters, in which case conformity to morality must itself be a 'very contingent and uncertain' thing if it is based on such considerations (Preface, see p. 169). Morality must have a more secure foundation if the possibility of moral collapse is to be excluded. Moreover, he argues, the untenability of the *idées fixes* is surely attested to by ordinary intuitions, by our 'common rational knowledge of morality'. Is it not apparent, first, that the moral worth of an action is totally independent of its results, in which luck plays such a part? Is it not clear, second, that the moral law cannot be determined by reference to human nature, since it is binding on *all* rational beings, whether or not they share our nature? And, finally, how can a person deserve *moral* praise if, by a mere 'gift of nature', he happens to prefer acting benevolently to acting selfishly?

It is, Kant proceeds, only 'a Good Will', the resolve to act for the sake of duty out of respect for the moral law, and independently of any other motives or goals, which has moral worth. What this entails is that the 'maxims' or principles on which alone I should act are those which conform to 'law in general' – which, that is, are binding on all rational creatures. Hence, in Section I, we find Kant formulating, without as yet using the actual expression, his famous 'categorical imperative': never to act upon a maxim unless I can 'will that my maxim should become a universal law' (p. 177). It would be wrong, for example, to act on the principle that promises may be broken when it is personally advantageous to do so. Such a principle could not become a general law, since the practice of promising would atrophy if people broke promises whenever it suited them. Kant goes on, in Section II, to argue that this imperative is equivalent to the demand to treat people as ends, 'never as means only': for to treat someone as a means is to act on a maxim which he or she could never rationally accept as a general law. Respect for persons and respect for the moral law are, therefore, two sides of the same coin.

In his own day and ever since, Kant's position has provoked many criticisms. One, pressed by the poet Friedrich Schiller, is that there is something chilling in the idea, which contradicts the whole Aristotelian tradition, that a natural inclination to virtuous behaviour is without moral worth.[1] Another, anticipated by Kant himself when he admitted the 'incomprehensible' mystery involved, is how mere knowledge of one's duty, unaccompanied by any other 'spring' to action, can serve to motivate one's behaviour. Wasn't Hume right to insist that reason without 'passion' is idle? Perhaps the key to answering these criticisms resides in the notion of 'respect'. Without becoming overtaxed about the meaning of the word 'moral', it might be admitted that a distinct kind of worth, overlooked since the Stoics, attaches to the person who acts against his inclinations, purely out of rational recognition of duty – a worth that elicits a special respect. And perhaps this special respect owed to rational beings, including oneself, for their capacity so to act is explanation enough of how a person can be moved to behave morally. Is it really such a mystery, once the leading ideas of Enlightenment moral psychology are unfixed, that I can be moved to act by a view of myself which, as Kant puts it elsewhere, 'infinitely elevates my worth, as an *intelligence*, through my personality, in which the moral law reveals to me a life independent of animality'?[2]

1 See the articles by Onora O'Neill and J. B. Schneewind in Paul Guyer (ed.), *The Cambridge Companion to Kant*, Cambridge: Cambridge University Press, 1992.
2 *Critique of Practical Reason*, Indianapolis: Bobbs-Merrill, 1976, pp. 161–2.

▶ ▶ ▶ **Preface**

Ancient Greek philosophy was divided into three sciences: physics, ethics and logic. This division is perfectly suitable to the nature of the thing, and the only improvement that can be made in it is to add the principle on which it is based, so that we may both satisfy ourselves of its completeness, and also be able to determine correctly the necessary subdivisions.

All rational knowledge is either *material* or *formal*: the former considers some object, the latter is concerned only with the form of the understanding and of the reason itself, and with the universal laws of thought in general without distinction of its objects. Formal philosophy is called logic. Material philosophy, however, which has to do with determinate objects and the laws to which they are subject, is again twofold; for these laws are either laws of *nature* or of *freedom*. The science of the former is physics, that of the latter, ethics; they are also called *natural philosophy* and *moral philosophy* respectively.

Logic cannot have any empirical part; that is, a part in which the universal and necessary laws of thought should rest on grounds taken from experience; otherwise it would not be logic, i.e. a canon for the understanding or the reason, valid for all thought, and capable of demonstration. Natural and moral philosophy, on the contrary, can each have their empirical part, since the former has to determine the laws of nature as an object of experience; the latter the laws of the human will, so far as it is affected by nature: the former, however, being laws according to which everything does happen; the latter, laws according to which everything ought to happen. Ethics, however, must also consider the conditions under which what ought to happen frequently does not.

We may call all philosophy *empirical*, so far as it is based on grounds of experience: on the other hand, that which delivers its doctrines from a priori principles alone we may call *pure* philosophy. When the latter is merely formal it is *logic*; if it is restricted to definite objects of the understanding it is *metaphysic*.

In this way there arises the idea of a twofold metaphysic – a *metaphysic of nature* and a *metaphysic of morals*. Physics will thus have an empirical and also a rational part. It is the same with ethics; but here the empirical part might have the special name of *practical anthropology*, the name *morality* being appropriated to the rational part. . . .

As my concern here is with moral philosophy, I limit the question . . . to this: Whether it is not of the utmost necessity to construct a pure moral philosophy, perfectly cleared of everything which is only empirical, and which belongs to anthropology? for that such a philosophy must be possible is evident from the common idea of duty and of the moral laws. Every one must admit that if a law is to have moral force, i.e. to be the basis of an obligation, it must carry with it absolute necessity; that, for example, the precept, 'Thou shalt not lie,' is not valid for men alone, as if other rational beings had no need to observe it; and so with all the other moral laws properly so called; that, therefore, the basis of obligation must not be sought in the nature of man, or in the circumstances in the world in which he is placed, but a priori simply in the conceptions of pure reason; and although any other precept which is founded on principles of mere experience may be in certain respects universal, yet in as far as it rests even in the least degree on an empirical basis, perhaps only as to a motive, such a precept, while it may be a practical rule, can never be called a moral law.

Thus not only are moral laws with their principles essentially distinguished from every other kind of practical knowledge in which there is anything empirical, but all moral philosophy rests wholly on its pure part. When applied to man, it does not borrow the least thing from the knowledge of man himself (anthropology), but gives laws a priori to him as a rational being. No doubt these laws require a judgement sharpened by experience, in order on the one hand to distinguish in what cases they are applicable, and on the other to procure for them access to the will of the man, and effectual influence on conduct; since man is acted on by so many inclinations that, though capable of the idea of a practical pure reason, he is not so easily able to make it effective *in concreto* in his life.

A metaphysic of morals is therefore indispensably necessary, not merely for speculative reasons, in order to investigate the sources of the practical principles which are to be found a priori in our reason, but also because morals themselves are liable to all sorts of corruption, as long as we are without that clue and supreme canon by which to estimate them correctly. For in order that an action should be morally good, it is not enough that it *conform* to the moral law, but it must also be done *for the sake of the law*, otherwise that conformity is only very contingent and uncertain; since a principle which is not moral, although it may now and then produce actions conformable to the law, will also often produce actions which contradict it. Now it is only in a pure philosophy that we can look for the moral law in its purity and genuineness (and, in a practical matter, this is of the utmost consequence): we must, therefore, begin with pure philosophy (metaphysic), and without it there cannot be any moral philosophy at all. That which mingles these pure principles with the empirical does not deserve the name of philosophy (for what distinguishes philosophy from common rational knowledge is that it treats in separate sciences what the latter only comprehends confusedly); much less does it deserve that of moral philosophy, since by this confusion it even spoils the purity of morals themselves, and counteracts its own end. . . .

Section 1: Transition from the Common Rational Knowledge of Morality to the Philosophical

Nothing can possibly be conceived in the world, or even out of it, which can be called good without qualification, except a Good Will. Intelligence, wit, judgement, and the other *talents* of the mind, however they may be named, or courage, resolution, perseverance, as qualities of temperament, are undoubtedly good and desirable in many respects; but these gifts of nature may also become extremely bad and mischievous if the will which is to make use of them, and which, therefore, constitutes what is called *character*, is not good. It is the same with the *gifts of fortune*. Power, riches, honour, even health, and the general well-being and contentment with one's condition which is called *happiness*, inspire pride, and often presumption, if there is not a good will to correct the influence of these on the mind, and with this also to rectify the whole principle of acting, and adapt it to its end. The sight of a being who is not adorned with a single feature of a pure and good will, enjoying unbroken prosperity, can never give pleasure to an impartial rational spectator. Thus a good will appears to constitute the indispensable condition even of being worthy of happiness.

There are even some qualities which are of service to this good will itself, and may facilitate its action, yet which have no intrinsic unconditional value, but always presuppose a good will, and this qualifies the esteem that we justly have for them, and does not permit us to regard them as absolutely good. Moderation in the affections and passions, self-control and calm deliberation are not only good in many respects, but even seem to constitute part of the intrinsic worth of the person; but they are far from deserving to be called good without qualification, although they have been so unconditionally praised by the ancients. For without the principles of a good will, they may become extremely bad, and the coolness of a villain not only makes him far more dangerous, but also directly makes him more abominable in our eyes than he would have been without it.

A good will is good not because of what it performs or effects, not by its aptness for the attainment of some proposed end, but simply by virtue of the volition, that is, it is good in itself, and considered by itself is to be esteemed much higher than all that can be brought about by it in favour of any inclination, nay, even of the sum total of all inclinations. Even if it should happen that, owing to special disfavour of fortune, or the niggardly provision of a stepmotherly nature, this will should wholly lack power to accomplish its purpose, if with its greatest efforts it should yet achieve nothing, and there should remain only the good will (not, to be sure, a mere wish, but the summoning of all means in our power), then, like a jewel, it would still shine by its own light, as a thing which has its own value in itself. Its usefulness or fruitfulness can neither add to nor take away anything from this value. It would be, as it were, only the setting to enable us to handle it the more conveniently in common commerce, or to attract to it the attention of those who are not yet connoisseurs, but not to recommend it to true connoisseurs, or to determine its value.

There is, however, something so strange in this idea of the absolute value of the mere will, in which no account is taken of its utility, that notwithstanding the thorough assent of even common reason to the idea, yet a suspicion must arise that it may perhaps really be the product of mere high-flown fancy, and that we may have misunderstood the purpose of nature in assigning reason as the governor of our will. Therefore we will examine this idea from this point of view.

In the physical constitution of an organized being, that is, a being adapted suitably to the purposes of life, we assume it as a fundamental principle that no organ for any purpose will be found but what is also the fittest and best adapted for that purpose. Now in a being which has reason and a will, if the proper object of nature were its *conservation*, its *welfare*, in a word, its *happiness*, then nature would have hit upon a very bad arrangement in selecting the reason of the creature to carry out this purpose. For all the actions which the creature has to perform with a view to this purpose, and the whole rule of its conduct, would be far more surely prescribed to it by instinct, and that end would have been attained thereby much more certainly than it ever can be by reason. Should reason have been communicated to this favoured creature over and above, it must only have served it to contemplate the happy constitution of its nature, to admire it, to congratulate itself thereon, and to feel thankful for it to the beneficent cause, but not that it should subject its desires to that weak and delusive guidance, and meddle bunglingly with the purpose of nature. In a word, nature would have taken care that reason should not break forth into *practical exercise*, nor have the presumption, with its weak insight, to think out for itself the plan of happiness, and of the means of attaining it. Nature would not only have taken on herself the choice of the ends, but also of the means, and with wise foresight would have entrusted both to instinct.

And, in fact, we find that the more a cultivated reason applies itself with deliberate purpose to the enjoyment of life and happiness, so much the more does the man fail of true satisfaction. And from this circumstance there arises in many, if they are candid enough to confess it, a certain degree of *misology*, that is, hatred of reason, especially in the case of those who are most experienced in the use of it, because after calculating all the advantages they derive, I do not say from the invention of all the arts of common luxury, but even from the sciences (which seem to them to be after all only a luxury of the understanding), they find that they have, in fact, only brought more trouble on their shoulders, rather than gained in happiness; and they end by envying, rather than despising, the more common stamp of men who keep closer to the guidance of mere instinct, and do not allow their reason much influence on their conduct. And this we must admit, that the judgement of those who would very much lower the lofty eulogies of the advantages which reason gives us in regard to the happiness and satisfaction of life, or who would even reduce them below zero, is by no means morose or ungrateful to the goodness with which the world is governed, but that there lies at the root of these judgements the idea that our existence has a different and far nobler end, for which, and not for happiness, reason is properly intended, and which must, therefore, be regarded as the supreme condition to which the private ends of man must, for the most part, be postponed.

For as reason is not competent to guide the will with certainty in regard to its objects and the satisfaction of all our wants (which it to some extent even multiplies), this being an end to which an implanted instinct would have led with much greater certainty; and since, nevertheless, reason is imparted to us as a practical faculty, i.e. as one which is to have influence on the *will*, therefore, admitting that nature generally in the distribution of her capacities has adapted the means to the end, its true destination must be to produce a *will*, not merely good as a *means* to something else, but *good in itself*, for which reason was absolutely necessary. This will then, though not indeed the sole and complete good, must be the supreme good and the condition of every other, even of the desire of happiness. Under these circumstances, there is nothing inconsistent with the wisdom of nature in the fact that the cultivation of the reason, which is requisite for the first and unconditional purpose, does in many ways interfere, at least in this life, with the attainment of the second, which is always conditional, namely, happiness. Nay, it may even reduce it to nothing, without nature thereby failing of her purpose. For reason recognizes the establishment of a good will as its highest practical destination, and in attaining this purpose is capable only of a satisfaction of its own proper kind, namely, that from the attainment of an end, which end again is determined by reason only, notwithstanding that this may involve many a disappointment to the ends of inclination.

We have then to develop the notion of a will which deserves to be highly esteemed for itself, and is good without a view to anything further, a notion which exists already in the sound natural understanding, requiring rather to be cleared up than to be taught, and which in estimating the value of our actions always takes the first place, and constitutes the condition of all the rest. In order to do this we will take the notion of duty, which includes that of a good will, although implying certain subjective restrictions and hindrances. These, however, far from concealing it, or rendering it unrecognizable, rather bring it out by contrast, and make it shine forth so much the brighter.

I omit here all actions which are already recognized as inconsistent with duty, although they may be useful for this or that purpose, for with these the question whether they are done *from duty* cannot arise at all, since they even conflict with it. I also set aside those actions which really conform to duty, but to which men have *no* direct *inclination*, performing them because they are impelled thereto by some other inclination. For in this case we can readily distinguish whether the action which agrees with duty is done *from duty*, or from a selfish view. It is much harder to make this distinction when the action accords with duty, and the subject has besides a *direct* inclination to it. For example, it is always a matter of duty that a dealer should not overcharge an inexperienced purchaser, and wherever there is much commerce the prudent tradesman does not overcharge, but keeps a fixed price for everyone, so that a child buys of him as well as any other. Men are thus *honestly* served; but this is not enough to make us believe that the tradesman has so acted from duty and from principles of honesty: his own advantage required it; it is out of the question in this case to suppose that he might besides have a direct inclination in favour of the buyers, so that, as it were, from love he should give no advantage to one over another. Accordingly the action was done neither from duty nor from direct inclination, but merely with a selfish view.

On the other hand, it is a duty to maintain one's life; and, in addition, everyone has also a direct inclination to do so. But on this account the often anxious care which most men take for it has no intrinsic worth, and their maxim has no moral import. They preserve their life *as duty requires*, no doubt, but not *because duty requires*. On the other hand, if adversity and hopeless sorrow have completely taken away the relish for life; if the unfortunate one, strong in mind, indignant at his fate rather than desponding or dejected, wishes for death, and yet preserves his life without loving it – not from inclination or fear, but from duty – then his maxim has a moral worth.

To be beneficent when we can is a duty; and besides this, there are many minds so sympathetically constituted that, without any other motive of vanity or self-interest, they find a pleasure in spreading joy around them and can take delight in the satisfaction of others so far as it is their own work. But I maintain that in such a case an action of this kind, however proper, however amiable it may be, has nevertheless no true moral worth, but is on a level with other inclinations, e.g. the inclination to honour, which, if it is happily directed to that which is in fact of public utility and accordant with duty, and consequently honourable, deserves praise and encouragement, but not esteem. For the maxim lacks the moral import, namely, that such actions be done *from duty*, not from inclination. Put the case that the mind of that philanthropist were clouded by sorrow of his own, extinguishing all sympathy with the lot of others, and that while he still has the power to benefit others in distress, he is not touched by their trouble because he is absorbed with his own; and now suppose that he tears himself out of this dead insensibility, and performs the action without any inclination to it, but simply from duty, then first has his action its genuine moral worth. Further still; if nature has put little sympathy in the heart of this or that man; if he, supposed to be an upright man, is by temperament cold and indifferent to the sufferings of others, perhaps because in respect of his own he is provided with the special gift of patience and fortitude, and supposes, or even requires, that others should have the same – and such a man would certainly not be the meanest product of nature – but if nature had not specially framed him for a philanthropist, would he not still find in himself a source from whence to give himself a far higher worth than that of a good-natured temperament could be? Unquestionably. It is just in this that the moral worth of the character is brought out which is incomparably the highest of all, namely, that he is beneficent, not from inclination, but from duty.

To secure one's own happiness is a duty, at least indirectly; for discontent with one's condition, under a pressure of many anxieties and amidst unsatisfied wants, might easily become a great *temptation to transgression of duty*. But here again, without looking to duty, all men have already the strongest and most intimate inclination to happiness, because it is just in this idea that all inclinations are combined in one total. But the precept of happiness is often of such a sort that it greatly interferes with some inclinations, and yet a man cannot form any definite and certain conception of the sum of satisfaction of all of them which is called happiness. It is not then to be wondered at that a single inclination, definite both as to what it promises and as to the time within which it can be gratified, is often able to overcome such a fluctuating idea, and that a gouty patient, for instance, can choose to enjoy what he likes, and to suffer what he may, since, according his calculation, on this occasion at least, he has [only] not sacrificed the enjoyment of the present moment to a possibly mistaken expectation of a happiness which is supposed to be found in health. But even in this case, if the general desire for happiness did not influence his will, and supposing that in his particular case health was not a necessary element in this calculation, there yet remains in this, as in all other cases, this law, namely, that he should promote his happiness not from inclination but from duty, and by this would his conduct first acquire true moral worth.

It is in this manner, undoubtedly, that we are to understand those passages of Scripture also in which we are commanded to love our neighbour, even our enemy. For love, as an affection, cannot be commanded, but beneficence for duty's sake may; even though we are not impelled to it by any inclination – nay, are even repelled by a natural and unconquerable aversion. This is *practical* love, and not *pathological* – a love which is seated in the will, and not in the propensions of sense – in principles of action and not of tender sympathy; and it is this love alone which can be commanded.

The second[1] proposition is: That an action done from duty derives its moral worth, *not from the purpose* which is to be attained by it, but from the maxim by which it is determined, and therefore does not depend on the realization of the object of the action, but merely on the *principle of volition* by which the action has taken place, without regard to any object of desire. It is clear from what precedes that the purposes which we may have in view in our actions or their effects regarded as ends and springs of the will, cannot give to actions any unconditional or moral worth. In what, then, can their worth lie, if it is not to consist in the will and in reference to its expected effect? It cannot lie anywhere but in the *principle of the will* without regard to the ends which can be attained by the action. For the will stands between its *a priori* principle, which is formal, and its *a posteriori* spring, which is material, as between two roads, and as it must be determined by something, it follows that it must be determined by the formal principle of volition when an action is done from duty, in which case every material principle has been withdrawn from it.

The third proposition, which is a consequence of the two preceding, I would express thus: *Duty is the necessity of acting from respect for the law.* I may have *inclination* for an object as the effect of my proposed action, but I cannot have *respect* for it, just for this reason, that it is an effect and not an energy of will. Similarly, I cannot have respect for inclination, whether my own or another's; I can at most, if my own, approve it; if another's sometimes even love it; i.e. look on it as favourable to my own interest. It is only what is connected with my will as a principle, by no means as an effect – what does not subserve my inclination, but overpowers it, or at least in case of choice excludes it from its calculation – in other words, simply the law of itself, which can be an object of respect, and hence a command. Now an action done from duty must wholly exclude the influence of inclination, and with it every object of the will, so that nothing remains which can determine the will except objectively the *law*, and subjectively *pure respect* for this practical law, and consequently the maxim* that I should follow this law even to the thwarting of all my inclinations.[2]

Thus the moral worth of an action does not lie in the effect expected from it, nor in any principle of action which requires to borrow its motive from this expected effect. For all these effects – agreeableness of one's condition, and even the promotion of the happiness of others – could have been also brought about by other causes, so that for this there would have been no need of the will of a rational being; whereas it is in this alone that the supreme and unconditional good can be found. The pre-eminent good which we call moral can therefore consist in nothing else than *the conception of law* in itself, *which certainly is only possible in a rational being*, in so far as this conception, and not the expected effect, determines the will. This is a good which is already present in the person who acts accordingly, and we have not to wait for it to appear first in the result.†

But what sort of law can that be, the conception of which must determine the will, even without paying any regard to the effect expected from it, in order that this will may be called good absolutely and without quali-

---

* A *maxim* is the subjective principle of volition. The objective principle (i.e. that which would also serve subjectively as a practical principle to all rational beings if reason had full power over the faculty of desire) is the practical *law*.

† It might be here objected to me that I take refuge behind the word *respect* in an obscure feeling, instead of giving a distinct solution of the question by a concept of the reason. But although respect is a feeling, it is not a feeling *received* through influence, but is *self-wrought* by a rational concept, and, therefore, is specifically distinct from all feelings of the former kind, which may be referred either to inclination or fear. What I recognize immediately as a law for me, I recognize with respect. This merely signifies the consciousness that my will is *subordinate* to a law, without the intervention of other influences on my sense. The immediate determination of the will by the law, and the consciousness of this is called *respect*, so that this is regarded as an *effect* of the law on the subject, and not as the *cause* of it. Respect is properly the conception of a worth which thwarts my self-love. Accordingly it is something which is considered neither as an object of inclination nor of fear, although it has something analogous to both. The *object* of respect is the *law* only, and that, the law which we impose on *ourselves*, and yet recognize as necessary in itself. As a law, we are subjected to it without consulting self-love; as imposed by us on ourselves, it is a result of our will. In the former respect it has an analogy to fear, in the latter to inclination. Respect for a person is properly only respect for the law (of honesty, etc.), of which he gives us an example. Since we also look on the improvement of our talents as a duty, we consider that we see in a person of talents, as it were, the *example of a law* (viz. to become like him in this by exercise), and this constitutes our respect. All so-called moral *interest* consists simply in *respect* for the law.

fication? As I have deprived the will of every impulse which could arise to it from obedience to any law, there remains nothing but the universal conformity of its actions to law in general, which alone is to serve the will as a principle, i.e. I am never to act otherwise than so *that I could also will that my maxim should become a universal law.* Here now, it is the simple conformity to law in general, without assuming any particular law applicable to certain actions, that serves the will as its principle, and must so serve it, if duty is not to be a vain delusion and a chimerical notion. The common reason of men in its practical judgements perfectly coincides with this, and always has in view the principle here suggested. Let the question be, for example: May I when in distress make a promise with the intention not to keep it? I readily distinguish here between the two significations which the question may have. Whether it is prudent, or whether it is right, to make a false promise. The former may undoubtedly often be the case. I see clearly indeed that it is not enough to extricate myself from a present difficulty by means of this subterfuge, but it must be well considered whether there may not hereafter spring from this lie much greater inconvenience than that from which I now free myself, and as, with all my supposed *cunning*, the consequences cannot be so easily foreseen but that credit once lost may be much more injurious to me than any mischief which I seek to avoid at present, it should be considered whether it would not be more *prudent* to act herein according to a universal maxim, and to make it a habit to promise nothing except with the intention of keeping it. But it is soon clear to me that such a maxim will still only be based on the fear of consequences. Now it is a wholly different thing to be truthful from duty, and to be so from apprehension of injurious consequences. In the first case, the very notion of the action already implies a law for me; in the second case, I must first look about elsewhere to see what results may often be combined with it which would affect myself. For to deviate from the principle of duty is beyond all doubt wicked; but to be unfaithful to my maxim of prudence may often be very advantageous to me although to abide by it is certainly safer. The shortest way, however, and an unerring one, to discover the answer to this question whether a lying promise is consistent with duty, is to ask myself, Should I be content that my maxim (to extricate myself from difficulty by a false promise) should hold good as a universal law, for myself as well as for others? and should I be able to say to myself, 'Every one may make a deceitful promise when he finds himself in a difficulty from which he cannot otherwise extricate himself'? Then I presently become aware that while I can will the lie, I can by no means will that lying should be a universal law. For with such a law there would be no promises at all, since it would be in vain to allege my intention in regard to my future actions to those who would not believe this allegation, or if they overhastily did so, would pay me back in my own coin. Hence my maxim, as soon as it should be made a universal law, would necessarily destroy itself.

I do not, therefore, need any far-reaching penetration to discern what I have to do in order that my will may be morally good. Inexperienced in the course of the world, incapable of being prepared for all its contingencies, I only ask myself: Canst thou also will that thy maxim should be a universal law? If not, then it must be rejected, and that not because of a disadvantage accruing from it to myself or even to others, but because it cannot enter as a principle into a possible universal legislation, and reason extorts from me immediate respect for such legislation. I do not indeed as yet *discern* on what this respect is based (this the philosopher may inquire), but at least I understand this, that it is an estimation of the worth which far outweighs all worth of what is recommended by inclination, and that the necessity of acting from *pure* respect for the practical law is what constitutes duty, to which every other motive must give place, because it is the condition of a will being good *in itself*, and the worth of such a will is above everything.

Thus, then, without quitting the moral knowledge of common human reason, we have arrived at its principle. And although, no doubt, common men do not conceive it in such an abstract and universal form, yet they always have it really before their eyes, and use it as the standard of their decision. Here it would be easy to show how, with this compass in hand, men are well able to distinguish, in every case that occurs, what is good, what bad, conformably to duty or inconsistent with it, if, without in the least teaching them anything new, we only, like Socrates, direct their attention to the principle they themselves employ; and that therefore we do not need science and philosophy to know what we should do to be honest and good, yea, even wise and virtuous. Indeed we might well have conjectured beforehand that the knowledge of what every man is bound to do, and therefore also to know, would be within the reach of every man, even the commonest. Here we cannot forbear admiration when we see how great an advantage the practical judgement has over the theoretical in the common understanding of men. In the latter, if common reason ventures to depart from the laws of experience and from the perceptions of the senses it falls into mere inconceivabilities and self-contradictions, at least into chaos of uncertainty, obscurity, and instability. But in the practical sphere it is just when the common understanding excludes all sensible springs from practical laws that its power of judgement begins to show itself to advantage. It then becomes even subtle, whether it be that it chicanes with its own conscience or with other claims respecting what is to be called right, or whether it desires for its own instruction to determine honestly the worth of actions; and, in the latter case, it may even have as good a hope of hitting the mark as any philosopher whatever can promise himself. Nay, it is almost more sure of doing so, because the philosopher cannot have any other principle, while he may easily perplex his judgement by a multitude of considerations foreign to the matter, and so turn aside from the right way. Would it not therefore be wiser in moral concerns to acquiesce in the judgement of common reason or at most only to call in philosophy for the purpose of rendering the system of morals more complete and intelligible, and its rules more convenient for use (especially for disputation), but not so as to draw off the common understanding from its happy simplicity, or to bring it by means of philosophy into a new path of inquiry and instruction?

Innocence is indeed a glorious thing, only, on the other hand, it is very sad that it cannot well maintain itself, and is easily seduced. On this account even wisdom – which otherwise consists more in conduct than in knowledge – yet has need of science, not in order to learn from it, but to secure for its precepts admission and permanence. Against all the commands of duty which reason represents to man as so deserving of respect, he feels in himself a powerful counterpoise in his wants and inclinations, the entire satisfaction of which he sums under the name of happiness. Now reason issues its commands unyieldingly, without promising anything to the inclinations, and, as it were, with disregard and contempt for these claims, which are so impetuous, and at the same time so plausible, and which will not allow themselves to be suppressed by any command. Hence there arises a natural *dialectic*, i.e. a disposition, to argue against these strict laws of duty and to question their validity, or at least their purity and strictness; and, if possible, to make them more accordant with our wishes and inclinations, that is to say, to corrupt them at their very source, and entirely to destroy their worth – a thing which even common practical reason cannot ultimately call good.

Thus is the *common reason of man* compelled to go out of its sphere, and to take a step into the field of a *practical philosophy*, not to satisfy any speculative want (which never occurs to it as long as it is content to be mere sound reason), but even on practical grounds, in order to attain in it information and clear instruction respecting the source of its principle, and the correct determination of it in opposition to the maxims which are based on wants and inclinations, so that it may escape from the perplexity of opposite claims, and not run the risk of losing all genuine moral principles through the equivocation into which it easily falls. Thus, when practical reason cultivates itself, there insensibly arises in it a dialectic which forces it to seek aid in philosophy, just as happens to it in its theoretic use; and in this case, therefore, as well as in the other, it will find rest nowhere but in a thorough critical examination of our reason.

Notes

1 The first proposition, which Kant did not explicitly state as such, was that only actions done from duty have moral worth.
2 It is worth noting that some commentators prefer 'reverence' to 'respect' as a translation of Kant's term *Achtung*.

Søren Kierkegaard, *Fear and Trembling*, Problema I

From Søren Kierkegaard, *Fear and Trembling*, trans. A. Hannay. Harmondsworth: Penguin, 1985, pp. 83–95 [note omitted]; copyright © Alastair Hannay 1985.

For Kant, we saw, the moral person acts on principles universally binding on rational beings. One criticism soon levelled, notably by G. W. F. Hegel, was that such principles, even if there are any, would be too abstract and empty to constitute a substantial ethical code by which anyone could live. For Hegel, an ethical system (*Sittlichkeit*) is 'universal' in the more restricted sense of comprising the laws and rules of the particular state or society by which its members are bound. Despite this important difference, Kant and most of his German successors were agreed on a number of crucial points. Ethical demands are, in some sense of the term, 'universal' and reason requires willing submission to them, at the expense, if need be, of a person's individuality. Or better, it is through such submission that human beings achieve their true individuality and dignity as rational beings. Moreover, such demands are sovereign: having no purpose or *telos* beyond them, there is nothing that could justify 'suspension of the ethical'.

That final expression is the Danish philosopher, Søren Kierkegaard's (1813–55), who, in the famous first 'Problema' of *Fear and Trembling*, raises the question, 'Is there a teleological suspension of the ethical?' Are there, that is, any circumstances in which a person is to be condoned, admired even, for overriding ethical imperatives? His answer – or rather, that of the pseudonymous 'author', Johannes de Silentio – is affirmative. Kierkegaard's strategy is to focus on an implication of the positions of Kant and Hegel. If we are always bound to act ethically, but also have a constant duty to God, this can only be because God is understood – by definition, as it were – as the endorser of the moral law, as 'a powerful moral lawgiver', to cite Kant.[1] This means, in turn, that a 'conscientious' person who imagines that God is calling on him to act unethically should conclude that he is mistaken – a point that Kant illustrates

[1] *Religion Within the Limits of Reason Alone*, San Francisco: Harper, 1960, p. 5.

with the story of Abraham's (mistaken) readiness to sacrifice his son in apparent accordance with God's command.

It is this story, which Kierkegaard takes to relate a genuine command of God, which is the centrepiece of *Fear and Trembling*, and his point is that, on Kantian and Hegelian premises, Abraham should indeed be simply condemned as a would-be murderer – something that Hegel, inconsistently, fails to do (p. 184 below). That failure is instructive: it suggests that Hegel, like many other people, cannot but admire Abraham. But this, of course, calls into question the whole insistence on the sovereignty of ethical demands. To show this, Kierkegaard needs to show that Abraham's sacrifice of Isaac would in *no* sense have been *ethically* justified. Thus we must distinguish Abraham's predicament from that of the so-called 'tragic hero', like Agamemnon, who is forced to choose between competing ethical demands – those of fatherhood and kingship. Nor is it that Abraham is acting on some general principle like 'If God tells you to do X, then do it!', for he 'feels no vain desire to show others the way' (p. 107). Nor, finally, is there anything rational in Abraham's willingness to sacrifice: on the contrary, he is a 'knight of faith' acting 'on the strength of the absurd' conviction that Isaac, though killed, will somehow be 'returned'. 'Faith begins precisely where thinking leaves off' (p. 82).

Unlike an ethical action, Abraham's is a purely 'private' and 'personal' one which he feels he must perform in virtue of *his* particular relation to God. And perhaps the main implication for moral philosophy, as distinct from theology, of Problema I is not that God, *pace* Kant and Hegel, may order us to defy the moral law, but that some 'private' and 'personal' convictions, religious or otherwise, may go so deep with an individual that he or she is justified in acting upon them despite their contradicting the requirements of ethics. The 'single individual', as Kierkegaard puts it, is 'higher than the universal' (p. 190 below). Despite the importance of always considering the demands of ethics, and despite the 'terrible solitude' of stepping 'outside the universal', the integrity of the individual is secured, not by identification with the ethical life of one's society, but by remaining 'true to oneself'.[2] What matters, Kierkegaard wrote in his *Journals*, is not to find a truth which 'can work upon men' in general, but one which is 'true *for me* . . . *for which I can live and die*' (1 August 1835).

In the end, perhaps, it is not important whether Kierkegaard is described as elevating certain demands *over* those of morality or as proposing a new and individualized conception of morality. Either way, his message was a revolutionary one: an early manifesto of that personal 'authenticity' which was to loom so large in the writings of later existentialist writers,[3] and which, more

[2] See Alastair Hannay, *Kierkegaard*, London: Routledge, 1982, *circa* p. 80.
[3] See, e.g., Karl Jaspers, *Philosophy*, Chicago: University of Chicago Press, 1969–71, on the 'boundary situations' where I am 'on my own', without guidance from general principles, thereby confirming that 'I am not a result of social configurations . . . I retain my own original potential' (vol. 2, p. 30).

importantly, was to enter the bloodstream of countless twentieth-century men and women disenchanted with, or 'alienated' by, the pretensions of universal recipes for the conduct of their lives.

Problema I. Is There a Teleological Suspension of the Ethical?

The ethical as such is the universal, and as the universal it applies to everyone, which can be put from another point of view by saying that it applies at every moment. It rests immanently in itself, has nothing outside itself that is its *telos* [end, purpose] but is itself the *telos* for everything outside, and when that is taken up into it, it has no further to go. Seen as an immediate, no more than sensate and psychic, being, the single individual is the particular that has its *telos* in the universal, and the individual's ethical task is always to express himself in this, to abrogate his particularity so as to become the universal. As soon as the single individual wants to assert himself in his particularity, in direct opposition to the universal, he sins, and only by recognizing this can he again reconcile himself with the universal. Whenever, having entered the universal, the single individual feels an urge to assert his particularity, he is in a state of temptation, from which he can extricate himself only by surrendering his particularity to the universal in repentance. If that is the highest that can be said of man and his existence, then the ethical and a person's eternal blessedness, which is his *telos* in all eternity and at every moment, are identical; for in that case it would be a contradiction to say that one surrendered that *telos* (i.e. suspended it *teleologically*) since by suspending the *telos* one would be forfeiting it, while what is said to be suspended in this sense is not forfeited but preserved in something higher, the latter being precisely its *telos*.

If that is the case, then Hegel is right in his 'Good and Conscience' where he discusses man seen merely as the single individual and regards this way of seeing him as a 'moral form of evil' to be annulled in the teleology of the ethical life,[1] so that the individual who stays at this stage is either in sin or in a state of temptation. Where Hegel goes wrong, on the other hand, is in talking about faith, in not protesting loudly and clearly against the honour and glory enjoyed by Abraham as the father of faith when he should really be remitted to some lower court for trial and exposed as a murderer.

For faith is just this paradox, that the single individual is higher than the universal, though in such a way, be it noted, that the movement is repeated, that is, that, having been in the universal, the single individual now sets himself apart as the particular above the universal. If that is not faith, then Abraham is done for and faith has never existed in the world, just because it has always existed. For if the ethical life is the highest and nothing incommensurable is left over in man, except in the sense of what is evil, i.e. the single individual who is to be expressed in the universal, then one needs no other categories than those of the Greek philosophers, or whatever can be logically deduced from them. This is something Hegel, who has after all made some study of the Greeks, ought not to have kept quiet about.

One not infrequently hears people who prefer to lose themselves in clichés rather than studies say that light shines over the Christian world, while paganism is shrouded in darkness. This kind of talk has always struck me as strange, since any reasonably deep thinker, any reasonably serious artist will still seek rejuvenation in the eternal youth of the Greeks. The explanation may be that they know not what to say, only that they have to say something. There is nothing wrong with saying that paganism did not have faith, but if this is to mean anything one must be a little clearer what one means by faith, otherwise one falls back into those clichés. It is easy to explain the whole of existence, faith included, and he is not the worst reckoner in life who counts on being admired for having such an explanation; for it is as Boileau says: '*un sot trouve toujours un plus sot, qui l'admire*' ['a fool can always find a greater fool who admires him'].

Faith is just this paradox, that the single individual as the particular is higher than the universal, is justified before the latter, not as subordinate but superior, though in such a way, be it noted, that it is the single individual who, having been subordinate to the universal as the particular, now by means of the universal becomes that individual who, as the particular, stands in an absolute relation to the absolute. This position cannot be mediated, for all mediation occurs precisely by virtue of the universal; it is and remains in all eternity a paradox, inaccessible to thought.[2] And yet faith *is* this paradox. Or else (these are implications which I would ask the reader always to bear in mind, though it would be too complicated for me to spell them out each time) – or else faith has never existed just because it has always existed. And Abraham is done for.

That the individual can easily take this paradox for a temptation is true enough. But one should not keep it quiet on that account. True enough, too, that many people may have a natural aversion to the paradox, but that is no reason for making faith into something else so that they too can have it; while those who do have faith should be prepared to offer some criterion for distinguishing the paradox from a temptation.

Now the story of Abraham contains just such a teleological suspension of the ethical. There has been no want of sharp intellects and sound scholars who have found analogies to it. Their wisdom amounts to the splendid principle that basically everything is the same. If one looks a little closer I doubt very much whether one will find in the whole world a single analogy, except a later one that proves nothing, for the fact remains that Abraham represents faith, and that faith finds its proper expression in him whose life is not only the most paradoxical conceivable, but so paradoxical that it simply cannot be thought. He acts on the strength of the absurd; for it is precisely the absurd that as the single individual he is higher than the universal. This paradox cannot be mediated; for as soon as he tries Abraham will have to admit that he is in a state of temptation, and in that case he will never sacrifice Isaac, or if he has done so he must return repentantly to the universal. On the strength of the absurd he got Isaac back. Abraham is therefore at no instant the tragic hero, but something quite different, either a murderer or a man of faith. The middle-term that saves the tragic hero is something Abraham lacks. That is why I can understand a tragic hero, but not Abraham, even though in a certain lunatic sense I admire him more than all others.

Abraham's relation to Isaac, ethically speaking, is quite simply this, that the father should love the son more than himself. Yet within its own compass the ethical has several rankings; let us see whether this story contains any such higher expression of the ethical which might explain his behaviour ethically, justify him ethically for suspending the ethical duty to the son, yet without thereby exceeding the ethical's own teleology.

When an enterprise involving a whole nation is prevented, when such an enterprise is brought to a halt by heaven's disfavour, when divine wrath sends a dead calm which mocks every effort, when the soothsayer performs his sad task and proclaims that the deity demands a young girl as a sacrifice – then it is with heroism that the father has to make that sacrifice.[3] Nobly will he hide his grief though he could wish he were 'the lowly man who dares to weep' and not the king who must bear himself as befits a king. And however solitarily the pain enters his breast, for he has only three confidants among his people, soon the entire population will be privy to his pain, but also to his deed, to the fact that for the well-being of the whole he was willing to offer that girl, his daughter, this lovely young maiden. Oh, what bosom! What fair cheeks! What flaxen hair! And the daughter will touch him with her tears, and the father avert his face, but the hero will raise the knife. And when the news of this reaches the ancestral home all the beauteous maidens of Greece will blush with animation, and were the daughter a bride the betrothed would not be angered but proud to have been party to the father's deed, because the maiden belonged to him more tenderly than to the father.

When that bold judge, who saved Israel in the hour of need binds God and himself in one breath with the same promise, then it is with heroism that he is to transform the young girl's jubilation, the beloved daughter's joy, to sorrow, and all Israel will grieve with her maidenly youth; but every free-born man will understand Jephthah, every stout-hearted woman admire him, and every maiden in Israel will want to do as his daughter; for what good would it be for Jephthah to triumph by making his promise but fail to keep it? Would the victory not be taken once more from the people?

When a son forgets his duty, when the State entrusts the father with the sword of judgement, when the laws demand punishment at the father's hand, then it is with heroism that the father must forget that the guilty one is his son. Nobly will he hide his pain, but in the nation there will be not one, not even the son, who fails to admire the father, and every time the laws of Rome are interpreted it will be recalled that many interpreted them more learnedly but none more gloriously than Brutus.

On the other hand, if it had been while his fleet was being borne by wind under full sail to its destination that Agamemnon had sent that messenger who brought Iphigenia to the sacrifice; if unbound by any promise that would decide the fate of his people Jephthah had said to his daughter: 'Sorrow now for two months henceforth over the short day of your youth, for I shall sacrifice you': if Brutus had had a righteous son and still called upon the lictors to execute him – who would understand them? If to the question, why did you do it?, these three had replied: 'It is a trial in which we are being tested', would one then have understood them better?

When at the decisive moment Agamemnon, Jephthah and Brutus heroically overcome their pain, have heroically given up the loved one, and have only the outward deed to perform, then never a noble soul in the world will there be but sheds tears of sympathy for their pain, tears of admiration for their deed. But if at that decisive moment these three men had added to the heroism with which they bore their pain the little words 'It won't happen', who then would understand them? If in explanation they added: 'We believe it on the strength of the absurd', who would understand them better? For who would not readily understand that it was absurd? But who would understand that for that reason one could believe it?

The difference between the tragic hero and Abraham is obvious enough. The tragic hero stays within the ethical. He lets an expression of the ethical have its *telos* in a higher expression of the ethical; he reduces the ethical relation between father and son, or daughter and father, to a sentiment that has its dialectic in its relation to the idea of the ethical life. Here, then, there can be no question of a teleological suspension of the ethical itself.

With Abraham it is different. In his action he overstepped the ethical altogether, and had a higher *telos* outside it, in relation to which he suspended it. For how could one ever bring Abraham's action into relationship with the universal? How could any point of contact ever be discovered between what Abraham did and the universal other than that Abraham overstepped it? It is not to save a nation, not to uphold the idea of the State, that Abraham did it, not to appease angry gods. If there was any question of the deity's being angry, it could only have been Abraham he was angry with, and Abraham's whole action stands in no relation to the universal, it is a purely private undertaking. While, then, the tragic hero is great through his deed's being an expression of the ethical life, Abraham is great through an act of purely personal virtue. There is no higher expression of the ethical in Abraham's life than that the father shall love the son. The ethical in the sense of the ethical life is quite out of the question. In so far as the universal was there at all it was latent in Isaac, concealed as it were in his loins, and it would have to cry out with Isaac's mouth: 'Don't do it, you are destroying everything.[4]

Then why does Abraham do it? For God's sake, and what is exactly the same, for his own. He does it for the sake of God because God demands this proof of his faith; he does it for his own sake in order to be able to produce the proof. The unity here is quite properly expressed in the saying in which this relationship has always been described: it is a trial, a temptation. A temptation, but what does that mean? What we usually call a temptation is something that keeps a person from carrying out a duty, but here the temptation is the ethical itself which would keep him from doing God's will. But then what is the duty? For the duty is precisely the expression of God's will.

Here we see the need for a new category for understanding Abraham. Such a relationship to the divine is unknown to paganism. The tragic hero enters into no private relationship with God, but the ethical is the divine and therefore the paradox in the divine can be mediated in the universal.

Abraham cannot be mediated, which can also be put by saying he cannot speak. The moment I speak I express the universal, and when I do not no one can understand me. So the moment Abraham wants to express himself in the universal, he has to say that his situation is one of temptation, for he has no higher expression of the universal that overrides the universal he transgresses.

Thus while Abraham arouses my admiration, he also appals me. The person who denies himself and sacrifices himself for duty gives up the finite in order to grasp on to the infinite; he is secure enough. The tragic hero gives up what is certain for what is still more certain, and the eye of the beholder rests confidently upon him. But the person who gives up the universal to grasp something still higher that is not the universal, what does he do? Can this be anything but temptation? And if it were something else but the individual were mistaken, what salvation is there for him? He suffers all the pain of the tragic hero, he brings all his joy in the world to nothing, he abandons everything, and perhaps the same instant debars himself from that exalted joy so precious to him that he would buy it at any price. That person the beholder cannot at all understand, nor let his eye rest upon him with confidence. Perhaps what the believer intends just cannot be done, after all it is unthinkable. Or if it could be done and the individual had misunderstood the deity, what salvation would there be for him? The tragic hero, he needs tears and he claims them; yes, where was that envious eye so barren as not to weep with Agamemnon, but where was he whose soul was so confused as to presume to weep for Abraham? The tragic hero has done with his deed at a definite moment in time, but in the course of time he achieves something no less important, he seeks out the one whose soul is beset with sorrow, whose breast cannot draw air for its stifled sighs, whose thoughts, weighed down with tears, hang heavy upon him; he appears before him, he breaks the spell of grief, loosens the corset, coaxes forth the tear by making the sufferer forget his own suffering in his. Abraham one cannot weep over. One approaches him with a *horror religiosus* [holy terror] like that in which Israel approached Mount Sinai. What if the lonely man who climbs the mountain in Moriah, whose peak soars heaven-high over the plains of Aulis, is not a sleepwalker who treads surefootedly over the abyss, while someone standing at the foot of the mountain, seeing him there, trembles with anxiety and out of respect and fear dares not even shout to him – what if he should be distracted, what if he has made a mistake? – Thanks! And thanks again, to whoever holds out to one who has been assaulted and left naked by life's sorrows, holds out to him the leaf of the word with which to hide his misery. Thanks to you, great Shakespeare!, you who can say everything, everything, everything exactly as it is – and yet why was this torment one you never gave voice to? Was it perhaps that you kept it to yourself, like the beloved whose name one still cannot bear the world to mention? For a poet buys this power of words to utter all the grim secrets of others at the cost of a little secret he himself cannot utter, and a poet is not an apostle, he casts devils out only by the power of the devil.

But now when the ethical is thus teleologically suspended, how does the single individual in whom it is suspended exist? He exists as the particular in opposition to the universal. Does this mean he sins? For this is the form of sin looked at ideally, just as the fact that the child does not sin because it is not conscious of its own existence as such does not mean that, looked at ideally, its existence is not that of sin or that the ethical does not make its demands of the child at every moment. If this form cannot be said to repeat itself in a way other than that of sin, then judgement has been delivered upon Abraham. Then how did Abraham exist? He had faith. That is the paradox that keeps him at the extremity and which he cannot make clear to anyone else, for the paradox is that he puts himself as the single individual in an absolute relation to the absolute. Is he justified? His justification is, once again, the paradox; for if he is the paradox it is not by virtue of being anything universal, but of being the particular.

How does the single individual assure himself that he is justified? It is a simple enough matter to level the whole of existence down to the idea of the State or to a concept of society. If one does that one can no doubt also mediate; for in this way one does not come to the paradox at all, to the single individual's as such being higher than the universal, which I can also put pointedly in a proposition of Pythagoras's, that the odd numbers are more perfect than the even. Should one happen to catch word of an answer in the direction of the paradox in our time, it will no doubt go like this: 'That's to be judged by the outcome.' A hero who has become the scandal of his generation, aware that he is a paradox that cannot be understood, cries undaunted to his contemporaries: 'The future will show I was right!' This cry is heard less frequently nowadays, for as our age to its detriment produces no heroes, so it has the advantage that it also produces few caricatures. Whenever nowadays we hear the words 'That's to be judged by the outcome' we know immediately with whom we have the honour of conversing. Those who speak thus are a populous tribe which, to give them a common name, I shall call the 'lecturers'. They live in their thoughts, secure in life, they have a *permanent* position and *sure* prospects in a well-organized State; they are separated by centuries, even millennia, from the convulsions of existence; they have no fear that such things could happen again; what would the police and the newspapers say? Their lifework is to judge the great, to judge them according to the outcome. Such conduct in respect of greatness betrays a strange mixture of arrogance and pitifulness, arrogance because they feel called to pass judgement, pitifulness because they feel their lives unrelated in even the remotest manner to those of the great. Surely anyone with a speck of *erectior ingenii* [nobility of mind] cannot become so completely the cold and clammy mollusc as to lose sight altogether, in approaching the great, of the fact that ever since the Creation it has been accepted practice for the outcome to come last, and that if one is really to learn something from the great it is precisely the beginning one must attend to. If anyone on the verge of action should judge himself according to the outcome, he would never begin. Even though the result may gladden the whole world, that cannot help the hero; for he knows the result only when the whole thing is over, and that is not how he becomes a hero, but by virtue of the fact that he began.

But in any case the outcome in its dialectic (in so far as it is finitude's answer to the infinite question) is totally incompatible with the existence of the hero. Or are we to take it that Abraham was justified in relating himself as the single individual to the universal by the fact that he got Isaac by a *marvel*? Had Abraham actually sacrificed Isaac, would that have meant he was less justified?

But it is the outcome that arouses our curiosity, as with the conclusion of a book; one wants nothing of the fear, the distress, the paradox. One flirts with the outcome aesthetically; it comes as unexpectedly and yet as effortlessly as a prize in the lottery; and having heard the outcome one is improved. And yet no robber of temples hard-labouring in chains is so base a criminal as he who plunders the holy in this way, and not even Judas, who sold his master for thirty pieces of silver, is more contemptible than the person who would thus offer greatness for sale.

It goes against my nature to speak inhumanity of greatness, to let its grandeur fade into an indistinct outline at an immense distance, or represent it as great without the human element in it coming to the fore – whence it ceases to be the great; for it is not what happens to me that makes me great, but what I do, and there is surely no one who thinks that anyone became great by winning the big lottery prize. Even of a person born in humble circumstances I ask that he should not be so inhuman towards himself as to be unable to think of the king's castle except at a distance and by dreaming of its grandeur indistinctly, wanting to exalt it and simultaneously destroying its grandeur by exalting it in such a debasing way. I ask that he be human enough to approach and bear himself with confidence and dignity there too. He should not be so inhuman as shamelessly to want to violate every rule of respect by storming into the king's salon straight from the street – he loses more by doing that than the king; on the contrary he should find pleasure in observing every rule of decorum with a glad and confident enthusiasm, which is just what will make him frank and open-hearted. This is only an analogy, for the difference here is only a very imperfect expression of the spiritual distance. I ask everyone not to think so inhumanly of himself as to dare not set foot in those palaces where not just the memory of the chosen lives on but the chosen themselves. He should not push himself shamelessly forward and thrust upon them his kinship with them, he should feel happy every time he bows before them, but be frank and confident and always something more than a cleaning woman; for unless he wants to be more than that he will never come in there. And what will help him are exactly the fear and distress in which the great are tried, for otherwise, at least if there is a drop of red blood in him, they will merely arouse his righteous envy. And whatever can only be great at a distance, whatever people want to exalt with empty and hollow phrases, that they themselves reduce to nothing.

Was there ever in the world anyone as great as that blessed woman, the mother of God, the Virgin Mary? And yet how do people speak of her? To say she was favoured among women doesn't make her great, and if it were not for the odd fact that those who listen can think as inhumanly as those who speak, surely every young girl would ask, why am I not favoured too? And had I nothing more to say I should by no means dismiss such a question as stupid; for as regards favours, abstractly considered, everyone is equally entitled. What is left out is the distress, the fear, the paradox. My thought is as pure as the next man's and surely the thought of anyone able to think in this way will be pure; if not, something dreadful is in store; for a person who has once called these images to mind cannot be rid of them again, and if he sins against them, then in their quiet wrath, more terrifying than the clamour of ten voracious critics, they will wreak their awful vengeance on him. No doubt Mary bore the child miraculously, but it went with Mary 'after the manner of women', and such a time is one of fear, distress and paradox. No doubt the angel was a ministering spirit, but he was not an obliging one who went round to all the other young girls in Israel and said: 'Do not despise Mary, something out of the ordinary is happening to her.' The angel came only to Mary, and no one could understand her. Yet what woman was done greater indignity than Mary, and isn't it true here too that those whom God blesses he damns in the same breath? This is the spirit's understanding of Mary, and she is not at all – as it offends me to say, though even more so that people have mindlessly and irresponsibly thought of her thus – she is not at all the fine lady sitting in her finery and playing with a divine child. Yet for saying notwithstanding, 'Behold the handmaid of the Lord' [Luke i.38 – Ed.], she is great, and it seems to me that it should not be difficult to explain why she became the mother of God. She needs no worldly admiration, as little as Abraham needs our tears, for she was no heroine and he no hero, but both of them became greater than that, not by any means by being relieved of the distress, the agony and the paradox, but because of these.

Great indeed it is when the poet presents his tragic hero for popular admiration and dares to say: 'Weep for him, for he deserves it'; for there is greatness in meriting the tears of those who deserve to shed them; great indeed for the poet to dare hold the crowd in check, dare discipline people into testing their own worthiness to weep for the hero, for the waste-water of snivellers is a degradation of the holy. But greater than all these is that the knight of faith dares to say even to the noble person who would weep for him: 'Do not weep for me, but weep for yourself.'

One is stirred, one harks back to those beautiful times, sweet tender longings lead one to the goal of one's desire, to see Christ walking about in the promised land. One forgets the fear, the distress, the paradox. Was it so easy a matter not to be mistaken? Was it not a fearful thought that this man who walked among the others was God? Was it not terrifying to sit down to eat with him? Was it so easy a matter to become an apostle? But the outcome, eighteen centuries, that helps; it helps that shabby deception wherein one deceives oneself and others. I do not feel brave enough to wish to be contemporary with such events, but for that reason I do not judge harshly of those who were mistaken, nor think meanly of those who saw the truth.

But now I return to Abraham. In the time before the outcome either Abraham was a murderer every minute or we stay with the paradox which is higher than all mediation.

So Abraham's story contains a teleological suspension of the ethical. He has, as the single individual, become higher than the universal. This is the paradox which cannot be mediated. How he got into it is just as inexplicable as how he stayed in it. If this is not how it is with Abraham, then he is not even a tragic hero but a murderer. To want to go on calling him the father of faith, to talk of this to those who are only concerned with words, is thoughtless. A tragic hero can become a human being by his own strength, but not the knight of faith. When a person sets out on the tragic hero's admittedly hard path there are many who could lend him advice; but he who walks the narrow path of faith no one can advise, no one understand. Faith is a marvel, and yet no human being is excluded from it; for that in which all human life is united is passion, and faith is a passion.

Notes

1 See Hegel's *Philosophy of Right*, Part 2, Section 3, Oxford: Clarendon Press, 1942, where he argues that 'morality (*Moralität*)', the 'subjective' sphere of individual conscience, must give way to 'the ethical life (*Sittlichkeit*)', the 'objective', 'universal' sphere of public duty.

2 'Mediation' is Hegel-speak for the resolving of contradictions or paradoxes.

3 In this and the following two paragraphs, Kierkegaard discusses three 'tragic heroes': Agamemnon, who must sacrifice his daughter Iphigenia in order to ensure a wind to take his fleet to Troy (the lines quoted are from Euripides' *Iphigenia*

in Aulis); Jephthah, who finds he must sacrifice his daughter as a burnt offering in gratitude for Jehovah's military assistance (Judges 11); and L. Junius Brutus, a Roman consul who executed his own sons for treason.

4 This alludes to the important point that, in killing Isaac, Abraham would not only be killing his son but the future leader of the nation. Unlike those of the tragic heroes, therefore, Abraham's deed would violate *both* paternal *and* patriotic duty.

From The Ethics of John Stuart Mill, ed. C. Douglas. Edinburgh: Blackwood & Sons, 1897, pp. 89–127 [notes and two paragraphs omitted].

Textbooks on Chinese philosophy report that 'the first utilitarian' was Mo Tzu in the fifth century BCE. Europe had to wait 2300 years, however, for the famous 'Principle of Utility' or 'Greatest Happiness Principle' to be proclaimed – by Jeremy Bentham in England and Claude-Adrien Helvétius in France – as the sole principle for judging the moral value of actions. Utilitarianism became the characteristic moral doctrine of radical eighteenth-century Enlightenment thought, its seemingly 'no nonsense' approach rooted in the predominant view of human nature 'under the governance', as Bentham put it, 'of two sovereign masters, *pain* and *pleasure*'.[1] If human beings *cannot* desire anything but happiness or pleasure, any religion or morality which tells them they *ought* to aim elsewhere must be so much pie-in-the-sky.

Despite the influence of utilitarianism on public policy in the early nineteenth century, its philosophical basis had come under fierce attack – from Kant, from Romantics like Coleridge, and from the pulpit – by the time Bentham's godson and the most important British philosopher of the century, John Stuart Mill (1806–73), wrote his famous book *Utilitarianism* in 1861. Chapter 2 of this work is intended as a rebuttal of 'the stock arguments against utilitarianism', which Mill characterizes as 'the creed which . . . holds that actions are right in proportion as they tend to promote happiness' (p. 208 and p. 195 below). These 'stock' objections ranged from the Kantian insistence that an action's consequences have no relevance to its moral worth to the accusation of 'swinishness' in regarding happiness and pleasure as our sole ends; and from the impracticability of guiding our behaviour by so grand a goal as 'the greatest happiness of the greatest number' to affirmation of the value 'for their own sake' of virtuous conduct and the performance of duty.

To these and other objections, Mill offers replies – whether by way of

[1] *A Fragment of Government and An Introduction to the Principles of Morals and Legislation*, Oxford: Blackwell, 1960, p. 125.

rebuttal, as when he accuses the Kantian objection of confusing the worth of actions with that of their agents; or by showing that the objectors misconstrue utilitarianism, wrongly imagining, for example, that the criterion of right action – the 'greatest happiness' – should always be our explicit motive; or by amending Benthamite doctrine in order to pre-empt an objection, as when he makes his famous distinction between 'higher' and 'lower' pleasures in response to the accusation of 'swinishness'.

There is little doubt that Mill articulates a more plausible moral philosophy than those of his utilitarian predecessors, not least through providing a more convincing moral psychology.[2] Although happiness or pleasure is our sole end, it should not be thought of as some 'hedonic state', susceptible to measurement by a 'felicific calculus', which we are constantly trying to produce. Rather, as for Aristotle, happiness is something we find in and through our actions. This enables Mill to lend sense to the idea of virtuous behaviour being good in itself: for when I help a friend in need, this is not a means to producing a state of pleasurable satisfaction, but something which does – or should – carry with it its own satisfaction.

Those looking for a decisive defence of utilitarianism, however, are liable to be disappointed. No more than Bentham does Mill genuinely *argue* for the Greatest Happiness Principle, both men leaving it obscure how a person is to move from valuing his or her own happiness to regard for the general happiness. On certain crucial issues, moreover, Mill is hard to pin down. Thus, while he is surely right to insist that any workable moral code must employ 'subordinate principles', such as 'Don't steal!', and not simply the 'ultimate' principle of the greatest happiness, he leaves the connection between the two opaque. What if I am convinced that, on this occasion, stealing will promote the general happiness? Should I steal? If, as Mill hints, I should not, is his position any longer one that deserves to be called utilitarian? This is a worry to which other of his remarks also give rise, notably the 'higher' *versus* 'lower' pleasures distinction. How, by reference to pleasure alone, can we make such an evaluative distinction among pleasures?[3]

Whether it mounts a successful defence or not, Mill's *Utilitarianism* was responsible for securing a central place for that doctrine in subsequent moral philosophy. Within a few years of its publication, British ethicists were divided between those, like Henry Sidgwick, who continued to refine the utilitarian tradition and those, like F. H. Bradley, to whom that whole tradition was anathema. As every First Year student of ethics today knows, the issues at the heart of such divisions show no sign of evaporating.[4]

---

[2] See John Skorupski, *John Stuart Mill*, London: Routledge, 1989.
[3] For doubts as to whether Mill really was a utilitarian, see Isaiah Berlin's essay on Mill in his *Four Essays on Liberty*, Oxford: Oxford University Press, 1969.

(*continued on next page*)

▷ ▷ ▷ Chapter 2: What Utilitarianism Is

A passing remark is all that needs be given to the ignorant blunder of supposing that those who stand up for utility as the test of right and wrong, use the term in that restricted and merely colloquial sense in which utility is opposed to pleasure. An apology is due to the philosophical opponents of utilitarianism, for even the momentary appearance of confounding them with any one capable of so absurd a misconception; which is the more extraordinary, inasmuch as the contrary accusation, of referring everything to pleasure, and that too in its grossest form, is another of the common charges against utilitarianism: and, as has been pointedly remarked by an able writer, the same sort of persons, and often the very same persons, denounce the theory 'as impracticably dry when the word utility precedes the word pleasure, and as too practicably voluptuous when the word pleasure precedes the word utility'. Those who know anything about the matter are aware that every writer, from Epicurus to Bentham, who maintained the theory of utility, meant by it, not something to be contradistinguished from pleasure, but pleasure itself, together with exemption from pain; and instead of opposing the useful to the agreeable or the ornamental, have always declared that the useful means these, among other things. Yet the common herd, including the herd of writers, not only in newspapers and periodicals, but in books of weight and pretension, are perpetually falling into this shallow mistake. Having caught up the word utilitarian, while knowing nothing whatever about it but its sound, they habitually express by it the rejection, or the neglect, of pleasure in some of its forms – of beauty, of ornament, or of amusement. Nor is the term thus ignorantly misapplied solely in disparagement, but occasionally in compliment; as though it implied superiority to frivolity and the mere pleasures of the moment. And this perverted use is the only one in which the word is popularly known, and the one from which the new generation are acquiring their sole notion of its meaning. Those who introduced the word, but who had for many years discontinued it as a distinctive appellation, may well feel themselves called upon to resume it, if by doing so they can hope to contribute anything towards rescuing it from this utter degradation.

(*continued from previous page*)
[4] Sidgwick, *Methods of Ethics*, London: Macmillan, 1962; Bradley, *Ethical Studies*, Oxford: Oxford University Press, 1962; and for more recent debates, see J. J. C. Smart and B. A. O. Williams (eds), *Utilitarianism: For and Against*, Cambridge: Cambridge University Press, 1973.

The creed which accepts as the foundation of morals, Utility, or the Greatest Happiness Principle, holds that actions are right in proportion as they tend to promote happiness, wrong as they tend to produce the reverse of happiness. By happiness is intended pleasure, and the absence of pain; by unhappiness, pain, and the privation of pleasure. To give a clear view of the moral standard set up by the theory, much more requires to be said: in particular, what things it includes in the ideas of pain and pleasure; and to what extent this is left an open question. But these supplementary explanations do not affect the theory of life on which this theory of morality is grounded – namely, that pleasure, and freedom from pain, are the only things desirable as ends; and that all desirable things (which are as numerous in the utilitarian as in any other scheme) are desirable either for the pleasure inherent in themselves, or as means to the promotion of pleasure and the prevention of pain.

Now, such a theory of life excites in many minds, and among them in some of the most estimable in feeling and purpose, inveterate dislike. To suppose that life has (as they express it) no higher end than pleasure – no better and nobler object of desire and pursuit – they designate as utterly mean and grovelling; as a doctrine worthy only of swine, to whom the followers of Epicurus were, at a very early period, contemptuously likened; and modern holders of the doctrine are occasionally made the subject of equally polite comparisons by its German, French and English assailants.

When thus attacked, the Epicureans have always answered that it is not they, but their accusers, who represent human nature in a degrading light; since the accusation supposes human beings to be capable of no pleasures except those of which swine are capable. If this supposition were true, the charge could not be gainsaid, but would then be no longer an imputation: for if the sources of pleasure were precisely the same to human beings and to swine, the rule of life which is good enough for the one would be good enough for the other. The comparison of the Epicurean life to that of beasts is felt as degrading, precisely because a beast's pleasures do not satisfy a human being's conceptions of happiness. Human beings have faculties more elevated than the animal appetites, and when once made conscious of them, do not regard anything as happiness which does not include their gratification. I do not, indeed, consider the Epicureans to have been by any means faultless in drawing out their scheme of consequences from the utilitarian principle. To do this in any sufficient manner, many Stoic as well as Christian elements require to be included. But there is no known Epicurean theory of life which does not assign to the pleasures of the intellect, of the feelings and imagination, and of the moral sentiments, a much higher value as pleasures than to those of mere sensation. It must be admitted, however, that utilitarian writers in general have placed the superiority of mental over bodily pleasures chiefly in the greater permanency, safety, uncostliness, &c., of the former – that is, in their circumstantial advantages rather than in their intrinsic nature. And on all these points utilitarians have fully proved their case; but they might have taken the other, and, as it may be called, higher ground, with entire consistency. It is quite compatible with the principle of utility to recognize the fact, that some *kinds* of pleasure are more desirable and more valuable than others. It would be absurd that while, in estimating all other things, quality is considered as well as quantity, the estimation of pleasures should be supposed to depend on quantity alone.

If I am asked what I mean by difference of quality in pleasures, or what makes one pleasure more valuable than another, merely as a pleasure, except its being greater in amount, there is but one possible answer. Of two pleasures, if there be one to which all or almost all who have experience of both give a decided preference, irrespective of any feeling of moral obligation to prefer it, that is the more desirable pleasure. If one of the two is, by those who are competently acquainted with both, placed so far above the other that they prefer it, even though knowing it to be attended with a greater amount of discontent, and would not resign it for any quantity of the other pleasure which their nature is capable of, we are justified in ascribing to the preferred enjoyment a superiority in quality, so far outweighing quantity as to render it, in comparison, of small account.

Now it is an unquestionable fact that those who are equally acquainted with, and equally capable of appreciating and enjoying, both, do give a most marked preference to the manner of existence which employs their higher faculties. Few human creatures would consent to be changed into any of the lower animals, for a promise of the fullest allowance of a beast's pleasures; no intelligent human being would consent to be a fool, no instructed person would be an ignoramus, no person of feeling and conscience would be selfish and base, even though they should be persuaded that the fool, the dunce or the rascal is better satisfied with his lot than they are with theirs. They would not resign what they possess more than he, for the most complete satisfaction of all the desires which they have in common with him. If they ever fancy they would, it is only in cases of unhappiness so extreme, that to escape from it they would exchange their lot for almost any other, however undesirable in their own eyes. A being of higher faculties requires more to make him happy, is capable probably of more acute suffering, and is certainly accessible to it at more points, than one of an inferior type; but in spite of these liabilities, he can never really wish to sink into what he feels to be a lower grade of existence. We may give what explanation we please of this unwillingness: we may attribute it to pride, a name which is given indiscriminately to some of the most and to some of the least estimable feelings of which mankind are capable; we may refer it to the love of liberty and personal independence, an appeal to which was with the Stoics one of the most effective means for the inculcation of it; to the love of power, or to the love of excitement, both of which do really enter into and contribute to it. But its most appropriate appellation is a sense of dignity, which all human beings possess in one form or other, and in some, though by no means in exact, proportion to their higher faculties, and which is so essential a part of the happiness of those in whom it is strong, that nothing which conflicts with it could be, otherwise than momentarily, an object of desire to them. Whoever supposes that this preference takes place at a sacrifice of happiness – that the superior being, in anything like equal circumstances, is not happier than the inferior – confounds the two very different ideas, of happiness and content. It is indisputable that the being whose capacities of enjoyment are low, has the greatest chance of having them fully satisfied; and a highly endowed being will always feel that any happiness which he can look for, as the world is constituted, is imperfect. But he can learn to bear its imperfections, if they are at all bearable; and they will not make him envy the being who is indeed unconscious of the imperfections, but only because he feels not at all the good which those imperfections qualify. It is better to be a human being dissatisfied than a pig satisfied; better to be Socrates dissatisfied than a fool satisfied. And if the fool, or the pig, is of a different opinion, it is because they only know their own side of the question. The other party to the comparison knows both sides.

It may be objected that many who are capable of the higher pleasures, occasionally, under the influence of temptation, postpone them to the lower. But this is quite compatible with a full appreciation of the intrinsic superiority of the higher. Men often, from infirmity of character, make their election for the nearer good, though they know it to be the less valuable; and this no less when the choice is between two bodily pleasures, than when it is between bodily and mental. They pursue sensual indulgences to the injury of health, though perfectly aware that health is the greater good. It may be further objected that many who begin with youthful enthusiasm for everything noble, as they advance in years sink into indolence and selfishness. But I do not believe that those who undergo this very common change, voluntarily choose the lower description of pleasures in preference to the higher. I believe that before they devote themselves exclusively to the one, they have already become incapable of the other. Capacity for the nobler feelings is in most natures a very tender plant, easily killed, not only by hostile influences, but by mere want of sustenance; and in the majority of young persons it speedily dies away if the occupations to which their position in life has devoted them, and the society into which it has thrown them, are not favourable to keeping that higher capacity in exercise. Men lose their high aspirations as they lose their intellectual tastes, because they have not time or opportunity for indulging them; and they addict themselves to inferior pleasures, not because they deliberately prefer them, but because they are either the only ones to which they have access, or the only ones which they are any longer capable of enjoying. It may be questioned whether any one who has remained equally susceptible to both classes of pleasures, ever knowingly and calmly preferred the lower; though many, in all ages, have broken down in an ineffectual attempt to combine both.

From this verdict of the only competent judges, I apprehend there can be no appeal. On a question which is the better worth having of two pleasures, or which of two modes of existence is the more grateful to the feelings, apart from its moral attributes and from its consequences, the judgement of those who are qualified by knowledge of both, or, if they differ, that of the majority among them, must be admitted as final. And there needs be the less hesitation to accept this judgement respecting the quality of pleasures, since there is no other tribunal to be referred to even on the question of quantity. What means are there of determining which is the acuter of two pains, or the intenser of two pleasurable sensations, except the general suffrage of those who are familiar with both? Neither pains nor pleasures are homogeneous, and pain is always heterogeneous with pleasure. What is there to decide whether a particular pleasure is worth purchasing at the cost of a particular pain, except the feelings and judgement of the experienced? When, therefore, those feelings and judgement declare the pleasures derived from the higher faculties to be preferable *in kind*, apart from the question of intensity, to those of which the animal nature, disjoined from the higher faculties, is susceptible, they are entitled on this subject to the same regard.

I have dwelt on this point, as being a necessary part of a perfectly just conception of Utility or Happiness, considered as the directive rule of human conduct. But it is by no means an indispensable condition to the acceptance of the utilitarian standard, for that standard is not the agent's own greatest happiness, but the greatest amount of happiness altogether; and if it may possibly be doubted whether a noble character is always the happier for its nobleness, there can be no doubt that it makes other people happier, and that the world in general is immensely a gainer by it. Utilitarianism, therefore, could only attain its end by the general cultivation of nobleness of character, even if each individual were only benefited by the nobleness of others, and his own, so far as happiness is concerned, were a sheer deduction from the benefit. But the bare enunciation of such an absurdity as this last renders refutation superfluous.

According to the Greatest Happiness Principle, as above explained, the ultimate end, with reference to and for the sake of which all other things are desirable (whether we are considering our own good or that of other people), is an existence exempt as far as possible from pain, and as rich as possible in enjoyments, both in point of quantity and quality; the test of quality, and the rule for measuring it against quantity, being the preference felt by those who, in their opportunities of experience, to which must be added their habits of self-consciousness and self-observation, are best furnished with the means of comparison. This, being, according to the utilitarian opinion, the end of human action, is necessarily also the standard of morality; which may accordingly be defined, the rules and precepts for human conduct, by the observance of which an existence such as has been described might be, to the greatest extent possible, secured to all mankind; and not to them only, but, so far as the nature of things admits, to the whole sentient creation.

Against this doctrine, however, rises another class of objectors, who say that happiness, in any form, cannot be the rational purpose of human life and action; because, in the first place, it is unattainable: and they contemptuously ask, What right hast thou to be happy? a question which Mr [Thomas] Carlyle clenches by the addition, What right, a short time ago, hadst thou even *to be*? Next, they say, that men can do *without* happiness; that all noble human beings have felt this, and could not have become noble but by learning the lesson of Entsagen, or renunciation; which lesson, thoroughly learnt and submitted to, they affirm to be the beginning and necessary condition of all virtue.

The first of these objections would go to the root of the matter were it well founded; for if no happiness is to be had at all by human beings, the attainment of it cannot be the end of morality, or of any rational conduct. Though, even in that case, something might still be said for the utilitarian theory, since utility includes not solely the pursuit of happiness, but the prevention or mitigation of unhappiness; and if the former aim be chimerical, there will be all the greater scope and more imperative need for the latter, so long at least as mankind think fit to live, and do not take refuge in the simultaneous act of suicide recommended under certain conditions by Novalis [pseudonym of Friedrich von Hardenberg (1772–1801) – Ed.]. When, however, it is thus positively asserted to be impossible that human life should be happy, the assertion, if not something like a verbal quibble, is at least an exaggeration. If by happiness be meant a continuity of highly pleasurable excitement, it is evident enough that this is impossible. A state of exalted pleasure lasts only moments, or in some cases, and with some intermissions, hours or days, and is the occasional brilliant flash of enjoyment, not its permanent and steady flame. Of this the philosophers who have taught that happiness is the end of life were as fully aware as those who taunt them. The happiness which they meant was not a life of rapture; but moments of such, in an existence made up of few and transitory pains, many and various pleasures, with a decided predominance of the active over the passive, and having, as the foundation of the whole, not to expect more from life than it is capable of bestowing. A life thus composed, to those who have been fortunate enough to obtain it, has always appeared worthy of the name of happiness. And such an existence is even now the lot of many, during some considerable portion of their lives. The present wretched education, and wretched social arrangements, are the only real hindrance to its being attainable by almost all.

The objectors perhaps may doubt whether human beings, if taught to consider happiness as the end of life, would be satisfied with such a moderate share of it. But great numbers of mankind have been satisfied with much less. The main constituents of a satisfied life appear to be two, either of which by itself is often found sufficient for the purpose – tranquillity, and excitement.[1] With much tranquillity, many find that they can be content with very little pleasure: with much excitement, many can reconcile themselves to a considerable quantity of pain. There is assuredly no inherent impossibility in enabling even the mass of mankind to unite both; since the two are so far from being incompatible that they are in natural alliance, the prolongation of either being a preparation for, and exciting a wish for, the other. It is only those in whom indolence amounts to a vice, that do not desire excitement after an interval of repose; it is only those in whom the need of excitement is a disease, that feel the tranquillity which follows excitement dull and insipid, instead of pleasurable in direct proportion to the excitement which preceded it. When people who are tolerably fortunate in their outward lot do not find in life sufficient enjoyment to make it valuable to them, the cause generally is, caring for nobody but themselves. To those who have neither public nor private affections, the excitements of life are much curtailed, and in any case dwindle in value as the time approaches when all selfish interests must be terminated by death: while those who leave after them objects of personal affection, and especially those who have also cultivated a fellow-feeling with the collective interests of mankind, retain as lively an interest in life on the eve of death as in the vigour of youth and health. Next to selfishness, the principal cause which makes life unsatisfactory is want of mental cultivation. A cultivated mind –

I do not mean that of a philosopher, but any mind to which the fountains of knowledge have been opened, and which has been taught, in any tolerable degree, to exercise its faculties – finds sources of inexhaustible interest in all that surrounds it: in the objects of nature, the achievements of art, the imaginations of poetry, the incidents of history, the ways of mankind past and present, and their prospects in the future. It is possible, indeed, to become indifferent to all this, and that too without having exhausted a thousandth part of it; but only when one has had from the beginning no moral or human interest in these things, and has sought in them only the gratification of curiosity.

Now there is absolutely no reason in the nature of things why an amount of mental culture sufficient to give an intelligent interest in these objects of contemplation, should not be the inheritance of every one born in a civilized country. As little is there an inherent necessity that any human being should be a selfish egotist, devoid of every feeling or care but those which centre in his own miserable individuality. Something far superior to this is sufficiently common even now, to give ample earnest of what the human species may be made. Genuine private affections, and a sincere interest in the public good, are possible, though in unequal degrees, to every rightly brought up human being. In a world in which there is so much to interest, so much to enjoy, and so much also to correct and improve, every one who has this moderate amount of moral and intellectual requisites is capable of an existence which may be called enviable; and unless such a person, through bad laws, or subjection to the will of others, is denied the liberty to use the sources of happiness within his reach, he will not fail to find this enviable existence, if he escape the positive evils of life, the great sources of physical and mental suffering – such as indigence, disease and the unkindness, worthlessness or premature loss of objects of affection. The main stress of the problem lies, therefore, in the contest with these calamities, from which it is a rare good fortune entirely to escape; which, as things now are, cannot be obviated, and often cannot be in any material degree mitigated. Yet no one whose opinion deserves a moment's consideration can doubt that most of the great positive evils of the world are in themselves removable, and will, if human affairs continue to improve, be in the end reduced within narrow limits. Poverty, in any sense implying suffering, may be completely extinguished by the wisdom of society, combined with the good sense and providence of individuals. Even that most intractable of enemies, disease, may be indefinitely reduced in dimensions by good physical and moral education, and proper control of noxious influences; while the progress of science holds out a promise for the future of still more direct conquests over this detestable foe. And every advance in that direction relieves us from some, not only of the chances which cut short our own lives, but, what concerns us still more, which deprive us of those in whom our happiness is wrapt up. As for vicissitudes of fortune, and other disappointments connected with worldly circumstances, these are principally the effect either of gross imprudence, of ill-regulated desires, or of bad or imperfect social institutions. All the grand sources, in short, of human suffering are in a great degree, many of them almost entirely, conquerable by human care and effort; and though their removal is grievously slow – though a long succession of generations will perish in the breach before the conquest is completed, and this world becomes all that, if will and knowledge were not wanting, it might easily be made – yet every mind sufficiently intelligent and generous to bear a part, however small and unconspicuous, in the endeavour, will draw a noble enjoyment from the contest itself, which he would not for any bribe in the form of selfish indulgence consent to be without.

And this leads to the true estimation of what is said by the objectors concerning the possibility, and the obligation, of learning to do without happiness. Unquestionably it is possible to do without happiness: it is done involuntarily by nineteen-twentieths of mankind, even in those parts of our present world which are least deep in barbarism; and it often has to be done voluntarily by the hero or the martyr, for the sake of something which he prizes more than his individual happiness. But this something, what is it, unless the happiness of others, or some of the requisites of happiness? It is noble to be capable of resigning entirely one's own portion of happiness, or chances of it: but, after all, this self-sacrifice must be for some end; it is not its own end; and if we are told that its end is not happiness, but virtue, which is better than happiness, I ask, would the sacrifice be made if the hero or martyr did not believe that it would earn for others immunity from similar sacrifices? Would it be made, if he thought that his renunciation of happiness for himself would produce no fruit for any of his fellow-creatures, but to make their lot like his, and place them also in the condition of persons who have renounced happiness? All honour to those who can abnegate for themselves the personal enjoyment of life, when by such renunciation they contribute worthily to increase the amount of happiness in the world; but he who does it, or professes to do it, for any other purpose, is no more deserving of admiration than the ascetic mounted on his pillar. He may be an inspiriting proof of what men *can* do, but assuredly not an example of what they *should*.

Though it is only in a very imperfect state of the world's arrangements that any one can best serve the happiness of others by the absolute sacrifice of his own, yet so long as the world is in that imperfect state, I fully acknowledge that the readiness to make such a sacrifice is the highest virtue which can be found in man. I will add, that in this condition of the world, paradoxical as the assertion may be, the conscious ability to do without happiness gives the best prospect of realizing such happiness as is attainable.[2] For nothing except that consciousness can raise a person above the chances of life, by making him feel that, let fate and fortune do their worst, they have not power to subdue him: which, once felt, frees him from excess of anxiety concerning the evils of life, and enables him, like many a Stoic in the worst times of the Roman empire, to cultivate in tranquillity the sources of satisfaction accessible to him, without concerning himself about the uncertainty of their duration, any more than about their inevitable end.

Meanwhile, let utilitarians never cease to claim the morality of self-devotion as a possession which belongs by as good a right to them, as either to the Stoic or to the Transcendentalist. The utilitarian morality does recognize in human beings the power of sacrificing their own greatest good for the good of others. It only refuses to admit that the sacrifice is itself a good. A sacrifice which does not increase, or tend to increase, the sum total of happiness, it considers as wasted. The only self-renunciation which it applauds is devotion to the happiness, or to some of the means of happiness, of others; either of mankind collectively, or of individuals within the limits imposed by the collective interests of mankind.

I must again repeat, what the assailants of utilitarianism seldom have the justice to acknowledge, that the happiness which forms the utilitarian standard of what is right in conduct is not the agent's own happiness, but that of all concerned. As between his own happiness and that of others, utilitarianism requires him to be as strictly impartial as a disinterested and benevolent spectator. In the golden rule of Jesus of Nazareth, we read the complete spirit of the ethics of utility. To do as one would be done by, and to love one's neighbour as oneself, constitute the ideal perfection of utilitarian morality. As the means of making the nearest approach to this ideal, utility would enjoin, first, that laws and social arrangements should place the happiness, or (as speaking practically it may be called) the interest, of every individual, as nearly as possible in harmony with the interest of the whole; and secondly, that education and opinion, which have so vast a power over human character, should so use that power as to establish in the mind of every individual an indissoluble association between his own happiness and the good of the whole; especially between his own happiness and the practice of such modes of conduct, negative and positive, as regard for the universal happiness prescribes: so that not only he may be unable to conceive the possibility of happiness to himself, consistently with conduct opposed to the general good, but also that a direct impulse to promote the general good may be in every individual one of the habitual motives of action, and the sentiments connected therewith may fill a large and prominent place in every human being's sentient existence. If the impugners of the utilitarian morality represented it to their own minds in this its true character, I know not what recommendation possessed by any other morality they could possibly affirm to be wanting to it; what more beautiful or more exalted developments of human nature any other ethical system can be supposed to foster, or what springs of action, not accessible to the utilitarian, such systems rely on for giving effect to their mandates.

The objectors to utilitarianism cannot always be charged with representing it in a discreditable light. On the contrary, those among them who entertain anything like a just idea of its disinterested character, sometimes find fault with its standard as being too high for humanity. They say it is exacting too much to require that people shall always act from the inducement of promoting the general interests of society. But this is to mistake the very meaning of a standard of morals, and to confound the rule of action with the motive of it. It is the business of ethics to tell us what are our duties, or by what test we may know them; but no system of ethics requires that the sole motive of all we do shall be a feeling of duty: on the contrary, ninety-nine hundredths of all our actions are done from other motives, and rightly so done, if the rule of duty does not condemn them. It is the more unjust to utilitarianism that this particular misapprehension should be made a ground of objection to it, inasmuch as utilitarian moralists have gone beyond almost all others in affirming that the motive has nothing to do with the morality of the action, though much with the worth of the agent. He who saves a fellow-creature from drowning does what is morally right, whether his motive be duty, or the hope of being paid for his trouble: he who betrays the friend that trusts him is guilty of a crime, even if his object be to serve another friend to whom he is under greater obligations. But to speak only of actions done from the motive of duty, and in direct obedience to principle: it is a misapprehension of the utilitarian mode of thought, to conceive it as implying that people should fix their minds upon so wide a generality as the world, or society at large. The great majority of good actions are intended, not for the benefit of the world, but for that of individuals, of which the good of the world is made up; and the thoughts of the most virtuous man need not on these occasions travel beyond the particular persons concerned, except so far as is necessary to assure himself that in benefiting them he is not violating the rights – that is, the legitimate and authorized expectations – of any one else. The multiplication of happiness is, according to the utilitarian ethics, the object of virtue: the occasions on which any person (except one in a thousand) has it in his power to do this on an extended scale, in other words, to be a public benefactor, are but exceptional; and on these occasions alone is he called on to consider public utility; in every other case, private utility, the interest or happiness of some few persons, is all he has to attend to. Those alone the influence of whose actions extends to society in general, need concern themselves habitually about so large an object. In the case of abstinences indeed – of things which people forbear to do, from moral considerations, though the consequences in the particular case might be beneficial – it would be unworthy of an intelligent agent not to be consciously aware that the action is of a class which, if practised generally, would be generally injurious, and that this is the ground of the obligation to abstain from it. The amount of regard for the public interest implied in this recognition is no greater than is demanded by every system of morals, for they all enjoin to abstain from whatever is manifestly pernicious to society.

The same considerations dispose of another reproach against the doctrine of utility, founded on a still grosser misconception of the purpose of a standard of morality, and of the very meaning of the words right and wrong. It is often affirmed that utilitarianism renders men cold and unsympathizing; that it chills their moral feelings towards individuals; that it makes them regard only the dry and hard consideration of the consequences of actions, not taking into their moral estimate the qualities from which those actions emanate. If the assertion means that they do not allow their judgement respecting the rightness or wrongness of an action to be influenced by their opinion of the qualities of the person who does it, this is a complaint not against utilitarianism, but against having any standard of morality at all; for certainly no known ethical standard decides an action to be good or bad because it is done by a good or a bad man, still less because done by an amiable, a brave, or a benevolent man, or the contrary. These considerations are relevant, not to the estimation of actions, but of persons; and there is nothing in the utilitarian theory inconsistent with the fact that there are other things which interest us in persons besides the rightness and wrongness of their actions. The Stoics, indeed, with the paradoxical misuse of language which was part of their system, and by which they strove to raise themselves above all concern about anything but virtue, were fond of saying that he who has that has everything; that he, and only he, is rich, is beautiful, is a king. But no claim of this description is made for the virtuous man by the utilitarian doctrine. Utilitarians are quite aware that there are other desirable possessions and qualities besides virtue, and are perfectly willing to allow to all of them their full worth. They are also aware that a right action does not necessarily indicate a virtuous character, and that actions which are blameable often proceed from qualities entitled to

praise. When this is apparent in any particular case, it modifies their estimation, not certainly of the act, but of the agent. I grant that they are, notwithstanding, of opinion, that in the long-run the best proof of a good
character is good actions; and resolutely refuse to consider any mental disposition as good, of which the predominant tendency is to produce bad
conduct. This makes them unpopular with many people; but it is an un-
popularity which they must share with every one who regards the distinction between right and wrong in a serious light, and the reproach is not one
which a conscientious utilitarian need be anxious to repel.

If no more be meant by the objection than that many utilitarians look on
the morality of actions, as measured by the utilitarian standard, with too
exclusive a regard, and do not lay sufficient stress upon the other beauties
of character which go towards making a human being loveable or admirable, this may be admitted. Utilitarians who have cultivated their moral
feelings, but not their sympathies nor their artistic perceptions, do fall into
this mistake; and so do all other moralists under the same conditions. What
can be said in excuse for other moralists is equally available for them, namely,
that if there is to be any error, it is better that it should be on that side. As
a matter of fact, we may affirm that among utilitarians, as among adherents
of other systems, there is every imaginable degree of rigidity and of laxity
in the application of their standard: some are even puritanically rigorous,
while others are as indulgent as can possibly be desired by sinner or by
sentimentalist. But, on the whole, a doctrine which brings prominently
forward the interest that mankind have in the repression and prevention
of conduct which violates the moral law is likely to be inferior to no other
in turning the sanctions of opinion against such violations. It is true, the
question, What does violate the moral law? is one on which those who
recognize different standards of morality are likely now and then to differ.
But difference of opinion on moral questions was not first introduced into
the world by utilitarianism, while that doctrine does supply, if not always
an easy, at all events a tangible and intelligible, mode of deciding such
differences. . . .

Again, defenders of utility often find themselves called upon to reply to
such objections as this – that there is not time, previous to action, for
calculating and weighing the effects of any line of conduct on the general
happiness. This is exactly as if any one were to say that it is impossible to
guide our conduct by Christianity, because there is not time, on every
occasion on which anything has to be done, to read through the Old and
New Testaments. The answer to the objection is, that there has been ample
time, namely, the whole past duration of the human species. During all
that time mankind have been learning by experience the tendencies of

actions; on which experience all the prudence, as well as all the morality, of life, is dependent. People talk as if the commencement of this course of experience had hitherto been put off, and as if, at the moment when some man feels tempted to meddle with the property or life of another, he had to begin considering for the first time whether murder and theft are injurious to human happiness. Even then I do not think that he would find the question very puzzling; but, at all events, the matter is now done to his hand. It is truly a whimsical supposition, that if mankind were agreed in considering utility to be the test of morality, they would remain without any agreement as to what *is* useful, and would take no measures for having their notions on the subject taught to the young, and enforced by law and opinion. There is no difficulty in proving any ethical standard whatever to work ill, if we suppose universal idiocy to be conjoined with it, but on any hypothesis short of that, mankind must by this time have acquired positive beliefs as to the effects of some actions on their happiness; and the beliefs which have thus come down are the rules of morality for the multitude, and for the philosopher until he has succeeded in finding better. That philosophers might easily do this, even now, on many subjects; that the received code of ethics is by no means of divine right; and that mankind have still much to learn as to the effects of actions on the general happiness, I admit, or rather, earnestly maintain. The corollaries from the principle of utility, like the precepts of every practical art, admit of indefinite improvement, and, in a progressive state of the human mind, their improvement is perpetually going on. But to consider the rules of morality as improvable, is one thing; to pass over the intermediate generalizations entirely, and endeavour to test each individual action directly by the first principle, is another. It is a strange notion that the acknowledgement of a first principle is inconsistent with the admission of secondary ones. To inform a traveller respecting the place of his ultimate destination, is not to forbid the use of landmarks and direction-posts on the way. The proposition that happiness is the end and aim of morality, does not mean that no road ought to be laid down to that goal, or that persons going thither should not be advised to take one direction rather than another. Men really ought to leave off talking a kind of nonsense on this subject, which they would neither talk nor listen to on other matters of practical concernment. Nobody argues that the art of navigation is not founded on astronomy, because sailors cannot wait to calculate the Nautical Almanack. Being rational creatures, they go to sea with it ready calculated; and all rational creatures go out upon the sea of life with their minds made up on the common questions of right and wrong, as well as on many of the far more difficult questions of wise and foolish. And this, as long as foresight is a human quality, it is to be presumed they will continue to do. Whatever we adopt as the fundamental principle of morality, we require subordinate principles to apply it by: the impossibility of doing without them, being common to all systems, can afford no argument against any one in particular. But gravely to argue as if no such secondary principles could be had, and as if mankind had remained till now, and always must remain, without drawing any general conclusions from the experience of human life, is as high a pitch, I think, as absurdity has ever reached in philosophical controversy.

The remainder of the stock arguments against utilitarianism mostly consist in laying to its charge the common infirmities of human nature, and the general difficulties which embarrass conscientious persons in shaping their course through life. We are told that an utilitarian will be apt to make his own particular case an exception to moral rules, and, when under temptation, will see an utility in the breach of a rule, greater than he will see in its observance. But is utility the only creed which is able to furnish us with excuses for evil-doing, and means of cheating our own conscience? They are afforded in abundance by all doctrines which recognize as a fact in morals the existence of conflicting considerations; which all doctrines do, that have been believed by sane persons. It is not the fault of any creed, but of the complicated nature of human affairs, that rules of conduct cannot be so framed as to require no exceptions, and that hardly any kind of action can safely be laid down as either always obligatory or always condemnable. There is no ethical creed which does not temper the rigidity of its laws, by giving a certain latitude, under the moral responsibility of the agent, for accommodation to peculiarities of circumstances; and under every creed, at the opening thus made, self-deception and dishonest casuistry get in. There exists no moral system under which there do not arise unequivocal cases of conflicting obligation. These are the real difficulties, the knotty points both in the theory of ethics and in the conscientious guidance of personal conduct. They are overcome practically with greater or with less success according to the intellect and virtue of the individual; but it can hardly be pretended that any one will be the less qualified for dealing with them, from possessing an ultimate standard to which conflicting rights and duties can be referred. If utility is the ultimate source of moral obligations, utility may be invoked to decide between them when their demands are incompatible. Though the application of the standard may be difficult, it is better than none at all: while in other systems, the moral laws all claiming independent authority, there is no common umpire entitled to interfere between them; their claims to precedence one over another rest on little better than sophistry, and unless determined, as they generally are, by the unacknowledged influence of considerations of utility, afford a free scope for the action of personal desires and partialities. We must remember that only in these cases of conflict between secondary principles is it requisite that first principles should be appealed to. There is no case of moral obligation in which some secondary principle is not involved; and if only one, there can seldom be any real doubt which one it is, in the mind of any person by whom the principle itself is recognized.

Notes

1 This paragraph might almost be a reply to Arthur Schopenhauer's 'pessimism'. According to him, it is the oscillation between the frenzied excitement of desire and the boredom of satiation that helps to make life so wretched. See, e.g., chapter 46 of volume 2 of *The World as Will and Representation*, New York: Dover, 1966.
2 This important point is frequently urged by Mill, e.g. in his *Autobiography*, Harmondsworth: Penguin, 1989, p. 118, where he writes, 'Ask yourself whether you are happy, and you cease to be so. The only chance is to treat, not happiness, but some end external to it, as the purpose of life.'

14

Friedrich Nietzsche, *On the Genealogy of Morals*, First Essay, Sections 2–14, 16

From Basic Writings of Nietzsche, trans. and ed. by Walter Kaufmann. New York: The Modern Library, 1968 [some passages omitted]; copyright © 1967 by Random House, Inc.; reprinted by permission of Random House, Inc.

Whether or not he was 'the greatest moral philosopher of the past century',[1] the German writer Friedrich Nietzsche (1844–1900) was surely that century's most powerful critic of morality – morality itself, that is, 'the moral point of view', and not simply the precepts and practices of his contemporaries. Nietzsche's ambition was a 'revaluation of all values', and the values of the future – those incarnate in the 'overman' (*Übermensch*) – are to be 'moraline-free', 'immoral'.

Since the Renaissance, at least, morality has come to be identified, Nietzsche argues, with 'Judaeo-Christian' morality and its various off-shoots, such as Enlightenment utilitarianism and Kant's ethics of duty. The main critical strategy Nietzsche deploys is what he calls 'genealogy', the 'unmasking' of beliefs by examining their forgotten historical origins and psychological motivations. He is aware, of course, that merely by uncovering the 'seedy' origin of a belief, one does not automatically invalidate it. 'The question of the origin of our evaluations . . . is not at all equivalent to their critique.'[2] Nevertheless, by demonstrating that people subscribe to moral values like charity and justice for reasons much less elevated than they imagine, any confidence that these values have a genuine grounding is dispelled. Moreover, it is Nietzsche's view that 'there are no moral facts', only moral 'interpretations',[3] and that interpretations necessarily reflect the needs and interests of interpreters. Hence if it can be shown that the ones to which moral values cater are to be despised, a genealogy of morality will in effect serve to discredit it.

In *On the Genealogy of Morals* (1887), Nietzsche attempts to 'unmask' the

[1] Bernard Williams, 'Nietzsche's centaur', *London Review of Books*, 3 October 1981, p.17.
[2] *The Will to Power*, New York: Vintage, 1968, §284.
[3] *The Twilight of the Idols*, in *The Portable Nietzsche*, New York: Viking, 1954, §6.1.

origins of a welter of moral concepts, including – in the First Essay – the notion of moral goodness itself. Against the 'English psychologists', such as Hume, Nietzsche argues that this notion does not reflect an original sympathetic concern for others. It arose, rather, as part of a defensive reaction, on the part of the 'weak' or the 'herd', against the proto-morality of the 'warrior-nobles', 'masters' and 'natural aristocrats' of earlier ages, such as Homeric Greece. Suffering from a sense of powerlessness and inferiority, the 'herd' successfully developed a morality of compassion, justice, and other Judaeo-Christian virtues, in order to emasculate and control the unbooted behaviour of the 'aristocrats'. In the mouth of the 'herd', Nietzsche argues, the words 'good' and 'bad' come to mean almost the precise opposite of what they meant for the 'nobles'.[4]

Implicit here is a challenge to one of the most central tenets of 'the moral point of view', apparent for example in Kant's ethics – that moral principles and duties are incumbent on *all* human beings. We encountered a limited challenge to this tenet in Kierkegaard for whom, in special circumstances, an individual may have to obey a higher calling than morality. Nietzsche's challenge is more radical. There is a 'rank order' among human beings, and moral values, which are suited for governing the behaviour of one type of person (the 'weak', the 'botched and bungled'), serve only to 'diminish' and 'choke' the lives of a higher, more exuberant type. The 'levelling' effect of moral universalism is, says Nietzsche, 'our greatest danger'. It is important to note, however, that elsewhere Nietzsche is not insensitive to the 'civilizing' effects of the emergence of morality, and that he does not deny the genuine benefits it has afforded the mass of men. It would be wrong, moreover, to suppose – as some Nazi ideologues did – that the 'warrior-nobles', the 'blond beasts of prey' referred to constitute Nietzsche's ideal type. They lack, for example, both the intelligence and self-discipline that must be ingredients in any such type.

In the famous and brilliant §13, we encounter a different aspect of Nietzschean genealogy. Here he reverses the usual assumption that morality presupposes various beliefs about human beings, such as that they are responsible 'subjects' possessed of free will. For Nietzsche, notions like freedom of the will are motivated by the same 'resentment' against the 'strong' as 'herd' values themselves are, and are needed in order to buttress those values. Rather than admit that they are *incapable* of exhibiting the strength of the 'nobles', the 'weak' pretend that they simply do not *choose* so to act – a ploy which enables them to congratulate themselves at the same time as blaming their enemies.

Alongside Marx and Freud, Nietzsche is one of the great 'masters of the hermeneutics of suspicion', to cite Paul Ricoeur's phrase, and it would be hard

---

[4] For more on *On the Genealogy of Morals*, see the articles by Arthur C. Danto and Frithjof Bergmann in *Reading Nietzsche*, ed. by R. C. Solomon and K. M. Higgins, Oxford: Oxford University Press, 1988.

to exaggerate the impact of his writings upon twentieth-century moral debate. More than any other philosopher, it is Nietzsche who has destroyed an older, unreflective confidence in the integrity of moral thought and talk. As many recent writers have remarked, Nietzsche is the man to wrestle against if any such confidence is to be restored.[5]

▷ ▷ ▷ First Essay: 'Good and Evil', 'Good and Bad'

2

. . . As is the hallowed custom with philosophers, the thinking of all of them is *by nature* unhistorical; there is no doubt about that. The way they have bungled their moral genealogy comes to light at the very beginning, where the task is to investigate the origin of the concept and judgement 'good'. 'Originally' – so they decree – 'one approved unegoistic actions and called them good from the point of view of those to whom they were done, that is to say, those to whom they were *useful*; later one *forgot* how this approval originated and, simply because unegoistic actions were always *habitually* praised as good, one also felt them to be good – as if they were something good in themselves.' One sees straightaway that this primary derivation already contains all the typical traits of the idiosyncrasy of the English psychologists – we have 'utility', 'forgetting', 'habit', and finally 'error', all as the basis of an evaluation of which the higher man has hitherto been proud as though it were a kind of prerogative of man as such. This pride *has* to be humbled, this evaluation disvalued: has that end been achieved?

Now it is plain to me, first of all, that in this theory the source of the concept 'good' has been sought and established in the wrong place: the judgement 'good' did *not* originate with those to whom 'goodness' was shown! Rather it was 'the good' themselves, that is to say, the noble, powerful, high-stationed and high-minded, who felt and established themselves and their actions as good, that is, of the first rank, in contradistinction to all the low, low-minded, common and plebeian. It was out of this *pathos of distance* that they first seized the right to create values and to coin names for values: what had they to do with utility! The viewpoint of utility is as remote and inappropriate as it possibly could be in face of such a burning eruption of the highest rank-ordering, rank-defining value

---

[5] See, e.g., Allen Bloom's *The Closing of the American Mind*, New York: Simon & Schuster, 1987.

judgements: for here feeling has attained the antithesis of that low degree of warmth which any calculating prudence, any calculus of utility, presupposes – and not for once only, not for an exceptional hour, but for good. The pathos of nobility and distance, as aforesaid, the protracted and domineering fundamental total feeling on the part of a higher ruling order in relation to a lower order to a 'below' – *that* is the origin of the antithesis 'good' and 'bad'. (The lordly right of giving names extends so far that one should allow oneself to conceive the origin of language itself as an expression of power on the part of the rulers: they say 'this *is* this and this', they seal every thing and event with a sound and, as it were, take possession of it.) It follows from this origin that the word 'good' was definitely *not* linked from the first and by necessity to 'unegoistic' actions, as the superstition of these genealogists of morality would have it. Rather it was only when aristocratic value judgements *declined* that the whole antithesis 'egoistic' 'unegoistic' obtruded itself more and more on the human conscience – it is, to speak in my own language, the *herd instinct* that through this antithesis at last gets its word (and its *words*) in. And even then it was a long time before that instinct attained such dominion that moral evaluation was actually stuck and halted at this antithesis (as, for example, is the case in contemporary Europe: the prejudice that takes 'moral', 'unegoistic', '*désintéressé*' as concepts of equivalent value already rules today with the force of a 'fixed idea' and brain-sickness).

3

In the second place, however: quite apart from the historical untenability of this hypothesis regarding the origin of the value judgement 'good', it suffers from an inherent psychological absurdity. The utility of the unegoistic action is supposed to be the source of the approval accorded it, and this source is supposed to have been *forgotten* – but how is this forgetting *possible*? Has the utility of such actions come to an end at some time or other? The opposite is the case: this utility has rather been an everyday experience at all times, therefore something that has been underlined again and again: consequently, instead of fading from consciousness, instead of becoming easily forgotten, it must have been impressed on the consciousness more and more clearly. How much more reasonable is that opposing theory (it is not for that reason more true –) which Herbert Spencer [1820–1903], for example, espoused: that the concept 'good' is essentially identical with the concept 'useful', 'practical', so that in the judgements 'good' and 'bad' mankind has summed up and sanctioned precisely its *unforgotten* and *unforgettable* experiences regarding what is useful-practical and what is harmful-impractical. According to this theory, that which has always proved itself useful is good: therefore it may claim to be 'valuable in the highest degree', 'valuable in itself'. This road to an explanation is, as aforesaid, also a wrong one, but at least the explanation is in itself reasonable and psychologically tenable.

4

The signpost to the *right* road was for me the question: what was the real etymological significance of the designations for 'good' coined in the various languages? I found they all led back to the *same conceptual transformation* – that everywhere 'noble', 'aristocratic' in the social sense, is the basic concept from which 'good' in the sense of 'with aristocratic soul', 'noble', 'with a soul of a high order', 'with a privileged soul', necessarily developed: a development which always runs parallel with that other in which 'common', 'plebeian', 'low' are finally transformed into the concept 'bad'. The most convincing example of the latter is the German word *schlecht* [bad] itself: which is identical with *schlicht* [plain, simple] – compare *schlechtweg* [plainly], *schlechterdings* [simply] – and originally designated the plain, the common man, as yet with no inculpatory implication and simply in contradistinction to the nobility. About the time of the Thirty Years' War, late enough therefore, this meaning changed into the one now customary.

With regard to a moral genealogy this seems to me a *fundamental* insight; that it has been arrived at so late is the fault of the retarding influence exercised by the democratic prejudice in the modern world toward all questions of origin. And this is so even in the apparently quite objective domain of natural science and physiology, as I shall merely hint here. But what mischief this prejudice is capable of doing, especially to morality and history, once it has been unbridled to the point of hatred is shown by the notorious case of [Henry Thomas] Buckle [1821–62] here the *plebeianism* of the modern spirit, which is of English origin, erupted once again on its native soil, as violently as a mud volcano and with that salty, noisy, vulgar eloquence with which all volcanos have spoken hitherto.

5

With regard to *our* problem, which may on good grounds be called a *quiet* problem and one which fastidiously directs itself to few ears, it is of no small interest to ascertain that through those words and roots which designate 'good' there frequently still shines the most important nuance by virtue of which the noble felt themselves to be men of a higher rank. Granted that, in the majority of cases, they designate themselves simply by their superiority in power (as 'the powerful', 'the masters', 'the commanders') or by the most clearly visible signs of this superiority, for example, as 'the rich', 'the possessors' (this is the meaning of *arya*; and of corresponding words in Iranian and Slavic). But they also do it by a *typical character trait*: and this is the case that concerns us here. They call themselves, for instance, 'the truthful'; this is so above all of the Greek nobility, whose mouthpiece is the Megarian poet Theognis [6th century BCE]. The root of the word coined for this, *esthlos*, signifies one who *is*, who possesses reality, who is actual, who is true; then, with a subjective turn, the true as the truthful: in this phase of conceptual transformation it becomes a slogan and catchword of the nobility and passes over entirely into the sense of 'noble', as distinct from the *lying* common man, which is what Theognis takes him to be and how he describes him – until finally, after the decline of the nobility, the word is left to designate nobility of soul and becomes as it were ripe and sweet.

. . . I believe I may venture to interpret the Latin *bonus* as 'the warrior', provided I am right in tracing *bonus* back to an earlier *duonus* (compare *bellum* = *duellum* = *duen-lum*, which seems to me to contain *duonus*). Therefore *bonus* as the man of strife, of dissention (*duo*), as the man of war: one sees what constituted the 'goodness' of a man in ancient Rome. Our German *gut* [good] even: does it not signify 'the godlike', the man of 'godlike race'? And is it not identical with the popular (originally noble) name of the Goths? The grounds for this conjecture cannot be dealt with here.

6

To this rule that a concept denoting political superiority always resolves itself into a concept denoting superiority of soul it is not necessarily an exception (although it provides occasions for exceptions) when the highest caste is at the same time the *priestly* caste and therefore emphasizes in its total description of itself a predicate that calls to mind its priestly function. It is then, for example, that 'pure' and 'impure' confront one another for the first time as designations of station; and here too there evolves a 'good' and a 'bad' in a sense no longer referring to station. One should be warned, moreover, against taking these concepts 'pure' and 'impure' too ponderously or broadly, not to say symbolically: all the concepts of ancient man were rather at first incredibly uncouth, coarse, external, narrow, straightforward and altogether *unsymbolical* in meaning to a degree that we can scarcely conceive. The 'pure one' is from the beginning merely a man who washes himself, who forbids himself certain foods that produce skin ailments, who does not sleep with the dirty women of the lower strata, who has an aversion to blood – no more, hardly more! On the other hand, to be sure, it is clear from the whole nature of an essentially priestly aristocracy why antithetical valuations could in precisely this instance soon become dangerously deepened, sharpened and internalized; and indeed they finally tore chasms between man and man that a very Achilles of a free spirit would not venture to leap without a shudder. There is from the first something *unhealthy* in such priestly aristocracies and in the habits ruling in them which turn them away from action and alternate between brooding and emotional explosions, habits which seem to have as their almost invariable consequence that intestinal morbidity and neurasthenia which has afflicted priests at all times; but as to that which they themselves devised as a remedy for this morbidity – must one not assert that it has ultimately proved itself a hundred times more dangerous in its effects than the sickness it was supposed to cure? Mankind itself is still ill with the effects of this priestly naïveté in medicine! Think, for example, of certain forms of diet (abstinence from meat), of fasting, of sexual continence, of flight 'into the wilderness' . . . : add to these the entire antisensualistic metaphysic of the priests that makes men indolent and overrefined, their autohypnosis in the manner of fakirs and Brahmins – Brahma used in the shape of a glass knob and a fixed idea – and finally the only-too-comprehensible satiety with all this, together with the radical cure for it, *nothingness* (or God – the desire for a *unio mystica* with God is the desire of the Buddhist for nothingness, Nirvana – and no more!). For with the priests *everything* becomes more dangerous, not only cures and remedies, but also arrogance, revenge, acuteness, profligacy, love, lust to rule, virtue, disease – but it is only fair to add that it was on the soil of this *essentially dangerous* form of human existence, the priestly form, that man first became *an interesting animal*, that only here did the human soul in a higher sense acquire *depth* and become *evil* – and these are the two basic respects in which man has hitherto been superior to other beasts!

7

One will have divined already how easily the priestly mode of valuation can branch off from the knightly-aristocratic and then develop into its opposite; this is particularly likely when the priestly caste and the warrior caste are in jealous opposition to one another and are unwilling to come to terms. The knightly-aristocratic value judgements presupposed a powerful physicality, a flourishing, abundant, even overflowing health, together with that which serves to preserve it: war, adventure, hunting, dancing, war games, and in general all that involves vigorous, free, joyful activity. The priestly-noble mode of valuation presupposes, as we have seen, other things: it is disadvantageous for it when it comes to war! As is well known, the priests are the *most evil enemies* – but why? Because they are the most impotent. It is because of their impotence that in them hatred grows to monstrous and uncanny proportions, to the most spiritual and poisonous kind of hatred. The truly great haters in world history have always been priests; likewise the most ingenious haters: other kinds of spirit hardly come into consideration when compared with the spirit of priestly vengefulness. Human history would be altogether too stupid a thing without the spirit that the impotent have introduced into it – let us take at once the most notable example. All that has been done on earth against 'the noble', 'the powerful', 'the masters', 'the rulers', fades into nothing compared with what the *Jews* have done against them; the Jews, that priestly people, who in opposing their enemies and conquerors were ultimately satisfied with nothing less than a radical revaluation of their enemies' values, that is to say, an act of the *most spiritual revenge*. For this alone was appropriate to a priestly people, the people embodying the most deeply repressed priestly vengefulness. It was the Jews who, with awe-inspiring consistency, dared to invert the aristocratic value-equation (good = noble = powerful = beautiful = happy = beloved of God) and to hang on to this inversion with their teeth, the teeth of the most abysmal hatred (the hatred of impotence), saying 'the wretched alone are the good; the poor, impotent, lowly alone are the good; the suffering, deprived, sick, ugly alone are pious, alone are blessed by God, blessedness is for them alone – and you, the powerful and noble, are on the contrary the evil, the cruel, the lustful, the insatiable, the godless to all eternity; and you shall be in all eternity the unblessed, accursed, and damned!'. . . One knows *who* inherited this Jewish revaluation [i.e., Christians – Ed.]. In connection with the tremendous and immeasurably fateful initiative provided by the Jews through this most fundamental of all declarations of war, I recall the proposition I arrived at on a previous occasion (*Beyond Good and Evil*, section 195) – that with the Jews there begins *the slave revolt in morality*: that revolt which has a history of two thousand years behind it and which we no longer see because it – has been victorious.

8

But you do not comprehend this? You are incapable of seeing something that required two thousand years to achieve victory? – There is nothing to wonder at in that: all *protracted* things are hard to see, to see whole. *That*, however, is what has happened: from the trunk of that tree of vengefulness and hatred, Jewish hatred – the profoundest and sublimest kind of hatred, capable of creating ideals and reversing values, the like of which has never existed on earth before – there grew something equally incomparable, a *new love*, the profoundest and sublimest kind of love – and from what other trunk could it have grown?

One should not imagine it grew up as the denial of that thirst for revenge, as the opposite of Jewish hatred! No, the reverse is true! That love grew out of it as its crown, as its triumphant crown spreading itself farther and farther into the purest brightness and sunlight, driven as it were into the domain of light and the heights in pursuit of the goals of that hatred – victory, spoil and seduction – by the same impulse that drove the roots of that hatred deeper and deeper and more and more covetously into all that was profound and evil. This Jesus of Nazareth, the incarnate gospel of love, this 'Redeemer' who brought blessedness and victory to the poor, the sick and the sinners – was he not this seduction in its most uncanny and irresistible form, a seduction and bypath to precisely those *Jewish* values and new ideals? Did Israel not attain the ultimate goal of its sublime vengefulness precisely through the bypath of this 'Redeemer', this ostensible opponent and disintegrator of Israel? Was it not part of the secret black art of truly *grand* politics of revenge, of a farseeing, subterranean, slowly advancing and premeditated revenge, that Israel must itself deny the real instrument of its revenge before all the world as a mortal enemy and nail it to the cross, so that 'all the world', namely all the opponents of Israel, could unhesitatingly swallow just this bait? And could spiritual subtlety imagine any *more dangerous* bait than this? Anything to equal the enticing, intoxicating, overwhelming and undermining power of that symbol of the 'holy cross', that ghastly paradox of a 'God on the cross', that mystery of an unimaginable ultimate cruelty and self-crucifixion of God *for the salvation of man*?

What is certain, at least, is that [under this sign] Israel, with its vengefulness and revaluation of all values, has hitherto triumphed again and again over all other ideals, over all *nobler* ideals.

9

'But why are you talking about *nobler* ideals! Let us stick to the facts: the people have won – or "the slaves" or "the mob" or "the herd" or whatever you like to call them – if this has happened through the Jews, very well! in that case no people ever had a more world-historic mission. "The masters" have been disposed of; the morality of the common man has won. One may conceive of this victory as at the same time a blood-poisoning (it has mixed the races together) – I shan't contradict; but this in-toxication has undoubtedly been *successful*. The "redemption" of the human race (from "the masters", that is) is going forward; everything is visibly becoming Judaized, Christianized, mob-ized (what do the words matter!). The progress of this poison through the entire body of mankind seems irresistible, its pace and tempo may from now on even grow slower, subtler, less audible, more cautious – there is plenty of time. . . .'

This is the epilogue of a 'free spirit' to my speech; an honest animal, as he has abundantly revealed, and a democrat, moreover; he had been listening to me till then and could not endure to listen to my silence. For at this point I have much to be silent about.

10

The slave revolt in morality begins when *ressentiment* [resentment] itself becomes creative and gives birth to values: the *ressentiment* of natures that are denied the true reaction, that of deeds, and compensate themselves with an imaginary revenge. While every noble morality develops from a triumphant affirmation of itself, slave morality from the outset says No to what is 'outside', what is 'different', what is 'not itself'; and *this* No is its creative deed. This inversion of the value-positing eye – this *need* to direct one's view outward instead of back to oneself – is of the essence of *ressentiment*: in order to exist, slave morality always first needs a hostile external world; it needs, physiologically speaking, external stimuli in order to act at all – its action is fundamentally reaction.

The reverse is the case with the noble mode of valuation: it acts and grows spontaneously, it seeks its opposite only so as to affirm itself more gratefully and triumphantly – its negative concept 'low', 'common', 'bad' is only a subsequently-invented pale, contrasting image in relation to its positive basic concept – filled with life and passion through and through – 'we noble ones, we good, beautiful, happy ones!' When the noble mode of valuation blunders and sins against reality, it does so in respect to the sphere with which it is *not* sufficiently familiar, against a real knowledge of which it has indeed inflexibly guarded itself: in some circumstances it misunderstands the sphere it despises, that of the common man, of the lower orders; on the other hand, one should remember that, even supposing that the affect of contempt, of looking down from a superior height, *falsifies* the image of that which it despises, it will at any rate still be a much less serious falsification than that perpetrated on its opponent – *in effigie* of course – by the submerged hatred, the vengefulness of the impotent. There is indeed too much carelessness, too much taking lightly, too much looking away and impatience involved in contempt, even too much joyfulness, for it to be able to transform its object into a real caricature and monster.

One should not overlook the almost benevolent nuances that the Greek nobility, for example, bestows on all the words it employs to distinguish the lower orders from itself; how they are continuously mingled and sweetened with a kind of pity, consideration and forbearance, so that finally almost all the words referring to the common man have remained as expressions signifying 'unhappy', 'pitiable' . . . – and how on the other hand 'bad', 'low', 'unhappy' have never ceased to sound to the Greek ear as one note with a tone-colour in which 'unhappy' preponderates: this as an inheritance from the ancient nobler aristocratic mode of evaluation, which does not belie itself even in its contempt. . . . The 'well-born' *felt* themselves to be the 'happy'; they did not have to establish their happiness artificially by examining their enemies, or to persuade themselves, *deceive* themselves, that they were happy (as all men of *ressentiment* are in the habit of doing); and they likewise knew, as rounded men replete with energy and therefore *necessarily* active, that happiness should not be sundered from action – being active was with them necessarily a part of happiness . . . all very much the opposite of 'happiness' at the level of the impotent, the oppressed, and those in whom poisonous and inimical feelings are festering, with whom it appears as essentially narcotic, drug, rest, peace, 'sabbath', slackening of tension and relaxing of limbs, in short *passively*.

While the noble man lives in trust and openness with himself (*gennaios* 'of noble descent' underlines the nuance 'upright' and probably also 'naïve'), the man of *ressentiment* is neither upright nor naïve nor honest and straightforward with himself. His soul *squints*; his spirit loves hiding places, secret paths and back doors, everything covert entices him as *his* world, *his* security, *his* refreshment; he understands how to keep silent, how not to forget, how to wait, how to be provisionally self-deprecating and humble. A race of such men of *ressentiment* is bound to become eventually *cleverer* than any noble race; it will also honour cleverness to a far greater degree: namely, as a condition of existence of the first importance; while with noble men cleverness can easily acquire a subtle flavour of luxury and subtlety – for here it is far less essential than the perfect functioning of the regulating *unconscious* instincts or even than a certain imprudence, perhaps a bold recklessness whether in the face of danger or of the enemy, or that enthusiastic impulsiveness in anger, love, reverence, gratitude and revenge by which noble souls have at all times recognized one another. *Ressentiment* itself, if it should appear in the noble man, consummates and exhausts itself in an immediate reaction, and therefore does not *poison*: on the other hand, it fails to appear at all on countless occasions on which it inevitably appears in the weak and impotent.

To be incapable of taking one's enemies, one's accidents, even one's misdeeds seriously for very long – that is the sign of strong, full natures in whom there is an excess of the power to form, to mould, to recuperate and to forget (a good example of this in modern times is [the Comte de] Mirabeau [1749–91], who had no memory for insults and vile actions done him and was unable to forgive simply because he – forgot). Such a man shakes off with a *single* shrug many vermin that eat deep into others; here alone genuine 'love of one's enemies' is possible – supposing it to be possible at all on earth. How much reverence has a noble man for his enemies! – and such reverence is a bridge to love. – For he desires his enemy for himself, as his mark of distinction; he can endure no other enemy than one in whom there is nothing to despise and *very much* to honour! In contrast to this, picture 'the enemy' as the man of *ressentiment* conceives him – and here precisely is his deed, his creation: he has conceived 'the evil enemy', '*the Evil One*', and this in fact is his basic concept, from which he then evolves, as an afterthought and pendant, a 'good one' – himself!

11

This, then, is quite the contrary of what the noble man does, who conceives the basic concept 'good' in advance and spontaneously out of himself and only then creates for himself an idea of 'bad'! This 'bad' of noble origin and that 'evil' out of the cauldron of unsatisfied hatred – the former an after-production, a side issue, a contrasting shade, the latter on the contrary the original thing, the beginning, the distinctive *deed* in the conception of a slave morality – how different these words 'bad' and 'evil' are, although they are both apparently the opposite of the same concept 'good'. But it is *not* the same concept 'good': one should ask rather precisely *who* is 'evil' in the sense of the morality of *ressentiment*. The answer, in all strictness, is: *precisely* the 'good man' of the other morality, precisely the noble, powerful man, the ruler, but dyed in another colour, interpreted in another fashion, seen in another way by the venomous eye of *ressentiment*.

Here there is one thing we shall be the last to deny: he who knows these 'good men' only as enemies knows only *evil enemies*, and the same men who are held so sternly in check *inter pares* [among equals] by custom, respect, usage, gratitude, and even more by mutual suspicion and jealousy, and who on the other hand in their relations with one another show themselves so resourceful in consideration, self-control delicacy, loyalty, pride and friendship – once they go outside, where the strange, the *stranger* is found, they are not much better than uncaged beasts of prey. There they savour a freedom from all social constraints, they compensate themselves in the wilderness for the tension engendered by protracted confinement and enclosure within the peace of society, they go *back* to the innocent conscience of the beast of prey, as triumphant monsters who perhaps emerge from a disgusting procession of murder, arson, rape and torture, exhilarated and undisturbed of soul, as if it were no more than a students' prank, convinced they have provided the poets with a lot more material for song and praise. One cannot fail to see at the bottom of all these noble races the beast of prey, the splendid *blond beast*[1] prowling about avidly in search of spoil and victory; this hidden core needs to erupt from time to time, the animal has to get out again and go back to the wilderness: the Roman, Arabian, Germanic, Japanese nobility, the Homeric heroes, the Scandinavian Vikings – they all shared this need. . . .

Supposing that what is at any rate believed to be the 'truth' really is true, and the *meaning of all culture* is the reduction of the beast of prey 'man' to a tame and civilized animal, a *domestic animal*, then one would undoubtedly have to regard all those instincts of reaction and *ressentiment* through whose aid the noble races and their ideals were finally confounded and overthrown as the actual *instruments of culture*; which is not to say that the *bearers* of these instincts themselves represent culture. Rather is the reverse not merely probable – no! today it is *palpable*! These bearers of the oppressive instincts that thirst for reprisal, the descendants of every kind of European and non-European slavery, and especially of the entire pre-Aryan populace – they represent the *regression* of mankind! These 'instruments of culture' are a disgrace to man and rather an accusation and counterargument against 'culture' in general! One may be quite justified in continuing to fear the blond beast at the core of all noble races and in being on one's guard against it: but who would not a hundred times sooner fear where one can also admire than *not* fear but be permanently condemned to the repellent sight of the ill-constituted, dwarfed, atrophied and poisoned? And is that not *our* fate? What today constitutes *our* antipathy to 'man'? – for we *suffer* from man, beyond doubt.

Not fear; rather that we no longer have anything left to fear in man; that the maggot 'man' is swarming in the foreground; that the 'tame man', the hopelessly mediocre and insipid man, has already learned to feel himself as the goal and zenith, as the meaning of history, as 'higher man' – that he has indeed a certain right to feel thus, in so far as he feels himself elevated above the surfeit of ill-constituted, sickly, weary and exhausted people of which Europe is beginning to stink today, as something at least relatively well-constituted, at least still capable of living, at least affirming life.

12

At this point I cannot suppress a sigh and a last hope. What is it that I especially find utterly unendurable? That I cannot cope with, that makes me choke and faint? Bad air! Bad air! The approach of some ill-constituted thing; that I have to smell the entrails of some ill-constituted soul!

How much one is able to endure: distress, want, bad weather, sickness, toil, solitude. Fundamentally one can cope with everything else, born as one is to a subterranean life of struggle; one emerges again and again into the light, one experiences again and again one's golden hour of victory – and then one stands forth as one was born, unbreakable, tensed, ready for new, even harder, remoter things, like a bow that distress only serves to draw tauter.

But grant me from time to time – if there are divine goddesses in the realm beyond good and evil – grant me the sight, but *one* glance of something perfect, wholly achieved, happy, mighty, triumphant, something still capable of arousing fear! Of a man who justifies *man*, of a complementary and redeeming lucky hit on the part of man for the sake of which one may still *believe in man*!

For this is how things are: the diminution and levelling of European man constitutes *our* greatest danger, for the sight of him makes us weary. – We can see nothing today that wants to grow greater, we suspect that things will continue to go down, down, to become thinner, more good-natured, more prudent, more comfortable, more mediocre, more indifferent, more Chinese, more Christian – there is no doubt that man is getting 'better' all the time.

Here precisely is what has become a fatality for Europe – together with the fear of man we have also lost our love of him, our reverence for him, our hopes for him, even the will to him. The sight of man now makes us weary – what is nihilism today if it is not *that*? – We are weary *of man*.

13

But let us return: the problem of the *other* origin of the 'good', of the good as conceived by the man of *ressentiment*, demands its solution.

That lambs dislike great birds of prey does not seem strange: only it gives no ground for reproaching these birds of prey for bearing off little lambs. And if the lambs say among themselves: 'these birds of prey are evil; and whoever is least like a bird of prey, but rather its opposite, a lamb – would he not be good?' there is no reason to find fault with this institution of an ideal, except perhaps that the birds of prey might view it a little ironically and say: '*we* don't dislike them at all, these good little lambs; we even love them: nothing is more tasty than a tender lamb.'

To demand of strength that it should *not* express itself as strength, that it should *not* be a desire to overcome, a desire to throw down, a desire to become master, a thirst for enemies and resistances and triumphs, is just as absurd as to demand of weakness that it should express itself as strength. A quantum of force is equivalent to a quantum of drive, will, effect – more, it is nothing other than precisely this very driving, willing, effecting, and only owing to the seduction of language (and of the fundamental errors of reason that are petrified in it) which conceives and misconceives all effects as conditioned by something that causes effects, by a 'subject', can it appear otherwise. For just as the popular mind separates the lightning from its flash and takes the latter for an *action*, for the operation of a subject called lightning, so popular morality also separates strength from expressions of strength, as if there were a neutral substratum behind the strong man, which was *free* to express strength or not to do so. But there is no such substratum; there is no 'being' behind doing, effecting, becoming; 'the doer' is merely a fiction added to the deed – the deed is everything. The popular mind in fact doubles the deed; when it sees the lightning flash, it is the deed of a deed: it posits the same event first as cause and then a second time as its effect. Scientists do no better when they say 'force moves', 'force causes', and the like – all its coolness, its freedom from emotion notwithstanding, our entire science still lies under the misleading influence of language and has not disposed of that little changeling, the 'subject' (the atom, for example, is such a changeling, as is the Kantian 'thing-in-itself'); no wonder if the submerged, darkly glowering emotions of vengefulness and hatred exploit this belief for their own ends and in fact maintain no belief more ardently than the belief that *the strong man is free* to be weak and the bird of prey to be a lamb – for thus they gain the right to make the bird of prey *accountable* for being a bird of prey.

When the oppressed, downtrodden, outraged exhort one another with the vengeful cunning of impotence: 'let us be different from the evil, namely good! And he is good who does not outrage, who harms nobody, who does not attack, who does not requite, who leaves revenge to God, who keeps himself hidden as we do, who avoids evil and desires little from life, like us, the patient, humble, and just' – this, listened to calmly and without previous bias, really amounts to no more than: 'we weak ones are, after all, weak; it would be good if we did nothing *for which we are not strong enough*'; but this dry matter of fact, this prudence of the lowest order which even insects possess (posing as dead, when in great danger, so as not to do 'too much'), has, thanks to the counterfeit and self-deception of impotence, clad itself in the ostentatious garb of the virtue of quiet, calm resignation, just as if the weakness of the weak – that is to say, their *essence*, their effects, their sole ineluctable, irremovable reality – were a voluntary achievement, willed, chosen, a *deed*, a *meritorious* act. This type of man *needs* to believe in a neutral independent 'subject', prompted by an instinct for self-preservation and self-affirmation in which every lie is sanctified. The subject (or, to use a more popular expression, the *soul*) has perhaps been believed in hitherto more firmly than anything else on earth because it makes possible to the majority of mortals, the weak and oppressed of every kind, the sublime self-deception that interprets weakness as freedom, and their being thus-and-thus as a *merit*.

14

Would anyone like to take a look into the secret of how *ideals are made* on earth? Who has the courage? – Very well! Here is a point we can see through into this dark workshop. But wait a moment or two, Mr Rash and Curious: your eyes must first get used to this false iridescent light. – All right! Now speak! What is going on down there? Say what you see, man of the most perilous kind of inquisitiveness – now I am the one who is listening.

– 'I see nothing, but I hear the more. There is a soft, wary, malignant muttering and whispering coming from all the corners and nooks. It seems to me one is lying; a saccharine sweetness clings to every sound. Weakness is being lied into something *meritorious*, no doubt of it – so it is just as you said'

– Go on!

– 'and impotence which does not requite into "goodness of heart"; anxious lowliness into "humility"; subjection to those one hates into "obedience" (that is, to one of whom they say he commands this subjection – they call him God). The inoffensiveness of the weak man, even the cowardice of which he has so much, his lingering at the door, his being ineluctably compelled to wait, here acquire flattering names, such as "patience", and are even called virtue itself; his inability for revenge is called unwillingness to revenge, perhaps even forgiveness ("for *they* know not what they do – we alone know what *they* do!"). They also speak of "loving one's enemies" – and sweat as they do so.'

– Go on!

– 'They are miserable, no doubt of it, all these mutterers and nook counterfeiters, although they crouch warmly together – but they tell me their misery is a sign of being chosen by God; one beats the dogs one likes best; perhaps this misery is also a preparation, a testing, a schooling, perhaps it is even more – something that will one day be made good and recompensed with interest, with huge payments of gold, no! of happiness. This they call "bliss".'

– Go on!

– 'Now they give me to understand that they are not merely better than the mighty, the lords of the earth whose spittle they have to lick (*not* from fear, not at all from fear! but because God has commanded them to obey the authorities) – that they are not merely better but are also "better off", or at least will be better off someday. [Allusion to Romans 13:1–2 – Ed.] But enough! enough! I can't take any more. Bad air! Bad air! This workshop where *ideals are manufactured* – it seems to me it stinks of so many lies.'

– No! Wait a moment! You have said nothing yet of the masterpiece of these black magicians, who make whiteness, milk and innocence of every blackness – haven't you noticed their perfection of refinement, their boldest, subtlest, most ingenious, most mendacious artistic stroke? Attend to them! These cellar rodents full of vengefulness and hatred – what have they made of revenge and hatred? Have you heard these words uttered? If you trusted simply to their words, would you suspect you were among men of *ressentiment*? . . .

– 'I understand; I'll open my ears again (oh! oh! oh! and *close* my nose). Now I can really hear what they have been saying all along: "We good men – *we are the just*" – what they desire they call, not retaliation, but "the triumph of *justice*"; what they hate is not their enemy, no! they hate "injustice", they hate "godlessness"; what they believe in and hope for is not the hope of revenge, the intoxication of sweet revenge ("sweeter than honey"

Homer called it), but the victory of God, of the *just* God, over the godless; what there is left for them to love on earth is not their brothers in hatred but their "brothers in love", as they put it, all the good and just on earth.'

– And what do they call that which serves to console them for all the suffering of life – their phantasmagoria of anticipated future bliss?

– 'What? Do I hear aright? They call that "the Last Judgement", the coming of *their* kingdom, of the "Kingdom of God" – meanwhile, however, they live "in faith", "in love", "in hope".'

– Enough! Enough!

16

Let us conclude. The two *opposing* values 'good and bad', 'good and evil' have been engaged in a fearful struggle on earth for thousands of years; and though the latter value has certainly been on top for a long time, there are still places where the struggle is as yet undecided. One might even say that it has risen ever higher and thus become more and more profound and spiritual: so that today there is perhaps no more decisive mark of a '*higher nature*', a more spiritual nature, than that of being divided in this sense and a genuine battleground of these opposed values. . . .

Note

1 That the 'blond beast' is found in Arabia and Japan is sufficient to show that, by this expression, Nietzsche does not intend 'Aryan man'. According to the translator, the reference is to the lion, a metaphor for the 'warrior-noble'.

G. E. Moore, *Principia Ethica*, chapter 1, sections 1–2, 5–15

From G. E. Moore, *Principia Ethica*. Cambridge: Cambridge University Press, 1960, pp. 1–3, 5–21; © Perry Moore, reproduced by permission of Mr Perry Moore and Cambridge University Press.

Nietzsche, self-proclaimed 'amoralist' and thinker of 'dynamite' thoughts, would not have been surprised at his role in engendering the irrationalist and icono-clastic views of morality which have prospered in twentieth-century continen-tal Europe. The mild-mannered and -speaking Cambridge philosopher G. E. Moore (1873–1958) would have been – indeed, was – perturbed at the way his 1903 book *Principia Ethica* helped to spawn a whole shoal of not so very different views – 'subjectivism', 'emotivism', 'non-cognitivism' etc. – in the English-language world. As he himself noted, his answer to the question 'What is good?' – namely, that 'good is good, and that is the end of the matter' (p. 232 below) – hardly sounds one to quicken the blood.

Moore was less vexed, presumably, by the dithyrambic welcome given by the Bloomsbury group to the final chapter of the book, with its proclamation of 'personal affections and aesthetic enjoyments [as] . . . by *far* the greatest goods (p. 189), which prompted J. M. Keynes to speak of the book as 'the beginning of a renaissance, the opening of a new heaven on earth'.[1] But among professional philosophers, for whom this personal credo rather betrayed Moore's own perception of the proper 'analytical' role of moral philosophy, it was not chapter 5 but chapter 1 which heralded a true renaissance. This is the chapter in which Moore launches his famous attack on the 'naturalistic fallacy'.

Three remarks on this expression, so much part of the contemporary ethical lexicon, are in order. First, it was a misnomer: for what Moore was attacking was the attempt to define 'good' by equating good with *any* other property, natural or otherwise. The 'fallacy' is as much committed by someone who

---

[1] From his *Two Memoirs*, quoted in John Skorupski, *English-Language Philosophy 1750–1945*, Oxford: Oxford University Press, 1993, p. 152.

equates 'good' with 'commanded by God' as by someone who identifies it with 'pleasurable'. Thus, it is perfectly possible to join in Moore's attack whilst remaining a 'naturalist' in the 'broad, useful' sense of adhering to an 'ethical view that stems from the general attitude that man is part of nature'.[2] Second, it is not clear that many earlier philosophers ever committed the 'fallacy' in the crass form that Moore characterizes it. Certainly it was unjust of him to accuse Mill of an 'artless use of the naturalistic fallacy', of simply *equating* the 'desirable' and the 'desired' by stipulative definition. But this, perhaps, matters less than it might seem. Moore's main objection to the 'fallacy' (§13) is that someone who defines 'good' as, say, 'pleasurable' reduces what is intended as a substantive moral claim, 'Pleasure alone is good', to the tautology 'Pleasure alone is pleasurable', and illegitimately precludes even raising the question 'Is pleasure good?'. Suitably amended, this objection would also be effective against philosophers who, without bluntly identifying good and pleasure, nevertheless insist that we could not really understand moral concepts except in terms of pleasure. And that is a kind of insistence very familiar in the history of ethics. Bentham, for example, denied that 'the word *right* can have any meaning without reference to utility'.

The third remark is that, if it was questionable to foist on Hume the thesis that 'ought' cannot be derived from 'is' – that evaluative judgements cannot be deduced from factual premises (see p. 150 above) – it is certainly wrong to suppose that this was Moore's thesis in rejecting 'the naturalistic fallacy'. (Unfortunately, the expression is often taken, these days, to refer to any attempt to derive an 'ought' from an 'is'). For Moore, 'good' is indefinable because it refers to an absolutely simple, 'non-natural' property. That certain things, such as friendship, have this property is a fact which we are able to 'see' or intuit, and one from which obligations can be deduced – for what a person ought to do, says Moore, is to produce good. As we will see in chapter 17, in connection with C. L. Stevenson's article, it is only when this 'intuitionist' thesis is rejected – as it was by the Logical Positivists in the 1920s – that dismissal of the 'naturalistic fallacy' can yield any general thesis about the impossibility of moving from statements of facts to the making of moral judgements.

In the short term, Moore's main impact was not upon iconoclastic thinkers, such as the 'emotivists' (whose doctrine he strongly opposed), but highly conservative philosophers standing in the 'moral sense' tradition of British ethics (see chapter 16 below).[3] But the time-bomb planted by Moore was ticking away, timed to go off during the era after the First World War when any confidence in a universally shared intuitive faculty capable of giving moral guidance to our lives had itself, and for obvious reasons, been exploded.

[2] Bernard Williams, *Ethics and the Limits of Philosophy*, London: Fontana, 1985, p. 121.
[3] For Moore's rejection of 'emotivism', see his 'Replies' in P. A. Schilpp (ed.), *The Philosophy of G. E. Moore*, Evanston, Ill.: Northwestern University Press, 1942.

▶ ▶ ▶ **Chapter 1: The Subject-matter of Ethics**

(1)   It is very easy to point out some among our everyday judgements, with the truth of which ethics is undoubtedly concerned. Whenever we say, 'So and so is a good man,' or 'That fellow is a villain'; whenever we ask, 'What ought I to do?' or 'Is it wrong for me to do like this?'; whenever we hazard such remarks as 'Temperance is a virtue and drunkenness a vice' – it is undoubtedly the business of ethics to discuss such questions and such statements; to argue what is the true answer when we ask what it is right to do, and to give reasons for thinking that our statements about the character of persons or the morality of actions are true or false. In the vast majority of cases, where we make statements involving any of the terms 'virtue', 'vice', 'duty', 'right', 'ought', 'good', 'bad', we are making ethical judgements; and if we wish to discuss their truth, we shall be discussing a point of ethics.

So much as this is not disputed; but it falls very far short of defining the province of ethics. That province may indeed be defined as the whole truth about that which is at the same time common to all such judgements and peculiar to them. But we have still to ask the question: what is it that is thus common and peculiar? And this is a question to which very different answers have been given by ethical philosophers of acknowledged reputation, and none of them, perhaps, completely satisfactory.

(2)   If we take such examples as those given above, we shall not be far wrong in saying that they are all of them concerned with the question of 'conduct' – with the question, what, in the conduct of us, human beings, is good, and what is bad, what is right, and what is wrong. For when we say that a man is good, we commonly mean that he acts rightly; when we say that drunkenness is a vice, we commonly mean that to get drunk is a wrong or wicked action. And this discussion of human conduct is, in fact, that with which the name 'ethics' is most intimately associated. It is so associated by derivation; and conduct is undoubtedly by far the commonest and most generally interesting object of ethical judgements.

Accordingly we find that many ethical philosophers are disposed to accept as an adequate definition of 'ethics' the statement that it deals with the question what is good or bad in human conduct. They hold that its enquiries are properly confined to 'conduct' or to 'practice'; they hold that the name 'practical philosophy' covers all the matter with which it has to do. Now, without discussing the proper meaning of the word (for verbal questions are properly left to the writers of dictionaries and other persons interested in literature; philosophy, as we shall see, has no concern with them), I may say that I intend to use 'ethics' to cover more than this – a usage, for which there is, I think, quite sufficient authority. I am using it to cover an enquiry for which, at all events, there is no other word: the general enquiry into what is good.

Ethics is undoubtedly concerned with the question what good conduct is; but, being concerned with this, it obviously does not start at the beginning, unless it is prepared to tell us what is good as well as what is conduct. For 'good conduct' is a complex notion: all conduct is not good, for some is certainly bad and some may be indifferent. And on the other hand, other things beside conduct may be good; and if they are so, then 'good' denotes some property that is common to them and conduct; and if we examine good conduct alone of all good things, then we shall be in danger of mistaking for this property, some property which is not shared by those other things: and thus we shall have made a mistake about ethics even in this limited sense; for we shall not know what good conduct really is. This is a mistake which many writers have actually made, from limiting their enquiry to conduct. And hence I shall try to avoid it by considering first what is good in general; hoping, that if we can arrive at any certainty about this, it will be much easier to settle the question of good conduct: for we all know pretty well what 'conduct' is. This, then, is our first question: What is good? and What is bad? and to the discussion of this question (or these questions) I give the name of ethics, since that science must, at all events, include it. . . .

(5)   But our question 'What is good?' may have still another meaning. We may, in the third place, mean to ask, not what thing or things are good, but how 'good' is to be defined. This is an enquiry which belongs only to ethics . . . and this is the enquiry which will occupy us first.

It is an enquiry to which most special attention should be directed; since this question, how 'good' is to be defined, is the most fundamental question in all ethics. That which is meant by 'good' is, in fact, except its converse 'bad,' the *only* simple object of thought which is peculiar to ethics. Its definition is, therefore, the most essential point in the definition of ethics; and moreover a mistake with regard to it entails a far larger number of erroneous ethical judgements than any other. Unless this first question be fully understood, and its true answer clearly recognized, the rest of ethics is as good as useless from the point of view of systematic knowledge. True ethical judgements . . . may indeed be made by those who do not know the answer to this question as well as by those who do; and it goes without saying that the two classes of people may lead equally good lives. But it is extremely unlikely that the *most general* ethical judgements will be equally valid, in the absence of a true answer to this question: I shall presently try to shew that the gravest errors have been largely due to beliefs in a false answer. And, in any case, it is impossible that, till the answer to this question be known, any one should know *what is the evidence* for any ethical judgement whatsoever. But the main object of ethics, as a systematic science, is to give correct *reasons* for thinking that this or that is good; and, unless this question be answered, such reasons cannot be given. Even, therefore, apart from the fact that a false answer leads to false conclusions, the present enquiry is a most necessary and important part of the science of ethics.

(6)   What, then, is good? How is good to be defined? Now, it may be thought that this is a verbal question. A definition does indeed often mean the expressing of one word's meaning in other words. But this is not the sort of definition I am asking for. Such a definition can never be of ultimate importance in any study except lexicography. If I wanted that kind of definition I should have to consider in the first place how people generally used the word 'good'; but my business is not with its proper usage, as established by custom. I should, indeed, be foolish, if I tried to use it for something which it did not usually denote: if, for instance, I were to announce that, whenever I used the word 'good', I must be understood to be thinking of that object which is usually denoted by the word 'table'. I shall, therefore, use the word in the sense in which I think it is ordinarily used; but at the same time I am not anxious to discuss whether I am right in thinking that it is so used. My business is solely with that object or idea, which I hold, rightly or wrongly, that the word is generally used to stand for. What I want to discover is the nature of that object or idea, and about this I am extremely anxious to arrive at an agreement.

But if we understand the question in this sense, my answer to it may seem a very disappointing one. If I am asked 'What is good?' my answer is that good is good, and that is the end of the matter. Or if I am asked 'How is good to be defined?' my answer is that it cannot be defined, and that is all I have to say about it. But disappointing as these answers may appear, they are of the very last importance. To readers who are familiar with philosophic terminology, I can express their importance by saying that they amount to this: that propositions about the good are all of them synthetic and never analytic; and that is plainly no trivial matter. And the same thing may be expressed more popularly by saying that, if I am right, then nobody can foist upon us such an axiom as that 'Pleasure is the only good' or that 'The good is the desired' on the pretence that this is 'the very meaning of the word'.

(7)   Let us, then, consider this position. My point is that 'good' is a simple notion, just as 'yellow' is a simple notion; that just as you cannot, by

any manner of means, explain to anyone who does not already know it, what yellow is, so you cannot explain what good is. Definitions of the kind that I was asking for, definitions which describe the real nature of the object or notion denoted by a word, and which do not merely tell us what the word is used to mean, are only possible when the object or notion in question is something complex. You can give a definition of a horse, because a horse has many different properties and qualities, all of which you can enumerate. But when you have enumerated them all, when you have reduced a horse to his simplest terms, then you can no longer define those terms. They are simply something which you think of or perceive, and to any one who cannot think of or perceive them, you can never, by any definition, make their nature known. It may perhaps be objected to this that we are able to describe to others objects which they have never seen or thought of. We can, for instance, make a man understand what a chimaera is, although he has never heard of one or seen one. You can tell him that it is an animal with a lioness's head and body, with a goat's head growing from the middle of its back, and with a snake in place of a tail. But here the object which you are describing is a complex object; it is entirely composed of parts with which we are all perfectly familiar – a snake, a goat, a lioness; and we know, too, the manner in which those parts are to be put together, because we know what is meant by the middle of a lioness's back, and where her tail is wont to grow. And so it is with all objects, not previously known, which we are able to define: they are all complex; all composed of parts, which may themselves, in the first instance, be capable of similar definition, but which must in the end be reducible to simplest parts, which can no longer be defined. But yellow and good, we say, are not complex: they are notions of that simple kind, out of which definitions are composed and with which the power of further defining ceases.

(8)   When we say, as Webster says, 'The definition of horse is "A hoofed quadruped of the genus *Equus*",' we may, in fact, mean three different things. (*a*) We may mean merely: 'When I say "horse", you are to understand that I am talking about a hoofed quadruped of the genus *Equus*.' This might be called the arbitrary verbal definition: and I do not mean that good is indefinable in that sense. (*b*) We may mean, as Webster ought to mean: 'When most English people say "horse", they mean a hoofed quadruped of the genus *Equus*.' This may be called the verbal definition proper, and I do not say that good is indefinable in this sense either; for it is certainly possible to discover how people use a word: otherwise, we could never have known that 'good' may be translated by *gut* in German and by *bon* in French. But (*c*) we may, when we define horse, mean something much more important. We may mean that a certain object, which we all of

us know, is composed in a certain manner: that it has four legs, a head, a heart, a liver, etc., etc., all of them arranged in definite relations to one another. It is in this sense that I deny good to be definable. I say that it is not composed of any parts, which we can substitute for it in our minds when we are thinking of it. We might think just as clearly and correctly about a horse if we thought of all its parts and their arrangement instead of thinking of the whole: we could, I say, think how a horse differed from a donkey just as well, just as truly, in this way as now we do, only not so easily; but there is nothing whatsoever which we could so substitute for good; and that is what I mean, when I say that good is indefinable.

(9)   But I am afraid I have still not removed the chief difficulty which may prevent acceptance of the proposition that good is indefinable. I do not mean to say that *the* good, that which is good, is thus indefinable; if I did think so, I should not be writing on ethics, for my main object is to help towards discovering that definition. It is just because I think there will be less risk of error in our search for a definition of 'the good', that I am now insisting that *good* is indefinable. I must try to explain the difference between these two. I suppose it may be granted that 'good' is an adjective. Well 'the good', 'that which is good', must therefore be the substantive to which the adjective 'good' will apply: it must be the whole of that to which the adjective will apply, and the adjective must *always* truly apply to it. But if it is that to which the adjective will apply, it must be something different from that adjective itself; and the whole of that something different, whatever it is, will be our definition of *the* good. Now it may be that this something will have other adjectives beside 'good' that will apply to it. It may be full of pleasure, for example; it may be intelligent: and if these two adjectives are really part of its definition, then it will certainly be true that pleasure and intelligence are good. And many people appear to think that if we say 'Pleasure and intelligence are good,' or if we say 'Only pleasure and intelligence are good,' we are defining 'good'. Well, I cannot deny that propositions of this nature may sometimes be called definitions; I do not know well enough how the word is generally used to decide upon this point. I only wish it to be understood that that is not what I mean when I say there is no possible definition of good, and that I shall not mean this if I use the word again. I do most fully believe that some true proposition of the form 'Intelligence is good and intelligence alone is good' can be found; if none could be found, our definition of *the* good would be impossible. As it is, I believe *the* good to be definable; and yet I still say that good itself is indefinable.

(10)   'Good', then, if we mean by it that quality which we assert to belong to a thing, when we say that the thing is good, is incapable of any

definition, in the most important sense of that word. The most important sense of 'definition' is that in which a definition states what are the parts which invariably compose a certain whole; and in this sense 'good' has no definition because it is simple and has no parts. It is one of those innumerable objects of thought which are themselves incapable of definition, because they are the ultimate terms by reference to which whatever *is* capable of definition must be defined. That there must be an indefinite number of such terms is obvious, on reflection; since we cannot define anything except by an analysis, which, when carried as far as it will go, refers us to something which is simply different from anything else, and which by that ultimate difference explains the peculiarity of the whole which we are defining: for every whole contains some parts which are common to other wholes also. There is, therefore, no intrinsic difficulty in the contention that 'good' denotes a simple and indefinable quality. There are many other instances of such qualities.

Consider yellow, for example. We may try to define it, by describing its physical equivalent; we may state what kind of light-vibrations must stimulate the normal eye in order that we may perceive it. But a moment's reflection is sufficient to shew that those light-vibrations are not themselves what we mean by yellow. *They* are not what we perceive. Indeed we should never have been able to discover their existence unless we had first been struck by the patent difference of quality between the different colours. The most we can be entitled to say of those vibrations is that they are what corresponds in space to the yellow which we actually perceive.

Yet a mistake of this simple kind has commonly been made about 'good'. It may be true that all things which are good are *also* something else, just as it is true that all things which are yellow produce a certain kind of vibration in the light. And it is a fact that ethics aims at discovering what are those other properties belonging to all things which are good. But far too many philosophers have thought that when they named those other properties they were actually defining good; that these properties, in fact, were simply not 'other', but absolutely and entirely the same with goodness. This view I propose to call the 'naturalistic fallacy' and of it I shall now endeavour to dispose.

(11) Let us consider what it is such philosophers say. And first it is to be noticed that they do not agree among themselves. They not only say that they are right as to what good is, but they endeavour to prove that other people who say that it is something else, are wrong. One, for instance, will affirm that good is pleasure; another, perhaps, that good is that which is desired; and each of these will argue eagerly to prove that the other is wrong. But how is that possible? One of them says that good is

nothing but the object of desire, and at the same time tries to prove that it is not pleasure. But from his first assertion, that good just means the object of desire, one of two things must follow as regards his proof:

(*a*)   He may be trying to prove that the object of desire is not pleasure. But, if this be all, where is his ethics? The position he is maintaining is merely a psychological one. Desire is something which occurs in our minds, and pleasure is something else which so occurs; and our would-be ethical philosopher is merely holding that the latter is not the object of the former. But what has that to do with the question in dispute? His opponent held the ethical proposition that pleasure was the good, and although he should prove a million times over the psychological proposition that pleasure is not the object of desire, he is no nearer proving his opponent to be wrong. The position is like this. One man says a triangle is a circle: another replies 'A triangle is a straight line, and I will prove to you that I am right: *for*' (this is the only argument) 'a straight line is not a circle.' 'That is quite true,' the other may reply; 'but nevertheless a triangle is a circle, and you have said nothing whatever to prove the contrary. What is proved is that one of us is wrong, for we agree that a triangle cannot be both a straight line and a circle: but which is wrong, there can be no earthly means of proving, since you define triangle as straight line and I define it as circle.' – Well, that is one alternative which any naturalistic ethics has to face; if good is *defined* as something else, it is then impossible either to prove that any other definition is wrong or even to deny such definition.

(*b*)   The other alternative will scarcely be more welcome. It is that the discussion is after all a verbal one. When A says 'Good means pleasant' and B says 'Good means desired,' they may merely wish to assert that most people have used the word for what is pleasant and for what is desired respectively. And this is quite an interesting subject for discussion: only it is not a whit more an ethical discussion than the last was. Nor do I think that any exponent of naturalistic ethics would be willing to allow that this was all he meant. They are all so anxious to persuade us that what they call the good is what we really ought to do. 'Do, pray, act so, because the word "good" is generally used to denote actions of this nature': such, on this view, would be the substance of their teaching. And in so far as they tell us how we ought to act, their teaching is truly ethical, as they mean it to be. But how perfectly absurd is the reason they would give for it! 'You are to do this, because most people use a certain word to denote conduct such as this.' 'You are to say the thing which is not, because most people call it lying.' That is an argument just as good! – My dear sirs, what we want to know from you as ethical teachers, is not how people use a word; it is not even, what kind of actions they approve, which the use of this word 'good' may certainly imply: what we want to know is simply what *is* good. We may indeed agree that what most people do think good, is actually so; we shall at all events be glad to know their opinions: but when we say their opinions about what *is* good, we do mean what we say; we do not care whether they call that thing which they mean 'horse' or 'table' or 'chair,' *gut* or *bon* or ἀγαθός; we want to know what it is that they so call. When they say 'Pleasure is good,' we cannot believe that they merely mean 'Pleasure is pleasure' and nothing more than that.

(12) Suppose a man says 'I am pleased'; and suppose that is not a lie or a mistake but the truth. Well, if it is true, what does that mean? It means that his mind, a certain definite mind, distinguished by certain definite marks from all others, has at this moment a certain definite feeling called pleasure. 'Pleased' *means* nothing but having pleasure, and though we may be more pleased or less pleased, and even, we may admit for the present, have one or another kind of pleasure; yet in so far as it is pleasure we have, whether there be more or less of it, and whether it be of one kind or another, what we have is one definite thing, absolutely indefinable, some one thing that is the same in all the various degrees and in all the various kinds of it that there may be. We may be able to say how it is related to other things: that, for example, it is in the mind, that it causes desire, that we are conscious of it, etc., etc. We can, I say, describe its relations to other things, but define it we can *not*. And if anybody tried to define pleasure for us as being any other natural object; if anybody were to say, for instance, that pleasure *means* the sensation of red, and were to proceed to deduce from that that pleasure is a colour, we should be entitled to laugh at him and to distrust his future statements about pleasure. Well, that would be the same fallacy which I have called the naturalistic fallacy. That 'pleased' does not mean 'having the sensation of red', or anything else whatever, does not prevent us from understanding what it does mean. It is enough for us to know that 'pleased' does mean 'having the sensation of pleasure', and though pleasure is absolutely indefinable, though pleasure is pleasure and nothing else whatever, yet we feel no difficulty in saying that we are pleased. The reason is, of course, that when I say 'I am pleased,' I do *not* mean that 'I' am the same thing as 'having pleasure'. And similarly no difficulty need be found in my saying that 'pleasure is good' and yet not meaning that 'pleasure' is the same thing as 'good', that pleasure *means* good, and that good *means* pleasure. If I were to imagine that when I said 'I am pleased,' I meant that I was exactly the same thing as 'pleased', I should not indeed call that a naturalistic fallacy, although it would be the same fallacy as I have called naturalistic with reference to ethics. The reason of this is obvious

enough. When a man confuses two natural objects with one another, defining the one by the other, if for instance, he confuses himself, who is one natural object, with 'pleased' or with 'pleasure' which are others, then there is no reason to call the fallacy naturalistic. But if he confuses 'good', which is not in the same sense a natural object, with any natural object whatever, then there is a reason for calling that a naturalistic fallacy; its being made with regard to 'good' marks it as something quite specific, and this specific mistake deserves a name because it is so common. As for the reasons why good is not to be considered a natural object, they may be reserved for discussion in another place. But, for the present, it is sufficient to notice this: Even if it were a natural object, that would not alter the nature of the fallacy nor diminish its importance one whit. All that I have said about it would remain quite equally true: only the name which I have called it would not be so appropriate as I think it is. And I do not care about the name: what I do care about is the fallacy. It does not matter what we call it, provided we recognize it when we meet with it. It is to be met with in almost every book on ethics; and yet it is not recognized: and that is why it is necessary to multiply illustrations of it, and convenient to give it a name. It is a very simple fallacy indeed. When we say that an orange is yellow, we do not think our statement binds us to hold that 'orange' means nothing else than 'yellow', or that nothing can be yellow but an orange. Supposing the orange is also sweet! Does that bind us to say that 'sweet' is exactly the same thing as 'yellow', that 'sweet' must be defined as 'yellow'? And supposing it be recognized that 'yellow' just means 'yellow' and nothing else whatever, does that make it any more difficult to hold that oranges are yellow? Most certainly it does not: on the contrary, it would be absolutely meaningless to say that oranges were yellow, unless yellow did in the end mean just 'yellow' and nothing else whatever – unless it was absolutely indefinable. We should not get any very clear notion about things, which are yellow – we should not get very far with our science, if we were bound to hold that everything which was yellow, *meant* exactly the same thing as yellow. We should find we had to hold that an orange was exactly the same thing as a stool, a piece of paper, a lemon, anything you like. We could prove any number of absurdities; but should we be the nearer to the truth? Why, then, should it be different with 'good'? Why, if good is good and indefinable, should I be held to deny that pleasure is good? Is there any difficulty in holding both to be true at once? On the contrary, there is no meaning in saying that pleasure is good, unless good is something different from pleasure. It is absolutely useless, so far as ethics is concerned, to prove, as Mr [Herbert] Spencer tries to do, that increase of pleasure coincides with increase of life, unless good *means* something different from either life or pleasure. He might just as well try to prove that an orange is yellow by shewing that it always is wrapped up in paper.

(13) In fact, if it is not the case that 'good' denotes something simple and indefinable, only two alternatives are possible: either it is a complex, a given whole, about the correct analysis of which there may be disagreement; or else it means nothing at all, and there is no such subject as ethics. In general, however, ethical philosophers have attempted to define good, without recognizing what such an attempt must mean. They actually use arguments which involve one or both of the absurdities considered in §11. We are, therefore, justified in concluding that the attempt to define good is chiefly due to want of clearness as to the possible nature of definition. There are, in fact, only two serious alternatives to be considered, in order to establish the conclusion that 'good' does denote a simple and indefinable notion. It might possibly denote a complex, as 'horse' does; or it might have no meaning at all. Neither of these possibilities has, however, been clearly conceived and seriously maintained, as such, by those who presume to define good; and both may be dismissed by a simple appeal to facts.

(*a*) The hypothesis that disagreement about the meaning of good is disagreement with regard to the correct analysis of a given whole, may be most plainly seen to be incorrect by consideration of the fact that, whatever definition be offered, it may be always asked, with significance, of the complex so defined, whether it is itself good. To take, for instance, one of the more plausible, because one of the more complicated, of such proposed definitions, it may easily be thought, at first sight, that to be good may mean to be that which we desire to desire. Thus if we apply this definition to a particular instance and say 'When we think that A is good, we are thinking that A is one of the things which we desire to desire,' our proposition may seem quite plausible. But, if we carry the investigation further, and ask ourselves 'Is it good to desire to desire A?' it is apparent, on a little reflection, that this question is itself as intelligible, as the original question 'Is A good?' – that we are, in fact, now asking for exactly the same information about the desire to desire A, for which we formerly asked with regard to A itself. But it is also apparent that the meaning of this second question cannot be correctly analysed into 'Is the desire to desire A one of the things which we desire to desire?': we have not before our minds anything so complicated as the question 'Do we desire to desire to desire to desire A?' Moreover any one can easily convince himself by inspection that the predicate of this proposition – 'good' – is positively different from the notion of 'desiring to desire' which enters into its subject: 'That we should desire to desire A is good' is *not* merely equivalent to 'That A should be good is good.' It may indeed be true that what we desire to desire is always also good; perhaps even the converse may be true: but it is very doubtful whether this is the case, and the mere fact that we understand very well what is meant by doubting it, shews clearly that we have two different notions before our minds.

(*b*)   And the same consideration is sufficient to dismiss the hypothesis that 'good' has no meaning whatsoever. It is very natural to make the mistake of supposing that what is universally true is of such a nature that its negation would be self-contradictory: the importance which has been assigned to analytic propositions in the history of philosophy shews how easy such a mistake is. And thus it is very easy to conclude that what seems to be a universal ethical principle is in fact an identical proposition; that, if, for example, whatever is called 'good' seems to be pleasant, the proposition 'Pleasure is the good' does not assert a connection between two different notions, but involves only one, that of pleasure, which is easily recognized as a distinct entity. But whoever will attentively consider with himself what is actually before his mind when he asks the question 'Is pleasure (or whatever it may be) after all good?' can easily satisfy himself that he is not merely wondering whether pleasure is pleasant. And if he will try this experiment with each suggested definition in succession, he may become expert enough to recognize that in every case he has before his mind a unique object, with regard to the connection of which with any other object, a distinct question may be asked. Every one does in fact understand the question 'Is this good?' When he thinks of it, his state of mind is different from what it would be, were he asked 'Is this pleasant, or desired, or approved?' It has a distinct meaning for him, even though he may not recognize in what respect it is distinct. Whenever he thinks of 'intrinsic value', or 'intrinsic worth', or says that a thing 'ought to exist', he has before his mind the unique object – the unique property of things – which I mean by 'good'. Everybody is constantly aware of this notion, although he may never become aware at all that it is different from other notions of which he is also aware. But, for correct ethical reasoning, it is extremely important that he should become aware of this fact; and, as soon as the nature of the problem is clearly understood, there should be little difficulty in advancing so far in analysis.

(14)   'Good', then, is indefinable; and yet, so far as I know, there is only one ethical writer, Professor Henry Sidgwick, who has clearly recognized and stated this fact. We shall see, indeed, how far many of the most reputed ethical systems fall short of drawing the conclusions which follow from such a recognition. At present I will only quote one instance, which will serve to illustrate the meaning and importance of this principle that 'good' is indefinable, or, as Professor Sidgwick says, an 'unanalysable no-

tion'. It is an instance to which Professor Sidgwick himself refers in a note on the passage, in which he argues that 'ought' is unanalysable.[1]

'Bentham,' says Sidgwick, 'explains that his fundamental principle "states the greatest happiness of all those whose interest is in question as being the right and proper end of human action"'; and yet 'his language in other passages of the same chapter would seem to imply' that he *means* by the word 'right' 'conducive to the general happiness'. Professor Sidgwick sees that, if you take these two statements together, you get the absurd result that 'greatest happiness is the end of human action, which is conducive to the general happiness'; and so absurd does it seem to him to call this result, as Bentham calls it, 'the fundamental principle of a moral system', that he suggests that Bentham cannot have meant it. Yet Professor Sidgwick himself states elsewhere that Psychological Hedonism is 'not seldom confounded with Egoistic Hedonism',[2] and that confusion, as we shall see, rests chiefly on that same fallacy, the naturalistic fallacy, which is implied in Bentham's statements. Professor Sidgwick admits therefore that this fallacy is sometimes committed, absurd as it is; and I am inclined to think that Bentham may really have been one of those who committed it. Mill, as we shall see, certainly did commit it. In any case, whether Bentham committed it or not, his doctrine, as above quoted, will serve as a very good illustration of this fallacy, and of the importance of the contrary proposition that good is indefinable.

Let us consider this doctrine. Bentham seems to imply, so Professor Sidgwick says, that the word 'right' *means* 'conducive to general happiness'. Now this, by itself, need not necessarily involve the naturalistic fallacy. For the word 'right' is very commonly appropriated to actions which lead to the attainment of what is good; which are regarded as *means* to the ideal and not as ends-in-themselves. This use of 'right', as denoting what is good as a means, whether or not it be also good as an end, is indeed the use to which I shall confine the word. Had Bentham been using 'right' in this sense, it might be perfectly consistent for him to *define* right as 'conducive to the general happiness', *provided only* (and notice this proviso) he had already proved, or laid down as an axiom, that general happiness was *the* good, or (what is equivalent to this) that general happiness alone was good. For in that case he would have already defined *the* good as general happiness (a position perfectly consistent, as we have seen, with the contention that 'good' is indefinable), and, since right was to be defined as 'conducive to *the* good', it would actually *mean* 'conducive to general happiness'. But this method of escape from the charge of having committed the naturalistic fallacy has been closed by Bentham himself. For his fundamental principle is, we see, that the greatest happiness of all concerned is the *right* and proper *end* of human action. He applies the word 'right', therefore, to the end, as such, not only to the means which are conducive to it; and, that being so, right can no longer be defined as 'conducive to the general happiness', without involving the fallacy in question. For now it is obvious that the definition of right as conducive to general happiness can be used by him in support of the fundamental principle that general happiness is the right end; instead of being itself derived from that principle. If right, by definition, means conducive to general happiness, then it is obvious that general happiness is the right end. It is not necessary now first to prove or assert that general happiness is the right end, before right is defined as conducive to general happiness – a perfectly valid procedure; but on the contrary the definition of right as conducive to general happiness proves general happiness to be the right end – a perfectly invalid procedure, since in this case the statement that 'general happiness is the right end of human action' is not an ethical principle at all, but either, as we have seen, a proposition about the meaning of words, or else a proposition about the *nature* of general happiness, not about its rightness or goodness.

Now, I do not wish the importance I assign to this fallacy to be misunderstood. The discovery of it does not at all refute Bentham's contention that greatest happiness is the proper end of human action, if that be understood as an ethical proposition, as he undoubtedly intended it. That principle may be true all the same; we shall consider whether it is so in succeeding chapters. Bentham might have maintained it, as Professor Sidgwick does, even if the fallacy had been pointed out to him. What I am maintaining is that the *reasons* which he actually gives for his ethical proposition are fallacious ones so far as they consist in a definition of right. What I suggest is that he did not perceive them to be fallacious; that, if he had done so, he would have been led to seek for other reasons in support of his Utilitarianism; and that, had he sought for other reasons, he *might* have found none which he thought to be sufficient. In that case he would have changed his whole system – a most important consequence. It is undoubtedly also possible that he would have thought other reasons to be sufficient, and in that case his ethical system, in its main results, would still have stood. But, even in this latter case, his use of the fallacy would be a serious objection to him as an ethical philosopher. For it is the business of ethics, I must insist, not only to obtain true results, but also to find valid reasons for them. The direct object of ethics is knowledge and not practice; and any one who uses the naturalistic fallacy has certainly not fulfilled this first object, however correct his practical principles may be.

My objections to Naturalism are then, in the first place, that it offers no reason at all, far less any valid reason, for any ethical principle whatever;

and in this it already fails to satisfy the requirements of ethics, as a scientific study. But in the second place I contend that, though it gives a reason for no ethical principle, it is a *cause* of the acceptance of false principles – it deludes the mind into accepting ethical principles, which are false; and in this it is contrary to every aim of ethics. It is easy to see that if we start with a definition of right conduct as conduct conducive to general happiness; then, knowing that right conduct is universally conduct conducive to the good, we very easily arrive at the result that the good is general happiness. If, on the other hand, we once recognize that we must start our ethics without a definition, we shall be much more apt to look about us, before we adopt any ethical principle whatever; and the more we look about us, the less likely are we to adopt a false one. It may be replied to this: Yes, but we shall look about us just as much, before we settle on our definition, and are therefore just as likely to be right. But I will try to shew that this is not the case. If we start with the conviction that a definition of good can be found, we start with the conviction that good *can mean* nothing else than some one property of things; and our only business will then be to discover what that property is. But if we recognize that, so far as the meaning of good goes, anything whatever may be good, we start with a much more open mind. Moreover, apart from the fact that, when we think we have a definition, we cannot logically defend our ethical principles in any way whatever, we shall also be much less apt to defend them well, even if illogically. For we shall start with the conviction that good must mean so and so, and shall therefore be inclined either to misunderstand our opponent's arguments or to cut them short with the reply, 'This is not an open question: the very meaning of the word decides it; no one can think otherwise except through confusion.'

(**15**) Our first conclusion as to the subject-matter of ethics is, then, that there is a simple, indefinable, unanalysable object of thought by reference to which it must be defined. By what name we call this unique object is a matter of indifference, so long as we clearly recognize what it is and that it does differ from other objects. The words which are commonly taken as the signs of ethical judgements all do refer to it; and they are expressions of ethical judgements solely because they do so refer. . . .

Notes

1 *Methods of Ethics*, London: Macmillan, 1962, book I, chapter iii, §1.
2 Ibid., book I, chapter iv, §1.

From W. D. Ross, *The Right and the Good*. Oxford: Clarendon Press, 1930, pp. 16–24, 28–37 [some notes and passages omitted]; reprinted by permission of Oxford University Press.

In my preamble to the previous chapter, I noted that G. E. Moore's immediate influence was upon some philosophically conservative moral philosophers, who were, in effect, rehabilitating the ethical intuitionism of such eighteenth-century writers as Richard Price, author of *A Review of the Principal Questions in Morals*.[1] The most prominent of these later intuitionists were the Oxford philosophers H. A. Prichard and W. D. (later Sir David) Ross. A more precise label for them would be 'deontological intuitionists': for while they agreed with Moore that good was an intuitable property, they rejected his view that deontological (from the Greek word meaning 'what is binding') concepts, such as 'right', 'duty' and 'obligation', could be reduced to, or understood in terms of, the notion of good. For both men, the right or obligatory is itself intuited or 'apprehended', and independently of any good that right action might produce. Consciously aping Moore's claim that 'good is good, and that is the end of the matter', Prichard held that no reasons can be given for why some action is right or obligatory, since its rightness is 'apprehended directly by an act of moral thinking'. Moral philosophy, if its aim is to search for such reasons, simply 'rests on a mistake'.[2]

Ross has been described as a 'less fanatical' intuitionist than Prichard, and this is because of a crucial amendment in the direction of common sense that he makes, in chapter 2 of *The Right and the Good* (1930), to his predecessor's position. An obvious objection to Prichard is that we do *not*, at all generally, just 'see' what our duty in some situation is. If we did, we would hardly confront the moral dilemmas we often do. Ross accommodates this objection by claiming that what a person directly apprehends is not that a certain action is

[1] Oxford: Oxford University Press, 1948.
[2] See Prichard's 'Does moral philosophy rest on a mistake?' (1912), in his *Moral Obligation*, Oxford: Oxford University Press, 1949.

actually a duty, but that performing it is a prima facie duty in virtue, say, of its being the repayment of a debt. That this action is prima facie obligatory is perfectly compatible with it also being prima facie non-obligatory: for it may at the same time be an action which involves breaking a promise or causing harm to an undeserving victim. A prima facie duty is explained as one that *would* be an actual duty, a 'duty *sans phrase*', in the absence of competing considerations (p. 250 below). Whereas our prima facie duties can be known for certain, verdicts as to our actual duties, where prima facie considerations collide, can only be a matter of 'probable judgement'.

Despite Ross's important concession to commonsense, he has come in for many criticisms. Some of these miss their mark. It is not, for example, Ross's view that one has only to hear a moral principle stated to 'see' its truth. For him, what we apprehend, in the first instance, is not the truth of principles, but the prima facie obligatoriness of particular actions. Another criticism, levelled against the whole idea of objective moral properties, will occupy us in chapter 17. A third criticism, predictable in the present climate, is that even the prima facie obligatoriness of actions is hardly the self-evident matter Ross assumes. It might be argued, for instance, that the duty to repay debts only exists in debt-incurring societies whose moral basis is questionable. More harshly, it has been held that Ross's ethics breathes a complacent, ivory tower confidence in a universal moral sense that was already seeming antediluvian by 1930.

Despite such criticisms, Ross is today enjoying renewed attention, partly because of his sharp arguments – several of which occur in the following pages – against utilitarian and teleological conceptions of right and duty. But his notion of prima facie duties is also frequently invoked as an antidote to the 'universalizability thesis', associated with R. M. Hare, that an action is right if and only if it falls under some exceptionless moral principle. This has not prevented the so-called 'particularist' critics of Hare from arguing that Ross is also too much of a 'generalist'. Not only, they argue, are there no features, such as being the keeping of a promise, which always make an action actually right, there are no features which always make it prima facie right. In some circumstances – those of a parlour-game in which breaking one's word is a crucial ingredient, say – the failure to keep one's word may be either morally irrelevant or even morally required.[3] Ross's views will surely continue to be discussed as long as this unresolved dispute between 'particularists' and 'generalists' continues.

[3] For R. M. Hare, see his *Freedom and Reason*, Oxford: Oxford University Press, 1963. For the 'particularist' criticism, see Jonathan Dancy, *Moral Reasons*, Oxford: Blackwell, 1993, chapters 5–6.

▶ ▶ ▶ **Chapter 2: What Makes Right Acts Right?**

The real point at issue between hedonism and utilitarianism on the one hand and their opponents on the other is not whether 'right' means 'productive of so and so'; for it cannot with any plausibility be maintained that it does. The point at issue is that to which we now pass, viz. whether there is any general character which makes right acts right, and if so, what it is. Among the main historical attempts to state a single characteristic of all right actions which is the foundation of their rightness are those made by egoism and utilitarianism. But I do not propose to discuss these, not because the subject is unimportant, but because it has been dealt with so often and so well already, and because there has come to be so much agreement among moral philosophers that neither of these theories is satisfactory. A much more attractive theory has been put forward by Professor Moore: that what makes actions right is that they are productive of more *good* than could have been produced by any other action open to the agent.[1]

This theory is in fact the culmination of all the attempts to base rightness on productivity of some sort of result. The first form this attempt takes is the attempt to base rightness on conduciveness to the advantage or pleasure of the agent. This theory comes to grief over the fact, which stares us in the face, that a great part of duty consists in an observance of the rights and a furtherance of the interests of others, whatever the cost to ourselves may be. Plato and others may be right in holding that a regard for the rights of others never in the long run involves a loss of happiness for the agent, that 'the just life profits a man'. But this, even if true, is irrelevant to the rightness of the act. As soon as a man does an action *because* he thinks he will promote his own interests thereby, he is acting not from a sense of its rightness but from self-interest.

To the egoistic theory hedonistic utilitarianism supplies a much-needed amendment. It points out correctly that the fact that a certain pleasure will be enjoyed by the agent is no reason why he *ought* to bring it into being rather than an equal or greater pleasure to be enjoyed by another, though, human nature being what it is, it makes it not unlikely that he *will* try to bring it into being. But hedonistic utilitarianism in its turn needs a correction. On reflection it seems clear that pleasure is not the only thing in life that we think good in itself, that for instance we think the possession of a good character, or an intelligent understanding of the world, as good or better. A great advance is made by the substitution of 'productive of the greatest good' for 'productive of the greatest pleasure'.

Not only is this theory more attractive than hedonistic utilitarianism, but its logical relation to that theory is such that the latter could not be true unless *it* were true, while it might be true though hedonistic utilitarianism were not. It is in fact one of the logical bases of hedonistic utilitarianism. For the view that what produces the maximum pleasure is right has for its bases the views (1) that what produces the maximum good is right, and (2) that pleasure is the only thing good in itself. If they were not assuming that what produces the maximum *good* is right, the utilitarians' attempt to show that pleasure is the only thing good in itself, which is in fact the point they take most pains to establish, would have been quite irrelevant to their attempt to prove that only what produces the maximum *pleasure* is right. If, therefore, it can be shown that productivity of the maximum good is not what makes all right actions right, we shall *a fortiori* have refuted hedonistic utilitarianism.

When a plain man fulfils a promise because he thinks he ought to do so, it seems clear that he does so with no thought of its total consequences, still less with any opinion that these are likely to be the best possible. He thinks in fact much more of the past than of the future. What makes him think it right to act in a certain way is the fact that he has promised to do so – that and, usually, nothing more. That his act will produce the best possible consequences is not his reason for calling it right. What lends colour to the theory we are examining, then, is not the actions (which form probably a great majority of our actions) in which some such reflection as 'I have promised' is the only reason we give ourselves for thinking a certain action right, but the exceptional cases in which the consequences of fulfilling a promise (for instance) would be so disastrous to others that we judge it right not to do so. It must of course be admitted that such cases exist. If I have promised to meet a friend at a particular time for some trivial purpose, I should certainly think myself justified in breaking my engagement if by doing so I could prevent a serious accident or bring relief to the victims of one. And the supporters of the view we are examining hold that my thinking so is due to my thinking that I shall bring more good into existence by the one action than by the other. A different account may, however, be given of the matter, an account which will, I believe, show itself to be the true one. It may be said that besides the duty of fulfilling promises I have and recognize a duty of relieving distress, and that when I think it right to do the latter at the cost of not doing the former, it is not because I think I shall produce more good thereby but because I think it the duty which is in the circumstances more of a duty. This account surely corresponds much more closely with what we really think in such a situation. If, so far as I can see, I could bring equal amounts of good into being by fulfilling my promise and by helping some one to whom I had made no promise, I should not hesitate to regard the former as my duty. Yet on the view that what is right is right because it is productive of the most good I should not so regard it.

There are two theories, each in its way simple, that offer a solution of such cases of conscience. One is the view of Kant, that there are certain duties of perfect obligation, such as those of fulfilling promises, of paying debts, of telling the truth, which admit of no exception whatever in favour of duties of imperfect obligation, such as that of relieving distress. The other is the view of, for instance, Professor Moore and Dr [Hastings] Rashdall, that there is only the duty of producing good, and that all 'conflicts of duties' should be resolved by asking 'by which action will most good be produced?' But it is more important that our theory fit the facts than that it be simple, and the account we have given above corresponds (it seems to me) better than either of the simpler theories with what we really think, viz. that normally promise-keeping, for example, should come before benevolence, but that when and only when the good to be produced by the benevolent act is very great and the promise comparatively trivial, the act of benevolence becomes our duty.

In fact the theory of 'ideal utilitarianism',[2] if I may for brevity refer so to the theory of Professor Moore, seems to simplify unduly our relations to our fellows. It says, in effect, that the only morally significant relation in which my neighbours stand to me is that of being possible beneficiaries by my action.* They do stand in this relation to me, and this relation is morally significant. But they may also stand to me in the relation of promisee to promiser, of creditor to debtor, of wife to husband, of child to parent, of friend to friend, of fellow countryman to fellow countryman, and the like; and each of these relations is the foundation of a prima facie duty, which is more or less incumbent on me according to the circumstances of the case. When I am in a situation, as perhaps I always am, in which more than one of these prima facie duties is incumbent on me, what I have to do is to study the situation as fully as I can until I form the considered opinion (it is never more) that in the circumstances one of them is more incumbent than any other; then I am bound to think that to do this prima facie duty is my duty *sans phrase* in the situation.

I suggest 'prima facie duty' or 'conditional duty' as a brief way of referring to the characteristic (quite distinct from that of being a duty proper) which an act has, in virtue of being of a certain kind (e.g. the keeping of a promise), of being an act which would be a duty proper if it were not at the

---

* Some will think it, apart from other considerations, a sufficient refutation of this view to point out that I also stand in that relation to myself, so that for this view the distinction of oneself from others is morally insignificant.

same time of another kind which is morally significant. Whether an act is a duty proper or actual duty depends on *all* the morally significant kinds it is an instance of. The phrase 'prima facie duty' must be apologized for, since (1) it suggests that what we are speaking of is a certain kind of duty, whereas it is in fact not a duty, but something related in a special way to duty. Strictly speaking, we want not a phrase in which duty is qualified by an adjective, but a separate noun. (2) 'Prima' facie suggests that one is speaking only of an appearance which a moral situation presents at first sight, and which may turn out to be illusory; whereas what I am speaking of is an objective fact involved in the nature of the situation, or more strictly in an element of its nature, though not, as duty proper does, arising from its *whole* nature. I can, however, think of no term which fully meets the case. . . .

There is nothing arbitrary about these prima facie duties. Each rests on a definite circumstance which cannot seriously be held to be without moral significance. Of prima facie duties I suggest, without claiming completeness or finality for it, the following division.*

(1) Some duties rest on previous acts of my own. These duties seem to include two kinds, (*a*) those resting on a promise or what may fairly be called an implicit promise, such as the implicit undertaking not to tell lies which seems to be implied in the act of entering into conversation (at any rate by civilized men), or of writing books that purport to be history and not fiction. These may be called the duties of fidelity. (*b*) Those resting on a previous wrongful act. These may be called the duties of reparation. (2) Some rest on previous acts of other men, i.e. services done by them to me. These may be loosely described as the duties of gratitude. (3) Some rest on the fact or possibility of a distribution of pleasure or happiness (or of the means thereto) which is not in accordance with the merit of the persons concerned; in such cases there arises a duty to upset or prevent such a distribution. These are the duties of justice. (4) Some rest on the mere fact that there are other beings in the world whose condition we can make better in respect of virtue, or of intelligence, or of pleasure. These are the

---

* I should make it plain at this stage that I am *assuming* the correctness of some of our main convictions as to prima facie duties, or, more strictly, am claiming that we *know* them to be true. To me it seems as self-evident as anything could be, that to make a promise, for instance, is to create a moral claim on us in someone else. Many readers will perhaps say that they do *not* know this to be true. If so, I certainly cannot prove it to them; I can only ask them to reflect again, in the hope that they will ultimately agree that they also know it to be true. The main moral convictions of the plain man seem to me to be, not opinions which it is for philosophy to prove or disprove, but knowledge from the start; and in my own case I seem to find little difficulty in distinguishing these essential convictions from other moral convictions which I also have, which are merely fallible opinions based on an imperfect study of the working for good or evil of certain institutions or types of action.

duties of beneficence. (5) Some rest on the fact that we can improve our own condition in respect of virtue or of intelligence. These are the duties of self-improvement. (6) I think that we should distinguish from (4) the duties that may be summed up under the title of 'not injuring others'. No doubt to injure others is incidentally to fail to do them good; but it seems to me clear that non-maleficence is apprehended as a duty distinct from that of beneficence, and as a duty of a more stringent character. It will be noticed that this alone among the types of duty has been stated in a negative way. An attempt might no doubt be made to state this duty, like the others, in a positive way. It might be said that it is really the duty to prevent ourselves from acting either from an inclination to harm others or from an inclination to seek our own pleasure, in doing which we should incidentally harm them. But on reflection it seems clear that the primary duty here is the duty not to harm others, this being a duty whether or not we have an inclination that if followed would lead to our harming them; and that when we have such an inclination the primary duty not to harm others gives rise to a consequential duty to resist the inclination. The recognition of this duty of non-maleficence is the first step on the way to the recognition of the duty of beneficence; and that accounts for the prominence of the commands 'thou shalt not kill', 'thou shalt not commit adultery', 'thou shalt not steal', 'thou shalt not bear false witness', in so early a code as the Decalogue. But even when we have come to recognize the duty of beneficence, it appears to me that the duty of non-maleficence is recognized as a distinct one, and as prima facie more binding. We should not in general consider it justifiable to kill one person in order to keep another alive, or to steal from one in order to give alms to another.

The essential defect of the 'ideal utilitarian' theory is that it ignores, or at least does not do full justice to, the highly personal character of duty. If the only duty is to produce the maximum of good, the question who is to have the good – whether it is myself, or my benefactor, or a person to whom I have made a promise to confer that good on him, or a mere fellow man to whom I stand in no such special relation – should make no difference to my having a duty to produce that good. But we are all in fact sure that it makes a vast difference.

One or two other comments must be made on this provisional list of the divisions of duty. (1) The nomenclature is not strictly correct. For by 'fidelity' or 'gratitude' we mean, strictly, certain states of motivation; and, as I have urged, it is not our duty to have certain motives, but to do certain acts. By 'fidelity', for instance, is meant, strictly, the disposition to fulfil promises and implicit promises *because we have made them*. We have no general word to cover the actual fulfilment of promises and implicit promises *irrespective of motive*; and I use 'fidelity', loosely but perhaps conveniently, to fill this gap. So too I use 'gratitude' for the returning of services, irrespective of motive. The term 'justice' is not so much confined, in ordinary usage, to a certain state of motivation, for we should often talk of a man as acting justly even when we did not think his motive was the wish to do what was just simply for the sake of doing so. Less apology is therefore needed for our use of 'justice' in this sense. And I have used the word 'beneficence' rather than 'benevolence', in order to emphasize the fact that it is our duty to do certain things, and not to do them from certain motives.

(2) If the objection be made, that this catalogue of the main types of duty is an unsystematic one resting on no logical principle, it may be replied, first, that it makes no claim to being ultimate. It is a prima facie classification of the duties which reflection on our moral convictions seems actually to reveal. And if these convictions are, as I would claim that they are, of the nature of knowledge, and if I have not misstated them, the list will be a list of authentic conditional duties, correct as far as it goes though not necessarily complete. The list of *goods* put forward by the rival theory is reached by exactly the same method – the only sound one in the circumstances – viz. that of direct reflection on what we really think. Loyalty to the facts is worth more than a symmetrical architectonic or a hastily reached simplicity. If further reflection discovers a perfect logical basis for this or for a better classification, so much the better.

(3) It may, again, be objected that our theory that there are these various and often conflicting types of prima facie duty leaves us with no principle upon which to discern what is our actual duty in particular circumstances. But this objection is not one which the rival theory is in a position to bring forward. For when we have to choose between the production of two heterogeneous goods, say knowledge and pleasure, the 'ideal utilitarian' theory can only fall back on an opinion, for which no logical basis can be offered, that one of the goods is the greater; and this is no better than a similar opinion that one of two duties is the more urgent. And again, when we consider the infinite variety of the effects of our actions in the way of pleasure, it must surely be admitted that the claim which *hedonism* sometimes makes, that it offers a readily applicable criterion of right conduct, is quite illusory.

I am unwilling, however, to content myself with an *argumentum ad hominem*, and I would contend that in principle there is no reason to anticipate that every act that is our duty is so for one and the same reason. Why should two sets of circumstances, or one set of circumstances, *not* possess different characteristics, any one of which makes a certain act our prima facie duty? When I ask what it is that makes me in certain cases sure that I have a prima facie duty to do so and so, I find that it lies in the fact that I have made a promise; when I ask the same question in another case, I find the answer lies in the fact that I have done a wrong. And if on reflection I find (as I think I do) that neither of these reasons is reducible to the other, I must not on any a priori ground assume that such a reduction is possible. . . .

It is necessary to say something by way of clearing up the relation between prima facie duties and the actual or absolute duty to do one particular act in particular circumstances. If, as almost all moralists except Kant are agreed, and as most plain men think, it is sometimes right to tell a lie or to break a promise, it must be maintained that there is a difference between prima facie duty and actual or absolute duty. When we think ourselves justified in breaking, and indeed morally obliged to break, a promise in order to relieve someone's distress, we do not for a moment cease to recognize a prima facie duty to keep our promise, and this leads us to feel, not indeed shame or repentance, but certainly compunction, for behaving as we do; we recognize, further, that it is our duty to make up somehow to the promisee for the breaking of the promise. We have to distinguish from the characteristic of being our duty that of tending to be our duty. Any act that we do contains various elements in virtue of which it falls under various categories. In virtue of being the breaking of a promise, for instance, it tends to be wrong; in virtue of being an instance of relieving distress it tends to be right. Tendency to be one's duty may be called a parti-resultant attribute, i.e. one which belongs to an act in virtue of some one component in its nature. *Being* one's duty is a toti-resultant attribute, one which belongs to an act in virtue of its whole nature and of nothing less than this.

Another instance of the same distinction may be found in the operation of natural laws. *Qua* subject to the force of gravitation towards some other body, each body tends to move in a particular direction with a particular velocity; but its actual movement depends on *all* the forces to which it is subject. It is only by recognizing this distinction that we can preserve the absoluteness of laws of nature, and only by recognizing a corresponding distinction that we can preserve the absoluteness of the general principles of morality. But an important difference between the two cases must be pointed out. When we say that in virtue of gravitation a body tends to move in a certain way, we are referring to a causal influence actually exercised on it by another body or other bodies. When we say that in virtue of being deliberately untrue a certain remark tends to be wrong, we are referring to no causal relation, to no relation that involves succession in time, but to such a relation as connects the various attributes of a mathematical figure. And if the word 'tendency' is thought to suggest too much a causal relation, it is better to talk of certain types of act as being prima facie right or wrong (or of different persons as having different and possibly conflicting claims upon us), than of their tending to be right or wrong.

Something should be said of the relation between our apprehension of the prima facie rightness of certain types of act and our mental attitude towards particular acts. It is proper to use the word 'apprehension' in the former case and not in the latter. That an act, *qua* fulfilling a promise, or *qua* effecting a just distribution of good, or *qua* returning services rendered, or *qua* promoting the good of others, or *qua* promoting the virtue or insight of the agent, is prima facie right, is self-evident; not in the sense that it is evident from the beginning of our lives, or as soon as we attend to the proposition for the first time, but in the sense that when we have reached sufficient mental maturity and have given sufficient attention to the proposition it is evident without any need of proof, or of evidence beyond itself. It is self-evident just as a mathematical axiom, or the validity of a form of inference, is evident. The moral order expressed in these propositions is just as much part of the fundamental nature of the universe (and, we may add, of any possible universe in which there were moral agents at all) as is the spatial or numerical structure expressed in the axioms of geometry or arithmetic. In our confidence that these propositions are true there is involved the same trust in our reason that is involved in our confidence in mathematics; and we should have no justification for trusting it in the latter sphere and distrusting it in the former. In both cases we are dealing with propositions that cannot be proved, but that just as certainly need no proof.

Some of these general principles of prima facie duty may appear to be open to criticism. It may be thought, for example, that the principle of returning good for good is a falling off from the Christian principle, generally and rightly recognized as expressing the highest morality, of returning good for evil. To this it may be replied that I do not suggest that there is a principle commanding us to return good for good and forbidding us to return good for evil, and that I do suggest that there is a positive duty to seek the good of all men. What I maintain is that an act in which good is returned for good is recognized as *specially* binding on us just because it is of that character, and that *ceteris paribus* any one would think it his duty to help his benefactors rather than his enemies, if he could not do both; just as it is generally recognized that *ceteris paribus* we should pay our debts rather than give our money in charity, when we cannot do both. A benefactor is not only a man, calling for our effort on his behalf on that ground, but also our benefactor, calling for our *special* effort on *that* ground.

Our judgements about our actual duty in concrete situations have none of the certainty that attaches to our recognition of the general principles of duty. A statement is certain, i.e. is an expression of knowledge, only in one or other of two cases: when it is either self-evident, or a valid conclusion from self-evident premises. And our judgements about our particular duties have neither of these characters. (1) They are not self-evident. Where a possible act is seen to have two characteristics, in virtue of one of which it is prima facie right, and in virtue of the other prima facie wrong, we are (I think) well aware that we are not certain whether we ought or ought not to do it; that whether we do it or not, we are taking a moral risk. We come in the long run, after consideration, to think one duty more pressing than the other, but we do not feel certain that it is so. And though we do not always recognize that a possible act has two such characteristics, and though there *may* be cases in which it has not, we are never certain that any particular possible act has not, and therefore never certain that it is right, nor certain that it is wrong. For, to go no further in the analysis, it is enough to point out that any particular act will in all probability in the course of time contribute to the bringing about of good or of evil for many human beings, and thus have a prima facie rightness or wrongness of which we know nothing. (2) Again, our judgements about our particular duties are not logical conclusions from self-evident premises. The only possible premises would be the general principles stating their prima facie rightness or wrongness *qua* having the different characteristics they do have; and even if we could (as we cannot) apprehend the extent to which an act will tend on the one hand, for example, to bring about advantages for our benefactors, and on the other hand to bring about disadvantages for fellow men who are not our benefactors, there is no principle by which we can draw the conclusion that it is on the whole right or on the whole wrong. In this respect the judgement as to the rightness of a particular act is just like the judgement as to the beauty of a particular natural object or work of art. A poem is, for instance, in respect of certain qualities beautiful and in respect of certain others not beautiful; and our judgement as to the degree of beauty it possesses on the whole is never reached by logical reasoning from the apprehension of its particular beauties or particular defects. Both in this and in the moral case we have more or less probable opinions which are not logically justified conclusions from the general principles that are recognized as self-evident.

There is therefore much truth in the description of the right act as a fortunate act. If we cannot be certain that it is right, it is our good fortune if the act we do is the right act. This consideration does not, however, make the doing of our duty a mere matter of chance. There is a parallel here between the doing of duty and the doing of what will be to our personal advantage. We never *know* what act will in the long run be to our advantage. Yet it is certain that we are more likely in general to secure our advantage if we estimate to the best of our ability the probable tendencies of our actions in this respect, than if we act on caprice. And similarly we are more likely to do our duty if we reflect to the best of our ability on the prima facie rightness or wrongness of various possible acts in virtue of the characteristics we perceive them to have, than if we act without reflection. With this greater likelihood we must be content.

Many people would be inclined to say that the right act for me is not that whose general nature I have been describing, viz. that which if I were omniscient I should see to be my duty, but that which on all the evidence available to me I should think to be my duty. But suppose that from the state of partial knowledge in which I think act *A* to be my duty, I could pass to a state of perfect knowledge in which I saw act *B* to be my duty, should I not say 'act *B* was the right act for me to do'? I should no doubt add 'though I am not to be blamed for doing act *A*'. But in adding this, am I not passing from the question 'what is right' to the question 'what is morally good'? At the same time I am not making the *full* passage from the one notion to the other; for in order that the act should be morally good, or an act I am not to be blamed for doing, it must not merely be the act which it is reasonable for me to think my duty; it must also be done for that reason, or from some other morally good motive. Thus the conception of the right act as the act which it is reasonable for me to think my duty is an unsatisfactory compromise between the true notion of the right act and the notion of the morally good action.

The general principles of duty are obviously not self-evident from the beginning of our lives. How do they come to be so? The answer is, that they come to be self-evident to us just as mathematical axioms do. We find by experience that this couple of matches and that couple make four matches, that this couple of balls on a wire and that couple make four balls: and by reflection on these and similar discoveries we come to see that it is of the nature of two and two to make four. In a precisely similar way, we see the prima facie rightness of an act which would be the fulfilment of a particular promise, and of another which would be the fulfilment of another promise, and when we have reached sufficient maturity to think in general terms, we apprehend prima facie rightness to belong to the nature of any fulfilment of promise. What comes first in time is the apprehension of the self-evident prima facie rightness of an individual act of a particular type. From this we come by reflection to apprehend the self-evident general principle of prima facie duty. From this, too, perhaps along with the apprehension of the self-evident prima facie rightness of the same act in virtue of its having another characteristic as well, and perhaps in spite of the apprehension of its prima facie wrongness in virtue of its having some third characteristic, we come to believe something not self-evident at all, but an object of probable opinion, viz. that this particular act is (not prima facie but) actually right.

In this respect there is an important difference between rightness and mathematical properties. A triangle which is isosceles necessarily has two of its angles equal, whatever other characteristics the triangle may have – whatever, for instance, be its area, or the size of its third angle. The equality of the two angles is a parti-resultant attribute. And the same is true of all mathematical attributes. It is true, I may add, of prima facie rightness. But no act is ever, in virtue of falling under some general description, necessarily actually right; its rightness depends on its whole nature and not on any element in it. The reason is that no mathematical object (no figure, for instance, or angle) ever has two characteristics that tend to give it opposite resultant characteristics, while moral acts often (as every one knows) and indeed always (as on reflection we must admit) have different characteristics that tend to make them at the same time prima facie right and prima facie wrong; there is probably no act, for instance, which does good to any one without doing harm to some one else, and vice versa.

Supposing it to be agreed, as I think on reflection it must, that no one *means* by 'right' just 'productive of the best possible consequences', or 'optimific', the attributes 'right' and 'optimific' might stand in either of two kinds of relation to each other. (1) They might be so related that we could apprehend a priori, either immediately or deductively, that any act that is optimific is right and any act that is right is optimific, as we can apprehend that any triangle that is equilateral is equiangular and vice versa. Professor Moore's view is, I think, that the coextensiveness of 'right' and 'optimific' is apprehended immediately. He rejects the possibility of any proof of it. Or (2) the two attributes might be such that the question whether they are invariably connected had to be answered by means of an inductive inquiry. Now at first sight it might seem as if the constant connection of the two attributes could be immediately apprehended. It might seem absurd to suggest that it could be right for any one to do an act which would produce consequences less good than those which would be produced by some other act in his power. Yet a little thought will convince us that this is not absurd. The type of case in which it is easiest to see that this is so is, perhaps, that in which one has made a promise. In such a case we all think that prima facie it is our duty to fulfil the promise irrespective of the precise goodness of the total consequences. And though we do not think it is necessarily our actual or absolute duty to do so, we are far from thinking that any, even the slightest, gain in the value of the total consequences will necessarily justify us in doing something else instead. Suppose, to simplify the case by abstraction, that the fulfilment of a promise to *A* would produce 1000 units of good for him, but that by doing some other act I could produce 1001 units of good for *B*, to whom I have made no promise, the other consequences of the two acts being of equal value; should we really think it self-evident that it was our duty to do the second act and not the first? I think not. We should, I fancy, hold that only a much greater disparity of value between the total consequences would justify us in failing to discharge our prima facie duty to *A*. After all, a promise is a promise, and is not to be treated so lightly as the theory we are examining would imply. What, exactly, a promise is, is not so easy to determine, but we are surely agreed that it constitutes a serious moral limitation to our freedom of action. To produce the 1001 units of good for *B* rather than fulfil our promise to *A* would be to take, not perhaps our duty as philanthropists too seriously, but certainly our duty as makers of promises too lightly.

Or consider another phase of the same problem. If I have promised to confer on *A* a particular benefit containing 1000 units of good, is it self-evident that if by doing some different act I could produce 1001 units of good for *A* himself (the other consequences of the two acts being supposed equal in value), it would be right for me to do so? Again, I think not. Apart from my general prima facie duty to do *A* what good I can, I have another prima facie duty to do him the particular service I have promised to do him, and this is not to be set aside in consequence of a disparity of good of the order of 1001 to 1000, though a much greater disparity might justify me in so doing.

Or again, suppose that *A* is a very good and *B* a very bad man, should I then, even when I have made no promise, think it self-evidently right to produce 1001 units of good for *B* rather than 1000 for *A*? Surely not. I should be sensible of a prima facie duty of justice, i.e. of producing a distribution of goods in proportion to merit, which is not outweighed by such a slight disparity in the total goods to be produced.

Such instances – and they might easily be added to – make it clear that there is no self-evident connection between the attributes 'right' and 'optimific'. The theory we are examining has a certain attractiveness when applied to our decision that a particular act is our duty (though I have tried to show that it does not agree with our actual moral judgements even here). But it is not even plausible when applied to our recognition of prima facie duty. For if it were self-evident that the right coincides with the optimific, it should be self-evident that what is prima facie right is prima facie optimific. But whereas we are certain that keeping a promise is prima facie right, we are not certain that it is prima facie optimific (though we are perhaps certain that it is prima facie bonific). Our certainty that it is prima facie right depends not on its consequences but on its being the fulfilment of a promise. The theory we are examining involves too much difference between the evident ground of our conviction about prima facie duty and the alleged ground of our conviction about actual duty.

The coextensiveness of the right and the optimific is, then, not self-evident. And I can see no way of proving it deductively; nor, so far as I know, has any one tried to do so. There remains the question whether it can be established inductively. Such an inquiry, to be conclusive, would have to be very thorough and extensive. We should have to take a large variety of the acts which we, to the best of our ability, judge to be right. We should have to trace as far as possible their consequences, not only for the persons directly affected but also for those indirectly affected, and to these no limit can be set. To make our inquiry thoroughly conclusive, we should have to do what we cannot do, viz. trace these consequences into an un-ending future. And even to make it reasonably conclusive, we should have to trace them far into the future. It is clear that the most we could possibly say is that a large variety of typical acts that are judged right appear, so far as we can trace their consequences, to produce more good than any other acts possible to the agents in the circumstances. And such a result falls far short of proving the constant connection of the two attributes. But it is surely clear that no inductive inquiry justifying even this result has ever been carried through. The advocates of utilitarian systems have been so much persuaded either of the identity or of the self-evident connection of the attributes 'right' and 'optimific' (or 'felicific') that they have not at-tempted even such an inductive inquiry as is possible. And in view of the enormous complexity of the task and the inevitable inconclusiveness of the result, it is worth no one's while to make the attempt. What, after all, would be gained by it? If, as I have tried to show, for an act to be right and to be optimific are not the same thing, and an act's being optimific is not even the ground of its being right, then if we could ask ourselves (though the question is really unmeaning) which we ought to do, right acts because they are right or optimific acts because they are optimific, our answer must be 'the former'. If they are optimific as well as right, that is interesting but not morally important; if not, we still ought to do them (which is only another way of saying that they *are* the right acts), and the question whether they are optimific has no importance for moral theory. . . .

Notes

1 The views of Moore on which Ross focuses are less those of *Principia Ethica* than the later (1912) *Ethics*, London: Oxford University Press, 1966.
2 The point of this term – which, despite being liable to mislead, has caught on – is that Moore's position shares with utilitarianism the idea that actions are right only in so far as they contribute to some good, while differing from classical utilitarianism in conceiving this good, not in terms of pleasure, but of certain 'ideals', like beauty.

17 Charles L. Stevenson, 'The Emotive Meaning of Ethical Terms'

From Charles L. Stevenson, *Facts and Values: Studies in Ethical Analysis.* New Haven: Yale University Press, 1963, pp. 10–31 [asterisked notes are Stevenson's; some notes omitted or shortened]; reproduced by permission of the publisher.

Both in English-language and 'continental' circles, the salient feature of twentieth-century moral philosophy since around 1930 has been the dominance of 'noncognitivist' theories. Whatever it is that moral judgements do – express emotions, register commitments, prescribe actions, or whatever – they do not, on these theories, state beliefs about reality. In the case of 'continental' trends, such as Existentialism, inspiration came from Kierkegaard and Nietzsche, with their emphases on the primacy of the will and the seedy genealogy of conventional moral norms. In English-language philosophy, 'noncognitivism' owed to a combination of G. E. Moore's exposure of the 'naturalistic fallacy' and later reflections, by thinkers far removed from Moore, on the nature of meaning. The dry character of much of the writing should not disguise the radical nature of the message. Time will doubtless tell whether, as one recent author sees it, the 'noncognitivist' 'den[ial] that anything is really worth struggling for, in the sense of "really" in which two and two really make four', poses one of those 'risks' which may hasten 'the end of the world'.[1] But that such views of twentieth-century ethics can be seriously held is itself testimony to its dominant and disturbing tone.

The Logical Positivists and others in the 1920s and 1930s agreed with Moore and Ross that moral judgements are not empirical statements, about what contributes to happiness, say. For them, however, the 'non-natural' properties to which Moore took moral terms to refer belong to metaphysical mythology. Indeed, if, as the Positivists held, the only meaningful statements are those which are empirically verifiable or the 'analytic' ones of logic, it followed that

[1] John Leslie, *The End of the World: The Sciences and Ethics of Human Extinction*, London: Routledge, 1996, p.11.

moral judgements are either meaningless or that they are not statements at all. The best-known product of this line of thought was the 'emotivist' – or 'Hurrah-Boo' – view of moral judgements. 'Stealing is bad', say, is 'merely an expression of a certain wish'; it is 'purely "emotive" . . . used to express feeling about certain objects'.[2]

The Positivists' remarks on ethics read as rather casual codas to what really interested them – the theory of meaning. And the same is true of other writers on language, such as Ogden and Richards, who were exploring the 'dynamic' roles which words can play over and above their informative and descriptive ones. It was left to the American philosopher, Charles L. Stevenson (1908–79), carefully to articulate a plausible version of the 'emotive', 'dynamic' meaning of moral language, one sensitive to the various constraints on a proper account of moral meaning. Two of the constraints on which he particularly dwells – ones which, he believes, earlier views have failed to honour – are that such an account must be able to accommodate the fact of genuine moral disagreement, and must do justice to the 'magnetic', action-influencing force of moral terms. His 1937 paper, which I have selected, is a paradigmatic example of much twentieth-century moral philosophizing in the 'analytical' vein. The philosopher's job is not the 'first order' one of proposing moral values, but the 'meta-ethical' one of analysing moral language – something Stevenson does in terms, not primarily of the personal feelings expressed by 'good', 'right', etc., but of the 'persuasive' effect of such words on audiences. Subscribing to Moore's rejection of 'naturalism', yet able to 'find no indefinable property' of goodness, Stevenson is of course following the prevailing 'noncognitivist' line.

A quarter of a century on, Stevenson wrote that 'no one, I suppose, continues to hold this [emotivist] view just as it stands' (*Facts and Values*, p. 79), but the long list he gives of philosophers who subsequently qualified and elaborated it bears witness to the remarkable grip exerted by the wider conviction that moral discourse belongs in a quite different category from that of informative or descriptive discourse.[3] Perhaps, though, this conviction is not so remarkable. For it cannot, of course, be denied how well 'emotivism' and its successors chime with the predilections – born of recent history rather than of the writings of philosophers – of a larger modern culture where it is apparently held, by many people, that morality is a 'personal' matter, one of 'opinion' or 'conviction' – at any rate, not a matter to be settled in the manner of '2 + 2 = 4'.

---

[2] Rudolf Carnap, *Philosophy and Logical Syntax*, London: Kegan Paul, 1935, p. 24; A.J. Ayer, *Language, Truth and Logic*, London: Gollancz, 1967, p. 108.
[3] For a detailed discussion of Stevenson, his precursors and successors, see W. D. Hudson, *Modern Moral Philosophy*, London: Macmillan, 1983.

▷ ▷ ▷ ▷ **The Emotive Meaning of Ethical Terms**

1

Ethical questions first arise in the form 'is so and so good?' or 'is this alternative better than that?' These questions are difficult partly because we don't quite know what we are seeking. We are asking, 'is there a needle in the haystack?' without even knowing just what a needle is. So the first thing to do is to examine the questions themselves. We must try to make them clearer, either by defining the terms in which they are expressed or by any other method that is available.

The present essay is concerned wholly with this preliminary step of making ethical questions clear. In order to help answer the question 'is *X* good?' we must *substitute* for it a question that is free from ambiguity and confusion.

It is obvious that in substituting a clearer question we must not introduce some utterly different kind of question. It won't do (to take an extreme instance of a prevalent fallacy) to substitute for 'is *X* good?' the question 'is *X* pink with yellow trimmings?' and then point out how easy the question really is. This would beg the original question, not help answer it. On the other hand, we must not expect the substituted question to be strictly 'identical' with the original one. The original question may embody hypostatization, anthropomorphism, vagueness, and all the other ills to which our ordinary discourse is subject. If our substituted question is to be clearer it must remove these ills. The questions will be identical only in the sense that a child is identical with the man he later becomes. Hence we must not demand that the substitution strike us, on immediate introspection, as making no change in meaning.

Just how, then, must the substituted question be related to the original? Let us assume (inaccurately) that it must result from replacing 'good' by some set of terms that define it. The question then resolves itself to this: How must the defined meaning of 'good' be related to its original meaning?

I answer that it must be *relevant*. A defined meaning will be called 'relevant' to the original meaning under these circumstances: Those who have understood the definition must be able to say all that they then want to say by using the term in the defined way. They must never have occasion to use the term in the old, unclear sense. (If a person did have to go on using the word in the old sense, then to this extent his meaning would not be clarified and the philosophical task would not be completed.) It frequently happens that a word is used so confusedly and ambiguously that we must give it *several* defined meanings, rather than one. In this case only the whole set of defined meanings will be called 'relevant', and any one of them will be called 'partially relevant'. This is not a rigorous treatment of *relevance*, by any means, but it will serve for the present purposes.

Let us now turn to our particular task – that of giving a relevant definition of 'good'. Let us first examine some of the ways in which others have attempted to do this.

The word 'good' has often been defined in terms of *approval*, or similar psychological attitudes. We may take as typical examples: 'good' means *desired by me* (Hobbes); and 'good' means *approved by most people* (Hume, in effect).* It will be convenient to refer to definitions of this sort as 'interest theories', following R. B. Perry, although neither 'interest' nor 'theory' is used in the most usual way.

Are definitions of this sort relevant?

It is idle to deny their *partial relevance*. The most superficial inquiry will reveal that 'good' is exceedingly ambiguous. To maintain that 'good' is *never* used in Hobbes' sense, and never in Hume's, is only to manifest an insensitivity to the complexities of language. We must recognize, perhaps, not only these senses, but a variety of similar ones, differing both with regard to the kind of interest in question and with regard to the people who are said to have the interest.

But that is a minor matter. The essential question is not whether interest theories are *partially* relevant, but whether they are *wholly* relevant. This is the only point for intelligent dispute. Briefly: Granted that some senses of 'good' may relevantly be defined in terms of interest, is there some *other* sense which is *not* relevantly so defined? We must give this question careful attention. For it is quite possible that when philosophers (and many others) have found the question 'is *X* good?' so difficult, they have been grasping for this *other* sense of 'good' and not any sense relevantly defined in terms of interest. If we insist on defining 'good' in terms of interest, and answer the question when thus interpreted, we may be begging *their* question entirely. Of course this *other* sense of 'good' may not exist, or it may be a complete confusion; but that is what we must discover.

Now many have maintained that interest theores are *far* from being completely relevant. They have argued that such theories neglect the very sense of 'good' that is most typical of ethics. And certainly, their arguments are not without plausibility.

---

* The definition ascribed to Hume is oversimplified, but not, I think, in a way that weakens the force of the observations that I am about to make. Perhaps the same should be said of Hobbes.

Only – what *is* this typical sense of 'good'? The answers have been so vague and so beset with difficulties that one can scarcely determine.

There are certain requirements, however, with which the typical sense has been expected to comply – requirements which appeal strongly to our common sense. It will be helpful to summarize these, showing how they exclude the interest theories:

In the first place, we must be able sensibly to *disagree* about whether something is 'good'. This condition rules out Hobbes' definition. For consider the following argument: 'This is good.' 'That isn't so; it's not good.' As translated by Hobbes, this becomes: 'I desire this.' 'That isn't so, for *I* don't.' The speakers are not contradicting one another, and think they are only because of an elementary confusion in the use of pronouns. The definition, 'good' means *desired by my community*, is also excluded, for how could people from different communities disagree?

In the second place, 'goodness' must have, so to speak, a magnetism. A person who recognizes *X* to be 'good' must *ipso facto* acquire a stronger tendency to act in its favour than he otherwise would have had. This rules out the Humian type of definition. For according to Hume, to recognize that something is 'good' is simply to recognize that the majority approve of it. Clearly a man may see that the majority approve of *X* without having, himself, a stronger tendency to favour it. This requirement excludes any attempt to define 'good' in terms of the interest of people *other* than the speaker.

In the third place, the 'goodness' of anything must not be verifiable solely by use of the scientific method. 'Ethics must not be psychology.' This restriction rules out all of the traditional interest theories without exception. It is so sweeping a restriction that we must examine its plausibility. What are the methodological implications of interest theories which are here rejected?

According to Hobbes' definition a person can prove his ethical judgements with finality by showing that he is not making an introspective error about his desires. According to Hume's definition one may prove ethical judgements (roughly speaking) by taking a vote. *This* use of the empirical method, at any rate, seems highly remote from what we usually accept as proof and reflects on the complete relevance of the definitions that imply it.

But are there not more complicated interest theories that are immune from such methodological implications? No, for the same factors appear; they are only put off for a while. Consider, for example, the definition: '*X* is good' means *most people would approve of 'X' if they knew its nature and consequences*. How, according to this definition, could we prove that a certain X was good? We should first have to find out, empirically, just what X was like and what its consequences would be. To this extent the empirical method as required by the definition seems beyond intelligent objection. But what remains? We should next have to discover whether most people would approve of the sort of thing we had discovered X to be. This could not be determined by popular vote – but only because it would be too difficult to explain to the voters, beforehand, what the nature and consequences of X really were. Apart from this, voting would be a pertinent method. We are again reduced to counting noses as a *perfectly final* appeal.

Now we need not scorn voting entirely. A man who rejected interest theories as irrelevant might readily make the following statement: 'If I believed that X would be approved by the majority, when they knew all about it, I should be strongly *led* to say that X was good.' But he would continue: '*Need* I say that X was good, under the circumstances? Wouldn't my acceptance of the alleged "final proof" result simply from my being democratic? What about the more aristocratic people? They would simply say that the approval of most people, even when they knew all about the object of their approval, simply had nothing to do with the goodness of anything, and they would probably add a few remarks about the low state of people's interests.' It would indeed seem, from these considerations, that the definition we have been considering has presupposed democratic ideals from the start; it has dressed up democratic propaganda in the guise of a definition.

The omnipotence of the empirical method, as implied by interest theories and others, may be shown unacceptable in a somewhat different way. G. E. Moore's familiar objection about the open question is chiefly pertinent in this regard.[1] No matter what set of scientifically knowable properties a thing may have (says Moore, in effect), you will find, on careful introspection, that it is an open question to ask whether anything having these properties is *good*. It is difficult to believe that this recurrent question is a totally confused one, or that it seems open only because of the ambiguity of 'good'. Rather, we must be using some sense of 'good' which is not definable, relevantly, in terms of anything scientifically knowable. That is, the scientific method is not sufficient for ethics.

These, then, are the requirements with which the 'typical' sense of 'good' is expected to comply: (1) goodness must be a topic for intelligent disagreement; (2) it must be 'magnetic'; and (3) it must not be discoverable solely through the scientific method.

2

I can now turn to my proposed analysis of ethical judgements. First let me present my position dogmatically, showing to what extent I vary from tradition.

I believe that the three requirements given above are perfectly sensible, that there is some *one* sense of 'good' which satisfies all three requirements, and that no traditional interest theory satisfies them all. But this does not imply that 'good' must be explained in terms of a Platonic Idea, or of a categorical imperative, or of a unique, unanalysable property. On the contrary, the three requirements can be met by a *kind* of interest theory. *But we must give up a presupposition that all the traditional interest theories have made.*

Traditional interest theories hold that ethical statements are *descriptive* of the existing state of interests – that they simply *give information* about interests. (More accurately, ethical judgements are said to describe what the state of interests is, was, or will be, or to indicate what the state of interests *would* be under specified circumstances.) It is this emphasis on description, on information, which leads to their incomplete relevance. Doubtless there is always *some* element of description in ethical judgements, but this is by no means all. Their major use is not to indicate facts but to *create an influence*. Instead of merely describing people's interests they *change* or *intensify* them. They *recommend* an interest in an object, rather than state that the interest already exists.

For instance: When you tell a man that he ought not to steal, your object is not merely to let him know that people disapprove of stealing. You are attempting, rather, to get *him* to disapprove of it. Your ethical judgement has a quasi-imperative force which, operating through suggestion and intensified by your tone of voice, readily permits you to begin to *influence*, to *modify*, his interests. If in the end you do not succeed in getting *him* to disapprove of stealing, you will feel that you have failed to convince him that stealing is wrong. You will continue to feel this, even though he fully acknowledges that you disapprove of it and that almost everyone else does. When you point out to him the consequences of his actions – consequences which you suspect he already disapproves of – these *reasons* which support your ethical judgement are simply a means of facilitating your influence. If you think you can change his interests by making vivid to him how others will disapprove of him, you will do so, otherwise not. So the consideration about other people's interest is just an additional means you may employ in order to move him and is not a part of the ethical judgement itself. Your ethical judgement does not merely describe interests to him, it directs his very interests. The difference between the traditional interest theories and my view is like the difference between describing a desert and irrigating it.

Another example: A munitions maker declares that war is a good thing. If he merely meant that he approved of it, he would not have to insist so strongly nor grow so excited in his argument. People would be quite easily convinced that he approved of it. If he merely meant that most people approved of war, or that most people would approve of it if they knew the consequences, he would have to yield his point if it were proved that this was not so. But he would not do this, nor does consistency require it. He is not *describing* the state of people's approval; he is trying to *change* it by his influence. If he found that few people approved of war, he might insist all the more strongly that it was good, for there would be more changing to be done.

This example illustrates how 'good' may be used for what most of us would call bad purposes. Such cases are as pertinent as any others. I am not indicating the *good* way of using 'good'. I am not influencing people but am describing the way this influence sometimes goes on. If the reader wishes to say that the munitions maker's influence is bad – that is, if the reader wishes to awaken people's disapproval of the man, and to make him disapprove of his own actions – I should at another time be willing to join in this undertaking. But this is not the present concern. I am not using ethical terms but am indicating how they *are* used. The munitions maker, in his use of 'good', illustrates the persuasive character of the word just as well as does the unselfish man who, eager to encourage in each of us a desire for the happiness of all, contends that the supreme good is peace.

Thus ethical terms are *instruments* used in the complicated interplay and readjustment of human interests. This can be seen plainly from more general observations. People from widely separated communities have different moral attitudes. Why? To a great extent because they have been subject to different social influences. Now clearly this influence does not operate through sticks and stones alone; words play a great part. People praise one another to encourage certain inclinations and blame one another to discourage others. Those of forceful personalities issue commands which weaker people, for complicated instinctive reasons, find it difficult to disobey, quite apart from fears of consequences. Further influence is brought to bear by writers and orators. Thus social influence is exerted, to an enormous extent, by means that have nothing to do with physical force or material reward. The ethical terms facilitate such influence. Being suited for use in *suggestion*, they are a means by which men's attitudes may be led this way or that. The reason, then, that we find a greater similarity in the moral attitudes of one community than in those of different communities is largely this: ethical judgements propagate themselves. One man says 'this is good'; this may influence the approval of another person, who then makes the same ethical judgement, which in turn influences another person, and so on. In the end, by a process of mutual influence, people take up more or less the same attitudes. Between people of widely separated communities, of course, the influence is less strong; hence different communities have different attitudes.

These remarks will serve to give a general idea of my point of view. We must now go into more detail. There are several questions which must be answered: How does an ethical sentence acquire its power of influencing people – why is it suited to suggestion? Again, what has this influence to do with the *meaning* of ethical terms? And finally, do these considerations really lead us to a sense of 'good' which meets the requirements mentioned in the preceding section?

Let us deal first with the question about *meaning*. This is far from an easy question, so we must enter into a preliminary inquiry about meaning in general. Although a seeming digression this will prove indispensable.

3

Broadly speaking, there are two different *purposes* which lead us to use language. On the one hand we use words (as in science) to record, clarify and communicate *beliefs*. On the other hand we use words to give vent to our feelings (interjections), or to create moods (poetry), or to incite people to actions or attitudes (oratory).

The first use of words I shall call 'descriptive', the second, 'dynamic'. Note that the distinction depends solely upon the *purpose* of the *speaker*.

When a person says 'hydrogen is the lightest known gas,' his purpose *may* be simply to lead the hearer to believe this, or to believe that the speaker believes it. In that case the words are used descriptively. When a person cuts himself and says 'damn', his purpose is not ordinarily to record, clarify or communicate any belief. The word is used dynamically. The two ways of using words, however, are by no means mutually exclusive. This is obvious from the fact that our purposes are often complex. Thus when one says 'I want you to close the door', part of his purpose, ordinarily, is to lead the hearer to believe that he has this want. To that extent the words are used descriptively. But the major part of one's purpose is to lead the hearer to *satisfy* the want. To that extent the words are used dynamically.

It very frequently happens that the same sentence may have a dynamic use on one occasion and not on another, and that it may have different dynamic uses on different occasions. For instance: A man says to a visiting neighbour, 'I am loaded down with work.' His purpose may be to let the neighbour know how life is going with him. This would *not* be a dynamic use of words. He may make the remark, however, in order to drop a hint. This *would* be dynamic usage (as well as descriptive). Again, he may make the remark to arouse the neighbour's sympathy. This would be a *different* dynamic usage from that of hinting.

Or again, when we say to a man, 'of course you won't make those mistakes any more,' we *may* simply be making a prediction. But we are more likely to be using 'suggestion', in order to encourage him and hence *keep* him from making mistakes. The first use would be descriptive, the second, mainly dynamic.

From these examples it will be clear that we can not determine whether words are used dynamically or not merely by reading the dictionary – even assuming that everyone is faithful to dictionary meanings. Indeed, to know whether a person is using a word dynamically we must note his tone of voice, his gestures, the general circumstances under which he is speaking, and so on.

We must now proceed to an important question: What has the dynamic use of words to do with their *meaning*? One thing is clear – we must not define 'meaning' in a way that would make meaning vary with dynamic usage. If we did, we should have no use for the term. All that we could say about such 'meaning' would be that it is very complicated and subject to constant change. So we must certainly distinguish between the dynamic use of words and their meaning.

It does not follow, however, that we must define 'meaning' in some non-psychological fashion. We must simply restrict the psychological field. Instead of identifying meaning with *all* the psychological causes and effects that attend a word's utterance, we must identify it with those that it has a *tendency* (causal property, dispositional property) to be connected with. The tendency must be of a particular kind, moreover. It must exist for all who speak the language; it must be persistent and must be realizable more or less independently of determinate circumstances attending the word's utterance. There will be further restrictions dealing with the interrelations of word in different contexts. Moreover, we must include, under the psychological responses which the words tend to produce, not only immediately introspectable experiences but *dispositions* to react in a given way with appropriate stimuli. I hope to go into these matters in a subsequent essay. Suffice it now to say that I think 'meaning' may be thus defined in a way to include 'propositional' meaning as an important kind.

The definition will readily permit a distinction between meaning and dynamic use. For when words are accompanied by dynamic purposes, it does not follow that they *tend* to be accompanied by them in the way mentioned above. E.g. there need be no tendency realizable more or less independently of the determinate circumstances under which the words are uttered.

There will be a kind of meaning, however, in the sense above defined, which has an intimate relation to dynamic usage. I refer to 'emotive' meaning (in a sense roughly like that employed by Ogden and Richards).[2] The emotive meaning of a word is a tendency of a word, arising through the history of its usage, to produce (result from) *affective* responses in people. It is the immediate aura of feeling which hovers about a word. Such tendencies to produce affective responses cling to words very tenaciously. It would be difficult, for instance, to express merriment by using the interjection 'alas'. Because of the persistence of such affective tendencies (among other reasons) it becomes feasible to classify them as 'meanings'.

Just *what* is the relation between emotive meaning and the dynamic use of words? Let us take an example. Suppose that a man tells his hostess, at the end of a party, that he thoroughly enjoyed himself, and suppose that he was in fact bored. If we consider his remark an innocent one, are we likely to remind him, later, that he 'lied' to his hostess? Obviously not, or at least, not without a broad smile; for although he told her something that he believed to be false, and with the intent of making her believe that it was true – those being the ordinary earmarks of a lie – the expression, 'you lied to her', would be emotively too strong for our purposes. It would seem to be a reproach, even if we intended it not to be a reproach. So it will be evident that such words as 'lied' (and many parallel examples could be cited) become suited, on account of their emotive meaning, to a certain kind of dynamic use – so well suited, in fact, that the hearer is likely to be misled when we use them in any other way. The more pronounced a word's emotive meaning is, the less likely people are to use it purely descriptively. Some words are suited to encourage people, some to discourage them, some to quiet them, and so on.

Even in these cases, of course, the dynamic purposes are not to be identified with any sort of meaning; for the emotive meaning accompanies a word much more persistently than do the dynamic purposes. But there is an important contingent relation between emotive meaning and dynamic purpose: the former assists the latter. Hence if we define emotively laden terms in a way that neglects their emotive meaning, we become seriously confused. *We lead people to think that the terms defined are used dynamically less often than they are.*

4

Let us now apply these remarks in defining 'good'. This word may be used morally or non-morally. I shall deal with the non-moral usage almost entirely, but only because it is simpler. The main points of the analysis will apply equally well to either usage.

As a preliminary definition let us take an inaccurate approximation. It may be more misleading than helpful but will do to begin with. Roughly, then, the sentence '*X* is good' means *we like 'X'*. ('We' includes the hearer or hearers.)

At first glance this definition sounds absurd. If used, we should expect to find the following sort of conversation: A: 'This is good.' B: 'But I *don't* like it. What led you to believe that I did?' The unnaturalness of B's reply, judged by ordinary word usage, would seem to cast doubt on the relevance of my definition.

B's unnaturalness, however, lies simply in this: he is assuming that 'we like it' (as would occur implicitly in the use of 'good') is being used descriptively. This will not do. When 'we like it' is to take the place of 'this is good,' the former sentence must be used not purely descriptively, but dynamically. More specifically, it must be used to promote a very subtle (and for the non-moral sense in question, a very easily resisted) kind of *suggestion*. To the extent that 'we' refers to the hearer it must have the dynamic use, essential to suggestion, of leading the hearer to *make* true what is said, rather than merely to believe it. And to the extent that 'we' refers to the speaker, the sentence must have not only the descriptive use of indicating belief about the speaker's interest, but the quasi-interjectory, dynamic function of giving direct expression to the interest. (This immediate expression of feelings assists in the process of suggestion. It is difficult to disapprove in the face of another's enthusiasm.)

For an example of a case where 'we like this' is used in the dynamic way that 'this is good' is used, consider the case of a mother who says to her several children, 'one thing is certain, *we all like to be neat.*' If she really believed this, she would not bother to say so. But she is not using the words descriptively. She is *encouraging* the children to like neatness. By telling them that they like neatness, she will lead them to *make* her statement true, so to speak. If, instead of saying 'we all like to be neat' in this way, she had said 'it's a good thing to be neat', the effect would have been approximately the same.

But these remarks are still misleading. Even when 'we like it' is used for suggestion, it is not quite like 'this is good'. The latter is more subtle. With such a sentence as 'this is a good book', for example, it would be practically impossible to use instead 'we like this book'. When the latter is used it must be accompanied by so exaggerated an intonation, to prevent its becoming confused with a descriptive statement, that the force of suggestion becomes stronger and ludicrously more overt than when 'good' is used.

The definition is inadequate, further, in that the definiens has been restricted to dynamic usage. Having said that dynamic usage was different from meaning, I should not have to mention it in giving the *meaning* of 'good'.

It is in connection with this last point that we must return to emotive meaning. The word 'good' has a laudatory emotive meaning that fits it for the dynamic use of suggesting favourable interest. But the sentence 'we like it' has no such emotive meaning. Hence my definition has neglected emotive meaning entirely. Now to neglect emotive meaning serves to foster serious confusions, as I have previously intimated; so I have sought to make up for the inadequacy of the definition by letting the restriction about dynamic usage take the place of emotive meaning. What I should do, of course, is to find a definiens whose emotive meaning, like that of 'good', simply does *lead* to dynamic usage.

Why did I not do this? I answer that it is not possible if the definition is to afford us increased clarity. No two words, in the first place, have quite the same emotive meaning. The most we can hope for is a rough approximation. But if we seek for such an approximation for 'good', we shall find nothing more than synonyms, such as 'desirable' or 'valuable'; and these are profitless because they do not clear up the connection between 'good' and favourable interest. If we reject such synonyms, in favour of non-ethical terms, we shall be highly misleading. For instance 'this is good' has something like the meaning of 'I *do* like this; do so as well.' But this is certainly not accurate. For the imperative makes an appeal to the conscious efforts of the hearer. Of course he cannot like something just by trying. He must be led to like it through suggestion. Hence an ethical sentence differs from an imperative in that it enables one to make changes in a much more subtle, less fully conscious way. Note that the ethical sentence centres the hearer's attention not on his interests but on the object of interest, and thereby facilitates suggestion. Because of its subtlety, moreover, an ethical sentence readily permits counter-suggestion and leads to the give and take situation that is so characteristic of arguments about values.

Strictly speaking, then, it is impossible to define 'good' in terms of favourable interest if emotive meaning is not to be distorted. Yet it is possible to say that 'this is good' is *about* the favourable interest of the speaker and the hearer or hearers, and that it has a laudatory emotive meaning which fits the words for use in suggestion. This is a rough description of meaning, not a definition. But it serves the same clarifying function that a definition ordinarily does, and that, after all, is enough.

A word must be added about the moral use of 'good'. This differs from the above in that it is about a different kind of interest. Instead of being about what the hearer and speaker *like*, it is about a stronger sort of approval. When a person *likes* something, he is pleased when it prospers and disappointed when it does not. When a person *morally approves* of something he experiences a rich feeling of security when it prospers and is indignant or 'shocked' when it does not. These are rough and inaccurate examples of the many factors which one would have to mention in distinguishing the two kinds of interest. In the moral usage, as well as in the non-moral, 'good' has an emotive meaning which adapts it to suggestion.

And now, are these considerations of any importance? Why do I stress emotive meanings in this fashion? Does the omission of them really lead people into errors? I think, indeed, that the errors resulting from such omissions are enormous. In order to see this, however, we must return to the restrictions, mentioned in section 1, with which the typical sense of 'good' has been expected to comply.

5

The first restriction, it will be remembered, had to do with disagreement. Now there is clearly some sense in which people disagree on ethical points, but we must not rashly assume that all disagreement is modelled after the sort that occurs in the natural sciences. We must distinguish between 'disagreement in belief' (typical of the sciences) and 'disagreement in interest'. Disagreement in belief occurs when A believes p and B disbelieves it. Disagreement in interest occurs when A has a favourable interest in X and when B has an unfavourable one in it. (For a full-bodied disagreement, neither party is content with the discrepancy.)

Let me give an example of disagreement in interest. A: 'Let's go to a cinema tonight.' B: 'I don't want to do that. Let's go to the symphony.' A continues to insist on the cinema, B on the symphony. This is disagreement in a perfectly conventional sense. They cannot agree on where they want to go, and each is trying to redirect the other's interest. (Note that imperatives are used in the example.)

It is disagreement in *interest* which takes places in ethics. When C says 'this is good,' and D says 'no, it's bad,' we have a case of suggestion and counter-suggestion. Each man is trying to redirect the other's interest.

There obviously need be no domineering, since each may be willing to give ear to the other's influence; but each is trying to move the other none the less. It is in this sense that they disagree. Those who argue that certain interest theories make no provision for disagreement have been misled, I believe, simply because the traditional theories, in leaving out emotive meaning, give the impression that ethical judgements are used descriptively only; and of course when judgements are used purely descriptively, the only disagreement that can arise is disagreement *in belief.* Such disagreement may be disagreement in belief *about* interests, but this is not the same as disagreement *in* interest. My definition does not provide for disagreement in belief about interests any more than does Hobbes'; but that is no matter, for there is no reason to believe, at least on common sense grounds, that this kind of disagreement exists. There is only disagreement *in* interest. (We shall see in a moment that disagreement in interest does not remove ethics from sober argument – that this kind of disagreement may often be resolved through empirical means.)

The second restriction, about 'magnetism', or the connection between goodness and actions, requires only a word. This rules out only those interest theories that do *not* include the interest of the speaker in defining 'good'. My account does include the speaker's interest, hence is immune.

The third restriction, about the empirical method, may be met in a way that springs naturally from the above account of disagreement. Let us put the question in this way: When two people disagree over an ethical matter, can they completely resolve the disagreement through empirical considerations, assuming that each applies the empirical method exhaustively, consistently, and without error?

I answer that sometimes they can and sometimes they cannot, and that at any rate, even when they can, the relation between empirical knowledge and ethical judgements is quite different from the one that traditional interest theories seem to imply.

This can best be seen from an analogy. Let us return to the example where A and B could not agree on a cinema or a symphony. The example differed from an ethical argument in that imperatives were used, rather than ethical judgements, but was analogous to the extent that each person was endeavouring to modify the other's interest. Now how would these people argue the case, assuming that they were too intelligent just to shout at one another?

Clearly, they would give 'reasons' to support their imperatives. A might say, 'but you know, Garbo is at the Bijou.' His hope is that B, who admires Garbo, will acquire a desire to go to the cinema when he knows what film will be there. B may counter, 'but Toscanini is guest conductor tonight, in an all-Beethoven programme'. And so on. Each supports his imperative ('*let's* do so and so') by reasons which may be empirically established.

To generalize from this: disagreement in interest may be rooted in disagreement in belief. That is to say, people who disagree in interest would often cease to do so if they knew the precise nature and consequences of the object of their interest. To this extent disagreement in interest may be resolved by securing agreement in belief, which in turn may be secured empirically.

This generalization holds for ethics. If A and B, instead of using imperatives, had said, respectively, 'it would be *better* to go to the cinema,' and 'it would be better to go to the symphony,' the reasons which they would advance would be roughly the same. They would each give a more thorough account of the object of interest, with the purpose of completing the redirection of interest which was begun by the suggestive force of the ethical sentence. On the whole, of course, the suggestive force of the ethical statement merely exerts enough pressure to start such trains of reasons, since the reasons are much more essential in resolving disagreement in interest than the persuasive effect of the ethical judgement itself.

Thus the empirical method is relevant to ethics simply because our knowledge of the world is a determining factor to our interests. But note that empirical facts are not inductive grounds from which the ethical judgement problematically follows. (This is what traditional interest theories imply.) If someone said 'close the door,' and added the reason 'we'll catch cold,' the latter would scarcely be called an inductive ground of the former. Now imperatives are related to the reasons which support them in the same way that ethical judgements are related to reasons.

Is the empirical method *sufficient* for attaining ethical agreement? Clearly not. For empirical knowledge resolves disagreement in interest only to the extent that such disagreement is rooted in disagreement in belief. Not all disagreement in interest is of this sort. For instance: A is of a sympathetic nature and B is not. They are arguing about whether a public dole would be good. Suppose that they discovered all the consequences of the dole. Is it not possible, even so, that A will say that it is good and B that it is bad? The disagreement in interest may arise not from limited factual knowledge but simply from A's sympathy and B's coldness. Or again, suppose in the above argument that A was poor and unemployed and that B was rich. Here again the disagreement might not be due to different factual knowledge. It would be due to the different social positions of the men, together with their predominant self-interest.

When ethical disagreement is not rooted in disagreement in belief, is there *any* method by which it may be settled? If one means by 'method' a *rational* method, then there is no method. But in any case there is a 'way'. Let us consider the above example again, where disagreement was due to A's sympathy and B's coldness. Must they end by saying, 'well, it's just a matter of our having different temperaments'? Not necessarily. A, for instance, may try to *change* the temperament of his opponent. He may pour out his enthusiasms in such a moving way – present the sufferings of the poor with such appeal – that he will lead his opponent to see life through different eyes. He may build up by the contagion of his feelings an influence which will modify B's temperament and create in him a sympathy for the poor which did not previously exist. This is often the only way to obtain ethical agreement, if there is any way at all. It is persuasive, not empirical or rational; but that is no reason for neglecting it. There is no reason to scorn it, either, for it is only by such means that our personalities are able to grow, through our contact with others.

The point I wish to stress, however, is simply that the empirical method is instrumental to ethical agreement only to the extent that disagreement in interest is rooted in disagreement in belief. There is little reason to believe that all disagreement is of this sort. Hence the empirical method is not sufficient for ethics. In any case, ethics is not psychology, since psychology does not endeavour to *direct* our interests; it discovers facts about the ways in which interests are or can be directed, but that is quite another matter.

To summarize this section: my analysis of ethical judgements meets the three requirements for the typical sense of 'good' that were mentioned in section 1. The traditional interest theories fail to meet these requirements simply because they neglect emotive meaning. This neglect leads them to neglect dynamic usage, and the sort of disagreement that results from such usage, together with the method of resolving the disagreement. I may add that my analysis answers Moore's objection about the open question. Whatever scientifically knowable properties a thing may have, it *is* always open to question whether a thing having these (enumerated) qualities is good. For to ask whether it is good is to ask for *influence*. And whatever I may know about an object, I can still ask, quite pertinently, to be influenced with regard to my interest in it.

6

And now, have I really pointed out the 'typical' sense of 'good'?

I suppose that many will still say 'no', claiming that I have simply failed to set down *enough* requirements that this sense must meet, and that my analysis, like all others given in terms of interest, is a way of begging the issue. They will say: 'When we ask "is X good?" we don't want mere influence, mere advice. We decidedly don't want to be influenced through persuasion, nor are we fully content when the influence is supported by a wide scientific knowledge of X. The answer to our question will, of course, modify our interests. But this is only because a unique sort of truth will be revealed to us – a truth that must be apprehended a priori. We want our interests to be guided by this truth and by nothing else. To substitute for this special truth mere emotive meaning and mere factual truth is to conceal from us the very object of our search.'

I can only answer that I do not understand. What is this truth to be *about*? For I recollect no Platonic Idea, nor do I know what to *try* to recollect. I find no indefinable property nor do I know what to look for. And the 'self-evident' deliverances of reason, which so many philosophers have mentioned, seem on examination to be deliverances of their respective reasons only (if of anyone's) and not of mine.

I strongly suspect, indeed, that any sense of 'good' which is expected both to unite itself in synthetic a priori fashion with other concepts and to influence interests as well, is really a great confusion. I extract from this meaning the power of influence alone, which I find the only intelligible part. If the rest is confusion, however, then it certainly deserves more than the shrug of one's shoulders. What I should like to do is to *account* for the confusion – to examine the psychological needs which have given rise to it and show how these needs may be satisfied in another way. This is *the* problem, if confusion is to be stopped at its source. But it is an enormous problem and my reflections on it, which are at present worked out only roughly, must be reserved until some later time.

I may add that if '*X* is good' has the meaning that I ascribe to it, then it is not a judgement that professional philosophers and only professional philosophers are qualified to make. To the extent that ethics predicates the ethical terms of anything, rather that explains their meaning, it becomes more than a purely intellectual study. Ethical judgements are social instruments. They are used in a cooperative enterprise that leads to a mutual readjustment of human interests. Philosophers have a part in this; but so too do all men.

Notes

1 See §13 of chapter 1 of Moore's *Principia Ethica* in this volume.
2 In their *The Meaning of Meaning*, London: Kegan Paul, 1923, p. 125,

C. K. Ogden and I. A. Richards in effect sketched the position that Stevenson elaborates and defends in the present article. They wrote: 'T[he] peculiar ethical use of "good" is, we suggest, a purely emotive one . . . it serves only as an emotive sign expressing our attitude . . . and perhaps evoking similar attitudes in other persons, or inciting them to actions . . .'.

Index

Abraham, 182–92
Ackrill, J.L., 30n
action,
  in the *Bhagavad Gita*, 94, 102–8
  good actions: Hume on, 150; and
    utilitarianism, 207–9
'actionless action', in Taoism, 78, 94
activity of the soul, in Aristotle, 29,
    37–8, 41, 44–6
Agamemnon, 182, 186, 188
Agrawal, M.M., 94n
amorality, in Plato's *Gorgias*, 11, 12
applied ethics, 1–2, 4, 5
Aquinas, St Thomas, 5
  and Bishop Butler, 126, 137
  and fundamental ethics, 4
  and moral grounds, 8
  and moral knowledge, 8
  Summa Theologica, 125–35
Aristotle, 58n, 135n
  and the activity of the soul, 29, 37–8,
    41, 44–6
  definition of ethics, 1, 2
  and the eighteenth-century
    Enlightenment, 166
  and Epicurus, 47, 48
  and *eudaimonia* (happiness), 7, 29,
    30, 32–4, 36–44
  and the function of man, 37–8
  and fundamental ethics, 4

  and meta-ethics, 3
  and moral grounds, 7–8
  and moral knowledge, 8
  and moral scope, 10
  Nicomachean Ethics, 10, 29–46
  and pleasure, 39–40
  and St Thomas Aquinas, 125–6
  and utilitarianism, 195
Arrington, Robert L., 7n
artisans, in Taoism, 78
Augustine, St, 125, 128
Ayer, A.J., 2n

bad, good and evil, Nietzsche on,
  214–29
Barnes, Jonathon, 30n
belief, disagreement in, Stevenson on,
  277–8
benevolence,
  in Bishop Butler, 141–5
  in Confucianism, 59
  in *The Book of Chuang Tzu*, 88–9, 90,
    91
Bentham, Jeremy, 6, 136, 194, 195,
  196
  and the naturalistic fallacy, 243–4
Bergmann, Frithjof, 213n
Berlin, Isaiah, 195n
Bernard, St, 125
Bhagavad Gita, The, 30, 93–109

and Buddhism, 110
and fundamental ethics, 4
and moral grounds, 8
and religion, 6
Bloom, Allen, 214n
Bloomsbury Group, 230
Book of Chuang Tzu, 77–92
Bradley, F.H., 195
Brahman, in the *Bhagavad Gita*, 94,
    101, 106–7, 109n
Brutus, 186
Buddhaghosa, 111n
Buddhism, 6, 110–24
    in the *Bodhicaryāvatāra* (Śāntideva),
        110, 111, 112–16, 118–19
    'four noble truths' in, 110–11
    Mahayana ('Great Vehicle') tradition,
        111
    and moral scope, 10, 110
    mother-recognition in, 118–24
    nirvana, 111, 112
    in 'The Second Path' (Tsongkapa),
        110, 117–24
    Theravada, tradition of, 111
business ethics, 1
Butler, Joseph,
    and Hume, 149
    and meta-ethics, 3
    Sermon 'Upon the Love of Our
        Neighbour', 136–48

Callicles, 11, 12–28
Carlyle, Thomas, 201
Carnap, Rudolf, 263n
caste,
    in the *Bhagavad Gita*, 8, 96, 109n
    Nietzsche on, 217–19
categorical imperative, in Kant, 167,
    177–8
character, ethics and, 1–2
Chinese philosophers,
    Chuang Tzu, 8, 77–92
    Hsun Tzu, 5, 8, 59–61, 70–6
    Mencius, 6, 59–61, 61–70
    Mo Tzu, 194

Christianity,
    and Aquinas, 125–6
    and Bishop Butler, 137, 147–8
    Kierkegaard, 184
Chuang Tzu,
    Book of, 77–92
    and moral knowledge, 8
Coleridge, Samuel Taylor, 194
Collins, Steven, 111n
compassion, in Buddhism, 110–14,
    120–1, 124
Confucianism, 6, 59–61, 64, 66
    in 'Human Nature is Good'
        (Mencius), 61–70
    in 'Man's Nature is Evil' (Hsun Tzu),
        70–6
    and Taoism, 77, 78, 85–6, 89–92
consequentialist ethics, 47, 166
contemplative life, in Aristotle, 30, 33,
    34
convention, and nature, in Plato's
    Gorgias, 12–14
Cooper, David E., 78n
Copleston, F.C., 126n
custom, ethics as, 1–2

Dancy, Jonathon, 247
Danto, Arthur, 95n, 213n
death,
    fear of, Epicurus on, 49–55
    and happiness, Aristotle on, 41–2
Democritus, 78
deontological ethics, 6, 7
deontological intuitionists, 246
Descartes, René, 149
desire,
    Epicurus on the classification of, 50,
        56
    Moore on good and, 241–2
Dharmakirti, *Commentary on Valid
    Perception*, 121
disagreement, Stevenson on ethical,
    275–8
Duncan-Jones, Austin, 137n
duty,

Kant's ethics of, 173–8, 179, 212, 250, 254
Ross on prima facie, 246–7, 249–61
and utilitarianism, 206

egoism *see* self-love
emotive meaning, of ethical terms, 264–80
emotivists, 231, 263
Empedocles, 27n
English Neo-Platonists, 149
enlightenment, in 'The Second Path' (Tsongkapa), 117–24
Enlightenment philosophers, 29, 48, 149, 166
and utilitarianism, 194
environmental ethics, and Taoism, 78
Epicureans, 47
and utilitarianism, 197
Epicurus,
and Bishop Butler, 136
and the eighteenth-century Enlightenment, 166
and fundamental ethics, 4
'Leading Doctrines', 47, 53–8
'Letter to Menoeceus', 47, 48–52
and moral grounds, 7–8
and utilitarianism, 196, 197
ethical life, in Aristotle, 30
ethical rationalism, in Hume, 149
ethical terms, emotive meaning of, 264–80
ethics,
defining, 1–2
in Moore, 232–3
eudaimonia see happiness
Eudoxus, 44
evil,
good and bad, Nietzsche on, 214–29
human nature as, in Hsun Tzu, 60–1, 70–6
and pain, in Plato's *Gorgias*, 24–6
returning good for, 255
Existentialism, 182, 262

faith, and the 'telelogical suspension of the ethical', 184–5, 187, 192
food, and Epicurus, 47, 51
free will, Nietzsche on, 213
Freud, Sigmund, 213
friendship, Epicurus on, 48, 56, 58
function of man, in Aristotle, 37–8
fundamental ethics, 2, 3–4, 6

Gandhi, Mahatma, 93
God, and the 'teleological suspension of the ethical', 125–6, 132–3, 181–2, 187
gods, Epicurus on the, 49, 52
good,
in Aristotle, 29, 30–46: idea of, 34–6
bad and evil, Nietzsche on, 214–29
human nature as, in Mencius, 60, 61–70
Moore on defining, 233–45, 267: and pleasure, 231, 234, 236, 239–41, 242, 248
returning good for, 255
Stevenson on defining, 265–8, 273–5, 279
good life, Epicurus on the, 50–2, 53–4, 55
Good Will, in Kant, 167, 170–1, 172–3
goodness, and pleasure, in Plato's *Gorgias*, 11, 12, 18–27, 47
Graham, A.C., 59n

Hannay, Alastair, 182n
Hansen, Chad, 61n, 77n
happiness,
in Aquinas, 126, 132–3
in Aristotle (*eudaimonia*), 7, 29, 30, 32–4, 36–44, 126
Bishop Butler on, 136, 137, 138–40, 147
in Epicurus, preconditions of, 49–50
Heavenly, in *The Book of Chuang Tzu*, 82
Hume on, 149
Kant on, 170, 172, 174–5, 179

and the naturalistic fallacy, 243–4
Nietzsche on, 222
and utilitarianism, 194, 195, 197,
    199, 200–7, 209
Hare, R.M., 10n, 247
'heart-mind', in Mencius, 60
Heaven, in *The Book of Chuang Tzu*,
    80–92
hedonism, 248–9
Hegel, G.W.F., 181, 182, 184, 192n
Heidegger, Martin, 78
Hellenistic Age, 47
Helvétius, Claude-Adrien, 194
Heracles, 14
Hesiod, 33
Hinduism, and the *Bhagavad Gita*,
    93–4
Hobbes, Thomas, 5, 136
    definition of good, 265, 266, 276
honour, and happiness, in Aristotle,
    33–4
Hsun Tzu, 5, 8, 59–61
    'Man's Nature is Evil', 70–6
Hudson, W.D., 263
human nature, 5
    Aquinas on, 134–5, 136
    Hsun Tzu on, 60–1, 70–6
    Kant on, 166
    Mencius on, 60, 61–70
    and utilitarianism, 194, 210–11
Hume, David,
    definition of good, 265, 266
    and Kant, 166, 167
    and meta-ethics, 3
    and the naturalistic fallacy, 231
    and Nietzsche, 213
    Treatise of Human Nature, 149–65
Hunter, Geoffrey, 150n
Hutcheson, Francis, 136

individual, the, and Kierkegaard, 182,
    183–4, 188–90
individualism, 29
injustice, Epicurus on, 57
interest, Stevenson on disagreement

in, 275–7
intuitionists, 9, 246
Islam, 125

Jaspers, Karl, 182n
Jesus of Nazareth, 205, 220
Jews, Nietzsche on, 219, 220
judgement,
    Hume on reason and, 153–4, 155
    and moral knowledge, 9
    Stevenson's analysis of ethical
        judgements, 268–70, 279
justice,
    Epicurus on, 55, 57
    in Hume, 149
    and the Sophists, 11

Kant, Immanuel,
    and Aquinas, 126
    and the *Bhagavad Gita*, 94–5
    on duty, 173–8, 179, 212, 250, 254
    and fundamental ethics, 3–4
    *Fundamental Principles of the
        Metaphysics of Morals*, 3–4,
        166–80
    Hegel's criticism of, 181
    and moral grounds, 7, 8
    and moral knowledge, 8
    and Nietzsche, 212, 213
    and utilitarianism, 194
Kantianism, and moral scope, 9
Keynes, J.M., 230
Kierkegaard, S., 262
    Fear and Trembling, 5–6, 181–93
    and individualism, 29
    and moral scope, 10
knowledge, in *Bhagavad Gita, The*, 94,
    107

language, Stevenson on the purpose of,
    270–1
Lao Tzu, 77, 85–7, 89–92
laws,
    Epicurus on just and unjust, 57
    see also natural law

Leslie, John, 262n
logic, Kant on, 168
Logical Positivists, 231, 262–3
Long, A.A., 48n
love (of self and neighbour),
    Bishop Butler on, 137–48
    Kant on, 175
    and utilitarianism, 205
Lucretius, 48
Luper, Steven, 48n

MacIntyre, Alasdair, 7n, 12n, 29n, 149n
Mahabharata, The, 93
Marx, Karl, 11, 213
Mary, Virgin, 191
meaning,
    Stevenson on meaning of ethical
        terms, 270–2
    theory of, 263
Mencius, 6, 59–61
    and fundamental ethics, 4
    'Human Nature is Good', 61–70
    and moral grounds, 7–8
    science and ethics in, 5
mental health, Epicurus on, 55
meta-ethics, 2, 3, 4, 6
metaphysic of morals, in Kant, 168,
    169–70
metaphysic of nature, in Kant, 168
Mill, John Stuart, 6, 137
    and fundamental ethics, 3, 4
    and moral knowledge, 8
    and the naturalistic fallacy, 231, 243
    Utilitarianism, 3, 194–211
Mirabeau, Comte de, 223
Mo Tzu, 60n, 194
Moore, G.E., 12, 261n
    on defining good, 233–45, 267
    and the deontological intuitionists,
        246
    and duty, 250
    and meta-ethics, 3
    and moral knowledge, 8–9
    and the noncognitivists, 262, 263
    Principia Ethica, 230–45

and right actions, 248, 258
moral and intellectual virtues, in
    Aquinas, 127–30, 133
moral grounds, 7–8
moral knowledge, 8–9
moral scope, 9–10
    in Buddhism, 10, 110
moral sense, in Hume, 161–5
moral sentiment, 61
Muslims, 125

natural law,
    in Aquinas, 126
    in Plato's Gorgias, 13
    Ross on the operation of, 254–5
natural right, in Plato's Gorgias, 14–18
Naturalism, Moore on, 244–5
naturalistic fallacy, Moore's attack on
    the, 230–1, 237–45, 262
nature,
    in the Book of Chuang Tzu, 78, 80
    and conventional morality, in Plato's
        Gorgias, 12–14
    in Epicurus, 47–8
    and moral principles, Hume on,
        163–4
    see also human nature
Neo-Platonists, 149
Nietzsche, F., 230, 262
    and fundamental ethics, 4
    and moral knowledge, 9
    and moral scope, 10
    On the Genealogy of Morals, 6, 212–29
    science and ethics in, 5
nirvana, 111, 112, 212–29
'noncognitivist' theories, 262
Novalis (Friedrich von Hardenberg),
    201

Ogden, C.K., 263, 272, 280n
O'Neill, Onora, 167n

pain,
    Epicurus on, 48, 50, 51, 53, 54, 55
    and happiness, Aristotle on, 42–3

and pleasure: Hume on, 162–3, 164;
    in Plato's *Gorgias*, 12, 22–7; and
    utilitarianism, 194, 196, 197,
    200, 201, 202
see also suffering
Parfit, Derek, 112n
Perry, R.B., 265
philosophes, 149
Pindar, 14
Plato, 33, 35, 46n, 58n, 248
    and Epicurus, 47
    Gorgias, 8, 11–28
    and meta-ethics, 3
pleasure,
    Aristotle on, 39–40
    Epicurus on, 47, 48, 51–5
    and good, in Moore, 231, 234, 236,
        239–41, 242
    and goodness, in Plato's *Gorgias*, 11,
        12, 18–27, 47
    and pain: Hume on, 162–3, 164; in
        Plato's *Gorgias*, 12, 22–7;
        and utilitarianism, 194, 196, 197,
        198–200, 248–9
political life, in Aristotle, 33–4
political philosophy, and ethics, 4–5
politics,
    in Aristotle, 30, 31–2, 41
    Epicurus on, 48
Positivists, 231, 262–3
Price, Richard, 246
Prichard, H.A., 246
priests, Nietzsche on, 217–19
Protagoras, 11
psychology, and ethics, 6, 59
punishment, in *The Book of Chuang Tzu*,
    83, 85
pure and impure, in Nietzsche, 217–18
Pythagoras, 27n

Radhakrishnan, S., 94n
Rashdall, Hastings, 250
realism and anti-realism in ethics, 151n
reason,
    in Aquinas, 127–8, 129–30

Epicurus on, 55
and faith, 125
Hume on morality derived from,
    149–50, 151–60
Kant on, 171–2, 179–80
religion,
    Epicurus on, 52
    and ethics, 5–6
    see also Christianity
respect, in Kant, 167, 175–6, 178
rewards, in the *Book of Chuang Tzu*, 83,
    85
Richards, I.A., 263, 272, 280n
Ricoeur, Paul, 213
right, natural right in Plato, 14–18
right acts, Ross on, 248–61
Rinpoche, Pabongka, and Tsongkapa,
    'The Second Path', 110, 111,
    117–24
ritual principles, Hsun Tzu on, 71, 73,
    74–5
Rochefoucauld, Duc de la, and Bishop
    Butler, 136
Roman Catholicism, and St Thomas
    Aquinas, 125
Ross, W.D., 262
    and moral knowledge, 8–9
    The Right and the Good, 246–61
Rousseau, Jean-Jacques, 2, 12

sages,
    in the *Book of Chuang Tzu*, 79, 80–1,
        84, 88, 90
    in Buddhism, 115
    Hsun Tzu on, 60, 71, 72, 73, 74–5
    Mencius on, 60, 61
    in Taoism, 78
Śaṃkara, 94
Śāntideva, *The Bodhicaryāvatāra*, 110,
    111, 112–16, 118–19
Schiller, Friedrich, 167
Schneewind, J.B., 167n
Schopenhauer, Arthur, 211n
Schweitzer, Albert, 94, 111
science,

in Aristotle, 31, 34–5
and ethics, 5
and the good life, Epicurus on, 54
security, Epicurus on, 53, 54
self, the
in the *Bhagavad Gita*, 94, 97–8, 108
'not-self' in Buddhism, 110–11,
112–13, 114–16, 119
self-love
and Bishop Butler, 137–48
and Hume, 149
self-sufficiency, in Aristotle, 37
Shih Cheng Chi, 86–7
Sidgwick, Henry, 195, 242–3
Skorupski, John, 2n, 195n
Socrates, 11, 12, 14–28, 128, 178, 199
Solon, 41
Sophists, 11
Spencer, Herbert, 215, 240
Sprigge, T.L.S., 136n
Stevenson, C.L., 231
and moral knowledge, 9
'The Emotive Meaning of Ethical
Terms', 262–80
Stoics, 47, 167
and utilitarianism, 199, 205, 207
suffering
in Buddhism, 110, 111, 112–14,
115–16, 119–20, 123
and utilitarianism, 204
see also pain

Tao Te Ching, 77, 78
Taoism, in *The Book of Chuang Tzu*,
77–92
teleological ethics, 6, 7, 166
'teleological suspension of the ethical',
Kierkegaard on, 181–92
Theognis, 217
theological virtues, in Aquinas, 127–30
Thrasymachus, 11
tragic hero, and the teleological
suspension of the ethical, 185, 186,
187, 188, 192

Tsongkapa,
'The Second Path', 110, 117–24
Three Principle Paths, 111, 117

universal scope of moral principles, 9–10
universalism, and Aristotle, 29
universalizability thesis, 247
utilitarianism, 194–211, 212
and fundamental ethics, 3
and moral scope, 9
Ross on, 248–9, 250, 253
and teleological ethics, 166

Vallée Poussin, Louis de la, 112n
virtue,
in the *Book of Chuang Tzu*, 79–80,
81, 82, 83, 84, 85, 89, 91
and reason, in Hume, 152
and religion, in Bishop Butler, 147–8
and utilitarianism, 206–7
virtues,
in Aquinas, 125–35: four cardinal
virtues, 131–2; moral and
intellectual virtues, 127–30, 133;
theological virtues, 126, 132–4
in Aristotle, 10, 29–30, 38–47
in Epicurus, 47, 52

Watson, Burton, 77n
Way, in *The Book of Chuang Tzu*, 78,
80
wealth, Epicurus on, 54
Weber, Max, 111
will,
in Kant, 167, 170–1, 172–3, 175–8
see also free will
William of Ockham, 126
Williams, Bernard, 4n, 212n, 231n
Williams, Paul, 111n
Wollaston, William, 149

Xinzhong Yao, 60n

Yin and Yang, 82, 92n